ESSAYS IN ENGLISH LEGAL HISTORY

S. E. THORNE

THE HAMBLEDON PRESS

LONDON   AND   RONCEVERTE

Published by The Hambledon Press 1985

35 Gloucester Avenue,
London NW1 7AX (U.K.)

309 Greenbrier Avenue,
Ronceverte, West Virginia (U.S.A.)

ISBN 0 907628 56 7

British Library Cataloguing in Publication Data

Thorne, Samuel E.
    Essays in English legal history. − (History
    series; 40)
    1. Law − England − History and criticism
    I. Title
    344.2   KD608

Library of Congress Cataloging in Publication Data

Thorne, Samuel Edmund, 1907-
    Essays in English legal history

    Includes index.
    1. Law − Great Britain − History and criticism −
Addresses, essays, lectures. I. Title.
KD606. T45   1985   349.42'09   85-5611
ISBN 0 907628 56 7   344.2009

Printed and bound in Great Britain
by Robert Hartnoll Ltd., Bodmin, Cornwall

CONTENTS

ACKNOWLEDGEMENTS

The articles reprinted here appeared first in the following places and are reprinted here by the kind permission of the original publishers.

1   *The English Historical Review*, xiii (1978), p. 794.

2   *Speculum*, xi (1936), pp. 452-61.

3   *Cambridge Law Journal* (1959), 193-209.

4   *Law Quarterly Review*, lii (1936), 345-64.

5   *Columbia Law Review*, xxxiii (1933), 428-36.

6   *West Virginia Law Quarterly*, 40 (1934), 347-59.

7   Lecture delivered in Exeter on 27th September, 1968 on the occasion of the 700th anniversary of the death of Henry de Bracton. Published by the University of Exeter (1970).

8   *Atti del II Congresso Internazionale della Società Italiana di Storia del Diritto (Venice, 18-22 September 1967)*, 803-20.

9   *University of Toronto Law Journal*, vii (1947), 1-26.

10   *Graya*, 50 (1959), 79-96.

11   *Illinois Law Review*, 31 (1936), 202-17.

12   *Bartolo da Sassoferrato: Studi e Documenti per il VI Centenario* (Giuffré, Milan, 1962), 675-89.

13   *La Storia del Diritto nel Quadro delle Scienze Storiche: Atti del I Congresso Internazionale della Società Italiana di Storia del Diritto* (Olschki, Milan, 1966), 437-45.

14   *New York University Law Review*, xxvi (1951), 10-23.

15   *The Library: Transactions of the Bibliographical Society* (1930), 421-6.

16   *Law Library Journal*, 29 (1936), 59-63.

17   Selden Society Lecture, 17th March, 1952. (Quaritch, London, 1957).

18   *Huntington Quarterly*, iv (1936), 85-8.

19   *University of Toronto Law Journal*, ii (1937), 24-49.

20   *Law Quarterly Review* (1938), 543-52.

BIBLIOGRAPHICAL NOTE

This collection of Professor Thorne's articles is inclusive with the exception of reviews and the pieces listed in section II below.

I. BOOKS

A Discourse upon the Exposicion and Understandinge of Statutes (Huntington Library, San Marino, 1942).

Prerogativa Regis. Tertia Lectura Roberti Constable de Lyncolnis Inne Anno II Henry VII (Yale University Press, New Haven, 1949).

Readings and Moots at the Inns of Court in the Fifteenth Century, vol. 1, Selden Society, vol. 71 (London, 1954).

Bracton on the Laws and Customs of England (De Legibus et Consuetudinibu Angliae), 4 vols. (Harvard University Press, Cambridge, Massachussetts, 1968-77.

II. ARTICLES NOT INCLUDED IN THIS COLLECTION

'Le droit canonique en Angleterre', *Revue Historique de Droit Français et Étranger*, xiii (1934), 499-513

Preface to W.O. Hassall, *A Catalogue of the Library of Sir Edward Coke* (Yale University Press, New Haven, 1950).

Preface to Edward Hake, *Epieikeia: A Dialogue on Equity*, edited by D.E.C. Yale (Yale University Press, New Haven, 1953).

'History of Law', in *Bibliography of British History, 1485-1603*, edited by Conyers Read (Oxford, 1959).

'Magna Carta', in *The Great Charter* (Pantheon, New York, 1962).

'Bibliografia', in *Charles Howard McIlwain e la Storia sulla Revoluzione Americana* (Mulino, Bologna, 1965).

1

HENRY I'S CORONATION CHARTER, CH.6

HENRY I's coronation charter, which had appeared in print some thirty-two times when Liebermann made his count in 1894, has received the attention of a number of distinguished editors, including (in modern times) Stubbs, Bémont and Liebermann himself, who drew its text from twenty-eight manuscripts.[1] The sixth chapter, essentially the same in all copies, printed and unprinted, reads as follows:

Omnia placita et omnia debita quae fratri meo debebantur condono, exceptis rectis firmis meis et exceptis illis quae pacta erant pro aliorum hereditatibus vel pro eis rebus quae justius aliis contingebant. Et si quis pro hereditate sua aliquid pepigerat, illud condono, et omnes relevationes quae pro rectis hereditatibus pactae fuerant.

It contains a number of puzzling statements, reflected in two recent translations which follow it closely.[2]

I pardon all pleas and debts that were owed to my brother, except my lawful farms and except those [payments] which were agreed on for the sake of others' inheritances or for those things that more rightly affected others. But if anyone has pledged anything for the sake of his own inheritance, that I pardon, as well as all reliefs that have been agreed on for the sake of rightful inheritances.

I forgive all pleas and all debts which were owing to my brother, except my own proper dues and except those things which were agreed to belong to the inheritance of others, or to concern the property which justly belonged to others. And if anyone had promised anything for his heritage, I remit it, and I also remit all reliefs which were promised for direct inheritance.

It is unlikely that Henry intended to remit all payments except those that belonged to the inheritances of others, or to pardon all reliefs, whether reasonable or not. A few simple emendations seem needed to restore the proper sense of the original, which, if they are acceptable, will then stand thus:

I remit all payments and debts owed to my brother, except my rightful dues and except those promised for the heirs [heredibus] of others or for the lands that belonged to others, and all rightful reliefs agreed upon for inheritances [et omnibus rectis relevationibus quae pro hereditatibus pactae fuerant]. If anyone has promised something more than is right [aliquid justius] for his inheritance, that I remit.

1. *Trans. Roy. Hist. Soc.* (N.S.), viii. 21; *Gesetze der Angelsachsen*, i. 521.
2. C. Stephenson and F. G. Marcham, *Sources of English Constitutional History* (1937), p. 47; *English Historical Documents, 1042–1891*, Eds. D. C. Douglas and G. W. Greenaway (1953), p. 401.

2

STATUTI IN THE POST-GLOSSATORS

I

THE facile and commonly drawn distinction between the Glossators who confined themselves to the study of Roman law as it stood in the actual text of Justinian, and the Commentators or Bartolists who sought to bring their studies to a practical point and to adapt Roman law principles to the needs of actual life, is a product of the sixteenth-century legal humanists who wished to understand Roman law as a historical fact of the past in terms of historical scholarship, and who thus were repelled by what Haloander described as 'die Barbarei der Commentarien und die scholastischen Zänkereien' and attracted by the earlier school which seemed to them to have shared their aim of a scientific reconstruction and interpretation of the text and even to have anticipated their cry 'zurück zu den Quellen.' But to the Glossators, no less than to their successors, the Roman law represented a living system of law in which dogmatic differences and discrepancies of thought, expression, and decision between every age and every jurist were not to be recovered and isolated in their classical purity but rather harmonized and explained away, and though often they did little more than restate the positions laid down by the jurisconsults of the second and third centuries or the editors of the sixth, they labored to explain what was difficult, to coördinate what seemed divergent or contradictory, and to show how these ancient principles or rules could be brought into relation with the existing conditions of society.[1] The School of Commentators, which rises in the latter part of the thirteenth century, aided by the developed scholastic method of the late mediaeval period, must of course be regarded as primarily responsible for the growth of the new Roman-Germanic customary law that triumphed in Italy and passed by reception to Germany, but it built upon a vigorous tradition antiquated only in method, and upon a living Roman law (into which mediaeval and Germanic elements had been absorbed) which as early as the end of the twelfth century had penetrated deeply and stubbornly into practice.[2] By the opening of

[1] Emil Seckel's brief sketch, 'Die Anfänge der europäischen Jurisprudenz im 11 und 12 Jahrhundert,' *Zeitschrift [der Savigny Stiftung] für Rechtsgeschichte [Röm. Abt.]* XLV (1925), p. 391, has now been expanded by E. Genzmer, 'Die Justinianische Kodifikation und die Glossatoren,' *Atti del congresso internazionale di diritto romano, Bologna* (Pavia, 1934), I, 345; see also in that volume, p. 431, E. M. Meijers, 'Sommes, Lectures, et Commentaires.' E. Seckel, 'Distinctiones Glossatorum,' *Festschrift d. Berliner jurist. Fakultät für F. von Martitz* (Berlin, 1911), p. 346. If the criticism of H. Kantorowicz (*Zeitschrift für Rechtsgeschichte [Rom. Abt.]* XLVI [1926,] p. 403) is noted, E. Best, *Storia del diritto italiano: Fonti* (Milan, 1923–25) is a useful book. H. Kantorowicz, 'Kritische Studien zur Quellen- und Literaturgeschichte der römischen Rechts im Mittelalter,' *Zeitschrift für Rechtsgeschichte (Rom. Abt.)* XLIX (1929), p. 55; J. Juncker, 'Summen und Glossen,' *ibid. (Kanon. Abt.)* XLV (1925), p. 384; E. Genzmer, 'Quare Glossatorum,' *Gedächtnisschrift für Emil Seckel* (Berlin, 1927), p. 1. The work of the Glossators may be seen to advantage in: G. Chevirer, *Essai sur l'histoire de la cause dans les obligations* (Paris, 1929), pp. 44–91; M. Zeijlmaker, *Overeenkomst en wilsovereenstemming* (Leyden, 1921); W. Taeuber, *Geld und Kredit im Mittelalter* (Berlin, 1933), pp. 117–245; E. Landsberg, *Die Glosse des Accursius und ihre Lehre vom Eigenthum* (Leipzig, 1883). For the influence of Abelard's *Sic et non*, in addition to M. Grabmann, *Die Geschichte der scholastischen Methode* (Freiburg i. Br., Herder, 1911), II, 200 f. and the 5th chapter in J. de Ghellinck, *Le mouvement théologique du XIIe siècle* (Paris, 1914), see: F. Thaner, *Abälard und das canonische Recht* (Graz, 1900); V. Rivalta, *Il Rinnovamento della giurisprudenza filosofica secondo la scolastica* (Bologna, 1888); E. Genzmer, 'Vorbilder für die Distinctionen der Glossatoren,' *Acta Congressus Iuridici Internationalis VII saeculo a Decretalibus Gregorii IX . . .* (Rome 1935), II, 343.

[2] We are concerned here neither with the problem of the survival of Roman law in local custom nor with the vexed question of continuity between the Roman jurists and Irnerius. The 'somnia Fittingiana' has received adequate criticism. M. Conrat (Cohn), *Geschichte der Quellen und Literatur des römischen Rechts im früheren Mittelalter* (Leipzig, 1891), p. 203 f.; E. Seckel, *Beiträge zur Geschichte beider Rechte im Mittelalter* (Tübingen, 1898), p. 377 note 5; H. Kantorowicz, *Ueber die Entstehung der Digestenvulgata* (Weimar: Böhlau, 1910), p. 20. That 'das wiedererschlossene römische Recht schon tiefer in die Praxis einzudringen begonnen hatte' seems clear (1) from the Glossator's practical legal opinions: E. Seckel, 'Ueber neuere Editionen juristischen Schriften aus dem Mittelalter,' *Zeitschrift für Rechtsgeschichte (Rom. Abt.)* XXI (1900), 305, note 1; F. de Zulueta, 'Footnotes to Savigny on Azo's Lectura in Codicem,' *Studi in onore di Pietro Bonfante* (Milan, 1930) III, 269; L. Chiappelli and Zdekauer *Un consulto d'Azone* (Rome, 1888); (2) from their numerous treatises and *summulae* on procedure in the courts: Genzmer, *Atti del congresso internazionale di diritto romano, cit. supra*, p. 404, note 249; H. Kantorowicz, 'Accursio e la sua biblioteca,' *Rivista di storia del diritto italiano*, II (1929), 35, 193; and (3) from the expansion of the Germanic Lombard feudal law under Roman law influence: E. Besta, *Storia, cit. supra*, I, 401 f.; J. Flach, *Etudes critiques sur l'histoire du droit romain au moyen âge* (Paris, 1890), p. 100 f.; E. M. Meijers, 'Les glossateurs et le droit féodal,' *Tijdschrift voor Rechtsgeschiedenis*, XIII (1934), p. 129. For the proverb 'chi non ha Azzo, non vada a palazzo,' and its variant,

the fourteenth century the mediaeval *Corpus iuris civilis* had achieved undoubted
recognition as a body of binding common law, to which the definitions and distinctions of three centuries of jurists had given great inward strength, but by its
side, in the Italian cities, there had evolved an equally binding mass of *statuti*—
legislative regulations of the communes—whose unquestioned validity in practice made it necessary that they receive a place in any comprehensive legal
theory, and that their relation to the *ius commune* find thoughtful consideration.[1]
Contrary to contemporary English common lawyers whose connection with the
legislature—whether that be the King in Council or in Parliament—was much
closer, and who therefore could find little suggestion of conflict between the judicature and the legislature,[2] the civilians were forced to interpret the written acts
of a legislator upon whose actual intention they could not draw, and in this way,
to the construction of an elaborate body of rules of statutory construction and interpretation that marks a distinct advance in juristic thought. For it is as true today as it was in the fourteenth century that the legislature cannot foresee all actual
cases, that the statute generally looks to the redress of a specific grievance and
does not give consideration to the effects of this change upon other parts of the
law, and that it must be interpreted and harmonized if it is to form an efficient
unit in an advanced legal system. But the full realization of this fact is reached
slowly: in England interpretation may be classified with covin and fraud as late
as 1336,[3] and similarly in Italy, at about the same period, efforts were made to
prohibit interpretation by express provision: in Brescia the Podestà swears
'Praedicta omnia et singula faciam et servabo toto tempore mei regiminis, re-
motis odio, amore, timore, pretio et precibus et omni alia interpretatione, inten-
tione et omni salvo et humana gratia,'[4] and in Siena statutes are to be understood 'secondo che sempricemente le parole giacciono et post sono, cosi semprice-

---

'Quidquid non agnoscit glossa nec agnoscit curia,' see E. Landsberg, *Ueber die Entstehung der Regel
'Quidquid non etc.'* (Bonn, 1890).

[1] F. Calasso, *La legislazione statutaria dell'Italia meridionale*, i: *Le basi storiche* (Rome, 1929).
Georg Dahm, whose analysis I follow here, has an excellent and important volume: *Das Strafrecht
Italiens im ausgehenden Mittelalter* (Berlin: de Gruyter, 1931). The Glossators, not without difficulty,
found a place for statutes in their political theory. O. v. Gierke, *Das deutsche Genossenschaftsrecht*
(Berlin, 1881), iii, 215–217; A. J. Carlyle, *A History of Mediaeval Political Theory in the West* (Edinburgh, 1928), ii, 1–91. The theories evolved by the post-Glossators to harmonize Roman sovereignty
and the undeniable validity of city statutes do not fall within the limits of this paper, but see C. N. S.
Woolf, *Bartolus of Sassoferrato* (Cambridge, 1913), pp. 146–160; Dahm, *Das Strafrecht Italiens*, pp.
45–49. Similarly we cannot deal here with their views upon the relation between statutes and (following the interpretation of Troeltsch) the absolute and relative laws of nature, but see A. Solmi,
'Alberto da Gandino e il diritto statutario nella giurisprudenza del sec. xiii,' *Rivista italiana per le
scienze giuridiche*, xxxii (1901), pp. 178–182; Dahm, *Das Strafrecht Italiens*, pp. 49–54.

[2] T. F. T. Plucknett, *Statutes and their interpretation in the first half of the fourteenth century* (Cambridge, 1922), pp. 164–169.

[3] 10 Edw. iii, stat. 3: 'And every man . . . shall keep and observe the aforesaid ordinances and
statutes . . . without addition, or fraud, by covin, evasion, art, or contrivance, ou par interpretation
des paroles.' Plucknett, *op. cit.*, p. 164.

[4] Statute i, 3 (1313) in *Hist. Patriae Mon.*, xvi, 2, col. 1585. But see Albericus de Rosciate, *Tractatus
de Statutis* (in *Tractatus utilissimi statutis* [Lyons, 1552]), i, 9, 62: 'Nec obstat quod statuta sint iurata
per potestates, quia etiam ipsum iuramentum recipit interpretationem.'

mente s'intenda senza alcuna interpretazione.'[1] But the Commentators, as practical jurists, realized very clearly indeed that a statute must be interpreted somehow and by some one if it is to serve a useful purpose, and that if that function is to be relinquished to a body other than the legislature, that rules must be drawn to prevent the application of a formless equity by judges faced with situations not within the statute's express words. But it must not be assumed, as Sohm, for example, assumes,[2] that statutes were interpreted in order to deprive them of validity; the problem rather was one of fitting into the symmetrical and coherent body of closely-knit and slowly-built doctrine that formed the common law, hundreds of diverse statutes dealing incompletely and unskilfully with many subjects, and frequently made on the spur of the moment to provide a remedy for a particular mischief without attention to the probable effect of the new provision upon the common law or indeed, upon the already existing statute law of the commune. It is with this process of accommodation and synthesis that we are concerned here.

That the common law was subsidiary to statute law is clear.[3] 'Ubi cessat statutum habet locum ius civile' is a well-recognized maxim which, however, is early understood to mean that not only where there is no statutory provision is the matter left to the disposition of the common law, but also that where the statute does not provide directly and expressly for the very type of case under consideration it will not be extended by analogy beyond the bounds of its exact words, and the matter therefore will be regarded as untouched by statute and as such to be decided by the *ius commune*. 'Casus omissus debet relinqui dispositioni iuris communis; casus omissus habetur pro omisso.'[4] But it was evident in practice that

---

[1] *Il costituto del Commune di Siena*, ed. A. Lisini (Siena, 1903) p. 498. *Statuto di Forli dell'anno 1359 . . .*, ed. E. Rinaldi (Milan, 1913), p. 277: 'statuta . . . intelligantur prout iacent verba et non recipiant aliquam interpretationem seu exteriorem intellectum, sed pure et sim[pliciter] ut verba eorum sonant, et quod a verbis ipsius statuti prout iacent minime recedatur.' Cf. W. Engelmann, 'Der geistige Urheber des Verbrechens nach dem italienischen Recht des Mittelalters,' *Festschrift für K. Binding* (Leipzig, 1911), ii, 574; G. Bohne, *Die Freiheitsstrafe in den italienischen Stadtrechten des 12 bis 16 Jahrhunderts* (Leipzig, 1922), i, §12, p. 165.

[2] R. Sohm, *The Institutes*, trans. J. C. Ledlie (3d ed., Oxford, 1907), pp. 143 ff.

[3] A. Solmi, 'Alberto da Gandino . . . ,' *Riv. ital. per le scienze giuridiche*, xxxii (1901), p. 189 f.; B. Brugi, 'Alcune osservazioni sul periodo storico dei post-glossatori in Italia,' *Archivio giuridico*, xxvi (1881), p. 421. The Roman law already had been regarded, a century earlier, as 'subsidiär geltendes Recht,' as 'lex omnium generalis,' by the Lombard jurists: M. Conrat (Cohn), *Geschichte*, p. 407, note 4; E. Besta, *Storia*, i, 401 f.; J. Flach, *Etudes critiques sur l'histoire du droit romain au moyen âge* (Paris, 1890), p. 100 f. A. Boretius (ed), *Liber Papiensis, M.G.H.*, LL., iv, lxxxviii–xc. Cf. the many statutory provisions that endeavor to exclude the common law by expressly permitting the judge to proceed *a simili* if the situation presented does not fall directly within the statute's words. *Il costituto del Commune di Siena*, p. 361; *Statuti di Perugia dell'anno 1342* (Corpus stat. Italicorum, ix) p. 67; *Statuta Patavina* (Padua, 1682), p. 191.

[4] Baldus [de Ubaldis], D 1.1. De iust. et iure 9.2; D 1.3 De leg. senatusque cons. 12.1. Albericus de Rosciate, *Tractatus de Statutis*, ii, 171, 8; i, 9, 1; Angelus [de Ubaldis], *Consilia* (Lyons, 1551) 72, 2; Bartolus [a Saxoferrato] D 39.4 De publ. et vect. 15.15; 15.18; 'cessat dispositio iuris communis, et ille casus esset lege non decisus, quod abhorret lex. . . . Sed in lege municipali secus, quia casus per eam non praevisus dispositioni iuris communis relinquitur.' And also, ' . . . non bene argumentatur de contractibus ad statuta, quia in contractibus magis consideramus mentem quam verba. . . . Sed

many statutes were little more than affirmations of existing common law, and it was difficult to consider the doctrine contained in them incapable of extension by analogy merely because it had been enacted into city law, when as common law it might clearly be extended *de similibus ad similia*.[1] Thus we arrive at the general rule of interpretation that statutes in derogation of the common law are to be literally and strictly construed, those which do not contradict common law may be interpreted other than strictly and extended beyond their literal word content.[2] But two so fundamentally different systems as statute and common law could not be brought into conformity so simply: a case in point is presented by Bartholomaeus de Saliceto[3] a statute fixed the punishment for adultery at 200*l*. but fixed no punishment for fornication; at common law the punishment for adultery was death, for fornication the confiscation of half the offender's goods. In other words, at common law fornication was considered the less serious crime and therefore subject to the less drastic penalty, yet this milder punishment itself was still more severe than the statute's punishment for adultery, the graver offense. Should this statute, clearly contradictory to the common law, be interpreted literally, and the unprovided case left to the disposition of the common law, the lesser crime would receive an absurdly large penalty.[4] Similarly it became clear that strict interpretation could meet with little success when applied to legislative acts drawn with the lack of care and the absence of attention to exact meaning and careful phraseology exhibited by most statutes of the period. Many read simply 'si quis occiderit' or 'si quis percusserit,' including no distinction between a wilful and a negligent homicide or battery, and if literally interpreted, making any plea by the defendant in confession and avoidance, such as self-defense, irrelevant. The most striking example of a statute drawn in this way may be seen in the statute of Bologna which set a death penalty upon one who let blood in the Palatio ('faciens sanguinem in Palatio'). A barber shaving a judge there negligently allowed himself to inflict a flesh wound that brought blood. An action was brought against him, and though he was acquitted, the matter was taken very earnestly indeed and aroused much interest among jurists. In the

---

in statutis consideramus verba: adeo, quia quod non est verbis expressum, relinquitur dispositioni iuris communis.' That this rule, especially when used in conjunction with that requiring a strict literal construction, led to extremely harsh results, will surprise no one. Albertus Gandinus in his *Tractatus de Maleficiis* (ed. H. Kantorowicz, *Albertus Gandinus und das Strafrecht der Scholastik* (1907–26), II, p. 374 gives cases in which a statute concerning corn was not extended to include farina, a statute on wine not extended to vinegar. In Solmi's words (*op. cit.*, p. 194) 'se lo statuto parla in singolare, non se allarga al plurale; se lo statuto dispone in maschile, non se deve credere che possa comprendere il femminile; se la disposizione statutaria indica la specie, non se dovrà estendere al genere.' Cf. Alb. de Rosc., *Tractus de Statutis*, I, 9, 5; II, 3, 1. Bonifacius de Vitalinis, *Tractatus super maleficiis* (Lyons, 1532) § Quid sit accusatio, 80.

[1] Baldus, *Consilia* (Lyons, 1589), IV, 3: ' . . . est ipsum ius commune ex quo a iure communi non discrepat.' Alb. de Rosc., D 39.4 De publ. et vect. 15.23: 'Dico . . . quod illa statuta sunt stricti juris quae sunt contra dispositionem iuris communis . . . , sed illa statuta quae totaliter imitarentur ius commune regulantur secundum ius commune.'

[2] Angelus, *Consilia*, 263, 2. Baldus, C 1.14 De leg. et const. 5.6; Gandinus (ed. Kantorowicz) p. 375; Bartolus, D 39.4 De publ. et vect. 15.21, 24, 26.   [3] C 3.41 De noxal. act. 2.28.

[4] C 1.3 De episc. et cler. 15.4: 'Puto quod poena iuris communis ut correcta non debeat imponi, ne absurdum insequatur.'

words of Rainerius de Forlivio, 'fuit magna contentio, tamen determinatum fuit quod non.'[1] This case and others similar to it led to the modification of the strict rule of interpretation by the formation of a corollary, namely, that statutes though contrary to common law nevertheless may be extended beyond their words if the application of their literal meaning leads to absurdity.[2]

This rule quite evidently is a practical compromise introduced to provide for cases similar to that presented by Salicetus and to furnish a means of escape from the dilemma of the Bolognese barber. If it be accepted in theory, the accepted rule that statutes in derogation of the common law are to be strictly construed no longer stands without exception. It was possible, however, to preserve both the old rule and the new by a distinction in the scholastic manner: the rule in the Bologna case is regarded as having been reached through an 'interpretatio declarativa' — a merely analytical examination of the statute's words — from which must be sharply distinguished the 'interpretatio extensiva' which is permitted only to statutes not contrary to common law and allows the judge to proceed by analogy in the recognized common law manner.[3] It will be observed, of course, that the distinction between these two methods of interpretation is a tenuous one, and that in reality the former looks not merely to the words of the statute but seeks to ascertain its meaning by an examination of its purpose and function. This seems especially clear when it becomes accepted doctrine that in the 'interpretatio declarativa' if the words as grammatically understood conflict with colloquial usage, usage is to prevail. This is interpretation in a real sense:

si communis usus loquendi repugnat propriae significationi, tunc mens legis est, quod intelligamus secundum communem usum loquendi, licet sit improprius. . . . In istis ergo casibus, si quis faceret contra mentem legis et non offenderet verba, incideret in legem et idem e converso, si quis faceret contra verba, non contra mentem, non incideret in legem.[4]

So too, Angelus de Ubaldis permits great latitude in the interpretation of statutes contrary to common law since he limits the definition of the word quite severely and defines as interpretation only that which goes beyond what may be found 'in verbis et in mente.' 'Interpretatio . . . proprie est, cum casus, de quo quaeritur, in verbis nec in mente continetur, sed solum propter identitatem rationis extendi potest ad casum, de quo quaeritur.'[5] But jurists were by no means agreed in accepting standard rules of statutory interpretation. There is much discussion of 'interpretatio declarativa,' 'intellectiva,' 'correctiva,' 'extensiva,' 'restrictiva,' and the words 'absurditas' and 'mens statuti' play a large part in the theories of many thinkers. A statement, however, upon which substantial agreement may be found is this: if the purpose of the statute is written into the statute proper it may be utilized, if it is not written, the result must be otherwise.[6]

[1] *Repetitio: lex Omnes populi* (D 1.1.9) in *Digestum Vetus* (Venice, 1585), 87.

[2] Bartolus, C 1.14 De leg. et const. 5.12: 'Non incidit in legem quia statutum sic intellectum contineret absurdum. Intelligatur ergo, si quis extraxerit sanguinem iniuriose, non autem si extraxerit alii providendo.' Bartolus, D 1.1 De iust. et iure 9.60. Angelus, *Consilia*, 234, 2.

[3] Gandinus (ed. Kantorowicz), p. 365. Alb. de Rosc., *Tract. de Stat.*, I, 9, 3; I, 9, 7; I, 9, 29; II, 99, 2.

[4] C 1.14 De leg. et const. 5.11. Alb. de Rosc., I, 84.   [5] D 48.8 Ad. 1 Corn. de Sic. 3.2.

[6] Bartolus, D 39.4 De publ. et vect. 15.19: 'Iacobus de Arena dicit, quod aut apparet ratio statuti et tunc illa attenditur, alias secus. . . . Circa hoc attende, si apparet de ratione statuti [et] est

Baldus, it is true, in one passage goes beyond this, and permits extension by analogy even though the purpose is not written, if it can be inferred by reason,[1] but we have been able to find no other jurist of the period who accepts this advanced view, and Baldus elsewhere adopts the orthodox view.

Just as they deal with the extension of a statute's words to include a situation not directly provided for, the commentators deal likewise with a statute's restriction to exclude cases which its general words seem to include. The former is regarded as 'interpretatio activa,' the latter, as 'interpretatio passiva,' and the problem raised is looked upon not as restricting the statute's words, but as 'utrum leges se extendant ad statuta' — whether common law will be read into statutes. There is little disagreement here: all jurists admit it necessary to read sound common law policy into loose and widely phrased statutory generalizations.

Si statutum dicit, quod si quis occiderit, occidatur, illud restringitur secundum ius commune, ut distinguatur dolus a culpa et an ad sui defensionem fecerit necne. . . .[2]

And the case of the Bolognese barber is placed upon a more logical foundation than that of absurdity upon which it had rested:

Et idem si dicat, si quis sanguinem fecerit in palatio, decapitetur, nam restringi debet ad facientem animo iniuriandi, non fleubotomandi causa ut in barbitonsore.[3]

Statuta debent benigne interpretari, et ideo si statutum dicit, quod si quis extraxerit sanguinem, puniatur, non intelligitur de medico vel barbitonsore.[4]

We may summarize our results as follows: common law policy is read into statutes; on the other hand, only those statutes may be freely extended beyond their literal word content that do not restrain the common law. Those which change common law rules may be extended only if their application leads to an absurd result or if their purpose is written into the statute and need not be inferred.[5]

---

scripti: confiteor una cum Iacobo praedicto. Si vero de ratione et mente apparet, non tamen est scripta in statutis, tunc non sto cum Iacobo.' Alb. de Rosc., 1, 9, 25, 59; Baldus, D 1.1 De iust. et iure 9.59: 'si talis intellectus est rationabilis et potest colligi ex verbis, vel intellectus contrarius est impossibilis, tunc debemus sequi mentem . . . secus, si ex verbis non potest elici nec presumi, quia tunc dicitur casus omissus.'

[1] *Consilia*, IV, 3, 2.

[2] Salicetus, C 1.3 De episc. et cler. 15.10. Baldus, c.1 X de constitut. 1, 2, 15: 'Hoc est dicere, quod ius commune informat statuta et vestit, sed non informatur nec vestitur ab eis, et hoc propter virtutem attractivam, quam habet ius commune ad municipale, non e contra.'

[3] Salicetus, *ibid.*   [4] Baldus, D 1.3 De leg. senatusque cons. 18.1.

[5] Alb. de Rosc., D 39.4 De publ. et vect. 15.30: 'aut statutum est nulla lege adiuvatum et hoc contingit, quando est reprobatum a iure, et tunc non valet, nec in casu expresso . . . , aut statutum est omni lege adiuvatum, ut quia est omnimodo secundum dispositionem iuris communis, et tunc puto servandum de statuto, quod observaretur de iure communi. . . . Aut statutum est lege generali adiuvatum . . . , sed non speciali, quia est contra dispositionem iuris communis . . . , et tunc dic: aut in statuto est scripta ratio, et tunc sto ratione. . . . Si vero ratio non est scripta in statuto, posito quod millies appareret de mente, non recedam a verbis nec extendam nec restringam et mentem. . . . Ex quibus omnibus videtur concludendum, quod statuta, quae sunt contra ius commune, non recipiant interpretationem extensivam vel restrictivam.'

II

The English development is remarkably similar, and it owes its similarity not to influence — for neither system influenced the other — but simply to the dictates of formal logic. There is no developed system of statutory interpretation in England until late in the fourteenth century, and the lateness of this development is due largely to the close union of powers which rendered it at first unnecessary. Later, with courts still able to refer disputed points to the council or parliament, the need for extending their technical equipment did not make itself felt.[1] But when the differentiation of court and *curia* finds judges no longer able to draw upon the legislature, and makes them dependent upon a document as the sole basis for their action, we find the doctrine of strict, literal interpretation adopted there as it had been in Italy. The first signs of the tendency appear in 1312,[2] and by 1346 it is well established.[3] The distinction made by the commentators between statutes that merely affirmed existing common law and those that restricted or contradicted it we likewise may find made by English common lawyers, though they make it in terms of a native doctrine of 'the equity of a statute' which we may define as the penumbra which, under favorable circumstances, the literal words of the statute may expand to fill.

Kingsmill — . . . Car ou un statut est fait que abrige le comon ley, nul chose sera pris per equite de ceo. Cest statut abrige le ley. . . . *Coningsby* — Al contrary; . . . le statut fuit fait par ouster delais . . . car il enlarge le comon ley . . . et si sic, il sera pris alarge. Et cases que sont in mesme le mischief pris per l'equite de ceo . . . mes si un statut abrige le comon ley out soit penal, la nul equite sera pris. . . .[4]

Thus statutes in derogation of the common law are strictly construed, those which do not contradict it may be extended beyond their literal word content by means of the doctrine of the statute's equity. But the application of the literal words of a penal statute did not always lead to justice, and in England, just as in Italy, though it is agreed that the literal words will not be extended, resort may be had to the 'interpretatio declarativa' or analytical examination of the statute's content to avoid an otherwise absurd result.

. . . by the statute of 25 Edw. III it is declared that if a servant kill his master it is treason. And in Hen. VI [Mich. 102] one was arraigned upon an indictment for killing the wife of

---

[1] H. G. Richardson and G. Sayles, 'The Early Statutes,' *Law Quarterly Rev.*, L (1934), 201, 540, 562. T. F. T. Plucknett, *Statutes and their interpretation in the first half of the fourteenth century* (Cambridge, 1922), pp. 55–56, 168.

[2] Belsham v. atte Street, Y.B. 5 Edw. II (Selden Soc. vol. XXXIII), p. 46: 'Nous ne deuoms autrement entendre lestatut qele ne parle mes statut ne parle si noun ou le tenant est en point de perdre par defaute mes le tenant ne etc. par defaute einz par defaute de noun seute vers lour garenter par quei demandoms iugement.' Le Warde v. Wullesthorpe, Y.B. 17 Edw. III (Rolls Ser.), p. 142 (1342–43); Sybeling v. Mussendene, Y.B. 17 and 18 Edw. III (Rolls Ser.), p. 446 (1343). Plucknett, *Statutes*, pp. 82–90, 164–169.

[3] Waghan v. Anon, Y.B. 20 Edw. III (2) [Rolls Ser.], p. 198: 'Nous ne poms prendre lestatut plus avant qe les paroles en ycele ne parle.'

[4] Y.B. 7 Hen. VI, Mich. 16 (1429). Y.B. 5 Edw. IV (Long Quinto) p. 62 (1466). Y.B. 18 Edw. IV, Mich. 18 (1479). Y.B. 11 Hen. VI, Trin. 23. Y.B. 5 Hen. VII, Mich. 11 (1490). Y.B. 7 Hen. VII, Pasch. 2 (1492). Y.B. 14 Hen. VII, Hil. 2 (1499). Y.B. 14 Hen. VII, Hil. 7 (1499). Y.B. 21 Hen. VII, Hil. 28 (1506).

his master, and he confessed, and there it came in question whether he should be drawn or hanged only, whereupon it is to be seen whether it be treason or not, and there it was adjudged, by the advice of all the justices of the one Bench and the other [in the Exchequer Chamber] that he should be drawn and hanged, because it was treason; and there it is not taken within the equity of the statute, which speaks only of killing his master, but rather within the words of the statute, for master and mistress are the same thing in effect. So that there the taking it to be treason is a declaration of the words of the statute rather than an equitable construction of it.[1]

The common lawyers, too, frequently were forced to restrict the scope of a statute by excepting particular cases from its operation. The most obvious were those in which the statute, though generally phrased, was not interpreted to include infants, married women, and persons *non compos mentis*, but other examples are numerous.[2]

These are halting methods of interpretation. In England (as in Italy) great reliance is placed upon the common law as the norm by which statutes are to be construed. Just as Iohannis Calderinus may say, 'certum est quod in dubio fieri debet interpretatio statuti secundum dispositionem iuris communis,' so Sir Edward Coke finds 'the surest construction of the statute to be by the rule and reason of the common law.' This often led to a narrow and jealous interpretation of statutes: judges were too willing to regard a statute contrary to common law as undesirable, but on the other hand, the rule acted as a guide without which the continuity of legal development would have been gravely imperilled. But by the close of the middle ages Englishmen may say with Plowden — though in practice the rule is not adopted — that 'words, which are no other than the verberation of the air, do not constitute the statute, but are only the image of it, and the life of the statute rests in the minds of the expositors of the words, that is, the makers of the statutes,'[3] just as the commentators said with Baldus, without adopting the rule in practice, that 'virtus enim legis consistit in substantia rationis, . . . quia mens legis idem est quod anima et spiritus ipsius scripture. Nam scriptura sine mente nihil est.'[4] Only slowly do judges begin to center attention upon the *ratio legis*, and then only when it can be collected from the statute itself. The rule formulated in the well-known dictum of Baron Parke in

---

[1] Partridge v. Strange and Croker, Plowd., pp. 77, 86. The matter was further expounded by Hales, J.—'The plural number contains in itself the singular number and more. And therefore the statute of 1 Hen. v, c. 3 recites "that whereas some people do of late use to forge divers false deeds and muniments, etc.," therefore it ordains that the party thereby grieved shall have his suit in that case, etc., here the statute speaks of false deeds in the plural number, yet if a man forge one deed, he shall be punished by the statute. So the statute of 5 Rich. II, c. 7 ordains, "that none shall make entry into any lands and tenements, except in case where entry is given by law," yet if a man enters into one tenement, he shall be punished notwithstanding the statute is in the plural number.' Cf. the exact situation in Alb. de Rosc., *Tract. de Statutis*, II, 28. There the production of false witnesses (producere testes) was punishable, but the defendant produced by one false witness.

[2] Y.B. 30 Edw. III, Mich. 6 (1356). Y.B. 36 Edw. III, Mich. (1362). Y.B. 19 Rich. II, Mich. (1396). Y.B. 11 Hen. IV, Hil. 28 (1410), Y.B. 1 Hen. VI (Selden Soc. vol. L) p. 30 (1422). Y.B. 4 Hen. VII, Trin. 6 (1489). Y.B. 21 Hen. VII, Hil. 28 (1506). [3] Partridge v. Strange and Croker, Plowd., 77, 82.

[4] C. 1 X De constitut. 1, 2, 15. Since this was written, I have treated the English material somewhat more fully in 'The Equity of a Statute and Heydon's Case,' *Illinois Law Review*, XXXI (1936), 202-217. See below, pp. 155-70.

1836 sums up the science of statutory interpretation both in England and in Italy during the late middle ages:

It is a very useful rule in the construction of a statute to adhere to the ordinary meaning of the words used, and to the grammatical construction, unless that is at variance with the intention of the legislature to be collected from the statute itself, or leads to any manifest absurdity or repugnance.[1]

Legislation comes late to both legal systems, and the problem of fitting diverse statutes into a body of closely knit doctrine is treated in the same way by both. The process is a striking one, especially in the absence of evidence of mutual dependence.

[1] Becke v. Smith, 2 M. & W. 191, 195.

3

ENGLISH FEUDALISM AND ESTATES IN LAND*

IT is fitting for a lecturer to pay his tribute to the man under whose auspices, so to speak, he lectures. That sometimes is a difficult matter, requiring the closing of an eye to many things, but in this case I am happily absolved from any such necessity, for there can be no doubt that Maitland was a man of genius. I hardly need say this in Cambridge, or in any other place where scholars come together, for his reputation has been long and securely established. It is now more than half a century since his death, and longer since his books were written, yet they are today more widely read than ever. The intensive researches of the last fifty years have made only the smallest alterations in the conclusions they reached. He himself was perhaps not quite as sure of them as we are. The most honest of men, he was always careful to reveal his doubts, and it is to a subject on which he had many doubts that I address myself today. I shall talk about the ownership and heritability of land in the twelfth century, in other words, about the emergence of the fee simple as an estate in land. I shall begin by setting before you Maitland's own account.

Maitland began by assuming that fiefs held by military service were heritable from the days of the Conquest.[1] That was universally assumed by the historians of his day and is still assumed by the most reputable, though, in the light of evidence discovered since Maitland's day, the heritability of military fiefs is now said to have been firmly established not at the Conquest but at the beginning of the twelfth century. The initial difficulty of this assumption, that Glanvill, writing at the end of the twelfth century, still knew nothing of the rules of inheritance, Maitland saw,[2] but in the face of evidence apparently making it quite clear that fiefs had descended from father to son from the beginning

3

* This is the first of the Frederic William Maitland Memorial Lectures given in Cambridge during February 1959. It was read again in Oxford in May. The lectures will appear in book form and I therefore have postponed any full citation of authorities, contenting myself with references to easily accessible books which may readily be consulted. It is a very pleasant duty to acknowledge here my indebtedness to the Managers of the F. W. Maitland Memorial Fund and to the Law and History Faculties of the University.

1 Pollock and Maitland, *History of English Law* (2nd ed.), i, 314–316.
2 P. & M., ii, 293–294.

of the twelfth century at the latest, Glanvill's ignorance had to
be explained in another way.[3]   Having thus begun by assuming
heritability, Maitland had to regard the tenant of military land as
its " owner "—I use this word in its ordinary sense—for obviously
one could hardly inherit from an ancestor who had held his fief
only for life.   But difficulties then presented themselves.   The documents of the twelfth century disclosed that a tenant by knight's
service was very far from being an " owner "—for example, he
apparently required the consent of his expectant heirs in order to
convey his land to third persons,[4] and many charters showed him
securing the consent, apparently the necessary consent, of his lord
as well.[5]   Such requirements would seem to reduce the tenant's
interest to something less than " ownership," perhaps to some
temporary interest in the land only, but if so, how could one
explain the heritability of fiefs which descended with regularity
from ancestor to heir?   The tenant had to be considered the
" owner " of his fief and the limitations upon him regarded not
as diminishing his " ownership " but merely as restraining his
power to alienate.[6]   The first restraint he found to derive from a
sort of family ownership, or more precisely, to be an indication
of a deeply rooted sentiment that land, even land held by military
service, should descend equally to all a man's sons.[7]   That is the
reason their consents were required when he sought, in his lifetime,
to alienate a portion to a stranger.   Dealings with land, however,
were few in the twelfth century, and the main purpose of the rule,
Maitland said, was to restrain a father from giving one of his sons
a larger portion than he could in due course expect.   The second
restraint, a tenant's need to secure his lord's consent to his alienations, Maitland attributed to some indeterminate right the lord had
to prevent alienations which would seriously impair his interests,
that is, his right to the services due him from the land.[8]

Now both these restrictions disappear in the last quarter of the
twelfth century; the requirement of the heir's consent, indeed, in
its last few years, for Glanvill, writing shortly before 1189, still
regarded such consent as necessary.[9]   Maitland was thus faced with
explaining their rapid disappearance.   In his view, the consent of
the expectant heir vanishes because of the introduction of primogeniture.   It would have been unfair to allow the eldest son to
object to gifts made to his brothers when their father's land had

[3] P. & M., i, 315–316.
[4] P. & M., ii, 13, 309–311.
[5] P. & M., i, 340 *et seq.*, 345.
[6] P. & M., ii, 13, 15, 17.
[7] P. & M., ii, 309, 312.
[8] P. & M., i, 332, 343.
[9] P. & M., ii, 308–309, 311, 313.

become no longer partible but inheritable only by him. The object of the rule had been to achieve an equal division among the sons. It was unbearable that it should continue, that the eldest should be able to prevent his father's gifts to his brothers, when, if none were made, all would come to him at his father's death.[10] Thus free alienation without the heir's consent comes in the wake of primogeniture. The disappearance of any need for the lord's consent is the result of a strong bias in favour of free alienation on the part of the king's justices. "They were disposed," Maitland said, "to concede to every tenant the fullest possible power in dealing with his land."[11]

There are grave difficulties in this ingenious analysis—the partibility of the knight's fee, the late appearance of primogeniture, the so-called bias of the king's justices in favour of freedom of alienation—which must remind one inevitably, as Professor Plucknett has said, of Adam Smith rather than of the *curia regis* of the late twelfth century. Its basic flaw was the assumption that military fiefs were heritable from the Conquest or soon thereafter, which made it necessary to regard the very first tenants by knight service as "owners" of their land. I propose to show that the military fief was not heritable until about the year 1200 and that its tenant held merely an estate for life. To the alienations of such a tenant, the consents of his lord and (if the gift was to continue after his death) of his heir were naturally necessary. If that is true, we may dispense with the theory of the partibility of knights' fees, equally divided among sons, for which there is no real evidence. Ownership and its concomitant heritability will then appear about the year 1200, and with ownership the consents formerly required will fall away. No further explanation for their disappearance is necessary and we may then return primogeniture to its proper place in the late eleventh century and discard the bias of the king's court toward freedom of alienation. When the tenant had become the owner of his fief, the judges naturally were disposed to concede to him the fullest possible power in dealing with his land.[12]

Let me turn first to the heritability of knights' fees. Maitland asked the question whether the followers of the Conqueror, who received great gifts of English land, held those lands heritably, and answered, writing before 1898 and thus in ignorance of evidence to be discovered later, that it was certain that they did so.[13] Professor Ganshof, writing within the last dozen years, says,

10 P. & M., ii, 20, 308–309, 312.
11 P. & M., i, 344.
12 P. & M., ii, 5, 6.
13 P. & M., i, 314.

"in England the heritability of fiefs was not generally established in the period immediately following the Norman Conquest. The two earliest charters of enfeoffment which we possess, dating from before 1087, seem to have contemplated nothing more than grants for life, though it is worth noting that in both cases the fiefs did become hereditary. By the twelfth century, however, heritability must be regarded as characteristic of the English fief." [14] And so Professor Plucknett: "By 1100 it therefore appears that the hereditary principle was admitted by the king in favour of his tenants in chief, and by them in favour of their sub-tenants." [15] And so Sir Frank Stenton: "In view of the number of tenancies, obviously military from the beginning, which can be traced from the Conqueror's time through the reigns of his sons, there is no room for doubt that knights' fees were in fact normally hereditary from the time of the first enfeoffments." [16]

Now in truth military tenancies often did pass from father to son, from ancestor to heir, but that does not necessarily imply heritability. If I hire my gardener's son after his father's death, and my son hires his son after him, the place as gardener has descended through three generations of the same family. Yet it is obvious that it has come to each by gift, and that the son and grandson of my gardener can in no way be said to have inherited it. What we have is a fief held by successive tenants in return for service, each succeeding by gift.

In feudal theory, a fief was given to a vassal in return for his homage and service. It was to provide his maintenance and give him the means of furnishing his lord with the service due.[17] Thus, it was his for no fixed period, but only as long as the personal relationship of vassalage, the tie of homage between lord and man which constituted his title, continued.[18] When that came to an end, as it did on the death of either of the parties, his fief came to an end with it. If it was the tenant who had died, the land reverted at once to the lord. Put more precisely, land which had been the lord's all along, subject to the tenant's interest, became his free of that interest. He could take it into his hand if he so wished, expelling the heir, but whether he did so or not, his rights in it revived in their entirety.[19] By the same token, the tenant's heir had no rights in the land but merely a claim to succeed his

14 *Feudalism* (1952), 120–121.
15 *Concise History of the Common Law* (5th ed.), 524. But p. 360: "The assize of mortdancestor (1176) played a large part in the final establishment of the hereditary principle."
16 *English Feudalism* (1932), 160.
17 Ganshof, *Feudalism*, 96, 121.
18 *Ibid.*, 38.
19 *Ibid.*, 121.

ancestor as the lord's feudal man, that is, to have the lord accept his homage and regrant to him the fief which had supported his ancestor's service and was now to support his own. This was a relationship into which the lord was not compelled to enter, and thus the regrant of his ancestor's fief to the heir not one he was required to make. To persuade him to do so a payment, a relief, might be offered.[20] When it was the lord who had died, his tenant still alive, homage came to an end in the same way and with it the fief it had guaranteed.[21] The tenant had merely a claim to be accepted as the feudal man of the new lord who had succeeded as heir and then to have regranted to him the land he had held. For this a payment might also be offered since the new lord was in no way bound to take his ancestor's tenant as his own.[22] What from below is a succession of lords is, of course, from above a succession of tenants. The new lord (let me call him B's heir, son of the former lord B) had come to the land not by descent but by virtue of a regrant made to him by his own lord A after the fief had returned to him at B's death. Thus, he took the fief free of any gifts B had made, all such estates having come to an end with the death of their warrantor B.

The acceptance by B, after his tenant C's death, of the homage of his heir, or if it was the lord B who had died, his heir's acceptance of C's homage, was the essential element in this scheme. It was the bond of homage between them, which barred the lord from himself retaking the land and obliged him to defend it against others, that constituted the tenant's title to his holding, the warrant by which he occupied his lord's land. In the absence of homage, or on its disappearance by death, disavowal or the commission of felony, he was without a warrantor, without title, and thus without defence.

By the second quarter of the twelfth century, the lands given by the Conqueror to his barons for their homage and service had been given again, by him or by his successors, first to their sons and then to their grandsons. In the same way, the fiefs given by such lords to their men for the service of a knight or knights had come into the hands of their descendants. This devolution, it seems likely, was neither dictated by law nor accomplished by agreement between the parties.[23] It was the result of expediency. It was essential that in military fiefs there should be a constant

[20] *Ibid.*, 122.
[21] *Ibid.*, 38, 39, 42, 124.
[22] *Ibid.*, 124–125.
[23] Douglas, *Feudal Documents from Bury St. Edmunds* (1932), cii–ciii; Plucknett, *Concise History*, 524; P. & M., i, 316: "the truth is that men gave lands and took lands and left the terms of the tenure to be decided by the course of events and their own strong wills."

and unbroken succession of men responsible for service. As they
were removed by death, replacements might be chosen at large,
but it must soon have become evident that, from a purely practical
point of view, no one was likely to be more readily available, or
more acceptable to the men of the fief, or (in the great majority
of cases) better prepared to undertake the duties required, than
the deceased tenant's eldest son. Primogeniture, all things considered, provided the best, if not always the most perfect solution
to the problem. The substitution of heir for ancestor, a practice
followed independently by many lords in many cases, gradually
established the general rule. For many years, however, though an
heir could look forward with increasing confidence to occupying
his ancestor's fief, he was far from being able to demand it as of
right. And on the lord's side, his regrant to the heir long retained
the character it had first had, that of a gift he might or might not
make. Made, perhaps, without enthusiasm, only because of the
absence of any practical alternative, as where I take on my
gardener's son after his father's death, it was a gift nonetheless;
it was only slowly borne in upon him that he was making a gift
required by law. But whatever the Conqueror's original grants
had contemplated and whatever the reasons which led to the introduction of primogeniture, by the second quarter of the twelfth
century tenants by military service had come to hold their fiefs
heritably. Their holdings devolved according to hereditary right.[24]
But the military fief had not gone in one long jump from a holding
which fell into the lord's hand at the tenant's death, thus requiring, if his heir was to have it, a gift or regrant by the lord,
to one that passed to such heir independently of the lord, descending to him directly from his ancestor. That position was only
slowly reached and had not yet been achieved by the third quarter
of the twelfth century.

A gift by B to C for his homage and service, even one to him
and his heirs in fee and inheritance, still gave C, in the first part
of the century, a fief of the traditional kind which came to an end
when the homage between himself and his lord B disappeared.
If it was C who had died, the land he had held fell into the hand
of his lord B, remaining his until he had taken the homage of
C's heir and given the land to him.[25] If the holding was by knight
service, this was a gift B was bound to make, but a gift nonetheless, for nothing descended to C's heir from his ancestor, whose

---

[24] See the charter of 1122 in Stenton, *English Feudalism*, 154–155; *Sir
Christopher Hatton's Book of Seals* (1950), No. 528.

[25] This long remained true of the king and his tenants in chief: *Book of Seals*,
No. 174. His position was not from the first exceptional: P. & M., i, 312,
n. 2.

life estate had come to an end, and he could come to the land in no other way. For it a relief might justifiably be asked, and if a charter were drawn the verbs "*reddo et concedo,*" even the verbs "*do et concedo*" proper to a new and original gift, were quite appropriate.[26] If it was B, the lord, who had died, his fief, of which C's holding was part, came to an end with his death and reverted to his own lord A. It was his until he had taken the homage of B's heir and given the fief to him. Before that had been done, if the heir, impatient of delay, entered upon the land, he was guilty of a wrongful intrusion.[27] If B's service had been military, A's gift was one he had become bound to make, but, as above, a gift nevertheless, for which a relief might legitimately be asked. After the regrant had been made, B's heir was not in by descent, his ancestor having held only a temporary estate, but, as any stranger might be, by gift. Thus, he took the holding free of the alienations his ancestor had made. With the death of B, their warrantor, the estates of his grantees had fallen to the ground. Thus, a new gift to C by his new lord was necessary. If C was a military tenant this was a gift B's heir had become bound to make, but here again, it was a gift nonetheless, for which a relief might be asked.

When it was C who had died, B was bound to regrant to C's heir if the holding was military, but only if he was of full age and on the land, ready to perform the service required. It often happened, however, that the heir was unascertained at his ancestor's death, or if known, was absent, or a minor incapable of homage and military service. Under such circumstances, where there was no one to do the service, the land had of necessity to remain in the lord's hand until such time as the heir had been ascertained or had made his appearance or reached full age. It would then be given to him in return for his homage.

By the middle of the twelfth century regrants regularly made had given tenants, whose lands had been held by their fathers and grandfathers before them, a more proprietary interest in their holdings. If the land they held was not yet wholly their own, it was no longer wholly the property of their lords; ownership was divided between them. Homage only half conferred a new title upon the tenant, half perfected a title already his. On his lord B's death C must still have his homage accepted by his new lord, but before that was done he was not entirely without right, as he once had been. And in the same way, though on his ancestor's

---

[26] Stenton, *English Feudalism*, 271, Nos. 24 and 25; 272, No. 26; 282, No. 43; Stenton, *Documents Illustrative of the Danelaw* (1920), Nos. 457, 518; *Book of Seals*, Nos. 50, 374.

[27] Here again the king's position is not at first exceptional: P. & M., i, 311.

death an heir had to have his homage accepted by B his lord before his ancestor's fief could properly become his, that no longer provided the sole warrant for his occupation. He had a title of a kind to his patrimony or heritage, a title prior to and independent of homage. The land was his as of right.[28] By the same token, lords had come to regard their fiefs as divided into two clearly distinguished portions: lands subinfeudated to others for military service and lands not so subinfeudated, *feudum* and *dominium*. A lord's rights in those of his lands which were in the hands of his tenants had weakened, as had their own in the lands they had themselves subinfeudated. And as their rights in the land they held in demesne had been strengthened at their lord's expense, so had his in his *dominium* at the expense of his own lord. But though his subinfeudated land was no longer his in the same sense that his *dominium* was, it had not slipped from his fingers completely, nor had his interest been reduced to that of being seised only of an incorporeal seignory. It was still recognisably his though by his gift it was presently in the hands of temporary tenants and though, after it had reverted to him at their deaths, it would in due course again be given to their heirs.

The future lay with the tenant, and here we must remember that all men were tenants except the king. In 1166 the interest of a tenant in demesne of the land was recognised by providing him with an action of his own for recovering land of which he had been disseised. He had not simply possession but "*une jouissance toute pénétrée d'éléments de droit.*" Nevertheless the lord's right remained as well. At his tenant's death the land fell at once into his hand; his rights had, in fact, been there all along; the tenant's rights had simply disappeared. There was, consequently, no reason why he might not enter upon it. He was required to give it to the tenant's heir, but until that gift had been made the heir, though of full age and on the land, could hardly be said to have his ancestor's holding, for he took nothing by descent. Technically the tenant still occupied another's land, and, if he was to have a title to it valid against his lord, his homage had to be accepted; it was that which barred the lord and provided, as long as it subsisted, the warrant for his occupation.

His lord's title was superior to the tenant's, but homage, as long as it continued, barred him from asserting it. It was along this line that legal theory began to accommodate itself to reality. Traditionally homage had disappeared with the death of either of the parties to it, but it now was regarded as continuing for a

---

[28] Stenton, *English Feudalism*, 271, No. 24; *Book of Seals*, No. 513.

longer time. It disappeared only when both were dead, subsisting as long as either survived.[29] Thus, when it was B, the lord, who had died, his heir when he came to the land (and if he died, his heir after him) was barred by the homage his ancestor had taken from entering upon the tenant C, who thus was guaranteed an estate for life which survived any change of lords. There was here no reversion and consequently no regrant and no relief. On C's death, however, the arrangement came to an end and his heir had to secure a new grant from B's heir.[30] And so when it was C, the tenant, who had died. If his heir was of full age and on the land at his ancestor's death, B was barred by the homage still subsisting from entering upon him, or if he died leaving an heir of full age, upon such heir. Despite the absence of actual homage between the tenant and his lord, B was barred as long as he lived. There was thus no reversion on C's death, no regrant and no relief. But on B's death the arrangement ended and C's heir had to secure a new grant from B's heir.[31] If the land was held by military service, both the above were regrants B's heir was bound to make, but he and C's heir were strangers and a new arrangement had to be entered into, through the renewal of homage or by a charter of gift. For either a relief might legitimately be asked. Homage, though preserved by a fiction, could not survive the deaths of both the parties to it and with its disappearance the tenant's title failed.

It was becoming very difficult, by the third quarter of the century, to see why, if at his ancestor's death he was of full age and ready to perform the service due, the land should not be the heir's at once, without a gift from his lord, before he had done the homage his lord was bound to accept and before he had paid his relief, a payment which no longer bore any relation to the value of the fief but had become a fixed charge reflecting the merely formal nature of the regrant for which it was the fee. The justice of this view was recognised by the Assize of Northampton in 1176. Such an heir need neither do homage nor pay a relief before having seisin of his ancestor's holding. This did not mean that he need never do homage nor pay relief nor that the lord had lost all interest in the land. It no longer reverted to him in fact, but it did so in theory; until the heir had done what was required of him both the fief and the heir were in his hand.[32] But the heir was seised of the land in demesne, the lord seised

---

[29] S. J. Bailey in Camb.L.J., viii, 278–280; ix, 88–93, 194.
[30] Stenton, *English Feudalism*, 159, 274, No. 31.
[31] *Ibid.*, 161, n. 2, 277, Nos. 34 and 35 (the word " *patre* " is omitted in line 5: " *de meo patre* "); *Book of Seals*, Nos. 88, 330.
[32] Glanvill, vii, 9; P. & M., i, 310.

only of an incorporeal interest. He suffered no loss since, as
before, the profits of the land were his until the heir had done
his homage and paid his relief. Nevertheless, there was no reversion in fact and thus no gift. The way had opened for the
idea that an heir inherited directly from his ancestor.

Seisin was not heritable nor did the land descend to the heir.
He was simply to have what his ancestor had held. Unless he
was of full age and on the land at his ancestor's death the land
still reverted to the lord, for the ancestor had held only for life.[33]
If he entered before the heir he committed no disseisin, and so if
he did not surrender it until required to do so by the assize he
need pay no damages; indeed, since the land was his, if he wasted
the tenement no damages were due to the heir. Except when the
heir was of full age and on the land at his ancestor's death, therefore, if the heir was to have the land a gift was still necessary,
but if the lord did not give it the sheriff would. It was thus no
longer a gift in any reasonable sense; it was the heir's right. If
a charter were drawn the proper words were " *concedo et confirmo*," denoting an act of confirmation, rather than the " *do et
concedo* " which had formerly been appropriate; though not found
earlier, charters of this kind have survived in considerable number
from the third quarter of the twelfth century.[34] Homage still
remained the basis of the tenant's title, but it had assumed a more
attenuated form: once taken, it subsisted as long as the tenant's
line continued, providing a permanent warrant for his heirs' occupation and barring the lord and his heirs from ever entering upon
them.[35] The lord's interest in the land, a real and undeniable
one, was not taken from him[36]; he was left his superior title; he
and his heirs were simply barred from asserting it against the
tenant and his heirs. The tenant had not yet become an " owner,"
holding in fee; he remained a life tenant only, his heirs succeeding
to life estates after him, no longer by successive gifts and homages
renewed but by force of the original gift made to him and his
heirs and the original homage. It would soon be seen that a
perpetual bar, which made the assertion of the only effective
superior title impossible, made the land the tenant's own; that
one who could give effectively an estate which might continue
indefinitely, without the need for subsequent regrants, was himself something more than a tenant for life; and that if one could
bar one's heirs from asserting their title and make them the
warrantors of the tenant and his heirs in perpetuity, such heirs

[33] P. & M., i, 310–311.
[34] Stenton, *English Feudalism*, 161.
[35] Bailey in (1958) 9 Camb.L.J. 194.
[36] P. & M., i, 237, n. 1.

did not take by virtue of the original gift, which would give them each a life interest in a knight's fee for a knight's service, but took only what their ancestor left, by inheritance from him. But that we have not reached that point by 1189 is evident from Glanvill's book.

Glanvill puts this case.[37] A father, whom we shall call F, has three sons, whom in order of their birth we call A, B and C. With the consent of A, F makes a feoffment to B for his service and takes his homage. Then B dies without issue, leaving F, A and C. To whom does the land go? This is a knotty problem, a *magna juris dubitatio*, which taxes the wisdom of the wisest lawyers. Though he is not quite sure whether A or C will prevail, Glanvill is clear that F, the father, cannot take and that his claim must be rejected. Why? He cannot possibly succeed to the land, Glanvill says, because he has taken the homage of B, which will bar him. This is the origin of the rule, law until 1833, that ascendants cannot inherit, but Glanvill does not formulate, nor, lacking the power to look into the future, could he be expected to formulate that rule. Had he seen the problem in that light, how much simpler to have said nothing of homage and to have explained that an elementary rule of the law of inheritance excludes all direct ascendants of the dead man.

As long as the ancestor had only a life estate there could be no inheritance, and that he had no more seems clear. In the assise of mortdancestor the question put to the recognitors was simply whether the ancestor had been seised in his demesne and " as of his fee." Had he, in other words, held it as one normally held a fief, or had he held it as a pledge, or as a loan, or in some other way that made it evident that the land was another's? If he had held it " as of his fee " his heir was to have seisin. But to hold land " as of one's fee " in the late twelfth century meant to hold an estate for one's life to which one's heirs would succeed by force of the original gift. That is the reason why Glanvill, though he considers many exceptions to the assize, objections that could be raised to defeat the demandant, does not contemplate the exception that the ancestor had held only for life. That would seem to us the most obvious objection to the heir's claim, that his action must fail because, since his father held only for life, nothing could descend to him. But Glanvill does not see it that way, for he is thinking of succession and not of inheritance. That one's father had held only for life is no objection to the assise of mortdancestor for everyone who holds in fee to himself and his heirs holds an estate for life, to which in due course his heirs will

[37] Glanvill, vii, 1; P. & M., ii, 286, 289–291, 292–295.

succeed. The same absence of any idea of heritability may be
seen in Glanvill's account of the writ of right for land brought
in the king's court. The demandant makes his claim to the land
as his right and his patrimony, of which his ancestor had been
seised in demesne and as of his fee. He traces no descent from
heir to heir into his own person, as he will have to do in the
thirteenth century, but simply alleges that his ancestor held " as
of fee " and that he is his heir. He is not claiming to succeed
his ancestor by inheritance, but claiming a right that is his by
the form of the original gift. Such is, indeed, the literal meaning
of the words " to his heirs." It is not until the next century
that they are taken to give the heir no rights and to mean simply
that the tenant has an estate in fee simple, one that will endure
as long as any heir of his is alive.[38] If so, on his ancestor's
death the heir can take only by inheritance. As Bracton says,
an heir acquires nothing by virtue of the gift made to his
ancestor, for he is not enfeoffed with him; he takes *ex causa
successionis* not *ex causa donationis*.[39] And so with the assise of
mortdancestor. It will then be said that the heir is entitled to
seisin because his father held an estate of inheritance, which
descended to him; if he did not, the heir's claim must fail.[40]

I have been concerned so far with gifts for homage and service.
If the heirs of lords and tenants alike had become bound to
recognise such gifts made by their ancestors they suffered no loss.
Instead of the land itself they got the service it owed. Subin-
feudations for service, indeed, were required by the system.
Grants made by a lord for military service were dictated by the
military requirements of his fief; they were made not for the personal profit or the convenience of the grantor but for the defence
of the realm. They met the permanent burden put upon the fief
and thus were an assurance to his heirs who likewise were faced
by the necessity of answering, with their required contingent of
knights, the king's summons to the feudal array. Gifts free of
service, however, were an entirely different matter. From the
lord's point of view, though his tenant remained responsible for the
services due from his holding, any gift that diminished the estate
charged with those services, or to put the matter in more modern
form, any gift that depleted the assets of the tenant's fief while
its fixed charges remained constant, made defaults on his part
more likely. From the heir's point of view, to expect him to
bear the burden of services when he succeeded only to an estate
substantially diminished by his father's generosity was to expect

---

[38] P. & M., ii, 13, 329.   [39] *Ibid.*, ii, 14.
[40] *Cf.* van Caenegem, *Royal Writs in England* (Selden Soc.), 322.

the impossible. On the other hand, some gifts free of services, particularly gifts to the church in free alms, were impossible to deny. The problem thus raised was a fundamental one, necessitating the reconciliation of two equally strong and conflicting claims. We may well imagine the many anxious meetings at which such matters were discussed. It is indeed no accident that the great majority of twelfth-century charters which show a lord acting in the presence of, and with the advice of, the men of his barony are concerned with gifts of land in free alms.[41]

In the twelfth century the tenant was in no sense the " owner " of his holding; he at first held land which was more his lord's than his own, then land the ownership of which was divided vaguely between them. Thus, his lord was at first the real donor, and later, if a valid gift was to be made, he had to join with his tenant in making it. If the lord's co-operation was to be secured, it was essential that any gift to the church, free of services, be reasonable. A gift of a very large portion of the tenant's holding was out of the question. A gift that was small, however, or one that was reasonable in the light of the fief's extent and resources, was possible, for there was a good deal of play in the joints of the average fee. What was needed was a judgment by the lord, often by the lord and his men, that the land which remained in the tenant's hand was sufficient to bear the burden fixed upon it, and thus that the total service owed by the lord would not be jeopardised. Giving land free of service when the grand object was to mobilise it for service, especially military service, was a difficult and dangerous matter.[42]

Such a gift was good without the heir's participation; the ancestor was the warrantor of his donee's estate, but with his death it came to an end. The heir, since he did not inherit from his ancestor, took the land free of any alienations his ancestor had made; if they were to take effect again a new grant by him was necessary. Gifts his ancestor had made for military service, for the defence of the realm, he was required to continue, but not those of other kinds unless he desired to do so. Gifts to the church fell into this category, but since they were prima facie reasonable and made for excellent and necessary purposes they were frequently renewed.[43] Certainly the monks would endeavour to see that he did so renew them, and that his heirs did so after him, for they succeeded to the fief in the same way that he had.[44]

---

[41] P. & M., i, 346; Stenton, *English Feudalism*, 89–90.
[42] P. & M., i, 340–343. Maitland did not distinguish sufficiently between gifts for service and gifts free of service; he saw the problem only in general terms: the tenant's capacity to alienate.
[43] *Book of Seals*, Nos. 107, 196, 199, 218, 354, 413, 507. [44] *Ibid.*, Nos. 518, 519.

Piety, simple or filial, usually made the monks' task an easy one, but to make the matter more certain the donor might solemnly order his heirs to respect his gift,[45] or set his curse on the head of any future heir who should attempt to destroy it. That was the function of the anathema clause, not uncommon in twelfth-century charters of gift to religious houses.[46] After the third quarter of the century the heir's charter becomes less a new grant and more a confirmation, the verb " *confirmo* " rather than " *concedo*," for reasons that will become plain in a moment, becoming ever more usual.

The best and most common method of binding one's heir, though it bound only the immediate heir and not his successors, was to have him join in the gift,[47] or secure his consent at the time the gift was made.[48] A great number of charters supply examples of expectant heirs joining in their ancestors' gifts.[49] It was not enough simply to secure the consent of the grantor's eldest son, for one could never be sure that he would in fact be the heir. If he consented and did succeed he could not afterwards complain; but if he died before his father his consent would not bar the actual successor. Thus an abbot, who could not get the consent of the donor's eldest brother, took the consents of his other brothers and of all his other kinfolk, but the eldest brother died in the donor's lifetime and his sons brought suit for the land—a suit the monks were glad to compromise. In some charters the heirs are put before us not merely as assenting to, but as joining in the gift: it is a gift by a man and his heir. In other cases the heirs are simply named among the witnesses. In all, however, there is every indication that actual consent was given: the names of each are supplied, and it is often said that they were present, witnessing and agreeing. But after the first half of Henry II's reign, in the third quarter of the century, the names disappear as does even the notation of consent.[50] Charters simply say " I and my heirs will warrant."

Now the mere use of the word " warrant " by a grantor, even the incorporation into his charter of the statement that he and his heirs will warrant, would earlier have had no special power to bar his immediate heir, to say nothing of his later ones. It is at this same time that we find the appearance of the rule that homage once taken will descend upon the donor's heirs, binding

[45] *Ibid.*, Nos. 153, 507, 510.
[46] P. & M., ii, 329, n. 2; Stenton, *Gilbertine Charters*, xxxiii; Douglas, *Feudal Documents*, 179; Stenton, *English Feudalism*, 37–39.
[47] Stenton, *English Feudalism*, 278, No. 36; 279, No. 38; *Book of Seals*, No. 143.
[48] *Ibid.*, 284, No. 46.
[49] P. & M., ii, 309–311.
[50] Stenton, *Gilbertine Charters*, xix, xxix; *Book of Seals*, No. 196n.

them to warrant the land to the donee and his heirs as long as they continue. These twin developments enabled tenants to bar their heirs from recovering lands they had alienated, but note that they are barred by the homage that descends upon them when their ancestor has given land for homage and by the express warranty that descends upon them when he has given land free of service. Nevertheless, we are moving rapidly toward ownership and heritability. The homage and warranty bars will soon be seen to be but partial expressions of principles that encompass them both. It will no longer be the homage and the warranty which bar an heir from succeeding to something to which he has a right; rather he has a right to nothing except what his ancestor leaves. By the same token, an ancestor can dispose of his land permanently not because the homage he has taken or the warranty he has given will bar his heirs, but because he has become, as he is in Bracton, the *verus dominus*, the real lord, the true owner of the land.[51]

This development may be dated within narrow limits. Glanvill does not yet accept it but it has been achieved by the early thirteenth century. The old distinction between conquest and heritage still finds a place in his book; a man may dispose of land he has acquired with greater ease than he may his patrimony. His patrimony he does not yet wholly own.[52] He may give a certain part of it with his daughter in (free) marriage, a certain part (free of service) as a reward to retainers, and a certain part to the church in free alms. If these are reasonable gifts, made with reference to the service due and the size and resources of his fief, they are good. But a father may not give any part of his heritage to his younger sons without the consent of the eldest. What this had once meant was that the heir must warrant the first gifts, that is, recognise them when he had succeeded to his ancestor's entire holding, even though they had been good only for his ancestor's lifetime; but that, when the fief had come into his hand free of his ancestor's gifts, he need not recognise a gift made to a younger son unless he had earlier consented to it. This was reasonable enough, for fathers were not often tempted to make gifts to strangers but had always been anxious to provide for their younger sons, and if the heir was to have a fief large enough to support the service fixed upon it such gifts must be made with his consent, otherwise he need not recognise them. Glanvill is puzzled by this, for if a father may make gifts to strangers without his eldest son's consent such persons are better off than legitimate younger sons. He is thinking of the father as the " owner "

[51] P. & M., ii, 4–6.
[52] *Ibid.*, ii, 308–309.

of his holding, not as a life tenant, all of whose gifts end with his death. Thus, he can no longer see why the heir's consent is necessary and provides a foolish explanation. The tenant was indeed becoming the " owner." In 1225, a son trying to get back a tenement his father had alienated, plaintively asks whether he could give away all the land he held by military service without retaining any service to himself and his heirs. His point is unavailing.[53] Bracton knows nothing of—or rather, having Glanvill's book before him, deliberately ignores—the old restraints; they are too obsolete to be worth a word. A tenant who holds in fee has become the owner of his fief, he may dispose of it all without consulting his heir, who takes only what his ancestor leaves, no more and no less.

But if a tenant may give away his land free of service and if his heir takes only what he leaves, no longer the fief free of his ancestor's alienations, gifts good only for his lifetime which required the heir's consent if they were to continue, how can the heir perform the services due? He cannot. By the late twelfth century it had already become impossible for the Crown to insist upon the production by the tenant in chief of the full contingent which he had recognised in the eleventh and early twelfth centuries. Since the heir's ability to control such alienations had disappeared, as had the lord's, the only means available were private agreement[54] and legislative fiat. Thus the Great Charter of 1217 provided that a man shall not give so much of his land (free of service) that he may not sufficiently do to the lord of the fee the service that pertains to that fee. This was unavailing. In 1258 the Petition of the Barons complained that men of religion have entered their fees without their consent. In 1259 the Provisions of Westminster declared it unlawful for religious men to enter into the fees of anyone without the licence of the chief lord of whom the thing is immediately held. But this did not end the matter and we finally have Edward I's Statute of Mortmain in 1279.

I must return to say a word about the disappearance of the need for the lord's consent. As you have seen from the statutes I have just quoted, his consent to his tenant's alienations, even to those in free alms, had become unnecessary by the thirteenth century. Indeed, it had become unnecessary by Glanvill's day, for he nowhere says or implies that a tenant may not alienate without his lord's consent. As long as his tenant had held only a life estate the lord's interest in the land had been evident. It was his, though temporarily in the hands of another. And so, though his tenant

---

[53] *Ibid.*, ii, 311.
[54] *Book of Seals*, No. 455; *Curia Regis Rolls*, viii, 138–139.

held it, it was his fee and consequently his consent or his confirmation that was the essential of any gift attempted by his tenant.[55] But as the tenant's proprietary interest grows, the lord's interest becomes incorporal. He has a right to the services for which the tenant is enfeoffed, he is seised of a seignory, of the homage and service of his tenant, but no longer of the land; the tenant is seised of that, he is seised in demesne, he is its owner. Similarly, what the tenant holds is no longer his lord's fee but his own. As an *addicio* to Bracton, written after the middle of the thirteenth century, says, when the lord's tenant B has alienated a portion of his land to another, who has entered into it, that other has not entered into the lord's fee, but into B's, for the lord has nothing in B's fee except his service. The fee of the lord, in truth, the writer adds, is this: homage and service and not a tenement in demesne. Only one who enters into his homage and service does him an injury, not one who enters into the tenement his tenant holds in demesne. Indeed, we have come full circle, for it is the lord whom Bracton uses to illustrate his statement that one who has no interest in the land cannot give it effectively. If a lord who has a tenant in demesne attempts to give the land to a stranger, the donee gets nothing. Thus we reach a logical position—one who has no interest in land need not consent to its alienation.

To sum up: by the end of the twelfth century one who holds to himself and his heirs is no longer a life tenant but the *verus dominus*, the real lord of the land. As such he no longer requires the consent of his lord or of his heir in dealing with it and thus restraints formerly existing fall away. There is no need to postpone primogeniture until this late date to explain their disappearance nor any need to postulate a strong bias on the part of the king's justices in favour of freedom of alienation, which is quite illusory. When he has become the *verus dominus* his heirs inherit from him; they no longer take by successive gifts from the lord and his heirs. Thus the heritability of land, which can hardly exist when the ancestor is a life tenant, then first appears—not in 1100 but very much closer to 1200. That the common law had already taken form, and that Glanvill's book had already been written, before the emergence of the heritable fee simple, when a life tenancy was the largest possible estate, explains a great many of the common law's anomalies: the curiously strong position of the life tenant, the maritagium, seisin of a free tenement as the touchstone of real property law, the absence of any outcry against reliefs until the thirteenth century, and many others. I shall treat of these matters in my succeeding lectures.

[55] P. & M., i, 345.

LIVERY OF SEISIN

BRACTON distinguishes very clearly the two elements in the thirteenth-century conveyance of freehold land: the *donatio* and the *traditio*, the feoffment and the livery, the declaration of the donor's will and the induction of the donee into seisin.[1] The *donatio* alone was powerless to transfer owner-ship; it was necessary that the donee be put into possession of the land by some actual delivery on or in view of the land itself, and until such livery had taken place nothing but an imperfect and unconsummated attempt to transfer had occurred.[2] There can be little doubt that the *donatio* preceded the *traditio* in time,[3] and that in the thirteenth-century it was usual, if not essential, that its terms be embodied in a written document, a charter of feoffment.[4] Yet this charter is always on its face a purely

---

[1] Bracton, De Legibus, fo. 39b, 40, 44, 44b. For his dependence upon Azo and the Corpus Iuris in his treatment of the land transfer see Woodbine, *The Roman Element in Bracton's De Adquirendo Rerum Dominio* (1922) 31 Yale L. Jour. 840ff.

[2] 2 Pollock & Maitland, History of English Law (1923) 84: 'The *donatio* itself will not entitle the donee to take seisin : if he does so, he will be guilty of disseising the donor. Nor does the *donatio* by itself create even a contractual right and bind the donor to deliver seisin. The charter of feoffment which pro-fessedly witnesses a completed gift, will not be read as an agreement to give. Until there has been livery, the feoffee, if such we may call him, has not even a *ius ad rem*.'

[3] That the *donatio* preceded the *traditio* seems clear from the order in which they are discussed in the texts of both Bracton and Britton, from the plea rolls (4 Curia Regis Rolls 39-40 (1205); 5 *ibid.* 28 (1207); 6 *ibid.* 85 (1210); Maitland, Bracton's Note Book (1887) pl. 1140), from the earliest Year Books (Y.B. 20 & 21 Edw. I (1292) 32, 256), and from the charters themselves (3 Historia et Cartularium Gloucestriae (Rolls Ser.) no. 1018/19). It is only through an incautious use of language that Holdsworth may seem to support a contrary view. Holdsworth, An Historical Introduction to the Land Law (1927) 113-14 : ' . . . the use of writing to show the intent with which seisin had been delivered became more common; and Bracton pointed out that it was convenient for the purpose of perpetuating testimony.' Similarly, Hazeltine, *Introduction* in Whitelock, Anglo-Saxon Wills (1930) xxxiii : 'The charter of feoffment was not a dispositive instrument; it was a pure evidence-document. It evidenced both the oral *donatio*, the feoffment, and the *traditio*. . . . ' To say that a document supplies evidence of an act that has not yet been performed is to describe it inaptly. See the cases in 5 Curia Regis Rolls 28 (1207) and 6 *ibid.* 85 (1210) in which the plaintiffs, when met by the defence of a charter, plead that there had been no livery of seisin, and therefore no valid gift.

[4] Though Bracton (De Legibus, fo. 11b, 398) is clear that the *donatio* need not be evidenced by a writing, and makes the point that the Norman lords and their under-tenants received no charters when the lands of England were first distributed after the Conquest (fo. 382; cf. Provisions of Marlborough, c. 9) there is much to be said for the position taken in Mr. G. J. Turner's *Bookland and Folkland* in Historical Essays in Honour of James Tait (1933) 358ff. Though

evidentiary document professing to witness a concluded transaction, and though there is clearly a further act necessary to complete the conveyance, it nevertheless will attest a completed gift in the clearest possible language.[5] An *ad hoc* explanation for this apparent contradiction is vouchsafed us by Bracton himself:

> 'Et per hoc quod dicit, *dedi*, vult quod res data fiat accipientis. Et per hoc quod dicit, *concessi*, perpendi poterit ex hoc quod donationi consensum praebuit, quia non multum differt dicere concessi quam dicere consensi. Item per hoc quod dicit, *praesenti carta mea confirmavi*, per hoc innuit quod vult quod voluntas sua, per quam res transfertur ad donatarium, et quae firma esse debet, praesenti carta sigilli sui munimine confirmetur. Est enim confirmare id quod prius firmum fuit simul firmare.'[6]

But this interpretation of the words of the charter has a hollow sound, and a careful reader cannot fail to note that Bracton is rationalizing an existing form in the light of contemporary usage rather than looking to its origin in fact. The charter is current soon after the Conquest in the exact form that Bracton knows it, and its persistence unchanged marks the slow process which attends the transformation of legal forms.[7] It is a reminder of the confirmatory character it possessed at an earlier period, during which its purpose was to record a transaction that had already taken place and which thus might rationally and appropriately be spoken of in the past tense. Further we may note that neither in the twelfth nor in the thirteenth century does the charter include a reference to livery of seisin in the sense of an actual delivery of possession, though this must seem strange in the light of Bracton's insistence upon it as a prerequisite to

a transfer of land without a charter was perhaps permissible in strict law, in the thirteenth century a prudent feoffee would be wise to insist upon a charter that would be presumptive evidence of his right and permit him to vouch to warranty. In some instances it apparently was prejudicial to have no charter: Chronicon de Bello (Anglia Christiana Soc., 1846) 50; Bracton's Note Book, pl. 272, 429, 851, 1565, 1843.

[5] Bracton reproduces the usual words; De Legibus, fo. 34b: 'Fit autem donatio in scriptura per haec verba, *Sciant praesentes et futuri quod ego talis dedi, concessi, et hac praesenti carta mea confirmavi tali, pro homagio et servitio suo, tantam terram cum pertinentiis in tali villa*, etcetera. . . .'

[6] Bracton, De Legibus, fo. 34b. The passage does not appear in the later condensations of Bracton: Britton and Fleta, nor to the best of my knowledge, in the Harvard Law School Library MS. of Gilbert of Thornton's *Summa*.

[7] Stenton, Charters relating to Gilbertine Houses (Lincoln Rec. Soc.) xviii: 'The phrase *dedi, concessi, et hac presenti carta confirmavi* was already well established in the earliest years of Henry II's reign.' Similarly: Wissman, *Förmlichkeiten bei den Landübertragungen in England während der anglonormannischen Periode* (1911) 3 Archiv für Urkundenforschung 286 n. 6; Douglas, Social Structure of Mediaeval East Anglia (1927) 11—12; Douglas, Feudal Documents from the Abbey of Bury St. Edmunds (Brit. Acad. Rec.) xl.

the complete transfer, an insistence that is amply borne out by the contemporary plea rolls. It is possible that here again we see the survival of an older use of the document, once quite suited to customs which did not make compulsory the actual delivery of seisin, but now outmoded in all but form. The fact that Bracton apparently is unfamiliar with a use of the document other than to evidence the terms of the *donatio* is not without importance for the solution of the problem of the antiquity of actual livery of seisin as an essential in the conveyance of free-hold land in England.

The descriptions of the transfer of seisin *inter vivos* found in our classical books bears a striking resemblance to those found in the customary law of the early Germanic period, and it is diffi-cult to resist drawing an analogy between them. So Maitland, in pointing out that the feoffee of Bracton's day must actually acquire seisin, adds ' it seems probable that in this respect our law represents or reproduces very ancient German law, that in the remotest age to which we can profitably recur a transfer of rights involved of necessity a transfer of things, and that a conveyance without livery of seisin was impossible and incon-ceivable.' [8] But it is easy to exaggerate this parallelism, and emphasis upon the purely formal features involved in the transfer of land has led historians to visualize a continuity between the eighth-century conveyance on the Continent and the thirteenth-century conveyance in England that is wholly imaginary. This in turn has served to elevate the actual delivery of seisin to an undeserved prominence in the transfer of freehold,[9] and to make plausible, in the face of clear evidence to the contrary, an in-sistence upon the uninterrupted necessity for livery since the Conquest.[10] It is only by minimizing the changes which occurred on the Continent in the centuries before the Conquest, and by concentrating attention upon the similarities between the

---

[8] 2 Pollock & Maitland, History of English Law (1923) 84; 3 Holdsworth, H. E. L. (1923) 221.
[9] Leake, Law of Property in Land (1909) 32; Challis, Law of Real Property (1911) 48; Bigelow, Introduction to the Law of Real Property (1919) 34; Bordwell, *Seisin and Disseisin* (1921) 34 Harvard L. Rev. 592, 593; 3 Holdsworth, History of English Law (1923) 225; An Historical Introduction to the Land Law (1927) 112-13.
[10] Holdsworth, An Historical Introduction to the Land Law (1927) 113: ' Abroad there was a tendency to confuse the actual delivery of seisin with symbolical observances (such as handing over a sod, a stick, a ring, or a knife), which were intended to evidence it. . . . But these developments did not take place in England. In England an actual livery of vacant seisin was required.' 3 Holdsworth, H. E. L. (1923) 224. Turner, *Bookland and Folkland* in Historical Essays in Honour of James Tait (1933) 359, 360, 361 : ' On a consideration of all the evidence . . . there can be little doubt that from the time of the Norman Conquest, and long afterwards, the usual method of transferring land was by a charter of feoffment followed by livery of (actual) seisin. . . .'

ancient Germanic conveyance and that described by Bracton, that it has been possible to overlook the very real differences between them.

Though studies upon the early Continental conveyance by no means agree among themselves in matters of detail, they point with some unanimity toward the view that the ancient Germanic land transfer may be resolved into two elements, at first undifferentiated, but later sharply divided, the *sala* and the *gewerida*. The *sala* was a public and oral declaration by the donor of his intention to transfer: the declaration of the terms of the gift, exchange, or sale; the *gewerida* the ritualistic handing over by the donor to the donee of the land itself, the formal entrance of the donee into possession as evidenced by acts indicative of his assumption of ownership, followed by the solemn abjuration (*auflassung*) of the land by the donor.[11] The origin of the formal and symbolic acts which constitute the *gewerida* or *investitura* lie in the fact that the concept of abstract ownership, of ownership unconnected with external manifestation in the form of possession or enjoyment, was foreign to the early ages. In an age that looked primarily to objective phenomena it was difficult to believe a man owner of land unless he actually enjoyed its benefits or at least possessed it. No more abstract idea as yet obtained, and to make this concept of ownership explicit it was essential not only that the donee enter into possession but that the donor surrender his own possession and enjoyment: a process which took the form of the transfer of material symbols representing the land (*Grundstücksbestandteilen*) and material symbols representing dominion over the land (*Herrschaftssinnbildern*) supplemented by abjuration. But these symbolic acts are not due solely to 'the incapacity of the primitive mind to conceive of a transfer of things without actual *traditio*,' but owe a substantial part of their continuing importance to the necessity for proof. The Germanic customary law required that transactions not only be capable of being heard and seen but that they be actually heard and seen. Change of ownership must be made publicly and visibly, otherwise it will be unwitnessed and unprovable. In the absence of written record,

---

[11] Stobbe, *Die Auflassung des deutschen Rechts* (1873) 12 Jherings Jahrbücher für Dogmatik 144; Haiss, Traditio und Investitura (1876); Sohm, *Zur Geschichte der Auflassung* in Festgab) für Thöl (1879) 96; 2 Heusler, Institutionen des deutschen Privatrechts (1885) 66f; 2 Gierke, Deutsches Privatrecht (1905) 268f; Schröder-von Kunssberg, Lehrbuch der deutschen Rechtsgeschichte (1922) 303; von Schwerin, Grundzüge des deutschen Privatrechts (1928) 113; Hübner, Grundzüge des deutschen Privatrechts (1930) 256; Planitz, Grundzüge des deutschen Privatrechts (1931) 73; *Konstitutivakt und Eintragung* in Festschrift Alfred Schultze (1934) 175.

an objective act or series of acts, incapable of ambiguity, such as those of the *gewerida*, which could be observed and remembered by witnesses must be the dominant element of the conveyance; and if witnesses must later testify not only to the fact of the gift but to its extent and boundaries, it is essential that these acts take place on the land.[12] With the growth of written record, however, it becomes possible to substitute written for oral memory, to provide testimony more permanent than that of mortal witnesses, by having a charter drawn at the conclusion of the ceremony on the land which can effectively be put in the place of the witnesses who attest it.[13] Thus both the fact of the gift and its extent may take permanent, and perhaps incontrovertible form.[14] The document cannot be substituted for the

---

[12] Discussion has centred about a capitulary of 818/19 (1 Capitularia Regum Francorum (ed. Boretius) 282). Sohm, Prozess der Lex Salica (1867) 221; *Zur Geschichte der Auflassung* in Festgabe für Thöl (1879) 91; Heusler, Gewere (1872) 1, 5, 482f; 2 Löning, Geschichte d. deutschen Kirchenrechts (1878) 754; Brunner, Zur Rechtsgeschichte d. römischen und germanischen Urkunde (1880) 277f; Forschungen z. deutschen und französischen Rechtes (1894) 35; 3 Ficker, Untersuchungen zur Erbenfolge der ostgermanischen Rechte (1896) 383; 5 *ibid.* (1902) 229; 2 Gierke, Deutches Privatrecht (1905) 271 n. 23; Mayer-Homberg, Fränkische Volksrechte im Mittelalter (1912) 356; Schröder-von Kunssberg, Lehrbuch d. deutschen Rechtsgeschichte (1922) 308; Schultze, Augustin und der Seelteil d. germanischen Erbrechts (1928) 52; Planitz, *Konstitutivakt und Eintragung* in Festschrift Alfred Schultze (1934) 175.

[13] Heusler, Gewere (1872) 15f; Merk, *Die Grundstücksübertragung nach dem alemannischen Volksrecht* in Festschrift Ernst Mayer (1932) 125, 136ff. The use of the document as a confirmatory instrument may be seen not only in the Lex Alamannorum (I, 1; II, 1; XIX) but also in the Lex Baiuvariorum (XVI, 15): 'Quicquid vendiderit homo aut comparaverit qualemcumque rem, omnia sint firmata aut per cartas aut per testes, qui hoc probare possent; hoc est de mancipiis, de terra, casis vel silvis; post accepto pretio aut per cartam aut per testes conprobetur firma emptio.' The conclusion that the document as described in the Lex Alamannorum and Lex Baiuvariorum is merely an instrument of corroboration is directly contrary to that reached by Brunner, who saw in the provisions official recognition of the validity of transfer by document alone (*traditio per cartam*). Brunner, Zur Rechtsgeschichte d. römischen und germanischen Urkunde (1880) 155, 266, 277ff; Forschungen zur Geschichte d. deutschen und französischen Rechtes (1894) 524ff. His view was widely accepted and is still current : Bresslau, *Urkundenbeweis und Urkundenschreiber im älteren deutschen Recht* (1886) 26 Forschungen z. deutschen Geschichte 60; Brissaud, Manuel d'histoire du droit français (1904) 1248; History of French Private Law (1912) 374 n. 4; 2 Gierke, Deutches Privatrecht (1905) 271 n. 22; Schuld und Haftung (1910) 379 n. 16; Schröder-von Kunssberg, Lehrbuch d. deutschen Rechtsgeschichte (1922) 306 n. 51. But Merk's study of the documents has now placed upon the provisions their proper interpretation : von Schwerin, Grundzüge d. deutschen Rechtsgeschichte (1934) 55; Schultze-von Lasaulx in (1934) 54 Zeitschrift für Rechtsgeschichte (Germ. Abt.) 408; cf. Meyer, Das Handgemal (1934) 95-6.

[14] Through the insertion of penal and excommunicatory clauses the charter was made firm (*firmitatem facere per cartam*) not only against disavowal by the donor but against the claims of third persons who might dispute the gift. Sjögren, Über die römische Konventionalstrafe und die Strafklauseln der fränkische Urkunde (1896); Boye, *Über die antiken Vorbilder der mittelalterlichen Pönformeln* (1914) 6 Archiv für Urkundenforschung 78f; Zatschek in (1927) 42 Mitteilungen des österreichischen Instituts für Geschichtsforschung 203; Fliniaux, *L'évolution du concept de clause pénale chez les canonistes du moyen âge* in Mélanges Paul Fournier (1929) 233; Studtmann, *Die Pönformeln der mittelalter-*

visible and public transfer of symbols which indicate and are in themselves the transference of possession, and thus of ownership. Actual or symbolic change of possession as an objective fact must take place : a recital in the document of the performance of these acts will serve no purpose other than to refresh the memories of witnesses who had observed them, and upon whom their proof must ultimately rest.[15] But the document will serve to retain the extent of the gift. The fact of transfer having been proved and the charter verified, the donee may rely upon the description contained in it. Witnesses need no longer be called to point out the boundaries that had been pointed out to them, but merely to attest the validity of the document in which the details doubtless were retained more clearly and precisely than would otherwise have been possible. The substitution of the document, in which the land might be described, for the witnesses, to whom it had been necessary to indicate its extent, removed an important reason for real or corporeal investiture.[16]

At least as early as the last quarter of the ninth century it becomes possible for donor and donee to avoid the ceremony on the land by the use of symbols whose transfer apart from the land will serve to effectuate the conveyance. But the growth of symbolic investiture must not be sought in the fact that 'one sod of turf is very like another, and since the bishop, who has just preached a soul-stirring sermon, would like to secure the bounties of the faithful while compunction is still at work, a sod from the churchyard will do, or a knife without any sod, or a glove, or indeed any small thing that lies handy '.[17] It is doubtless true that it becomes no longer necessary that turf and twig

---

lichen Urkunde (1931) 12 Archiv f. Urkundenforschung 251; Merk, *Die Grundstücksübertragung nach dem alemannischen Volksrecht* in Festschrift Ernst Mayer (1932) 151-60.

[15] 2 Brunner-von Schwerin, Deutsche Rechtsgeschichte (1928) 499, 532, 560f; 1 Bresslau, Handbuch der Urkundenlehre (1912) 640f; Thorne, *Notes on Courts of Record in England* (1934) 40 West Virginia L. Quart. 347-50; Wigmore, Treatise on Evidence (1923) § 2426; Merk, *Grundstücksübertragung* (1932) 150.

[16] Note 14, *supra.* Though Merk (*Grundstücksübertragung* (1932) 155-60) claims complete indisputability of private charters through the insertion of excommunicatory and penal clauses and stipulations, it may be doubted whether anything more than the land boundaries were rendered incontrovertible. Hübner, Der Immobiliarprozess der fränkische Zeit (1893) 177ff; Beyerle, Das Entwicklungsproblem im germanischen Rechtsgang (1915) 175f; Mayer, Geschworenengericht und Inquisitionsprozess (1916) 12; Mayer-Homberg, Beweis und Wahrscheinlichkeit nach älteren deutschen Recht (1921) 220f; Ruth, Zeugen und Eideshelfer in den deutschen Rechtsquellen des Mittelalters (1922) 20. The charters cited by Merk from the St. Gallen *Urkundenbuch* seem to support this view, but whether the complete charter or only the description of the transferred land was indisputable is immaterial for our present purpose.

[17] 2 Pollock & Maitland, History of English Law (1923) 86. Hübner (History of Germanic Private Law (1918) 243) likewise stresses convenience as the reason for the institution of symbolic investiture.

taken from the very land to be transferred be handed to the donee: a sod may be taken from a nearby field, a convenient knife or staff formally passed; soon any tangible object (*corporeum quodlibet*) whose transfer may be observed will serve to satisfy the requirement.[18]   But this is not due to a tardy realization that sods of turf are remarkably similar, but to the fact that the necessity for a visit to the land and for an elaborate ceremony there that would fix the extent of the gift in the memories of witnesses had been removed.   We may well believe that neither donor nor donee required a survey of the land boundaries at the time of transfer to make clear the land that was being passed: long before preliminary negotiations must have settled this to their satisfaction.   But except for the fact that it need not take place on the land, the symbolic investiture did not differ essentially from the real investiture it superseded. There is the same insistence that possession be transferred in symbolic form, upon the publicity and visibility of the transfer that would permit interested third parties to voice their objections and help to prevent the frauds secrecy of conveyance renders possible, and upon the requirement of an act or series of acts incapable of ambiguity.   The symbolic transfer must be made *in presentia omnium*, in the market-place, church, or court [19]: there the act of handing over the symbol must be as

---

[18] Mayer, *Die Einkleidung im germanischen Recht* in 2 Festschrift für Wach (1913) 47ff; Brissaud, History of French Private Law (1912) 369-71.   There are many instances scattered through the notes to Sohm, *Zur Geschichte der Auflassung* (1879) and Planitz, *Konstitutivakt und Eintragung* (1934) cited *supra*; one of the most striking may be found in 1 Cartulaire de l'Yonne (ed. Quantin) 162 : '. . . conventio facta est. . . .   Tunc Adam (the donor) de equo suo descendens et accepto uno ex lapidibus in via jacentibus dedit in manum episcopi in signum et confirmationem hujus relictionis, sub praesentia horum testium. . . . Deinde ipsum lapidum ad Fontismense monasterium Adam ipse afferens, obtulit super altare.'   Though it is by no means clear, there is some support for the view that the document itself might be considered a symbol whose transfer would effectuate investiture : see the summary of Brunner's work in Wigmore, Treatise on Evidence (1923) § 2426; Hazeltine, *Introduction* in Whitelock, Anglo-Saxon Wills (1930) xxxii-xxxv; 1 Freundt, Wertpapiere im antiken und frühmittelalterlichen Rechte (1910) 189-92; Tangl, *Urkunde und Symbol* in Festschrift Heinrich Brunner (1910) 761.   But Brunner's writings upon the *traditio per cartam* have recently been subjected to very telling criticism : Heuberger, Allgemeine Urkundenlehre für Deutschland und Italien (1921) 19f, 24f, 29f, 32f, 40f, 51ff; Steinacker, Die antiken Grundlagen der frühmittelalterlichen Privaturkunde (1927) 81ff, esp. 89-90; Brandileone, *La Stipulatio nell'età imperiale Romana e durante il medio evo* (1928) 1 Rivista di Storia del Diritto Italiano 1, 51.   See especially the material collected in Merk, *Grundstücksübertragung* (1932) *cit. supra* and the careful but too cautious resumé in Schultze-von Lasaulx, Beiträge zur Geschichte des Wertpapierrechts (1931) 5ff, 25ff.

[19] The pertinent provisions of the various Germanic codes are collected in Brissaud, History of French Private Law (1912) 368 n. 5.   The controversy as to whether the word ' publice' signifies simple publicity or 'in open court' is reviewed in Merk, *Grundstücksübertragung* (1932) 146-49; cf. Cap. Aquisgranense (809) in 1 Capitularia Regum Francorum (ed. Boretius) 149 : 'De traditionibus ut in abscondito non fiant propter conturbationes diversas.'

clear and well defined as it had been on the land.   It is natural that the transfer appear in conjunction with the *sala*, and the *sala* with the absorption of the (symbolic) *investitura* will include in itself the transfer of what will later be called right and seisin, and thus the complete conveyance.[20]   The agreement to alienate by gift, exchange, or sale generally will immediately be followed by some symbolic transfer before witnesses, who will act as witnesses to the symbolic transfer and also as witnesses to the charter which will then be drawn attesting the conveyance.   It will, of course, remain possible to transfer land by actual livery: to visit the land and convey it to the donee in accordance with older custom.   In both instances the charter will contain a description of the transferred land agreed upon by the parties in interest, and will witness a completed act.[21]

---

[20] The *sala* was taking place off the land as early as 819 : see the material collected in Beyerle, *Die Anfänge des Kölner Schreinwesens* (1931) 51 Zeitschrift für Rechtsgeschichte (Germ. Abt.) 385ff. It is still a *streitfrage* whether the *sala* plus symbolic investiture conferred complete ownership.   Sohm (p. 102) is not clear that it does : ' Der mit symbolischer Investitur verbundene Veräusserungsvertrag ist beides zugleich : ist der Rechtsgrund und das Datum für den Ewerb des Eigenthums. Alle Rechtswirkungen des Eigenthums sind schon mit diesem Akt verbunden.   Die nun noch nachfolgende thatsächliche Besitzergreifung kann den Eigenthum wohl noch seine Ausübung, aber nicht mehr seine Entstehung geben.'   Cf. Heymann, *Zur Geschichte des jus ad rem* in Festschrift Otto Gierke (1911) 1167 ; Hazeltine, *Introduction* in Whitelock, Anglo-Saxon Wills (1930) xxvi.   But this view is due to the anticipatory destruction of the old Germanic-Frankish seisin : it interprets the older seisin in the light of its later status when, under the influence of Roman law, it had been reduced to the measure of the Roman possession.   Champeaux, Essai sur la Vestitura ou Saisine (1899).

[21] The charters may be phrased in the present, but nevertheless they are merely dispositively-phrased evidence of a completed gift.   Merk, *Grundstücksübertragung nach dem alemannischen Volksrecht* (1932) 159 : 'In Bezug auf die Übereignung selbst ist die alemannische *carta* lediglich ein dispositiv gefasstes Zeugnis über die schon unabhängig von der Urkunde sich vollziehende mündliche Übertragungshandlung.'   The dispositive or diploma form is used by the draughtsman to perpetuate the actual moment, the very words of grant in all their solemnity.   Galbraith, *Monastic Foundation Charters of the Eleventh and Twelfth Centuries* (1934) 4 Cambridge Hist. Jour. 209.   Hazeltine, *Introduction* in Whitelock, Anglo-Saxon Wills (1930) xxx-xxxi calls attention to the fluctuations in the personal pronoun and in the tense which is a marked feature of the Anglo-Saxon wills.   It is explainable only if we remember that the scribe, acting a passive rôle, has sometimes taken down the words as from dictation ; while, at other times, giving perhaps his own version of the transaction, he has indicated the grantor by using the third personal pronoun and has employed the past tense instead of the present in referring to the transaction as a whole. The distinction between documents in diploma form, phrased in the present, and those in charter form, phrased in the past, stems from Brunner's *Carta und Notitia* in Commentationes in honorem Th. Mommseni (1877) 570 ; 1 Abhandlungen zur Rechtsgeschichte (1931) 458.   Redlich pointed out in 1901 that the distinction was not reflected in practice (Mitteilungen des österreichischen Instituts für Geschichtsforschung 6 Ergänzungsband (1901) 1ff.) but the weight of Brunner's authority led to its wide acceptance.   Though many texts still adhere to this classification of documents, note the recent criticism in : Steinacker, *Der Ursprung der traditio cartae und das westgotische Urkundenwesen* in Festschrift d. Akad. Vereins deutscher Historiker in Wien (1914) 7, 10 ; Heuberger, *Cartam tradidi* in Festschrift O. Redlich (1928) 91ff ; Schultze-von Lasaulx, Beiträge z. Geschichte d. Wertpapierrechts (1931) 35f.

The words of gift in the normal English charter are well established early in the twelfth century, and there is reason to believe that the words *dedi, concessi, et hac praesenti carta confirmavi* relate to a complete transfer and confirm an act which already lay in the past.[22] The transaction was complete without the charter; written evidence of the conveyance was not essential. The only object of the document was to provide testimony more permanent than that of mortal witnesses, to supply written evidence against any who might hereafter challenge the gift to which it relates. It must be true that the words 'I have given, etc.' frequently hide the form the transfer had taken, but charters describing the ceremonial acts of the donation are not wholly lacking, and from them we may note the presence of symbolic investiture in England. Thus in 1112 Edric the interpreter gave his land in full chapter of the Abbey of Bury St. Edmunds, and afterwards offered it with a knife on the altar.[23] Robert gives a carucate of land to Whiteby Abbey by a staff placed on the altar.[24] Land is transferred by a text of the gospels,[25] or by the formal transfer of the charter itself.[26] Nor

---

[22] Stenton, Charters relating to Gilbertine Houses (Lincoln Rec. Soc.) xvi-xix; Documents illustrative of the Social and Economic History of the Danelaw (Brit. Acad. Records of Soc. and Econ. Hist.) ciii-cvi; Facsimiles of Early Charters (Northamptonshire Rec. Soc.) Introd.; Douglas, The Social Structure of Medieval East Anglia (1927) 12; Feudal Documents from the Abbey of Bury St. Edmunds (Brit. Acad. Records of Soc. and Econ. Hist.) xl-xlii; Stenton, English Feudalism (1932) 152.

[23] Douglas, Feudal Documents from the Abbey of Bury St. Edmunds, no. 172 : Ipse Aedricus . . . dedit terram . . . in capitulo coram omnibus monachis prius et postea ipsam optulit super altare Sancti Aedmundi cum cultello.' *Ibid.* no. 173 (1135) : 'et quia hoc donum propria manu presente comitissa cum cultello meo super altare Sancti Aedmundi posui.' 2 Historia et Cartularium Gloucestriae (Rolls Ser.) 166 (1139—1161) : 'vidimus etiam, quod domina mea Matilda regina ipsum Robertum Gernun usque ad altare S. Petri Gloucestriae conduxit, ubi ipse astante regina pluribusque aliis per cultellum super altare donationem illam confirmavit.' Facsimiles of Royal and other Charters in the British Museum (1903) no. 32 : 'Quam donationem in praesentia prioris et conventus eiusdem ecclesie per hunc cultellum confirmavi.' West, The Register of the Abbey of St. Benet of Holme (Norfolk Rec. Soc.) no. 139 (1134-40) : 'Istamque donacionem ipse Walterus cum quodam cultello super altare sancti Benedicti optulit.' Madox, Formulare Anglicanum (1702) no. 400 : 'Donatio vero facta est in sequenti festivitate Sancti Martini . . . super altare Sanctae Mariae per unum cultellum.' Bigelow, Placita Anglo-Normannica (1879) 70—71 : 'rex per cultellum eburneum quod in manu tenuit et abbati porrexit hoc donum peregit apud curiam . . .' cf. Select Civil Pleas (Selden Soc.) no. 16 (1200).

[24] 1 Cartularium Abbathiae de Whiteby (1879) no. 93 : 'donavi Deo et Fratribus de Wyteby, et per unum baculum . . . multis videntibus, quam super altare optuli.' A good deal of material is collected in Wissman, *Förmlichkeiten bei den Landübertragungen in England während der anglonormannischen Periode* (1911) 3 Archiv für Urkundenforschung 280ff., but his conclusion, based upon Bracton, that actual livery of seisin was required in the early twelfth century, cannot be supported.

[25] 1 Historia et Cartularium Gloucestriae (Rolls Ser.) no. 104 (1121) : 'Helyas Giffardus dedit . . . et super altare S. Petrie de Gloucestria per textum posuerunt terram de Bocholte.' 2 *ibid.* 151 (1148-79) : 'Hanc autem concessionem sigilli mei impressione munitam feci in praesentia abbatis et totius conventus

may symbolic investiture take place only at the altar. Seisin may be transferred in the hundred court,[27] in the county court,[28] in the baron's court,[29] or in the king's court.[30] In the twelfth century, then, the gift was attended or executed by some ceremony of livery, but there is evident no legal doctrine of livery of seisin in contradistinction to the act of giving. The gift may be strengthened by ceremonies, by giving in the hands of a bishop, by laying the gift symbolically upon the altar, by making an oath, or by the process of affidavit. But to give and to give seisin seem very much the same thing:

> 'Ego . . . concessi et hac praesenti carta confirmavi, quando feci dedicare ecclesiam S. Pancratii; et de decima denariorum . . . dotavi ipsam ecclesiam et inde saisivi eam per capillos capitis mei et fratris mei, Radulphi de Warenna; quos abscidit cum cultello de capitibus nostris ante altare Henricus episcopus Wintoniensis.'[31]

And even after Glanvill's clear distinction between *saisina* and *ius*, jurors will continue to regard as undifferentiated seisin in Court and seisin on the land.

> 'Iuratores dicunt quod . . . dedit ei per cartam predic-

Gloucestriae et super altare S. Petri multis astantibus per textum obtuli.' Salter, Oxford Charters (1929) no. 9 (1153) : '. . . ego Radulfus de Sancto Audoeno . . . donavi salinam meam . . . et per textum sancti euuangelii super altare beati Petrus . . .' Facsimiles of Royal and other Charters in the British Museum (1903) no. 62 : 'Willelmus de Belmeis . . . salutem . . . me dedisse . . . Fulcherio presbitero ecclesiam S. Pancratii . . . Hanc donationem in pleno capitulo feci et investituram praedicto Fulcherio per textum solemniter coram capitulo faciente.'

[36] 2 Historia et Cartularium Gloucestriae (Rolls Ser.) 51 (1149-83) : 'Et ut donati mea rata et irrefragabilis perseveret, donationem meam carta mea sigillo impressa confirmavi, et in die S. Martini coram omni parochia super altare S. Gundlei ad oblationem cartam praesentavi; et Robertus praedictae ecclesiae vicarius huius facti totam parochiam in testimonium vocavit.' 1 *ibid.* 106, 354; 2 *ibid.* 29. 1 Cartularium Abbathiae de Whiteby (1879) 125, 141. 1 Priory of Hexham (Surtees Soc.) 162. Madox, Formulare Anglicanum (1702) no. 415.

[27] Registrum Monasterii de Winchelcumba (1892) 101 : 'Thomas Capellanus coram hundredo quando saisinam suam recepit, super missale iuratoriam praestitit cautionem.' 1 Historia et Cartularium Gloucestriae, no. 69 (1148-79) : '. . . misi etiam eos in plenam saysinam eiusdem terrae coram hundredo Gloucestriae.'

[28] Maitland, Bracton's Note Book (1887) pl. 1838 (1227) : 'Fulco pater suus dedit ei terram illam per cartam suam in pleno comitatu et ei seisinam fecit per fustum et baculum.' *Ibid.* pl. 1189 (1236) : '. . . quia idem Galfridus numquam coram comitatu vel alibi comparuit ad faciendum eis seisinam.'

[29] Madox, Formulare Anglicanum (1702) 100 : 'Et ipse Alexander . . . per unum ramum arboris eam terram michi quietam reddidit in manum, ad saisiendum predictum Thomam de illa : et ego saisivi Thomam inde per eundem ramum arboris.' 1 Historia et Cartularium Gloucestriae, no. 380 : '. . . Ego vero de Everardo et eadem terra feci eidem ecclesiae . . . plenam seysinam in curia mea apud Lamburne . . .'

[30] Madox, Formulare Anglicanum (1702) xi-xii.

[31] Facsimiles of Royal and other Charters in the British Museum (1903) no. 25. See : Galbraith, *Monastic Foundation Charters of the Eleventh and Twelfth Centuries* (1934) 4 Cambridge Hist. Jour. 205ff.

> tam terram cum pert. et in pleno hundredo fecit ei seisinam et donum et ostendit cartam quam fecerat ei de feoffamento et cepit inde homagium, et postea accessit ad terram illam et fecit ei seisinam. . . .' [32]

It is difficult to believe that the distinction between seisin and right, firm in Glanvill, has been drawn in the early twelfth century. To give seisin is to transfer the object to the donee; seisin is not the pure Roman possession, but a purely medieval concept not easily distinguishable from right. Seisin in this sense includes enjoyment by the donee—possession must pass to him—but just as on the Continent, a symbolic transfer of possession will serve the purpose. In the language of Bracton a century later, 'incipit donatarius habere liberum tenementum propter coniunctionem iuris et seisinae, et mutuum utriusque partis consensem.' [33] The donee begins immediately to have a freehold due to the conjunction of right, seisin, and mutual consent. The theory that the ceremonies described above did not obviate the necessity for further livery on the land has authoritative support,[34] but in the face of a mass of evidence recording some sort of livery as part of the process of grant, it is more than difficult to believe in the necessity of a separate legal ceremony on the land for which hardly a decisive instance can be found in the course of several centuries.[35]

In the late twelfth and early thirteenth centuries all the expedients of symbolic livery give way before the growth of actual livery, and for the origin of this requirement we need not look beyond the growth of royal jurisdiction over land. At the beginning of Henry II's reign the enforcement of the land law was largely a private matter, appropriately confined to the barons' courts. Toward the end of that same century Glanvill still can recognize private jurisdictions over land as a most fundamental matter: so much so that Adams can picture him saying, 'We are going to build up a royal judicial system. We have got to do it in the teeth of private jurisdictions which occupy in civil cases a very important part, almost the whole, of the field. We therefore lay down at the outset the fundamental principle that, on petition of the complainant, by the writ of *praecipe*, the king may draw into his court any plea he wishes concerning land

---

[32] Maitland, Bracton's Note Book (1887) pl. 754 (1233). See: note 28 *supra*. Bracton's Note Book pl. 1169; Madox, Formulare, no. 301.

[33] De Legibus, fo. 39b.

[34] Note 10, p. 33 , *supra*.

[35] Galbraith, *Monastic Foundation Charters* (1934) 4 Camb. Hist. Jour. 208. But *cf.* Stenton, Documents illustrative of the Social and Economic History of the Danelaw (Brit. Acad. Rec. of Soc. and Econ. Hist.) cv, n. 1; West, The Register of the Abbey of St. Benet of Holme (Norfolk Rec. Soc.) no. 164.

feudally held or any free tenement.' [36]   The four assizes of novel
disseisin, mort d'ancestor, darrein presentment, and *utrum* which
are increased in scope soon after the middle of the twelfth century, all force the defendant to appear and answer before the
king's justices.[37]   The writ of right allowed the lord to try the
case if he would, but default of right would permit the plaintiff
to have it transferred to the king's court.   If the lord did
attempt to try it, the grand assize allowed the tenant to throw
the case into the king's court, as soon as the issue was joined, by
a demand that proof take the form of a verdict of twelve knights
rather than trial by battle.   By these provisions practically any
case concerning land could be taken out of the old and transferred to the courts of the new system.   The transfer was not
compulsory: it lay wholly within the choice of the individual,
but the advantages of the new were many and not easily disregarded.   At the end of the century the possessor of land might
be almost certain that a contest as to its possession or ownership
would take him at some stage of the proceedings into the king's
court; by the middle of the next, cases concerning title to land
and seisin go there as a matter of course.[38]

A public symbolic transfer of land familiar to all witnessing
the transfer, and which, if disputed, would be heard in the
baron's court in the presence of suitors who themselves had been
the witnesses, would regard as superfluous the requirement that
the gift be supplemented by the actual handing over of possession.   In all probability the donee would go into immediate
possession, but the fact of the gift and the placing of the donee
into symbolic enjoyment and possession was the essence of the
conveyance there as on the Continent.[39]   The royal justices,
however, were dependent in the assizes upon a group of recognitors, in the grand assize upon twelve knights, who might be
expected to have knowledge of an open and notorious change of
possession—an objective, indisputable, and easily-ascertained
fact—but who could hardly know of a symbolic transfer not

---

[36] Council and Courts in Anglo-Norman England (1926) 173.
[37] The sworn inquest has its origin in a prerogative procedure for the sovereign
and for those with whom he shares its benefits. Haskins, Norman Institutions
(1918) 196—238. It is probable that Henry's first step toward the centralization
of justice was to extend this procedure to the determination of the question
whether land was lay fee or alms. Thorne, *The Assize Utrum and Canon Law
in England* (1933) 33 Columbia L. Rev. 428; *Le droit canonique en Angleterre*
(1934) 13 Revue historique de droit français et étranger 499. The assizes of
novel disseisin and mort d'ancestor are instituted in 1166 and 1176 respectively.
1 Pollock & Maitland, H. E. L. (1923) 145—150; Stenton, *England: Henry II*
in 5 Cambridge Mediaeval History (1926) 586f. A small body of ancient custom
forms their base.
[38] Adams, Council and Courts in Anglo-Norman England (1926) 174.
[39] Note 20, p. 38, *supra*; cf. note 35, last page.

followed by such change. Actual delivery of possession is insisted upon by the king's justices: as Maitland has pointed out, hardly a question is commoner in the Note Book and the earliest Year Books than whether there has been a real and honest change of possession. The justices examine the jurors about the relevant facts and will not be put off with ceremonies.[40] Proof is what is wanted—some unambiguous, manifest action that the recognitors when summoned to Westminster may know and tell —and anyone at all concerned with land will be careful to adhere to the formalities of conveyance prescribed by the justices, for it is they who will be called upon to decide the validity of the conveyance in case of dispute. ' Sed qualiter perpendi poterit quo animo donator donationem fecerit, cum solus deus cor hominis intueatur, et homo secundum faciem iudicare oportet?' is a tag found several times in Bracton's treatise, and since man must judge by externals, it is necessary that there be a real and evident change of possession, for otherwise, as far as we may know, the donor has not fully consented.[41] Only by his overt acts can we know his intention—or a question more frequently raised—the limits of his intention, and it is with this in mind that Bracton stresses the importance of the *traditio*.

But the importance of actual livery in a system that worked with the jury, though an essential part of the picture, is not the picture *in toto*. The assize of novel disseisin, with its stress upon seisin as distinguished from ownership, made seisin in the sense of possession a clear and definite term, and contributed to the necessity for its presence in the conveyance. We have noted above that in the early twelfth century, to give and to give seisin seem very much the same thing: seisin is an enjoyment of property not essentially distinguishable from right.[42] But seisin in this sense was quite outside the field of royal control: its determination was a question of seignorial justice and wholly within the jurisdiction of the feudal court, where it was safe-guarded by an action whose later representative was the writ of right, based upon the best and oldest seisin. It is true that the assizes of novel disseisin and mort d'ancestor led to a sharp dis-

---

[40] 2 Pollock & Maitland, H. E. L. (1923) 84 n. 3. Add to the citations there given: Bracton's Note Book pl. 428, 1865, 1922. In this connexion note that the gagee of land in the late twelfth century must get actual possession of the gaged land; an agreement not accompanied by change of possession will be unenforceable in the King's Court. Glanvill, De Legibus (ed. Woodbine) 139, 170, 252, 286.

[41] De Legibus, fo. 42.

[42] Joüon des Longrais, La conception anglaise de la Saisine (1925); summarized by Plucknett in (1927) 40 Harvard L. Rev. 921-25; Plucknett, Concise History of the Common Law (1929) 274f.

tinction between seisin in this sense and seisin as pure possession, and also that they brought seisin in the latter sense completely under royal protection, but to say that Henry deliberately set out to protect possession in order to deprive the baronial courts of their jurisdiction is completely to misunderstand the conditions of the time.[43]   The assizes have an undoubted political background: their motive in part is the royal policy that would draw the sub-tenant into the king's court and would even put in his hands a weapon to turn against the lord.   But their primary aim is to quell the disorder of self-help and to provide a summary remedy for the man unjustly dispossessed of his tenement or prevented from entering into his inheritance.   The unfavourable position of the plaintiff in the writ of right placed a valuable premium upon violence.   The defendant had the choice of proof, the duel or the Grand Assize; likewise the defendant had the land during the years that might elapse before the matter received final settlement in the slow-moving feudal courts.   There was surely place for an action that would save the possessor, wrongfully evicted by violent means, from being put to his writ of right, and men, sure of the fact that they had been unjustly disseised or prevented from entering upon their inheritance, could afford to forgo the security which a judgment in their favour in a writ of right would give, well content with a rapid judgment by which they could be put into immediate possession, into seisin, of the land.   If the action would prevent the disseisee from resorting to self-help and private war to repossess himself of his land, it would fill a necessary place.   Disseisin was looked upon partly as a crime, and thus within the jurisdiction of the king, nor must the element of tort it contains be overlooked.[44]   But to the lawyers of the time, to whom the Roman distinctions were becoming familiar, the assizes protected possession and no more.   For them, though ownership of land will remain a matter for the feudal courts, the king himself will

---

[43] Barons used the new procedure which meant as much to them as to the humblest freeman. Stenton, *England: Henry II* in 5 Cambridge Med. Hist. (1926) 589; Mitteis, Lehnrecht und Staatsgewalt (1933) 369f. Magna Carta demanded that the judges be sent four times a year into the counties to take assizes.

[44] The plaintiff very soon recovers damages which become normal in the assize: Woodbine, *Origins of the action of Trespass* (1924) 33 Yale L. Jour. 807f; Lincolnshire Assize Rolls (Lincoln Rec. Soc.) lxxvi-lxxvii. The fact that the assize could be brought against the disseisor but not his heir likewise throws light upon the tort basis of the action. The element of crime is visible in the fine imposed upon the guilty defendant, and his imprisonment when the disseisin had taken place with force and arms. Joüon des Longrais, La conception anglaise de la Saisine (1925) 54 n. 2.

protect by royal writ and inquest of neighbours every possession
of a free tenement. The analogy between *possessio* and *saisina*
was most apt. Though the distinction between the assizes and
the writ of right may not have been firmly grounded upon the
private law of the early twelfth century, the basis for a separation of seisin from right can be found there. Seisin in its new
Roman sense of strict possession had played some part in the
purely medieval concept of seisin as ' une jouissance toute
pénétrée d'éléments de droit,' as ' le droit réel conçu sous la
forme d'une jouissance ' [45]; a distinction between seisin and
right was perhaps already crystallizing within the single, un-
abstract concept of seisin-ownership. The introduction of an
action based upon seisin (possession) served to bring seisin out
sharply against *ius*, and at the same time to reaffirm its importance as a component element of *ius*. It reasserted the necessity
for real livery of seisin in the conveyance, a necessity which had
always been present but which, long before both on the Continent and in England, had become attenuated into symbolic
livery. Seisin in its new sense therefore becomes again a prerequisite for a valid conveyance.

The rise of livery of seisin may be approximately dated by the
corresponding decline of the charter witness. To all appear-
ances a change came over men's conception of the function of a
witness during the twelfth century. It would seem that originally he bore his testimony to some definite act that took place in
his presence. We have noted above the ceremonies performed
by Edric the interpreter in the chapter and at the altar of the
church. After describing them the document proceeds ' hii sunt
testes qui erant prius in capitulo ad donationem et postea in
monasterio ad oblationem,' and then follows a list of names of
men who clearly were actually present at the ritual.[46] Similarly
in the grant of Ralf de Sancto Audoeno of a salt-pan at Anning-

---

[45] Joüon des Longrais, Saisine (1925) 45, 57. His thesis that in the late
twelfth century seisin was equivalent not to possession but to right has been
subjected to careful criticism by Woodbine. Glanvill, De Legibus (1932) 262,
281-82. There can be little doubt that earlier the distinction between seisin
(right) and seisin (possession) was not clear cut; the presence of the distinction
after Glanvill is difficult to deny. Maitland explained the necessity for actual
livery by the influence of classical Roman law which was making itself felt at the
time the common law was taking shape. 2 Pollock & Maitland, H. E. L., 89.
It is true that the quotation ' Traditionibus et usucapionibus dominia rerum, non
nudis pactis, transferuntur ' from the Code 2. 3. 20 is found in an *addicio* to
Bracton's text, and that the *addicio* may have been written by Bracton himself
(Woodbine, *Roman elements in Bracton* (1922) 31 Yale L. Jour. 824) but Bracton
is here applying Roman distinctions to English law. That the law in England
influenced by wholly different considerations had come to approximate the Roman
distinction between *proprietas* and *possessio*, without the influence of that distinction playing any part, we have tried to show above.
[46] Douglas, Feudal Documents from the Abbey of Bury St. Edmunds, no. 172.

ton there is an addition ' audientibus et videntibus plurimis.' [47]
But as the reign of Henry II (1154—1189) draws towards its
close, formulae which assert the physical presence of the witness
steadily become less frequent until at last the introductory *his
testibus* has become a matter of common form. Already before
1200 there is conclusive evidence that the witnesses to a charter
might be ignorant of its provisions until they were afterwards
informed of them by the donor; a person might be asked by
letter to attest a charter that had already been made. The
charter-witness, in fact, bore his testimony to the terms of the
gift as expressed in the charter, he need not have been present at
its execution or transfer. The formula *Isti sunt vocati in
testimonium* which repeatedly occurs expresses this function of
the witness with admirable precision; presence at the ceremonial
acts of donation is no longer required. [48] This change reflects
the increasing stress upon actual delivery of the land that was
being fostered by the royal justices. The testimony of witnesses
at the ceremony of donation was no longer of importance in
deciding the validity of a transfer. On the question of the
donor's sanity, the terms of the *donatio*, the tenor of the document, the identification of the donor's seal, their word continued
to be valuable; but whether or not there had been livery of seisin
was a question for the *iuratores*. It is clear from the earliest
recorded cases that jury and witnesses are regarded as quite
separate entities, [49] and that the questions as to livery of seisin
were put not to the charter-witnesses but to the jury itself. [50]
Charter-witnesses will continue to present their testimony to the

---

[47] Note 25, p. 39, *supra*.

[48] Stenton, Gilbertine Charters (Lincoln Rec. Soc.) xxxi; Documents illustrative
of the Social and Economic History of the Danelaw (Brit. Acad.) ciii-cvi;
Douglas, Feudal Documents from the Abbey of Bury St. Edmunds (Brit. Acad.)
xlii-xliii; The Social Structure of Medieval East Anglia (1927) 14.

[49] Richardson in (1934) 50 Law Quarterly Rev. 579. Brunner, Entstehung
der Schwurgerichte (1872) 434-36; Thayer, Preliminary Treatise on Evidence
(1898) 97ff; 2 Pollock & Maitland, H. E. L. (1923) 628; Glanvill, De Legibus
(ed. Woodbine) 257. Charter-witnesses take a decreasingly important part in the
ceremonies attendant upon the formulation of the charter, and as their special
knowledge decreases there remains no reason for distinguishing them from the
inquest to which they are joined. Bracton describes them answering the questions put to the summoned inquest. Bracton, De Legibus, fo. 396, 398. In
1318 a statute enabled the Court, when the witnesses did not appear, to proceed
to the inquest without them. The introduction of the seal is largely responsible
for this loss of importance. Witnesses are no longer needed to verify the produced
charter which is authenticated by the donor's seal. If the seal was disputed, it
was usual to resort to the practice of collating seals : Glanvill, De Legibus (1932)
257.

[50] 5 Curia Regis Rolls 272 (1208) : ' . . . et inde ponit se super comitem
Rogerum, qui nominatus est in carta, et super alios testes carte illius et super
legalem juratam patrie. Consideratum est quod jurata fiat utrum ipsa priorissa
inde saisita [fuit] die qua etc.' Maitland, Bracton's Note Book (1887) pl. 250,
286.

justices, and we find them doing so as late as 1227, but the annotator of Bracton's Note Book adds, ' Nota quod solempnitas et simulata donatio in comitatu per fustum et bastonem et per hostium et haspam non valet sine seisina continua usque ad mortem donatoris.' [51] Likewise, the custom of transferring a symbol as part of the *donatio* continues, but now that it no longer serves to transfer seisin it is looked upon as a gage or pledge by which the donor can be constrained to deliver possession of the land, or in other words, to proceed to the *traditio*.[52] Thus the functions of both the charter-witness and symbol have been transformed and adapted to the new requirement of actual livery; seisin itself has been contracted to correspond almost completely to the Roman *possessio*.

But though livery of actual seisin is thus a necessary element of the conveyance, it is far from being its predominant element.[53] The requirement that the conveyance be perfected upon the land had proved burdensome upon the Continent centuries before, and in England incorporeal investiture apart from the land had long been well established. The new requirement insisted upon by the royal justices tended to make land transfer again a cumbersome and unwieldy process. To be sure, real investiture had continued to play an important part both in England and abroad in the conveyance of holdings; upon men accustomed to this mode of transfer the revived importance of delivery of actual possession would be without noticeable effect. But the importance which had attached to the *sala*, or declaration of intention, when used in conjunction with symbolic investiture, and the undoubted convenience of this method of transfer, were not easily superseded. In the early twelfth century it may be believed that the donee entered upon actual possession soon after receiving symbolic investiture. His ownership did not depend upon this entry : seisin and right, still partly undifferentiated, had been given him by the ceremony. Under the new rule, a necessary element of ownership was not his until he had entered upon and taken possession of the land, and he therefore cannot be regarded as owner until that act has taken place. But the preliminary transaction—the *sala*, or as it will now be called, the *donatio*—still retains its predominant place in the conveyance. It is the intention to transfer, an intention usually embodied in

---

[51] Bracton's Note Book pl. 1838.
[52] As signum : 2 Chronicon Monasterii de Abingdon (Rolls Ser.) 189; as *vades* : 2 *ibid*. 100, 168; as *pignus* : *ibid*. 161; as *donum* : *ibid*. 123, 145; as *signum pactionis* : 1 Landboc Monasterii Winchelcumba (Rolls Ser.) 212. For a similar development on the Continent see Heusler, Gewere (1872) 18.
[53] Note 9, p. 33, *supra*.

a written document, that is the element of the conveyance
uppermost in Bracton's mind. 'Nihil enim tam conveniens est
naturali aequitati quam desiderium domini volentis in alium res
suam transferre ratam haberi.'[54] The donee by entering into
possession perfects or solidifies, so to speak, the donation. He
receives possession which is necessary to ownership, but the
taking of possession is no juristic act: it is clearly not the *causa
efficiens* but merely the *causa sine qua non* of the transfer. This
has been obscured by the fact that seisin in its older sense persists: as a concept signifying ownership it is never replaced by
the Roman *proprietas* or *dominium*. The law will contrast the
seisin protected by the writ of right with that protected by the
novel disseisin, but more definite than that it does not become.
Thus Bracton may speak of one who is in seisin yet not seised,
'sunt quidam in seisina et non seisiti,'[55] and still remain perfectly understandable to his contemporaries. The seisin protected
by the assize is possession; likewise the seisin conferred by livery
is possession. But that possession, if added to right given by
the *donatio*, will place the donee into seisin in its proprietal
sense. It is important that this distinction be made clearly:
livery does not give seisin in the sense of ownership, but merely
seisin in the sense of possession.[56]

Bracton includes in his treatise a description of the *traditio*
on the land: by the door, the hasp, or the ring of the house (per
ostium et per haspam vel per anulum) or, if the land contained
no building, by means of the staff and wand (per fustum et per
baculum),[57] but how necessary this procedure was in practice is
problematical. If the land were within the view of the parties
when the *donatio* was made, and the donee made an actual entry
upon it while the donor was yet alive, there was a sufficient
feoffment.[58] Similarly, if the donee, after the *donatio*, goes

---

[54] De Legibus, fo. 39b.
[55] De Legibus, fo. 206, 209. Similarly, those seised but not in possession;
despite the termor's occupation, the lessor is seised. 2 Pollock & Maitland,
H. E. L. 37f. A person in occupation of land as guardian is 'seisitus de
terra illa ut de warda': Glanvill, De Legibus (1932) 164, 165. For a careful
description of Bracton's terminology: Joüon des Longrais, Saisine (1925) 178–
200.
[56] Turner, *Bookland and Folkland* in Historical Essays in Honour of James
Tait (1933) 358-59: 'When the plea rolls refer to a transfer of land by livery
of seisin alone, they almost always—in my observation always—refer to transfers,
the validity of which was in dispute. Livery of seisin might pass the possession,
and be a good answer to a writ of novel disseisin or any other possessory writ:
but it is at least doubtful whether the right as opposed to the mere possession
could pass without a charter.' Cf. 369-70.
[57] De Legibus, fo. 40.
[58] De Legibus, fo. 41; Y. B. 20—21 Edw. I 257 (1292): 'The assise came
and said that N. the father of Alice made a good charter to Alice, and came to
the lord's Court and delivered the charter in the presence of good men, and said

upon the land and takes seisin, though he will be guilty of a technical disseisin, in the absence of objection by the donor there is likewise a sufficient feoffment.[59] If the donee is already in possession, either as tenant of the donor or holding adversely to him, the donor can pass ownership to him by a *donatio* without more.[60] For the donee is already in possession and it is unnecessary that he leave and be reinstated by the donor. In short, livery of seisin is little more than the requirement that the donor make public his gift, that he be prevented from seeming to give and yet retain; it is an expression in concrete form of the maxim *donner et retiner ne vaut*. Nor must seisin be transferred by the donor in person: it may be done by anyone authorized by him; indeed, authorizations to give seisin become a recognized part of the normal character of feoffment. But even this formality may be dispensed with by placing an agent of the donee into possession and releasing the property to the donee by deed. At the time Bracton is writing this method of transfer by release and quit-claim is coming into frequent use; shortly afterwards it will replace the transfer by charter of feoffment and livery. Actual livery thus becomes merely a temporary, additional element in conveyancing, from which the ingenuity of lawyers soon found a way of escape. The *donatio* and not the *traditio* of possession was the essential element of the conveyance after as well as before the introduction of real livery. A running commentary upon the continuing importance of the *donatio* is afforded by the growth of more precise language in the charter. Despite a seeming return to actual livery which would indicate the extent of the gift to witnesses, the boundaries are written with more and more care into the body of the instrument.

To sum up: though the land transfer in thirteenth-century England is superficially similar to that in use on the Continent in the eighth century, the differences between the two are very marked. On the Continent, the ceremony on the land was the jural act that transferred ownership; in England, livery of seisin conferred upon the donee simple possession: the jural act of transfer is found in the *donatio*. Stress placed upon livery of seisin as the essential element of the conveyance has been due

---

thus, " Alice, go to that land and take seisin thereof " . . . *Cave, J.*: Was N. the feoffor in that will where the land lay, and so near the land that he could see the land or point it out with his finger? and if he did so or not, then tell us : or if the land was so near the Court that he could see the land or point it out with his finger when he said in Court " Alice, go to that land and take seisin." *The Assise:* No sir; he was a league distant.'

[59] De Legibus, fo. 40, 44.
[60] De Legibus, fo. 41; Woodbine, *Roman elements in Bracton* (1922) 31 Yale L. Jour. 841-42; 2 Pollock & Maitland, H. E. L. 91 n. 1.

to an incomplete distinction between seisin in the sense of possession and seisin in the sense of ownership. The reversion to the old ideas which required an actual livery of vacant seisin was due to a set of circumstances quite outside the necessities of real property law, nor is its reappearance completely explained by the incapacity of the primitive mind to conceive of a transfer of things without actual *traditio*. Lastly, symbolic investiture was as well established in England during the early twelfth century as it was on the Continent: permanent evidence of its presence is found in the continuing importance of the *donatio* and in the formulae of the normal charter which inconsistently continues to witness a completed gift before the transaction of gift is concluded.

5

THE ASSIZE *UTRUM* AND CANON LAW IN ENGLAND

Henry II began his struggle with the church by invoking the ancient customs of the realm,[1] and it is now generally established that in the Constitutions of Clarendon he presented not innovations under the guise of *avitae leges* but an accurate description of the customary practice in the reign of Henry I.[2] In the matter of the clergy's exclusive jurisdiction over land held in frank almoign,[3] however, the evidence though frag-

---

[1] Henry could do nothing until the death of Theobald, but in 1162 at a great council held at Rouen he ordered that the canons of the council of Lillebonne (1080) be observed. 1 ROBERT DE TORIGNI, CHRONICA (ed. Delisle, 1872) 336; *cf.* HASKINS, NORMAN INSTITUTIONS (1918) 30 ff.; DAVIS, ENGLAND UNDER THE NORMANS AND ANGEVINS (1915) 527 ff.; BÖHMER, KIRCHE UND STAAT IN ENGLAND UND IN DER NORMANDIE (1899) 33 ff. The Constitutions of Clarendon (1164) were based upon a 'recordatio vel recognitio cujusdam partis consuetudinum et libertatum et dignitatum antecessorum suorum, videlicet regis Henrici avi sui.' STUBBS-DAVIS, SELECT CHARTERS (1913) 161, 163; 5 ROBERTSON, MATERIALS FOR THE HISTORY OF THOMAS BECKET (Rolls Series) 71. At the council of Woodstock (1163) Becket had opposed Henry's proposal that the *auxilium vicecomitis* be paid into the treasury on the ground that the custom was otherwise. Round, *An Alleged Debate on Danegeld in 1163* (1890) 5 ENG. HIST. REV. 750; FEUDAL ENGLAND (1909) 497. *Cf.* Innocent III (1208) in 3, 6, and 8, X, 1, 4. For a similar appeal to history by John: POWICKE, STEPHEN LANGTON (1928) 83 ff.

[2] Stenton, *Henry II* (1926) 5 CAMBRIDGE MEDIAEVAL HISTORY 554 ff., 895. BROOKE, THE ENGLISH CHURCH AND THE PAPACY (1931) 206 ff. Attention has centered upon the question of criminous clerks—the crucial point in the Henry-Becket controversy—but even here, in spite of the obscurity which surrounds the problem in the eleventh and early twelfth century, there is much to be said for the truth of Henry's contention. NISSL, DER GERICHTSSTAND DES CLERUS IM FRÄNKISCHEN REICH (1886) 79-82; MAITLAND, CANON LAW IN THE CHURCH OF ENGLAND (1898) 132 ff.; Génestal, *La dégradation des clercs et le droit normand* (1911) BULL. DU COMITÉ DES TRAVAUX HIST. ET SCIENT. (Section des Sciences Écon. Et Soc.) 231, 235 ff.; 2 GÉNESTAL, LE PRIVILEGIUM FORI EN FRANCE (1924) 102, 106; GABEL, BENEFIT OF CLERGY IN ENGLAND (1929) 15 ff. It has not been hitherto noted that Henry had offered to submit the question to the scholars at the University of Paris [1 CHARTULARIUM UNIVERSITATIS PARISIENSIS (1889) 21-3], surely not the offer of one against whom the authorities are legion. But Maitland and others underestimate the weight which the Biblical text: 'non punit Deus bis in idipsum' (NAHUM I, 9) and its quotation by Gratian [Decr. C. 12, qu. 2, c. 30: 1 CORPUS IURIS CANONICI (ed. Friedberg) col. 731] would have had for the doctors of the twelfth century.

[3] This is admitted by c. 9 of the Constitutions: 'Si calumnia emerserit inter clericum et laicum, vel inter laicum et clericum, de ullo tenemento quod clericus attrahere velit ad elemosinam, laicus vero ad laicum feudum, recognitione duodecim legalium hominum, per capitalis Justitiae regis considerationem terminabitur, utrum tenementum sit pertinens ad elemosinam sive ad feudum laicum, coram ipso Justitia regis. Et si recognitum fuerit ad elemosinam pertinere, placitum erit in curia ecclesiastica, si vero ad laicum feudum, nisi ambo de eodem episcopo vel barone advocaverint, erit placitum in curia regia. Sed si uterque advocaverit in feudo illo eundem episcopum vel baronem, erit placitum in curia ipsius; ita quod propter factam recognitionem saisinam non amittit, qui prior saisitus fuerat, donec per placitum dirationatum fuerit.' *Cf.* 1 POLLOCK AND MAITLAND (1903) 246; MAITLAND, DOMESDAY BOOK AND BEYOND (1897) 280.

mentary is sufficient to indicate that under Henry I and his predecessors the English church had enjoyed no such exclusive control.[4] The principle that church land is free of all secular judicial supervision, which must be sharply distinguished from the charter-right of a particular bishop-immunist to exclude royal ministers,[5] finds its origin in the writings of the canonists of the Gregorian reform,[6] and is confined for a time to the chain of canonical collections mainly Italian compiled under Gregory's influence. It does not appear in the earlier pseudo-Isidorian *Decretales* nor in the *Decretum* of Burchard of Worms;[7] strangely enough, though it has not been traced in the collections of Yvo of Chartres, it finds a place in several collections based upon his work.[8] It is difficult to see how it could have been introduced into England

---

[4] ROUND, CALENDAR OF DOCUMENTS PRESERVED IN FRANCE (1899) nos. 26, 78, 119, 122, 127, 132; REGISTRUM ANTIQUISSIMUM (Lincoln Rec. Soc.) nos. 28, 100; DELISLE-BERGER, RECUEIL DES ACTES DE HENRI II (1916) 586; 2 FARRER, EARLY YORKSHIRE CHARTERS (1915) nos. 1113, 1177, 1178; Stenton, *An Early Inquest* (1917) 32 ENG. HIST. REV. 47. •

[5] Pivano, *Le Immunità ecclesiastiche* (1908) FESTSCHRIFT FÜR EMIL FRIEDBERG; 2 PÖSCHL, BISCHOFSGUT UND MENSA EPISCOPALIS (1909).

[6] Fournier, *Les collections canoniques romaines de l'époque de Grégoire VII* (1918) 41 MÉM. DE L'ACAD. DES INSCRIPT. ET BELLES-LETTRES 271; *Un tournant de l'Histoire du Droit* (1917) 41 REV. HIST. DE DROIT FRANÇ. ET ÉTRANGER 129; *Le premier manuel canonique de la réform de XIᵉ siècle* (1894) 14 MÉLANGES D'ARCHEOL. ET D'HIST. DE L'ÉCOLE FRANÇ. DE ROME 147; *Un groupe de recueils italiens des Xᵉ et XIᵉ siècles* (1915) 40 MÉM. DE L'ACAD. DES INSCRIPT. ET BELLES-LETTRES 95; *Observations sur diverses recensions de la collection canonique d'Anselme de Lucques* (1901) 13 ANNALES DE L'UNIVERSITÉ DE GRENOBLE 427; *Le Liber Tarraconensis* (1895) MÉLANGES JULIAN HAVET; Valls-Taberner, *Les coleccions canóniques a Catalunya durant la época comtal* (1925) FESTGABE HEINRICH FINKE; Fournier, *Les sources canoniques du Liber de Vita Christiana de Bonizo de Sutri* (1917) 78 BIB. DE L'ÉCOLE DES CHARTES 117; 1 SECKEL, TEXTE ZUR GESCHICHTE DES RÖMISCHEN UND KANONISCHEN RECHTS IM MITTELALTER (1930) xxi ff. See in general: 2 FLICHE, LA RÉFORM GRÉGORIENNE (1925); DE GHELLINCK, LE MOUVEMENT THÉOLOGIQUE DE XIIᵉ SIÈCLE (1914); 2 FOURNIER & LE BRAS, HISTOIRE DES COLLECTIONS CANONIQUES EN OCCIDENT (1932); HÜFFER, BEITRÄGE ZUR GESCHICHTE DER QUELLEN DES KIRCHENRECHTS UND DES RÖMISCHEN RECHTS IM MITTELALTER (1862). It is closely connected with the growing papal claim to temporal power. VOOSEN, PAPAUTÉ ET POUVOIR CIVIL A L'ÉPOQUE DE GRÉGOIRE VII (1927) 158 ff; BERNHEIM, MITTELALTERLICHE ZEITANSCHAUUNGEN IN IHREM EINFLUSS AUF POLITIK UND GESCHICHTSSCHREIBUNG (1918) 110 ff.; Arquillière, *Sur la formation de la 'théocratie pontificale'* (1925) MÉLANGES D'HIST. DU MOYEN ÂGE OFFERTS À FERDINAND LOT 1.

[7] Fournier, *Études critiques sur le 'Décret' de Burchard de Worms* (1910) 34 NOUVELLE REV. HIST. DE DROIT FRANÇ. ET ÉTRANGER 41, 213, 289, 564; *Le décret de Burchard de Worms* (1910) 12 REV. D'HIST. ECCLÉSIASTIQUE. It may be noted in passing that Maitland's designation of Burchard as the source from which the author of the Leges Henrici Primi extracted his ecclesiastical law [1 POLLOCK AND MAITLAND (1903) 99] is not founded on fact. LIEBERMANN, UEBER DAS ENGLISCHE RECHTSBUCH LEGES HENRICI (1901) 23. The absence of the principal from the False Decretals makes it unlikely that it appears in the collection brought into England by Lanfranc. BROOKE, THE ENGLISH CHURCH AND THE PAPACY (1931) 57-83; BÖHMER, DIE FÄLSCHUNGEN ERZBISCHOF LANFRANKS VON CANTERBURY (1902) 61-70.

[8] Fournier, *La collection canonique dite Caesaraugustana* (1921) 45 NOUV. REV. HIST. DROIT. FRANÇ. ET ÉTRANGER 53. *Cf. Les collections canoniques attribuées à Yves de Chartres* (1896) 57 BIB. DE L'ÉCOLE DES CHARTES 648.

much before Stephen's reign.[9]   That Henry II, nevertheless, was willing
to grant this comparatively recent dictate the status of ancient custom
points to the extent to which papal doctrine had been received under
Stephen, but more significantly, to the essentially innocuous nature of
the concession.   The acute conflict between secular and ecclesiastico-
papal jurisdiction was still in the future, and though the problem of
church land had become an important one,[10] Henry claims merely the
right to decide, by an assize under the eye of his justiciar, the preliminary question whether *(utrum)* the land in dispute is lay fee or
alms.[11]   Toward the end of the twelfth century Glanvill so describes

---

[9] I have in preparation a paper on the origin of this claim and its introduction
into England.   Makower's contention [CONSTITUTIONAL HISTORY OF THE CHURCH
OF ENGLAND (1895) 433-34] that Stephen's charter of 1136 granted jurisdiction over
such disputes to the church is unfounded.   *Cf.* Appendix II, and § 4, n. 32.

[10] The great transference of churches from lay to monastic ownership which
marks the twelfth century was one of the most notable administrative achievements of the English Middle Ages.   Böhmer, *Das Eigenkirchentum in England*
(1921) TEXTE UND FORSCHUNGEN ZUR ENGLISCHEN KULTURGESCHICHTE 301-53;
Cf. Stutz, (1923) 43 ZEIT. DER SAVIGNY-STIFTUNG FÜR RECHTSGESCHICHTE
(Kanon. Abt.) 409.   The movement toward monastic foundation quickens in the
eleventh century and receives a sudden acceleration under Stephen: gifts of men
and women of rank form the greater portion of the endowments, but villeins and
free peasants contribute proportionately.   STENTON, DOCUMENTS ILLUSTRATIVE OF
THE SOCIAL AND ECONOMIC HISTORY OF THE DANELAW (Brit. Acad. Records of Soc.
and Econ. Hist.) lii ff.; no. 101.   In the later twelfth century, due to the influence
upon private deeds of the completed writ-charter documents of the royal chancery
[DOUGLAS, FEUDAL DOCUMENTS FROM THE ABBEY OF BURY ST. EDMUNDS (Brit.
Acad. Records of Soc. and Econ. Hist.) xxxv-xxxvii, xlv-xlvii; DOUGLAS, SOCIAL
STRUCTURE OF MEDIAEVAL EAST ANGLIA (1927) 12], difference in rank is unre-
flected in any formal differences in the charters themselves [STENTON, CHARTERS
RELATING TO GILBERTINE HOUSES (Lincoln Rec. Soc.) xxxiii-xxxv] yet there is
no reason to doubt the continuance of gifts from all members of society.   Chapter
2 of the Constitutions puts a check upon grants and it is one of the clauses tolerated
by the Pope.   *Cf.* ROUND, DOCUMENTS PRESERVED IN FRANCE (1899) nos. 665,
755, 1045 and 1112.

[11] Henry claims this as ancient custom but no instance of a recognition of this
question by sworn inquest has been found in England prior to 1164.   In Normandy
it is impossible to say how clearly this principle was established before the appearance of the assize *utrum* in the Constitutions of Clarendon.   HASKINS, NOR-
MAN INSTITUTIONS (1918) 172-3.   The claim made by an ardent Norman for
priority seems indefensible.   Blum, *Les origines du bref de fief lai et d'aumône*
(1925) TRAVAUX DE LA SEMAINE D'HISTOIRE DU DROIT NORMAND 369, 390-91.
In the latter part of Henry II's reign the principle is equally well established in
both parts of Henry's kingdom.   HASKINS, 172-3, n. 95, 96. Liebermann, *Zum
Kirchenstaatsrecht der Normandie* (1926) 46 ZEIT. DER SAVIGNY-STIFT. FÜR
RECHTSGESCHICHTE (Kanon. Abt.) 532-4.   In England the bountiful use of his
prerogative procedure by Henry to ascertain rights, liberties, customs, and possessions which had vanished or increased during the reign of Stephen must have made
the process a familiar one.   HASKINS, 234-37; Galbraith, *Royal Charters to Winchester* (1920) 35 ENG. HIST. REV. 398, *cf.* 385 n. 1.   For an interesting example
of this procedure in the absence of ducal writ see: 1 ANTIQUUS CARTULARIUS
ECCLESIAE BAIOCENSIS (1902) no. 63.   The pope disapproved this seemingly in-
offensive method of deciding the preliminary question of competency (5 ROBERT-
SON, MATERIALS, 74) ; the assumption which underlies Henry's provision and made
it distasteful to Alexander was his implied claim that both secular and ecclesiastical courts were subject to the king's authority, and it was therefore for him to
decide to which court cases should be brought.   *Cf.* Brooke, *Effect of the Murder
of Becket on Papal Authority in England* (1928) 2 CAMBRIDGE HIST. J. 216.

the procedure,[12] but in Bracton the assize *utrum* has become merely an ordinary proprietary action in the king's court limited to rectors of parochial churches and enabling them to obtain lands held by their predecessors: it has become *singulare beneficium* introduced by a benevolent sovereign to remedy a defect in the writ system:[13] it is "the parson's writ of right."[14] A profound change has thus occurred in the nature of the action: this transformation is the result of the growth of papal canon law in England.

Under William I and William II the king's authority over the church in England portrays a supremacy to which the eleventh century affords no equal.[15] Henry I seems to have adhered in general to the policy of his father, and though he was forced to surrender lay investiture, otherwise retained all essential authority.[16] Thus under the first

[12] GLANVILL, DE LEGIBUS (ed. Woodbine) XIII, 23, 24, 25; *cf.* XII, 25. Glanvill gives us little beside the form of the writ which is almost identical with that given by Bracton. It is doubtful whether the process it gives rise to is simply one of deciding competency. See *infra* note 28.

[13] BRACTON, DE LEGIBUS, f. 285b, f. 286.

[14] 2 BRITTON (ed. Nichols) 207.

[15] The literature is voluminous. For this and the following note see in general: MAKOWER, CONSTITUTIONAL HISTORY OF THE CHURCH OF ENGLAND (1895); HASKINS, NORMAN INSTITUTIONS; BÖHMER, KIRCHE UND STAAT; BROOKE, ENGLISH CHURCH AND THE PAPACY; Corbett, *England* (1926) 5 CAMB. MED. HIST. 521 ff. EADMER, HISTORIA NOVORUM (Rolls Series). No bishops allowed to visit Rome, no appeals allowed to go out of, or papal legates or bulls allowed to come into the country without the king's consent. GREGORII VII REGISTRUM (ed. Caspar) vii, 1; *cf.* Brooke, *Pope Gregory VII's Demand for Fealty from William the Conqueror* (1911) 26 ENG. HIST. REV. 225, but see: 2 FLICHE, LA RÉFORM GRÉGORIENNE 345. The holding of ecclesiastical synods and the canons passed by them were likewise under royal control. Is it evident that the king and not the pope was the master of the church of England. In Normandy the situation was similar. The tradition that the Conqueror had threatened to hang to the highest tree any monk who dared obey a papal legate was very much alive [2 ODERICUS VITALIS, HISTORIA ECCLESIASTICA (ed. Le Prévost) 84]. Papal legates could not travel through the duchy without ducal permission, much less could they exercise their legatine functions within its borders [STUBBS, HISTORICAL INTRODUCTIONS TO THE ROLLS SERIES (1902) 251]. The Norman clergy might upon occasion attend a great council, but Henry I was careful to instruct them not to bring innovations into his lands (4 ODERICUS VITALIS, 373). As to appointments to ecclesiastical office, theory was disregarded and the duke's will carried out. 2 VIOLLET, HISTOIRE DES INSTITUTIONS POLITIQUES (1890) 340. Even Henry II, fresh from the spectacular humiliation at Avranches, caused his nominee to be placed upon the archepiscopal throne. CHESNEL, LE COTENTIN ET L'AVRANCHIN SOUS LES DUCS DE NORMANDIE (1912) 59-63, 179-80. William I had degraded an archbishop of Rouen (1 ODERICUS VITALIS, 184) and members of the ducal household could not be excommunicated with royal license (ROUND, CALENDAR, no. 1318).

[16] Henry's reign is complicated by his stubborn controversy with Anselm of Canterbury. HASSE, ANSELM VON CANTERBURY (1843, 52); SCHMITZ, DER ENGLISCHE INVESTITURSTREIT (1884); Liebermann, *Anslem von Canterbury und Hugo von Lyon* (1896) HISTORISCHE AUFSÄTZE AN G. WAITZ GEWIDMET 156. But that he retained royal control is evident from two letters of Paschal II in 1115 [EADMER, HISTORIA NOVORUM (Rolls Series) 228, 232; JAFFÉ-LÖWENFELD, REGESTA PONTIFICUM ROMANORUM (1885) 6450, 6453] in which the pope complains that no papal nuncios or letters are admitted except by the king's express permission; that no appeal, no ecclesiastical suit, is brought from England to the papal court; and that ecclesiastical synods are being held and bishops translated to other sees without the pope's consent, even without his knowledge.

three Norman kings papal influence is excluded *in toto,* ecclesiastical causes are decided not by judges delegate acting under a papal rescript, but by bishops who have their place in the royal *curia,* do homage to the king for their temporalities, and act as the king's justiciar in their provinces.[17] Most important of all, the king and not the pope is the final court of appeal in both ecclesiastical and secular cases.[18] It is significant that the appeal to the pope was opposed as much by the bishops who were jealous of their own independent status as by the crown. Under such conditions there is good reason to believe that the English ecclesiastical courts administered English ecclesiastical law and proceeded in accordance with English ecclesiastical custom:[19] and though the growth of papal control during the weak reign of Stephen must not be minimized,[20] there is available evidence sufficient to support the contention that it was not until after Henry II's concession at Avranches in 1172 that the ecclesiastical jurisdiction of England was altered, the lost law of Theobald's primacy swept away, and the canon law received in its place.[21] But whether this is true or not, it is certain

---

[17] Stenton (1929) 3 CAMBRIDGE HIST. J. 4 ff.

[18] Henry II claims this as ancient custom in the Constitutions of Clarendon, c. 8: 'De appellationibus si emerserint, ab archidiacono debent procedere ad episcopum ab episcopo ad archiepiscopum. Et si archiepiscopus defuerit in justitia exhibenda ad dominum regem perveniendum est postremo, ut praecepto ipsius in curia archiepiscopi controversia terminetur, ita quod non debeat ulterius procedere absque assensu domini regis.' And enforces it. MAKOWER, CONSTITUTIONAL HISTORY OF THE CHURCH OF ENGLAND, 228 n. 8, 240 n. 2. For documents suggesting that no acute opposition between secular and ecclesiastical justice can have developed by Stephen's reign and Theobald's primacy see: Stenton, *Acta Episcoporum* (1929) 3 CAMBRIDGE HIST. J. 1.

[19] The Maitland-Stubbs-Ogle controversy summarized by Davis in *The Canon Law in England* (1913) ZEIT. DER SAVIGNY-STIFT. FÜR RECHTSGESCHICHTE (Kanon. Abt.) 344 is concerned mainly with a later period, yet Davis correctly points out (at 357) the purely hypothetical nature of what Stubbs called the common law of the English church courts. The subject is a dangerous one, but it seems to me that the wholesale reception of papal instruction upon canon law and procedure which takes place during the period of 1172-1185 admits of no other explanation. It is safe to say that whatever law was administered under the first three Norman kings was enacted by bishops who were the king's feudal men and whose judgments in the final analysis would have to stand in the king's court.

[20] Brooke, *The Effect of Becket's Murder on Papal Authority in England* (1928) 2 CAMBRIDGE HIST. J. 213, 223; cf. GRAHAM, ENGLISH ECCLESIASTICAL STUDIES (1929) 185. Stenton, *Acta Episcoporum,* 3.

[21] At Avranches Henry was reconciled with the Pope, but not before he had made two concessions, one of which was the freedom of appeal to Rome. Appeals, and the consequent appointment of bishops as judges-delegate to hear them, became frequent. That the English bishops were largely ignorant of the canonical doctrine they were to enforce, and of the procedure they were to observe, may be inferred from the mass of inquiries sent by them to the Pope, and the amount of law that was clarified for their benefit. MAITLAND, CANON LAW IN ENGLAND, 122 ff.; Brooke, *The Effect of Becket's Murder,* 218 ff.; BROOKE, ENGLISH CHURCH AND THE PAPACY, 212 ff.; The preponderance of decretal-letters addressed to England in papal letters between 1172 and 1185 is striking. In particular, the letters Alexander III (1159-81) wrote to English bishops in the period 1172-81 form more than half the letters he wrote during his entire pontificate. In the *Decretales,* of Alexander's 424 decretals 219 were directed to England, the same proportion is

that after 1172 ecclesiastical cases, even small cases, go directly to Rome and are laid before the supreme tribunal without ever having come before any lower court.[22] William of Drogheda writing in 1239, a good decade before Bracton, though he knows that England is full of judges ordinary, assumes and steadily maintains the assumption that all large and much small litigation will be brought in the first instance to a court constituted for the occasion by a papal *breve*.[23] Thus declaring land to be alms will no longer mean that it will be subject to the ruling of a bishop's or archbishop's court in England and to the final decision of the king on appeal, but rather that title and possession to English land will be settled at Rome in accordance with the *ius papale*.[24] Henry's recognition of

found in the letters of Lucius III (1181-85), his successor. But this does not hold true of either Alexander's predecessors or the popes who followed Lucius, including Innocent III whose 600 decretals form the largest portion of the *Decretales*. In the *Quinque Compilationes* among the papal letters not included in the official collection the contrast is clearer. Seventy-one of the 115 decretals of Alexander go to England, 7 out of the 9 of Lucius, but in the case of the other popes the proportion is quite a small one. A good part of this abnormal quota must be due to the fact that the machinery of the appeal had been unknown: what Alexander has to say about judges-ordinary, judges-delegate, and papal legates is almost exclusively (24 out of 30 decretals, 13 out of 18 on judges-delegate) for Englishmen. But English bishops ask advice on almost every canonically settled point of law; they are often rebuked (MAITLAND, *supra,* 126), but nevertheless continue to send long examination papers to the Pope often comprising 50 or 60 questions of law, generally unconnected with any litigation. That they were unfamiliar with the Roman custom and procedure is plain; whether they were ignorant of substantive canon law is more doubtful, but, at least, a *prima facie* case may be made out.

[22] Examples are common in any collection of documents. An interesting case of a very small suit referred to Urban III (c. 1186): STENTON, FACSIMILES OF EARLY CHARTERS (Northamptonshire Rec. Soc.) 76.

[23] Maitland, *William of Drogheda and the Universal Ordinary* (1897) 12 ENG. HIST. REV. 625, 633. Wahrmund, *Die* Summa Aurea *des Wilhelmus de Drokeda* (1914) 2 QUELLEN ZÜR GESCHICHTE DES RÖMISCH-KANONISCHEN PROCESSES IM MITTELALTER xix ff., *cf.* de Zulueta, *William of Drogheda* (1926) 2 MÉLANGES CORNIL 641. Maitland remarked that Drogheda's description of the opening of a suit began by impetrating a papal writ and compared it to BRACTON, f. 235b. Interesting light is shed on the word in (1930) 40 MOYEN ÂGE 8.

[24] Alexander III did not hesitate to do this, though he admits he had gone too far in ordering his delegates to give possession in a dispute between laymen who had come into the ecclesiastical courts on a question of bastardy. 1 POLLOCK AND MAITLAND, 247 n. 1. It is noteworthy that due to the fact that in impetrating a papal writ judges could be named, and not always impartial judges, many monasteries and religious houses ask for the 'ne pro aliqua causa ponantur in placitum de tenementis suis nisi coram me' clause in their charters of confirmation from the king. DELISLE-BERGER, RECUEIL DES ACTES DE HENRI II, nos. 463, 514, 560, 561, 565, 567, 572, 657, 659, 667, 686, 704, 768. There are earlier examples [SALTER, OXFORD CHARTERS (1929) no. 30; ROUND, CALENDAR, no. 129] but the years after 1172 see a large increase. A charter of 1175 (DELISLE-BERGER, nos. 588, 589) reads: 'Prohibemus [sic] ne pro aliqua causa ponantur in placitum de tenementis suis nisi coram me vel capitali justitia mea, quia non permitterem judicium fieri de elemosina mea et antecessorum meorum, nisi coram me . . .' It is significant that in 1172-3 Henry II introduces the 'Dei Gratia' into his style [DELISLE, RECUEIL DES ACTES DE HENRI II, INTRODUCTION (1909) 32]. This is similar to the remark of the Emperor Frederick Barbarossa in 1157. MIRBT, QUELLEN ZUR GESCHICHTE DES PAPSTTUMS (1924) 169; *cf.* KERN, GOTTESGNADENTUM UND WIDERSTANDSRECHT (1915) 304-07. In general: SCHMITZ, URSPRUNG UND GESCHICHTE DER DEVOTIONSFORMELN (Kirchenrechtliche Abh. 81).

the clergy's right to exclusive jurisdiction over land held in alms has changed radically in content, and in this change lies the reason for the transformation of the assize *utrum*. This preliminary action, which is the only hold the king retains upon his once complete power over church land, tends more and more finally to decide the case.[25] An assize under his justiciar decides according to English common law' not the abstract question whether the land in dispute is lay fee or alms, but the actual proprietary question, is the land the lay fee of *A* or the alms of *B*. So a layman impleaded before judges-delegate will ask a writ of prohibition forbidding them from intermeddling with lay fee, and have his right to the land decided under the common law by means of the assize. Nor is this introduction of appeal to the pope unconnected with Bracton's surprising statement that land may be lay fee though it be held in pure, free and perpetual alms,[26] and the general rapid limitations placed about the word *elemosina,* nor with, perhaps, the origin of the rule laid down by Glanvill that no man need answer for his free tenement without the king's writ.[27]

The paucity of material makes it difficult to trace the process of judicial legislation by which, in the ninety years between the Constitutions of Clarendon and Bracton's *De Legibus,* the action is first made proprietary and then limited to a definite class of churchmen. In Glanvill's day it is at least questionable whether the assize still served the

---

[25] In Normandy at the very end of the twelfth century [Trés Ancien Coutumier (ed. Tardif) 46] the corresponding writ *de feodo et elemosina* is proprietary. Blum, *Les origines du bref de fief lai et d'aumône* (1925) Travaux de la Semaine d'Histoire du Droit Normand 1923, 369, 382 ff.; Mitteis, *Beaumanoir und die geistliche Gerichtsbarkeit* (1914) 35 Zeit. der Savigny-Stift. für Rechtsgeschichte (Kanon. Abt.) 319-21. In the event that the recognitors were unable to decide definitely that the land was the lay fee of *A* or the alms of *B* the case was sent to the church court, though the author adds: 'Tamen multociens inter dominum Rothomagensem archiepiscopum et Willelmum senescallum [placitum] inde audivimus.' But the ecclesiastical bias of the author is evident throughout. Viollet, *Les Coutumiers de Normandie* (1912) 33 Histoire Littéraire de la France 53. The English procedure of the time must have approximated this. 1 Rotuli Curia Regis (1199) 436. Later on the Continent the writ acquired a wholly new status. Blum, *Le fonctionnement du bref de fief lai et d'aumône* (1924) 35 Moyen Âge 118.

[26] Bracton, De Legibus, f. 407. The contrast to lay fee is no longer *elemosina* but consecrated soil, the sites of churches and monasteries and their church-yards, to which Bracton adds their dower—lands given to them at the time of their dedication. *Cf.* f. 207b.

[27] Glanvill, XII, 25: 'Praeterea sciendum quod secundum consuetudinem regni nemo tenetur respondere in curia domini sui de aliquo libero tenemento suo sine praecepto domini regis vel eius capitali justitiae. Ita dico si laicum fuerit feodum petitum.' *Cf.* Glanvill (ed. Woodbine) 272-4; Adams, Origin of the English Constitution (1920) 96-105; Council and Courts in Anglo-Norman England (1926) 166-7. This would, of course, exempt a lay freeholder from appearing before a court constituted by papal writ. In the present state of our knowledge as to the origin of the principle, any dogmatic statement regarding it must be a mere guess, but that the provision was aimed at papal interference is one of the possibilities which must be considered.

purpose for which it was created in 1164.[28] Scarcely ten years after his treatise the action resembles the more familiar possessory assizes of *novel disseisin* and *mort d'ancestor*;[29] Glanvill himself lumps them all together. That Bracton can regard the assize as "a singular benefit which has been introduced in favor of an individual parson claiming land in the name of his church"[30] is evidence both that its proprietary force was no novelty and that its change had not been recent. The scope of the action on the Continent is in accord. In Glanvill and in the earliest Register of Writs the assize may be brought by either layman or clerk: this rule fluctuates but by 1227 Patteshull seems to have decided against allowing the layman the assize, a ruling to which Bracton registers a lively dissent.[31] It may be inferred that the necessity for the assize as a method for aiding the layman in evading papal appeals had passed. In 1220 it was urged that the assize was not a remedy for the patron or for the vicar, and there is both authority for the view and evidence that tenants in frank almoign are suing for lands in the temporal courts by the ordinary actions.[32] By Bracton's day the transformation of the assize *utrum* is completed and stands as another example of the practical adaptation of the available means to a given end so characteristic of the formative period of our law. The growth of this assize accompanied by severe restrictions upon the definition of

---

[28] In view of the rapid growth of the appeal to Rome it is not likely that the writs in Glanvill present a truer picture than do the writs in Bracton. They are almost similar, and but for Bracton's explanatory remarks, could both indicate the process described in the Constitutions of Clarendon. It is clear that there has been change by 1250 and the late twelfth century cases cited by Woodbine (GLANVILL, DE LEGIBUS, 286) point toward change before 1187. Just a few years after Glanvill the procedure on the Continent resembles Bracton more than it does the procedure contemplated in 1164. The divergence of the Norman *breve de feodo et elemosina* from the English assize *utrum* [BRUNNER, ENSTEHUNG DER SCHWUR-GERICHTE (1871) 236, 324-26; 2 MAITLAND, COLLECTED PAPERS (1911) 216; BIGELOW, HISTORY OF PROCEDURE (1880) 4; HASKINS, NORMAN INSTITUTIONS, 173; 1 POLLOCK AND MAITLAND, 247] has been overstressed. Blum, *Les origines du bref de fief lai et d'aumône* (1925) TRAVAUX, 377 f.; *Le fonctionnement du bref de fief lai et d'aumône* (1924) 35 MOYEN ÂGE 123 ff.

[29] 1 ROTULI CURIA REGIS 190, 436.

[30] BRACTON, f. 286b: 'Et cum habeant tales personae (churchmen) omnia remedia generalia, quae quidem laicus haberet, non habebunt recursum ad singulare beneficium, quod introductum est in favore alicujus singularis personae terram petentis nomine ecclesiae suae . . .' For a discussion of the reasons why parsons of parochial churches were unable to use the ordinary proprietary remedies for the recovery of land see: 1 POLLOCK AND MAITLAND, 248 ff.

[31] GLANVILL, XIII, 23. Maitland, *The History of the Register of Original Writs* (1889) 3 HARV. L. REV. 97, 111; MAITLAND, BRACTON'S NOTE BOOK (1887) nos. 368, 1020, 1923. *Cf.* BRACTON, f. 285b: 'Sed cum restringendae sunt lites potius quam laxandae, ut vitentur duella et magnae assisae, et placitum maturius terminetur, oportet hodie quod breve istud et assisa locum teneat in persona utriusque, tam laici quam rectoris, secundum quod olim fuit observatum . . .'

[32] BRACTON'S NOTE BOOK, nos. 308, 539; 1 CURIA REGIS ROLLS (1200) 325; THE EARLIEST LINCOLNSHIRE ASSIZE ROLL (Lincoln Rec. Soc.) lxxv-lxxvii.

elemosina,[33] and the rise of the writs of prohibition,[34] did much to keep the title and possession of English land a matter for decision by the common law courts.[35]

---

[33] BRACTON'S NOTE BOOK, nos. 547, 755, 1143; BRACTON, f. 407. In Normandy in 1208 permission not to plead except in church courts with respect to their *elemosina* is granted to the Templars. DELISLE, RECUEIL DE JUDGEMENTS DE L'ECHIQUIER (1864) 48, cited Mitteis, *Beaumanoir und die geistliche Gerichtsbarkeit* (1914) 35 ZEIT DER SAVIGNY-STIFT. FÜR RECHTSGESCHICHTE (Kanon. Abt.) 263, 276 n. 3. *Cf.* FOURNIER, OFFICIALITÉS AU MOYEN ÂGE (1880) 84, 85.

[34] GLANVILL, XII, 21, 22; BRACTON, f. 402 ff.; *cf.* RIOLLOT, LE DROIT DE PRÉVENTION DES JUGES ROYAUX SUR LES JUGES SEIGNEURIAUX (1931) c. 1. It is mainly concerned, however, with a later period.

[35] Miss Kimball's article, *The Judicial Aspects of Frank Almoign Tenure* (1932) 47 ENG. HIST. REV. 1, escaped my attention during the writing of this paper. She makes no mention of the introduction of the appeal to Rome and gives little attention to the history of the assize after 1164. Her canonical researches, starting as they do with the *Decretales* of Gregory IX, give no indication of the papal origin of the distinction between ecclesiastical and lay fee, and leave unexplained the introduction of the claim into England.

6

NOTES ON COURTS OF RECORD IN ENGLAND*

Heinrich Brunner long ago found the origin of courts of record in an extension to the records of their courts of the privilege of incontestable documentation possessed by the Frankish kings.[1] It had long been a commonplace that the documents of the Merovingian and Carolingian kings as contrasted with contemporary private documents dispense with witnesses, but Brunner first pointed out that the absence of witnesses was due to the incontestability of these documents which made the *rogatio testium* and hence the *subscriptio testium* superfluous.[2] But, though it was therefore impossible to question the material content (*sachliche Inhalt*) of the document, it was always possible to dispute its

---

* Professor Plucknett has pointed out that curious modern definition of a court of record as one which can fine and imprison (*per*. Lord Holt in Groenvelt v. Burwell (1697) 1 Ld. Raym. 454, 467) is itself evidence that the term 'court of record' has had a tortuous history. The purpose of these notes is not to trace that history in detail but rather to throw some light upon two of the many facets the problem presents. The enormous scope of the problem and the absence of any treatment of the subject must explain both the presence of what may seem two distinct papers under one title and the publication of two parts of a homogeneous work before the connecting framework has been fully completed.

[1] *Zeugen- und Inquisitionsbeweis der karolingischen Zeit* in 15 SITZUNGS-BERICHTE DER PHIL-HIST. KLASSE DER WIENER AKADEMIE (1866) 343, 384-85= FORSCHUNGEN ZUR GESCHICHTE DES DEUTSCHEN UND FRANZOSISCHEN RECHTES (1894) 88, 128; *Wort und Form im altfranzosischen Prozess* in 57 *ibid*. (1868) 655, 664-68=FORSCHUNGEN (1894) 260, 268ff; DIE ENTSTEHUNG DER SCHWURGERICHTE (1872) 50, 189-95; *Das Gerichtszeugnis und die frankische Konigsurkunde* in FESTGABEN FUR A. W. HEFFTER (1873) 133=1 ABHAND-LUNGEN ZUR RECHTSGESCHICHTE (1931) 417; *Carta und Notitia* in COM-MENTATIONES IN HONOREM TH. MOMMSENI (1877) 570=1 ABHANDLUNGEN ZUR RECHTSGESCHICHTE (1931) 458; *Die Zulassigkeit der Anwaltschaft im franzosischen, normannischen und englischen Rechts des Mittelalters* (1878) 1 ZEITSCHRIFT FUR VERGLEICHENDE RECHTSWISSENSCHAFT 321, 356ff.=FOR-SCHUNGEN (1894) 389, 418ff; ZUR RECHTSGESCHICHTE DER ROMISCHEN UND GERMANISCHEN URKUNDE (1880) 157ff; 1 DEUTSCHE RECHTSGESCHICHTE (1906) 563f; 2 *ibid*. (1928) 560.

[2] *Das Gerichtszeugnis und die frankische Konigsurkunde*, 438-441; 1 DEUTSCHE RECHTSGESCHICHTE, 566-67; and his explanation has been adopted by diplomatists: Redlich, *Allgemeine Einleitung zur Urkundenlehre* in ERBEN-SCHMITZ-KALLENBERG, URKUNDENLEHRE (1907) 31; HEUBERGER, ALLGEMEINE URKUNDENLEHRE (1921) 30f; GIRY, MANUEL DE DIPLOMATIQUE (1925) 821ff; STEINACKER, DIE ANTIKEN GRUNDLAGEN DER FRUHMITTELALTERLICHEN PRIVATURKUNDE (1927) 8. Bresslau (2 HANDBUCH DER URKUNDENLEHRE (1915) 204) expresses the distinction succinctly: '*Die Grunde fur diesen Unterschied* (between private witnessed and royal unwitnessed documents) *erhellen aus dem, was fruher uber die Stellung und den Wert der Konigsurkunde im Beweisverfahren bemerkt worden ist* (1 *ibid*. (1912) 640ff.); *die Anfechtung ihres sachlichen Inhalts war rechtlich unmoglich und ihrer formale Echtheit wurde nicht durch Zeugenbeweis, sondern durch die Aussagen des koniglichen Kanzleipersonals oder des Konigs selbst erwiesen*.'

authenticity, in other words, its formal genuineness (*formale Echtheit*) and this question was resolved at first by the chancellor or a chancery clerk, later by an examination of the king's seal attached to the document.[3] Brunner further remarked the fact that the unofficial court-documents (*Gerichtsurkunde*) of the Frankish period sometimes bore the subscription of witnesses, sometimes were unwitnessed, sometimes were sealed with the king's seal, and in the sealed *gerichtsurkunde* of the royal court found an extension of the privilege of indisputability from the king's charters to a more general class of royal documents which included the records of the royal court.[4] He was of the opinion that this privilege was Frankish in origin, that with the breakdown of the Frankish empire and its law it passed to Normandy and persisted in the courts of the Norman dukes, that it was brought to England by the Conquest.[5]

---

[3] Although Seeliger (11 MITTEILUNGEN DES OSTERREICHISCHEN INSTITUTS FUR GESCHICHTSFORSCHUNG (1890) 398) takes the opposite view, Brunner (2 DEUTSCHE RECHTSGESCHICHTE (1928) 426) and Bresslau (1 HANDBUCH DER URKUNDENLEHRE (1912) 643) hold that in the Germanic law the challenge to a document was a single act in which material and formal characteristics were undistinguished. But *ex hypothesi* the challenge to a royal document could go only to its formal validity. The question is settled by the referendar, clerk, or chancellor who had written the document, perhaps by the king himself. BRESSLAU, 644. This is of course only possible as long as the author of the document or the king is available. As a substitute the question of authenticity is made dependent upon the seal (1 BRESSLAU, 688; REDLICH, DIE PRIVATURKUNDE DES MITTELALTERS (1911) 106) and it is only by a later extension that this means of identification includes proof of the credibility of the document's content.

[4] *Das Gerichtszeugnis und die Frankische Konigsurkunde*, 441: '*Was von der Konigsurkunde im allgemeinen, gilt auch von der uber ein konigliches Placitum ausgestellten Urkunde. Die Placita- so werden die Urkunden uber Placita gleichfalls gennant- sind ja im Namen des Konigs und unter koniglichem Siegel ausgestellt. Da aber die Urkunde nach den Grundsatzen des Zeugenbeweises behandelt wird, so muss der unscheltbaren Konigsurkunde ein unscheltbares Zeugnis des Konigsgerichtes, also ein Gerichtszeugnis entsprechen.*' 1 DEUTSCHE RECHTSGESCHICHTE 566 ff; 2 *ibid.*, 560. ff. For *gerichtsurkunde* see: REDLICH, DIE PRIVATURKUNDE, 64ff; Bresslau, *Urkundenbeweis und Urkundenschreiber im alteren deutschen Recht* (1886) 26 FORSCHUNGEN ZUR DÉUTSCHEN GESCHICHTE 1ff; 1 BRESSLAU, HANDBUCH DER URKUNDENLEHRE, 591ff. (no repetition of authorities cited in earlier article); but compare: Heuberger, *Frankische Pfalzgrafenzeugnis und Gerichtsschreibertum* (1926) 41 MITTEILUNGEN DES OSTERREICHISCHEN INSTITUTS FUR GESCHICHTSFORSCHUNG 46, 56-62. Sohm (DIE FRANKISCHE REICHS-UND GERICHTSVERFASSUNG (1871) 527 n. 5) gives an example of a witnessed *gerichtsurkunde;* for sealed *gerichtsurkunde*: SICKEL, ACTA REGUM ET IMPERATORUM KAROLINORUM (1867) 192, 364; MAYER-HOMBERG, DIE FRANKISCHEN VOLKSRECHTE (1912) 245 ff.

[5] DAS GERICHTSZEUGNIS UND DIE FRANKISCHE KONIGSURKUNDE, 434, 440; DIE ENTSTEHUNG DER SCHWURGERICHTE (1872) 50; FORSCHUNGEN (1894) 419, 424. Liebermann (3 GESETZE DER ANGELSACHSEN (1916) 290) adopts his view: '*Von der Curia des Frankischen Konigs ging dies Vorrecht der Unanfechtbarkeit uber auf die des Normann. Herzogs und des Anglonorman. Konigs.*' Record is not the only English institution whose roots Brunner found in the Frankish empire and which he traced through Normandy to England: both equity and the jury he regarded as having followed a similar path. The

But before the Conquest there is in Normandy no evidence of the incontestable king's charter: there is neither a chancery nor a seal to answer for the formal genuineness of the document,[6] nor the absence of the *subscriptio testium* to indicate that proof by witnesses was unnecessary.[7] Evidence of written judicial records, either private or public, is likewise lacking: the Frankish notarii, cancellarii (*gerichtsschreiber*) found no foothold in Normandy nor do official court rolls appear until long after the Conquest.[8]

---

former has been vigorously attacked by Kirn in *Uber die angebliche Billigkeitsjustiz des frankischen Konigs* (1927) 47 ZEITSCHRIFT FUR RECHTSGESCHICHTE (GERMANISTISCHE ABTEILUNG) 115 and in *Aequitatis iudicium von Leo dem Grossen bis zu Hinkmar von Reims* (1932) 52 *ibid.* 53. As to the latter, evidence of continuity between the Frankish *inquisitio per testes* and the Norman jury remain undiscovered (HASKINS, NORMAN INSTITUTIONS (1918) 226) as does evidence of the existence of the assize in Normandy before 1164, the date of its appearance in England. Thorne, *The Assize Utrum and Canon Law in England* (1933) 33 COL. L. REV. 430 n. 11. With regard to courts of record Brunner (ENTSTEHUNG, 50 n. 2; *Gerichtszeugnis*, 426, 432) is forced to admit with Sohm (DIE FRANKISCHE REICHS-UND GERICHTSVERFASSUNG (1871) 436) that they were unknown to the Frankish law and for their existence in Normandy prior to the Conquest produces no evidence earlier than the SUMMA DE LEGIBUS NORMANNIE (c. 1250).

[6] But two Norman charters before 1066 make mention of a chancellor (HASKINS, NORMAN INSTITUTIONS (1918) 52 n. 248). These are charters of Richard II (c. 1006) but the chancellor early disappears (HASKINS, 59-60). None of William's charters bears the attestation of a chancellor, few the attestation of a chaplain, only one mentions its author (LOT, ETUDES CRITIQUES SUR L'ABBAYE DE ST. WANDRILLE (1913) no. 20) who seems to have been a monk at St. Wandrille (*ibid.* nos. 30, 31). In general the variation of style and form preclude the existence of an effective chancery and indicate that the charters were generally drawn up by the recipients. Stevenson, *An Old-English Charter of William the Conqueror* (1896) 11 ENG. HIST. REV. 731, 733 n. 5; HASKINS, 52-54, 274. Under the Conqueror's son in Normandy the situation is similar. HASKINS, 72-74. Anterior to 1066 there is no trace or mention of a ducal seal. Stevenson, *Yorkshire Surveys and other Eleventh Century Documents* (1912) 27 ENG. HIST. REV. 1, 4; HASKINS, 53 n. 255. In fact the seal in use in lower Italy disappeared under Norman domination. 1 BRESSLAU 942.

[7] The charters of William in the most important cartularies and collections are witnessed: LE PROVOST, MEMOIRES POUR SERVIR A L'HISTOIRE DU DEPARTEMENT DE L'EURE (1862-69) LOT, ETUDES CRITIQUES SUR L'ABBAYE DE SAINT-WANDRILLE (1913); ROUND, CALENDAR OF DOCUMENTS PRESERVED IN FRANCE (1899); SAUVAGE, L'ABBAYE DE SAINT-MARTIN DE TROARN (1911); VERNIER, CHARTES DE L'ABBAYE DE JUMIEGES (1916); ANTIQUUS CARTULARIUS ECCLESIAE BAIOCENSIS (1902-03); HASKINS, NORMAN INSTITUTIONS (1918) appendices. The witnesses to Willim's charters sign in attestation rather than assent. HASKINS, 54-55; *cf.* MAITLAND, DOMESDAY BOOK AND BEYOND (1897) 247-52.

[8] HALBEDEL, FRANKISCHE STUDIEN (1915) 42f; Bresslau, *Der Ambasciatorenvermerk in der Urkunden der Karolinger* (1908) 1 ARCHIV FUR URKUNDENFORSCHUNG 177; MAYER-HOMBERG, FRANKISCHEN VOLKSRECHTE IM MITTELALTER (1912) 245f; 1 TOUT, CHAPTERS IN MEDIAEVAL ADMINISTRATIVE HISTORY (1920) 122ff; VALIN, LE DUO DE NORMANDIE (1910) 103f. The decisions of Norman courts in the period anterior to the Fench conquest have reached us only in charters preserved by the interested parties; there are no plea rolls or feet of fines. DELISLE, RECUEIL DE JUGEMENTS DE L'ECHIQUIER

In England before the Conquest the situation is only slightly more propitious: the Anglo-Saxon kings have not established Brunner's necessary concomitant to record, the incontrovertible king's charter,[9] and though there is a chancery,[10] there is no private or official systematic written record of litigation.

The absence of written court documents makes it impossible to find the origin of courts of record in England in Brunner's theory of the transmission of the king's privilege of incontestable documentation. The germ of record must lie either in the delegation to his court of the king's privilege of oral indisputability,[11]

DE NORMANDIE (1864) 247ff; PERROT, ARRESTA COMMUNIA SCACCARII (1910); MARNIER, ESTABLISSEMENTS ET COUTUMES, ASSISES ET ARRETS DE L'ECHIQUIER DE NORMANDIE *au* XIIIe *siecle* (1839).

[9] BRUNNER, ZUR RECHTSGESCHICHTE D. ROMISCHEN UND GERMANISCHEN URKUNDE (1880) 158-59; MAITLAND, DOMESDAY BOOK AND BEYOND, 250. This must follow solely from the *subscriptio testium* for both Maitland and Brunner's statements as to the non-existence of the Anglo-Saxon chancery must be discarded. The seal is in use under Edward the Confessor. 27 ENG. HIS. REV. 6-7. ARONIUS, DIPLOMATISCHE STUDIEN UBER DIE ALTEREN ANGELSACHSISCHEN URKUNDEN (1883) 12. Earlier Brunner (GERICHTSZEUGNIS, 434) attributed the lack of record among the Anglo-Saxons to the presence of court-witnesses: '*Das angelsachsische Recht kennt den Rekord nicht, es benutzt vielmehr besonders ernannte Urkundspersonen als Zeugen sowohl uber Rechtsgeschafte als auch uber gerichtliche Akte,*' citing EDWARD II, 2; AETHELSTAN V, 1 § 5; EDGAR IV, 3-6. These are taken directly from SCHMID, GESETZE DER ANGELSACHSEN (1858) 649 s. v. *recordatio*, and are applicable only in so far as they describe transaction witnesses used to corroborate business transactions of sale, gift, and exchange. Bechert, *Die Einleitung des Rechtsgang nach angelsachsischem Recht* (1927) 47 ZEIT. F. RECHTSGESCHICHTE (GERMANISTISCHE ABT.) 31f. Liebermann, *Die Eideshufen bei den Angelsachsen* (1910) HISTORISCHE AUFSATZE FUR ZEUMER 557.

[10] See the two articles of Stevenson cited *supra* n. 6. DAVIS, REGESTA REGUM ANGLO-NORMANNORUM (1913) xi ff. The diplomatic examination urged by Haskins to determine the extent to which the Anglo-Norman chancery was influenced by Anglo-Saxon precedents has been made by Galbraith for Winchester (*Royal Charters to Winchester* (1920) 35 ENG. HIST. REV. 382-400) by Douglas for Bury St. Edmunds (FEUDAL DOCUMENTS FROM THE ABBEY OF BURY ST. EDMUNDS [1932] both indicate the dependence of the A-N writ charter on the A-S writ and the continuity between the A-S and A-N royal scriptoria. *Cf.* Galbraith, *An Episcopal Land Grant of 1085* (1929) 44 ENG. HIST. REV. 355-56; 1 TOUT, CHAPTERS IN MEDIAEVAL ADMINISTRATIVE HISTORY (1920) 131.

[11] 2 POLLOCK & MAITLAND, HISTORY OF ENGLISH LAW (1923) 669-70; quoted 5 HOLDSWORTH, H. E. L. (1934) 157. Add to n. 2, p. 699 the remark of Willoughby, J.: '*Quant le Roi recorde ascume chose de sa vewe demesne cel record ne serra jammes anienti.*' Y. B. 12-13 EDW. III (Rolls Ser) 101 (1338). The incontestability of the king's oral word may have Anglo-Saxon roots: in Kent (c. 695) a bishop or a king's word though unsupported by oath is incontrovertible. Withraed c, 16 (1 LIEBERMANN, GESETZE, 13). *Cf. Les Costumes d'Oleron*, c. 40 in 2 BLACK BOOK OF THE ADMIRALTY (1873) 311: '*Li mayres est creguz de tout ceu que il dit comment que il dient comme iuges, ou comme clamis, ou comme garenz . . . . quar le maires est tenguz par son saigrement de iuger dreit et de dire verite et de faire leaute.*' Brunner claims oral indisputability in the Frankish law (2 DEUTSCHE RECHTSGESCHICHTE (1928) 16): '*Das frankische Recht hatte den Grundsatz: der Konig lugt nicht. Sein Wort besass erhohte Glaubwurdigkeit... Sein schriftliches und*

or in the delegation of his privilege to have all that has transpired in his presence incontrovertible.[12] It may seem gratuitous to distinguish between either or both of these and the king's written word, and to fail to regard all three as instances of the same fundamental claim, but nevertheless the distinction seems sound. The oral record in England is completely disconnected from the written tradition of the Frankish court.[13] In Glanvill there is mention of record but none of rolls:[14] the record lies in the memories of the justices,[15] and after the introduction of rolls the situation remains

---

sein mundliches Zeugnis durfte im Rechtsgang bei Verwirkung des Lebens nicht angefochten werden.' But he cites only the Kentish law *supra*.

[12] Leis Willelme c. 24 (1 LIEBERMANN, GESETZE 510): '*De hume ki plaided en ki curt que ceo seit, fors la u le cors le rei seit, e hom lui met sure k'il ad dit chose qu'il ne voille conuistre, s'il pot deredhner par un entendable hume del plait oant e veant qu'il ne l'averad dit, recovre ad sa parole.*' DIALOGUS DE SCACCARIO I, c. 4: 'For there sits the Chief Justice of the lord king . . . . as well as the greatest men of the kingdom . . . . so that whatever has been established in the presence of such great men subsists by an inviolable right.' GLANVILL (ed. Woodbine, 119) VIII, 5: '*Necesse est enim quod id quod aliquis in curia domini Regis coram domini regis vel eius institiis cognoverit, vel quod se facturum in manum ceperit, teneant is qui hoc in manu cepit vel cognovit.*'

[13] The presence or absence of a written record had no effect upon the status of the court as a court of record. The county court was not of record (n. 27 *infra*) yet it might have a written record. 6 C. R. R. 228 (1212); Y. B. 8 EDW. II 219 (1314); Y. B. 19 EDW. III 479-80 (1345); Manorial courts and hundred courts in private hands were in a similar position. Y. B. 30-31 EDW. I 500 (1302). This point is well made by Woodbine (*County Court Rolls and County Court Records* (1930) 43 HARVARD L. REV. 1096 n. 36; his edition of GLANVILL, DE LEGIBUS (1932) 238-45) but his statement that 'for such of the king's court as have a roll, that roll is the record' must be taken with caution.

[14] GLANVILL, DE LEGIBUS (ed. Woodbine, 54, 82, 120-23) I, 31; V, 11; VIII, 5-11. The earliest plea-roll evtant is that of 1194. Round, *The Earliest Plea Rolls* (1896) 11 ENG. HIST. REV. 102. Maitland (SELECT PLEAS OF THE CROWN (1888) xxvi-xxvii) brought forward evidence to show the existence of such rolls as early as 1181, but see Round, *The First-Known Fine* in FEUDAL ENGLAND (1909) 509. There is evidence of a roll for the first year of Richard I (1189). Woodbine, *Proof of Existence of Plea Rolls before 1194* (1926) 35 YALE L. J. 345; 3 C. R. R. 45. The date of Glanvill is thus earlier than 1189, perhaps than 1181. The Dialogus de Scaccario mentions the rolls of the justices: see n. 21 *infra*, but whether these were more than a record of amercements or the passage an interpolation in the Dialogus is unknown. Richardson, *Richard Fitz Neal and the Dialogus de Scaccario* (1928) 43 ENG. HIST. REV. 161, 321.

[15] Before 1195 the justices might bear record of a fine levied before them, and if they did so theor record was conclusive; but their record was based upon their memory. GLANVILL, DE LEGIBUS (ed. Woodbine, 121) VIII, 8; *cf. ibid.* 236 *s. v.* finalem concordiam. In 1344 (Y. B. 18-19 EDW. III 299) an inquest had been taken at nisi prius '*et nota qen le recorde ny ad pas mencion fait que enquys fut des damages*'. But Willoughby who had taken the inquest and was now one of the judges sitting '*recorda de bouche*' that the jury assessed the damages. Y. B. 30-31 EDW. I 329 (1902); I ROTULI PARLIAMENTORUM (1292) 84. Record is regarded as something that had taken place before justices, and long after the introduction of rolls the emphasis of the serjeants in court is still so placed. Examples are numerous: '*encontre*

unchanged, for though the rolls may serve to refresh the memories
of the justices they do not completely substitute for them. The
rolls vary among themselves,[16] and may be altered and supplemented
by the justices without further formality.[17] It is true that where
there are written records litigants often vouch the rolls and records
of the justices, but rolls and records are used in no technical sense,
and it seems to have been immaterial whether the litigant vouched
the justices or their rolls.[18] It may be said without fear of contradiction that the *recordum* and the roll are not yet synonymous.[19]

sa reconysance demene en court ke porte record' (Y. B. 20-21 EDW. I (1292)
309 *bis*); '*en curt ke porte record*' Y. B. 21-22 EDW. I (1293) 33, 35); '*devant
Justice ky portunt Record*' (*ibid.* (1293) 145); '*conisance fet en court*' (*ibid.*
(1293) 146 *bis*); '*ne put dire qe nous ly avoms acquite en court que porte
record*' (Y. B. 4 EDW. II (1310) 77); '*jugement si vous encountre vostre
conissaunce demene en court qe porte record pusez dire . . . .*' (Y. B. 4
EDW. II (1311) 169); '*Record est de chose fet en court*' (Y. B. 9 EDW. II
(1315) 38); '*par sa . . . . conissaunce . . . . en court qe porte record*' (*ibid.*
(1316) 103); '*en court qe porte recorde*' (*ibid.* (1316) 128, 129); '*vous no
posz dire qe nous en court qe porte recorde vous eoins l'acquitaunce conu*'
(*ibid.* (1316) 132). For an instance in which it seems clear that the acknowledgment in court and not the entry on the roll was of the essence see: Y. B.
2-3 EDW. II (1308-09) 42 in which it was claimed that the Statute of Westminster II (13 EDW. I) c. 18 limited an acknowledgment to matter in dispute
and not to any acknowledgment made before justices. *Cf.* Y. B. 21-22 EDW.
I (R. S.) 146.

[16] 3 C. R. R. 301 (1205): '*. . . . et preceptum est justiciariis quod tunc
habeant recordum tocius loquele et quod possint tunc certificare quorum rotuli
aliis adversantur de recordo illo, ut dicitur.*' 3 C. R. R. 334 (1205): '*Unde
dominus rex precepit ut justiciarii scire facerent ei que diversitas in quibus
rotulis invenitur.*'

[17] Frounceys v. Latimer, Y. B. 4 EDW. II 114 (1310).

[18] '*ponit se super justiciarios et rotulos corum*' (1 C. R. R. (1200) (177);
'*vocat rotulos domini regis*' (*ibid.* 181); '*ponit se super rotulos curie domini
regis*' (*ibid.* (1201) 402); '*vocat ad warantum rotulos*' (*ibid.* 408): '*vocaverat
recordum illorum justiciariorum*' (*ibid.* 418); '*ponit se super rotulos domini
regis. Et quoniam justiciarii recordantur . . . .*' (2 C. R. R. (1201) 19);
'*ponit se super rotulos anni primi regmi Riccardi et super recognitores*' (3 C.
R. R. (1203) 45); '*et inde vocat justiciarios et rotulos ad warantum*' (*ibid.*
(1204) 168); '*petit recordum curie et rotulorum*' (*ibid.* 170); '*vocat ad
warantum justiciarios et rotulos domini regis*' (4 C. R. R. (1205) 36); '*dies
data . . . . quia justiciarii volunt interim inspicere rotulos suos et certificari
. . . .*' (*ibid.* (1206) 210); '*petit recordum curie domini regis . . . . curia
ergo recordantur* (*ibid.* 264); '*vocat rotulos et recordum justiciariorum*' (6 C
R. R. (1212) 260); '*ponit se super recordum justiciariorum*' (*ibid.* 308).
Similarly, to vouch the unenrolled record of the county court: '*vocavit inde
recordum comitatus*' (1 C. R. R. 72); '*ponit se super recordum comitatus*'
(*ibid.* 100); '*vocat curiam ad warantum*' (*ibid.* 400). This voucher to warranty is an appeal to the court's memory (2 POLLOCK & MAITLAND, H. E. L.
(1923) 670 n. 7) and may be seen in the later plea rolls: *vocavit curiam
domini regis ad warantum*' (BRACTON'S NOTE BOOK, pl. 88); '*vocat ad
warantum rotulos ipsorum iustitiariorum*' (*ibid.* pl. 829).

[19] For the contrast between roll and record see the interesting case *Abbess
of Barking v. Sutton,* Y. B. 16 EDW. III (2) 120, 128, 132, 593-97 (1342)
in which counsel draws the distinction: '*Sire, il vous sourmit bien coment la
defaute vous fut mustre; par quei, Sire, ceo quest ore entre en roulle ne put
neynt estre recorde; par quei, Sire, nous prioms qe vous voillez recorder la*

The rolls of pleas did not early obtain a position similar to that of the formal Pipe Roll,[20] but by the middle of the fourteenth century the court rolls begin to reflect a like formality and precision.[21] This, however, is not at all dependent upon the indisputability of the king's documents, for though the concept is well recognized in Anglo-Norman England and probably took form soon after the Norman kings had adopted the Anglo-Saxon chancery to their new

---

chose tiel com il fut.' Cf. Y. B. 16 EDW. III (2) 94; for fine and record: Y. B. 9 EDW. II 42 (1315).

[20] DIALOGUS DE SCACCARIO I, 5: 'The roll is of such authority that in nothing may it be altered or changed except in the case of obvious error plan to all, and then only by the common counsel of all the barons. Moreover the roll of a past year, or a roll of the current year after the payment to the Exchequer, no one can alter except the King.' The rolls of the Pipe were the only continuous record kept by the king's court and even after the retention of feet of fines in the Treasury, fines are inscribed upon the Pipe roll (after due payment) for greater security. Richardson, *An Early Fine* (1932) 48 LAW Q. REV. 415, 416. That the rolls kept by the justices were not held in as high esteem as the Pipe Rolls either because they were not subject to as careful treatment or because they could be altered by the justices and did not in themselves necessarily comprise the complete *recordum* is indicated by the fact that litigants make payments to have cases entered on the Pipe Rolls even after the case has been entered on the plea-roll. P. R. 6 RICH. I (1194) 163; MAITLAND, THREE ROLLS OF THE KING'S COURT (1194). See the cases collected in Langbein, *The Jury of Presentment and the Coroner* (1933) 33 COL. L. REV. 1361 n. 126.

[21] No amendment of an enrolled plea. Y. B. 20 EDW. III (1) 108, 112 (1345/6); 329, 331 (1346); *Cf.* Y. B. 20 EDW. III (1) 192. The increasing emphasis upon the rolls is illustrated by Scrope, C. J. in a report of an Eyre at Northhampton in 1329 (Y. B. 8 EDW. II (Selden Soc. no. 37) xxi-xxiv). When urged to reduce an amercement he refused the petition, saying that 'he could not do this, for the fine had been entered on the roll; and he told how the king was angry with Sir Ralph de Hengham and put him on his trial on many charges, and did all that he could do, but he could find no fault in him save that he had remitted half a mark of a fine and had made an alteration in his rolls to that effect, and for this trespass the King fined him eight thousand marks.' But this would have been permissible after 1290 when Hengham was tried (Y. B. 4 EDW. II (1310) 114) and earlier DIALOGUS DE SCACCARIO II, 2; 'Let the judges take care that they deliver the rolls to the treasurer correct and in order, for it is not allowed even to the judges to change one iota *after the rolls have been given in*, even though all the judges agree therein.' Nor does Scrope's account conform to the account of Hengham's trial in the official records. RADULPHI DE HENGHAM SUMMAE (ed. Dunham) liii-lvi. The change is reflected in the physical make-up of the rolls and in the discontinuance of separate rolls. Bracton (DE LEGIBUS, fo. 352b) in speaking of variance in the rolls says we are to be guided by the roll of the protonotary 'cuius irrotulacionem debent *omnes* alii rotuli . . . .' Thus so many rolls were made that they may be referred to as 'all'. In 4 HENRY III there were five rolls available. Powicke in (1924) 39 ENG. HIST. REV. 268. For the reign of Edward II and later there are but two rolls: the Rex roll and that of the Chief Justice kept by the custos rotulorum. Y. B. 6 EDW. II (1) xxiv; Y. B. 5 Edw. II xi-xviii. In Edward III's reign the Rex roll is about one-tenth as complete as the C. J. roll and is obviously not used to bear record (Y. B. 16 EDW. III (2) xxv-xxix) though it might on rare occasions contain matter supplementing the roll of the justice.

needs and increased powers,[22] it seems to have had no influence upon the rolls. The formality seems to be due to the spread of the administrative practice of the Exchequer,[23] to the increased business of the court which made it impossible to rely further upon memory, and to the elaborate procedure which by about 1340 the court of Common Pleas had developed. The very real connection between the king and record persists though the transfer of the seal to administrative officers serves to blur the issue.[24] Emphasis

---

[22] During Henry II's reign the chancery had begun to break up royal acts into two chief categories: charters and writs. Charters retained the list of witnesses, writs were witnessed by the king himself. DELISLE, RECUEIL DES ACTES DE HENRI II, INTRODUCTION (1909) 325-26. But Tout (1 CHAPTERS IN MEDIAEVAL ADMINISTRATIVE HISTORY (1920) 135 n. 3) seems to follow Poole (15 SCOTTISH HIST. REV. (1918) 265-68) in believing that the '*teste me ipso*' appears first in the royal charters of Richard I, and with respect to royal charters Miss Prescott has shown this to be true. *The Early Use of 'Teste Me Ipso'* (1920) 35 ENG. HIST. REV. 214. From the reign of Henry III letters patent and letters close are attested by the king alone, but charters strictly so called continue to be attested by a varying number of ministers and courtiers. MAXWELL-LYTE, THE GREAT SEAL OF ENGLAND (1926) 234ff. It is clear that Brunner's statement (ZUR RECHTSGESCHICHTE D. ROMISCHEN U. GERMANISCHEN URKUNDE, 158) that the '*teste me ipso*' comes in from Normandy is unfounded, and that perhaps his theory that the *subscriptio testium* denotes disputability may be inapplicable to England. Despite the witnesses the king's charters are incontrovertible: '*Nota quod contra protestationem Regum per cartas suas non procedit placitum nec duellum nec magna assisa.*' (BRACTON'S NOTE BOOK pl. 226); *cf.* BRACTON, DE LEGIBUS (ed. Woodbine, 109) fo. 34; BRACTON'S NOTE BOOK pl. 239; *cf.* BRACTON, DE LEGIBUS, fo. 24; BRACTON'S NOTE BOOK pl. 1236; Y. B. 33-35 EDW. I 185; Y. B. 20 EDW III (2) 421 (1346).

[23] Plucknett (CONCISE HISTORY (1929) 10) hints at Domesday Book as the origin of the technical concept of record, and traces the idea to the rolls of the Exchequer and thence to the rolls of the law courts. But his discussion must be confined to the growth of indisputability of the *rolls*.

[24] Bolland (Y. B. 6-7 EDW. II (Selden Soc.) xxv-xxvii) was amazed to find that the roll of a manorial court (not a roll of record) might be made into an incontestable document by having a transcript made and sealed with the foot of the Great Seal. He quotes Thorpe, C. J. (1354) in a case in which the tenant in an assize of novel disseisin pleaded in bar of the assize on the ground that he himself had recovered by a writ of right patent brought in a manorial court the very same lands as were claimed in the assize. He offered no proof of this assertion and was instructed by the Chief Justice '*sil ust sue a faire venir la record en le Chancery et ore est mis auant le record sub pede sigilli il ust este bon barre*'. LIBER ASSISARUM, 147 n. 14; BROOKE'S ABRIDGEMENT, *Monstrans de faites*, no. 97. But this is little more than an application of Glanvill's (DE LEGIBUS (ed. Woodbine p. 122) VIII, c. 9) statement that the king may summon any court to make a record before his court so that that record may be indisputable: '*Item recordum potest habere quaelibet curia, ex beneficio principis, quemadmodum si rex aliqua rationabili cause motus fecerit aliquam curiam summoneri ad recordum faciendum in curia sua, ita quod velit dominus rex non liceat eius recordo contradici.*' For the transformation of a bishop's certificate of legitimacy into a record by the half seal see Y. B. 17 EDW. III (1343) 393-95. In 1501 it was held that if what purported to be a record bore any seal except that of the king *nul tiel record* would be a good plea: '*Devant les Justices del Comon Banc . . . . fuit dit per totam curiam pur ley et par Keble. On dira bien envers tiel record certifie desous le seel d'Eschiquier ou del Comon Banc Nul tiel record*

is placed more and more on the roll as indisputable evidence of the record and as the distinguishing feature of the court of record.[25] In line with this development the entire concept of record changes from that of incontestable evidence to that of public policy.[26]

II

At least as early as Glanvill the county court, in which the suitors were judges, the sheriff the presiding officer, was not a court of record.[27] But a distinction must be drawn between proceedings conducted by the county court and proceedings conducted by the sheriff in the county court. In the latter case the sheriff heard pleas not as sheriff but as *iustitiarius regis* by virtue of a delegation of authority from the king and as such had record.[28] The Norman kings distrusted the ancient customary process of the county court but were not able completely to dispense with it until their own control over local justice was secure. Thus they gave county court judgments a provisional validity. But for local cases in which it would be impossible or impractical to send a royal

car ce nest forsque un transcript del record: mes incontre le Grand Seel del Roy in le Chancerie nemy'. Y. B. 16 HEN. VII, 11, no. 5, cf. Y. B. 16 EDW. III (2) 354 (1342). Edward II claimed the power to convert into a legal record of conviction anything of the nature of treason which he held to be notorious. Y. B. 11-12 EDW. III xxxiii; Y. B. 12-13 EDW III 97-101 (1338/9). 'The King is of record in whatever part of the world he may be.' Y. B. 12-13 EDW. III 183 (1339).

[25] TERMS DE LA LEY *s. v. Record* defines a court of record by reference to the formal characteristics of its records: see the quotation 5 HOLDSWORTH, H. E .L. 159 n. 1.

[26] Hynde's Case, 4 REP. 70b, 71a; Floyd v. Barker, 12 REP. 23, 24: 'Records are of so high a nature, that for their sublimity they import verity in themselves; and none shall be received to aver anything against the record itself; and in this point the law is founded upon great reason; for if the judicial matters of record should be drawn in question, by partial or sinister supposals and averments of offenders, or any on their behalf, there will never be an end to causes; but, controversies will be infinite.' Cf. PLOWDEN, 491a; Salmond, *The Superiority of Written Evidence* (1890) 6 LAW Q. REV. 83. For a similar shift in emphasis in the doctrine of judicial immunity: Holdsworth, *Immunity for Judicial Acts* (1924) JOURNAL OF THE SOC. OF PUBLIC TEACHERS OF LAW, 17.

[27] GLANVILL, DE LEGIBUS (ed. Woodbine, 121) VIII, 9; BRACTON, DE LEGIBUS (ed. Woodbine, 441-42) fo. 156b; HENGHAM, SUMMA MAGNA (ed. Dunham, 8-10, 12-13) c. 4; *Modus Componendi Brevis* in WOODBINE, FOUR THIRTEENTH CENTURY LAW TRACTS (1910) 154; STAT. WESTMINSTER II (13 Edw. I) c. 2. If in accordance with Fleta (II, 43) and Hengham (SUMMA MAGNA c. 4) the fact that the suitors are judges indicates the absence of a writ to the sheriff and therefore of record, the court was not of record as early as 1180: Pipe Rolls 26 HEN. II 57; 34 HEN. II 43.

[28] BRACTON, DE LEGIBUS (ed. Woodbine, 307f, 438-39) fo. 108f, 155b-156; HENGHAM, SUMMA MAGNA (ed. Dunham) c. 4; FLETA II, 43; BRITTON (ed. Nichols) 135-136; GILBERT DE THORNTON, SUMMA (Harvard Law School Library MS 2.2) fo. 46b. Woodbine, *County Court Rolls and County Court Records* (1930) 43 HARV. L. REV. 1107f.

justice, they pressed into service the newly-reconstituted sheriff, invested him with the requisite authority, his court with the attribute of record.[29]   The list of causes, then, which could be heard in the county court has its roots in at least two separate jurisdictions, but it was not long before all proceedings in the same court were mingled and their different histories forgotten.   The history of the decline of the county court has never been written, and an insight into the shrinking jurisdiction of the sheriff with emphasis upon his loss of record may not be without value.

In 1370 it was already a moot question whether the sheriff was judge when commissioned by writ,[30] and though it was held he was, in 1461 when the question came before the Common Bench the opposite result was reached.   The plaintiff had recovered a judgment for damages in a court of ancient demesne but had been unable to have execution due to the fact that the defendant had neither goods nor chattels within the jurisdiction.   He had then sued a *certiorari* out of the Chancery directed to the bailiff of the lord demanding that the record be certified into the Chancery, and from there it had come into the Common Bench by *mittimus*.   With the record now before the justices the plaintiff prayed execution:

> *"Littleton*: It appears that this recovery was in ancient demesne; in that case no execution can be awarded here, for no execution will be awarded except on matter of record, and the record of ancient demesne is not such, for on it one can only have false judgment, which proves that it is not matter of record.   *Moyle*: We do not have jurisdiction to hold pleas of land in ancient demesne, but we can award execution of damages, for that is matter of record, since the plea was held by the king's writ, and just as in a writ of right in court baron, if the record comes before us we can award execution because it is matter of record since the plea was held by writ. In such case a writ of error lies as it does in *justicies*.   *Quod Prisot negavit* and said: in neither case would a writ of error lie but only false judgment, for the suitors and not the bailiff

---

[29] MORRIS, THE MEDIAEVAL ENGLISH SHERIFF (1927) 73, 198.   The action *de vetitio namii* was of this sort: BRACTON, DE LEGIBUS (ed. Woodbine, 439) fo. 155b: '*Detentio namii pro districtione facienda pertinet ad coronam domini regis, et vix aliqui conceditur terminandum praeterquam ipsi domino regi vel iustitiariis suis. Sed quia placitum istud dilationem non capit, propter animalia muta et propter damnum quod evenire posset si diu detinerentur inclusa, donec placitum de vetitio namii terminaretur, ideo placitum de vetitio namii vicecomiti concedetur terminandum, hac necessitate, quod quidem non habet ex officio vicecomitis, sed sicut institiarius ipsius domini regis.*'   Cf. SELECT PLEAS IN MANORIAL COURTS (1888) xxv.

[30] Y. B. 44 EDW. II Pasch. 12 p. 11: the sheriff may be judge in admeasurement of dower where authority delegated by writ.

are judges. *Moyle*: If the plea is held in the county by plaint then the suitors are judges, but if it is held by writ, as *justicies*, the sheriff is judge. *Quod fuit negatum*. *Prisot*: The judgment is not of record until we affirm or disaffirm it; then it is of record and execution may be awarded or a writ of error had.'[81]

Some few years later the question was again raised. A writ of admeasurement of pasture had been brought, the admeasurement made, and then removed to the Common Bench by *certiorari*. A writ *de secunda superoneratione* was then granted by the court. The defendant claimed that the admeasurement could not be removed by *certiorari* but only by *pone, recordari,* or false judgment since the admeasurement was not made before justices but before the sheriff:

> "*Jenney* (counsel for the defendant): The admeasurement was made by the sheriff who is not a justice, for the suitors are judges in the county court, just as in a writ of *justicies*. *Danby*: In *justicies* the sheriff is judge, not the suitors, for the writ reads *quod justicies T etc.*, and thus is a commission and command to the sheriff who holds the plea as a justice, and well he may, for the plea is not *in pleno comitatu* . . . . *Littleton*: On the contrary, neither in *justicies* not in any viscontiel action is the sheriff judge, but only the suitors, for he has no court except the county court and can hold no pleas except there — if he does it is *coram non judice*. And thus in replevin the command is *replegiari facias* yet is it held in the county and the suitors are judges, in a writ of right to the lord *quod plenum rectum teneas etc.* the suitors, are judges, and so here for the *justicies* has no other effect than to allow him to hold pleas involving more than forty shillings. And if they (the suitors) were not judges then one could not have false judgment, for this writ lies only against suitors, but on a judgment given under *justicies* false judgment lies, proving that the suitors are judges. *Quod Choke and Needham affirmavit*.'[82]

---

[81] Y. B. 39 HEN. VI, Mich. 5; BROOKE'S ABRIDGEMENT (1573) *Justicies* 6: '*Nota que in Court baron, hundred, et county, les suitors sont judges, et hoc cibien in brief de droit patent direct al court baron, in justicies, come sur auters suites, que sont la per plaint sans brief.*' See Y. B. 3 HEN. VI, Pasch. 2 (1402); Y. B. 7 HEN. VI, Mich. 17 (1429); Y. B. 34 HEN. VI, Pasch. 2 (1456); Y. B. 21 EDW. IV, Mich. 46 (1482); Y. B. 16 HEN. VII, Mich. 6 (1501).

[82] Y. B. 7 EDW. IV, Hil. 27 (1468). *Cf.* Y. B. 34 HEN. VI, Trin. 13 (1456): '*Littleton*: If a *justicies* is sent to the sheriff, even though it is an original writ, the party will never be allowed a writ of error on it, but only false judgment. But if judgment is given in a franchise, there error will lie. *Moyle*: On a judgment given in the county under *justicies*, as you say, false judgment and not error lies. But if the writ of *justicies* is removed here by *pone*, as

Similarly, the sheriff's court in the county was not considered a court of record within the meaning of the doctrine of merger,[33] nor was the litigant unable to go behind the records of this court in order to find the sheriff civilly or criminally liable for an abuse of jurisdiction.[34]

By the middle of the fifteenth century, then, the suitors and not the sheriff were the judges in the county court even in proceedings under writ. The distinction between proceedings by the county court and proceedings in the county court had been lost, or in other words, the king's county court and the sheriff's county court had become one and the same institution. With this merger went the loss of the sheriff's privilege of record. As evidence that the change must have taken place long before this period it may be pointed out that the learned Littleton knows nothing of any extraordinary jurisdiction of the sheriff and that he explains the writ of *justicies* as a means of granting jurisdiction to an amount greater than forty shillings, though the writ long antedated

---

can well be done pending the plea, Sir, in that case after the plea and judgment given in this court, the party will doubtless have a writ of error and not false judgment. Thus the nature of the court changes the nature of the writ.' *Semble*: Y. B. 6 EDW. IV, Mich. 9 (1467). If the plaintiff in the writ of false judgment be nonsuited, the other party can sue execution immediately. FITZHERBERT'S NATURA BREVIUM (ed. Hale, (1730) 40) 18g.

[33] Y. B. 9 EDW. IV, Hil. 10 (1470): '*Moyle*: In debt it cannot be pleaded that the plantiff had recovered before on the same bill or contract in the county under a *justicies*, or in any other court not of record, unless he had sued execution. But the matter is otherwise in a court of record.' Whether the plaintiff had recovered below was matter in *pais*: Y. B. 34 HEN. VI, Trin. 15 (1456): 'If one recovers on a writ of right in ancient demesne by assize or otherwise, so that damages are recovered, and if a writ of debt is sued on this record. the defendant can plead *nul tiel record* and it will be tried by the country.' However in Y. B. 9 EDW. IV, Mich. 27 (1470) Choke, J. said: 'There is diversity between recovery in a court of record and in those courts which are not of record, as ancient demesne or court baron, for against a recovery there one cannot plead *nul tiel record*, for there is no record, but one can plead *nul tiel recovery*, and it will be tried by *pais, quod fuit concessum*.' See also Y. B. 10 HEN. VII, Mich. 20 (1495).

[34] Y. B. 9 HEN. VI, Hil. 9 (1413): '*Martyn*: If a sheriff returns three or four exactions on an *exigent* when in truth there are five, will not the party have an action against the sheriff because of this? (*Quasi diceret, sic*) yet he is sheriff of record and the *exigent* is of record, but he is not a justice of record. And all the justices were of the opinion that the action would well lie.' 2 HEN. IV, Mich. 14 (1401); Y. B. 22 EDW. IV, Mich. 11 (1483). In the case of courts of record it had been held as early as the reign of Edward III that a litigant could not go behind the record in order to show the judge liable for an abuse of jurisdiction. 27 ASSISARUM 18. *Cf.* Y. B. 10 HEN. VI, Mich. 22 (1414); Y. B. 7 HEN. VI, Pasch. 22 (1429). Holdsworth, *Immunity for Judicial Acts* (1924) JOURN. OF THE SOCIETY OF PUBLIC TEACHERS OF LAW 17; 6 H. E. L. (1924) 235ff.

the statutory limitation.[35] By the time of Crompton and Coke the view advanced by Littleton was well established,[36] though it may be noted that Coke's explanation of the rule is little more than a repetition of Littleton's argument *supra*.[37] The loss of the sheriff's record must be contemporaneous with the appearance of the suitors as judges in cases instigated by writ as contrasted with plaint, and with that of the writ of false judgment from the sheriff's court.[38] The lack of cases points toward the solution. The growth of local royal jurisdiction made it unnecessary for the litigant longer to invoke the procedure of special writ to the sheriff.

---

[35] The interpretation put upon the Statute of Gloucester (6 EDW. I) c. 8 deprived the county court of jurisdiction if the amount in question was more than 40s. BRITTON (ed. Nichols) 155; POLLOCK & MAITLAND, H. E. L. (1923) 554. The writ of *justicies* occurs in Glanvill (DE LEGIBUS (ed. Woodbine, 174) XIII, 39) and in John's reign: Maitland, *The History of the Register of Original Writs* (1889) 3 HARV. L. REV. 112.

[36] COKE LITT. 117b; 2 COKE INST. (1662) 312; 4 COKE INST. c. 55; CROMPTON, L'AUTHORITIE ET JURISDICTION DES COURTS (1594) 230-32.

[37] *Jentleman's Case* 6 Rep. 11b (1583). The question as there raised was whether in a writ of right *patent* directed to the lord of the manor, or in a writ of right *close* directed to the lord of ancient demesne, or in a writ of *justicies* directed to the sheriff, the court held by virtue of the writ was or was not a court of record. It was argued that the lord, the bailiff, or the sheriff was constituted judge by the writ since it was sent to him and not to the suitors, and that 'as the writ is of record and constitutes a new judge, then the authority of the judge being by the king's writ, the court must also be of record.' This Coke vigorously denied: the reason why the writ is sent to the lord or sheriff is because the court baron is the lord's court, the county court the sheriff's, and the writ is sent to him to whom the court belongs. Further (1) the suitors are judges (implying that if the writ to the sheriff made him judge the court would have record, but since the suitors who hold no king's writ are judges, they hold no king's court) and (2) a writ of false judgment and not error lies whether the plea is held by king's writ or not, and as false judgment lies only from a court which is not of record, these courts are not of record.

[38] Y. B. 15 EDW. III 58 (1341); Y. B. 13 RICH. II 123 (1390). Vinogradoff's citation (Y. B. 6 EDW. II (1) xxxvii) is incorrect: the case referred to is 7 Edw. II (Vulgate) 244 (droit). It is interesting to note that the reverse of the process that had taken place in the county court was occurring in the merchant courts. The suitors are judges in 1344 (1 LITTLE RED BOOK OF BRISTOL (1900) 70, 71) but in 1467 the steward or chief officer of the court was considered judge and the party might have a writ of error but not of false judgment. Y. B. 6 EDW. IV, Mich. 9.

THE best account of Bracton's life was written by Maitland in 1887. Succeeding years and the printing of many records enable us to add some few new facts, but nothing of great consequence. We still have no definite information about the years prior to 1240, where most of the difficulties lie. Of his later life, we now know that he was a justice *coram rege* for two periods of four years each, 1247-51 and 1253-57, though we do not know why he left or why he was recalled. Before his first appointment, he had already served once as a justice in eyre, in 1245, and often as a justice of assise, particularly in the south-western counties. Positions of that kind were not entrusted to beginners, nor is it likely that Bracton acquired the necessary learning and experience outside the courts. Thus when in 1240 we find the Exchequer ordered to pay Henry de Bratton forty marks for his maintenance in the king's service—our earliest piece of evidence—we may assume that he was already filling some office connected with the courts. Just what it was is not specified, as was often the case, but the sum named is large, not far removed from the salaries received by justices of the Bench, and we may take it that he was then an experienced man, holding a responsible position, who had been connected with the courts for some years. Taken by itself, the writ is consistent with the view that it was only in 1239 that he first entered the royal service, as a young man of perhaps 25, whose patrons, William Ralegh, the eminent judge, and Richard of Cornwall, the king's brother, had opened to him, at one bound, the higher ranks of the royal service. But though it is doubtless true that a well connected man might easily pass into the royal service, from what we know of Henry III's judges, even the best connexions were unlikely to give him a place on a court within seven years, or send him on eyre in five. So far as the records show, a man needed a longer period of training in English law, and an acquaintance with the complexities of an eyre had first to be acquired by attendance at others, in some less exalted capacity, generally as a clerk. In the year 1239, Bracton was in fact filling the office of senior clerk in the court *coram rege*, and we may assume that he, like others, had reached it in the ordinary way.

Clerks in the courts of Henry III's reign were of two kinds, as Mr. Meekings has shown us. The differences between them may be seen in the contrasting careers of two contemporary Williams, who both became justices of the Bench and justices *coram rege*, William Ralegh and William of York. Ralegh was from 1219, probably from some years earlier, the close associate, confidential clerk and right-hand man of Martin of Pateshull, the eminent judge. The relation between them was personal rather than official. When Pateshull went on eyre, Ralegh accompanied him invariably; when he sat in Westminster, Ralegh assisted him there. William of York, on the other hand, seems unconnected with any particular judge; his services were impersonal and official. He sometimes went on eyre with Pateshull, but he also served with other judges, as the chancellor instructed him. Toward the end of his clerical career he was assigned for a few eyres as justice, with Segrave and others, then returned to his work as clerk. Ralegh never interrupted his clerical career, serving continuously with Pateshull until his retirement. The distinction between the two forms of service cannot be drawn more sharply, for example, by seeing whether one received a salary chargeable to the royal revenue and one did not. Both were in orders and both were beneficed clerks, and both had papal dispensations dispensing them from the canons against pluralism, as indeed had Pateshull.

Pateshull retired in 1229 and died shortly thereafter. Within a few weeks Ralegh had been appointed to the Bench, with precedence over some who had sat as justices while he was a clerk. Two years later, in 1231, William of York was promoted to the Bench. They had been clerks for 13 or 14 years. In 1234 Ralegh moved to the court *coram rege*, retiring from it in 1239, when he was elected bishop of Norwich; in 1242 he was translated to Winchester. William of York moved to the court *coram rege* in 1242, resigning from it in 1247 on his election as bishop of Salisbury. In that year Bracton was appointed to the court. On his election to Salisbury, William of York vacated his ecclesiastical offices, including canonries at York and Wells. To his place at Wells, Bracton was soon appointed.

Bracton seems not to have been as widely known in his lifetime as Ralegh or William of York, nor does his career have quite the brilliance of theirs. Perhaps he was less the administrator and man of action and more the thoughtful scholar, as his treatise would lead us to believe. But be that as it may, it seems unlikely that he would have been appointed a justice in less time than it took the two Williams to rise to that office. If we assume that he served as clerk for precisely as long as they had, he would have come to the courts in about 1234, the year Ralegh left the Bench for the court *coram rege*. If so, he never saw Pateshull, yet he often tells us what Martin, for so he names him, used to do and say, and he quotes Pateshull's letters and papers, nowhere enrolled. That he knew Ralegh there can be no doubt, and from what better source could he have acquired his knowledge of Pateshull than from his confidential clerk of so many years. They are the real heroes of the treatise: as Maitland remarked, we are almost justified in saying that Bracton's is a book on the law of England as administered by two judges, Pateshull and Ralegh.

If we assume that Bracton, with no previous training in English law, first came to the courts in 1239, after Ralegh had left them, that leaves too short a time for his appointments as judge. Nor do visits and talks with Ralegh in Norwich and Winchester seem sufficient to account for his knowledge of Pateshull's judicial work and Ralegh's own. The evidence seems to point to a close connexion for some years, in a legal not an ecclesiastical atmosphere. In all probability, he began his career in 1234 as the personal clerk of his fellow Devonian, the already famous judge, who may be the same Ralegh who was presented to the church of Bratton Fleming in 1212. That would explain how he secured and used Pateshull's rolls, which Ralegh had kept, and Ralegh's own rolls, which he may have written. He was in orders and his academic career lay behind him. If we may make a guess, he was then about 26, which would make him about 60 at his death.

But we remember Bracton, and commemorate his memory today, not because he was a judge *coram rege*, for were that his only claim to fame he, like his fellow justices, Jeremy de Caxton, Henry de la Mare, and the others, would be long forgotten. Even the names of the much more eminent Martin of Pateshull and William Ralegh would be no better remembered, for it is Bracton's book that has kept the names of his masters fresh. It is on his book, of course, that his reputation rests, as he himself hoped. A statement of native English law, written when other men, in other parts of Europe, were also attempting to state the principles of their own native legal systems, Bracton's treatment is so detailed and accurate that there is nothing to match it in the whole legal literature of the middle ages. It is also a difficult book, offering its critics many occasions for the display of folly and many opportunities to make scarecrows of themselves, not always resisted. From the very first, the *De Legibus* had an unfortunate career. Left at Bracton's death with no competent guardian, it fell almost at once into well-intentioned but ignorant hands, and in the years succeeding found few to befriend it. The choice of its first modern editor was only one of the several disasters that overtook it, the chief of which was Maitland's *Bracton and Azo*, a scrupulously honest book, but one which failed, surprisingly, in view of its author, to look beneath the surface. Thus it is no wonder that Bracton fell into disrepute, and that even the unoriginal *Fleta*, the poor man's Bracton, came to be thought a superior production. Maitland, as he wrote to Bigelow in 1885, lived in fear that it would be no Englishman, but a Russian or a German, who would edit Bracton and shame the nation which had produced a six volume edition of rubbish. That was more than a possibility, for no one at home seemed anxious to undertake the long and troublesome task. Nor was his fear unfounded, for some 25 years later, no volunteer having yet appeared, a new edition was begun, not indeed by a Russian or a German, but by an American, George E. Woodbine, who brought it to completion some 35 years later. But Maitland was essentially if not technically correct, for Bracton's chief champions did indeed come from the Continent, to find a welcome in England and to spend the remainder of their lives there, fortunately for Bracton studies. I speak of Vinogradoff, Kantorowicz and Schulz, whose efforts on behalf of Bracton's text ought not to go unmentioned today.

One of the glories of Bracton's book is that it has not merely an insular but a European character, for he drew not only on his native English materials, but on the writings of Continental jurists and canonists. It thus takes its place in the mainstream of European development, the last English law book of which that can be said. Like his contemporaries abroad, Bracton was endeavouring to reduce his native materials to order, using the principles and distinctions of Roman law to rationalize the results reached in the English courts. It provided him not only with a number of concepts under which his English matter could be subsumed, and thus fashioned, for the first time, into an articulated system of principles, but with a precise technical vocabulary, infinitely more subtle than that of the plea rolls, with which to describe and analyze it. His *De Legibus*, the first heroic attempt to show the coherence and essential rationality of English law, was a book with a grand design and a noble purpose. It is not too much to say that it is one of the most remarkable contributions of a remarkable age. To Sir Henry Maine, however, Bracton had simply, 'put off on his countrymen as a compendium of pure English law a treatise of which the entire form and a third of its contents were directly borrowed from the Corpus Juris'. This extravagant and unfounded statement, which ought properly to have gone unanswered, unfortunately led Maitland to formulate an equally extravagant and unfounded reply. Far from being Roman, almost the whole of the treatise was pure English law, for Bracton owed only two small portions, some 22 folios of almost 450, to Roman law sources, and those he took not from the Corpus Juris but from the elementary manual Azo had written on the Institutes and from the Institutes themselves. The two portions were the jurisprudential introduction he thought a book on law required, and some generalities on obligations and actions, both borrowed to provide the theoretical background his practical native materials failed to give him. They were Roman flourishes added to a book complete without them. Furthermore, though his task was simply that of copying relevant portions of the books open before him, he frequently miscopied them, making it only too evident that the point of the passage had escaped him, or when abridging his source omitted essential words and phrases, without apparently realizing that their omission made nonsense of the passage abstracted. He was not guilty of sophisticated errors, those a man who was not expert might make in constructing a doctrine out of contradictory fragments in the Digest, but mistakes of a much more elementary kind. Indeed, his work showed him to be no more than an uninstructed Romanist, a beginner to whom even the elements of Roman Law were new and strange; not the experienced borrower Maine had imagined. To make his ineptitude clear it was only necesssary to place the passages in the treatise by the side of the sources from which Bracton had drawn them. But once he had finished with speculative questions and had put his foreign materials aside, the text was of an entirely different character.

He no longer stumbles and blunders but writes with the confidence and mastery one would expect of an English justice expounding the law he himself administers. In the one case we see a beginner groping his way among uncouth terms and alien ideas; in the other a master at his ease.

Maitland had simply not recognized the extent to which Bracton had used Roman law, for many passages appear throughout the treatise. He consequently misconceived Bracton's purpose in using it, for he was not simply a practical English lawyer supplying his book with an ostentatious introduction, or prefacing his discussion of actions with a few learned generalities. Nor was he engaged in copying or making an abstract of the texts open before him. To reproduce the teachings of Justinian and Azo was not his aim, but to use the ideas and language there found for English purposes. Departures from them were thus not distortions or perversions of the texts he was using, for a treatise on English law required some modification of Roman material, some remodelling of Roman doctrines, some adaptation of Roman terms to English institutions. It was not, therefore, altogether proper to place his work and Azo's side by side and draw the plausible but misleading conclusion that the differences were due to ignorance and misunderstanding. Nor when he omitted portions of Azo's text, or failed to reproduce some of his arguments, was there any need to assume that the matter was beyond his comprehension. The conflicting opinions expressed by Italian jurists were simply outside the scope of his book. Indeed, Maitland saw mistakes where there were none, misunderstandings where none existed, and approached Bracton's text with considerably less than his usual perceptiveness. We can hardly now understand how he could have asked 'What does English law know of the *hereditas iacens?*', when it clearly knew the thing if not the word and distinguished sharply between an abator and a disseisor; or how he could have written 'It is not improbable that the classical use of *obligatio* perplexes Bracton. The word is only known to English practitioners as the word which describes a bond, a written and sealed confession of a debt. How, then, can bonds arise *ex maleficio?*'

Not all scholars were willing to accept Bracton's ignorance as the true reason for the mistakes in the text, but the parallel passages adduced in proof seemed unanswerable. Furthermore, the new edition, which appeared in 1922, made it evident that the defective passages Maitland had noted appeared in all the surviving manuscripts, and must thus have been present in their common ancestor, Bracton's original. On the other hand, Bracton did not always err. There were a number of instances in which he showed himself capable of following a complex text, of abstracting it intelligently, and of handling without difficulty the technical vocabulary of Roman law. His book thus reflected a puzzling mixture of competence and appalling incompetence.

The first attempt to resolve this contradiction was made in 1941 by Hermann Kantorowicz, who proposed the thesis that the errors were not Bracton's, but had been introduced, after his death, by the editor or redactor who had prepared his manuscript for publication. It was his inaccurate copy, not Bracton's original, which .was the common ancestor of the manuscripts, and thus responsible for the errors they all contained. His thesis, in advance of its time, rested essentially on two points: new evidence, unknown to Maitland, which showed Bracton using Roman materials skilfully, drawing them from various parts of the Corpus Juris, and combining them intelligently, and an explanation of the blunders Maitland had noted as nothing more than the ordinary errors normally made by scribes in copying texts. Bracton thus appeared to be a competent Romanist, at least competent enough to be excused the elementary blunders and disastrous omissions which left his text meaningless. Kantorowicz was unable, however, to produce the real evidence his critics demanded, that is, Bracton's original, free of the faults found in the manuscripts—an impossible requirement since his original was universally acknowledged to be no longer extant. Since his proof failed and conjecture was inadmissible, Kantorowicz seemed to them to be creating an ideal text by the too-simple means of attributing any and all errors to a hypothetical redactor, for whose existence only the well-known errors in the text were alleged as proof. The redactor was thus a scapegoat, an invention, an imaginary figure introduced to take responsibility for Bracton's errors, to arrest the judgment we ought properly to pass on Bracton himself. Moreover, the far larger English law portions of the treatise showed no sign of similar blunders. If there had indeed been a redactor, he had there been able to copy accurately what he had before him.

Was it not reasonable to believe that he had done the same in the civil law portions?

Kantorowicz was already dead when his book appeared in 1941. In 1943 and the years immediately following a succession of important papers considerably enhanced Bracton's standing as a civilian. It now appeared that he had been familiar with a number of Roman and canon law treatises, quotations from which, not before identified, appeared in many portions of his book. Roman law had evidently played a larger part in his work than Maitland had thought, and far from being thought an uninstructed Romanist, he could now be regarded as a civil lawyer who had received his formal training at a university. The defects Maitland had noted, however, continued to be an embarrassment. If they could not be attributed to the redactor's inaccurate copy, they had perforce to be attributed to Bracton himself. Thus we reach the view that though trained, he was only imperfectly trained, though he had studied at a university, his studies had been interrupted, though he was learned, he was not deeply learned, though he was more than an uninstructed Romanist, he was not an accomplished one.

But there was now a presumption in Bracton's favour, and thus correspondingly more to be said for Kantorowicz's thesis. Not all the mistakes Maitland had charged against him were now thought to be his, supported though they were by the unanimous testimony of the manuscripts—some were too grievous. If they were not Bracton's, however, the manuscripts must not have derived from his original; indeed, Kantorowicz's most intemperate antagonist now adopted his view that the manuscripts descend from an inaccurate intervening copy. It had not been made by a redactor, however, but by a scribe, who sometimes failed to copy Bracton's original accurately. Since none of the manuscripts gave the correct reading, none derived from Bracton's original, which must have disappeared immediately on being copied, never to be used again.

Bracton was not an accomplished Romanist because, though he knew and used the Institutes and the secondary manuals, the textbooks, of Roman law, his acquaintance with the primary sources, the Digest and Code, the mark of an accomplished jurist, was slight. That view, first expressed by Maitland eighty years ago and often repeated, may now be put aside, for quotations from almost 500 different sections of the Digest and Code have now been identified in Bracton's book. They have no accompanying citation, but are, for the most part, accurately reproduced, and unless we assume that Bracton was quoting from memory, which was some-times the case, he clearly had those volumes by his side and knew how to use them. Further proof of his civil law training, if such is needed, appears in the language he uses, even when his subject is completely English. It is the unmistakable technical vocabulary of the schools, hardly to be acquired elsewhere.

As evidence of Bracton's competence as a Romanist increases, it becomes ever more likely that the mistakes and omissions which disfigure the Roman law portions of his text were introduced by another, the redactor. One of the strongest arguments against his existence, mentioned before, was the fact, often asserted, that the English law portions of the book were well transmitted. If the redactor had there reproduced Bracton's original accurately, had he not also done so in the Roman portions. Was not Bracton's skill as an English jurist and his lack of knowledge of Roman law the best explanation for the difference between the bad Roman and the good English law portions of his work?

When we turn to the English law portions, however, we find that they contain the same defects as the Roman, and in far greater numbers. If Bracton can write meaningless passages on obligations and actions, he can do so as well on gifts, attornment, dower, novel disseisin, outlawry, homicide by misadventure, theft, and many other purely English matters. Whatever reservations we may have as to his knowledge of Roman law, there is a strong presumption that he did not have an indifferent understanding of English law, and that what he wrote was sensible and understandable. He was, as Maitland said, writing about matters he understood, about law he administered. If the manuscripts do not bear that out, and if the defects to which they testify cannot reasonably be attributed to ignorance or inadequate training, they constitute a valid argument for the existence of a redactor. There would thus seem to be evidence enough to sustain the view that the text as we have it is not simply a copy of Bracton's original, but shows the intervention of another hand. Yet we may still meet the view that no copy intervened between Bracton's original and the extant manuscripts, and that we have it as he wrote it, mistakes and all. We are thus back once more with Maitland in 1895, perhaps a little behind him, for he had confined his remarks to the Roman law portions only. It depends, of course, on how many blemishes one has found, and how grievous they are, and how willing one is to charge them all to Bracton's account. But putting such questions aside, the number of slightly erroneous words and phrases, obviously mistakes in the copyist's eye, not in the author's mind, is so large that it seems difficult, if not impossible, to believe that we have his text as he wrote it. And simple omissions which leave a passage meaningless, are generally not made by an author in the first instance, but rather by a scribe mechanically copying another's work.

But there is no need to depend on such arguments, for there is more than sufficient evidence to show that the *De Legibus*, as we have it, is not simply a copy of the text Bracton wrote, for neither he nor anyone else could have written it as it now stands. It abounds in inconsecutive passages and impossibly long parentheses, which, interrupting as they do the sequence of thought, have clearly been inserted by another hand. Independent paragraphs, sometimes several, have been thrust into the middle of sentences, or pieced into them by connective phrases, or placed between sentences which before had followed one another. Paragraphs are often found in the wrong place, or in the wrong order; sometimes a single paragraph has been divided in half and incorporated separately, or two carelessly combined into one. Paragraphs have been inexpertly conflated. that is, they have been worked into an existing text, or combined to form a text, often with disastrous results.

These once independent paragraphs, still recognizable as such, strongly resemble the *addiciones*, also inserted at inappropriate places in the text. Originally in the margin of the archetype, they were taken into the body of the work by later copyists, working independently, and thus appear at different places in different manuscripts. Unlike them, the paragraphs I have just described stand at the same place in all the manuscripts, and clearly had that place in their common ancestor. If that was Bracton's own copy, he must have written the text as it now appears, or if the passages were later additions, inserted them where they now stand. Since neither seems possible, the archetype from which the manuscripts descend cannot be his original, but a copy of his work recast by another hand.

That would explain the mysterious disappearance of his original, which, having given birth to an inaccurate archetype, made by a redactor or a scribe, promptly disappeared, never to be copied again. If it was in another form, it had simply been superseded by the new work, arranged in a more acceptable way. It would also explain the many passages which cannot be made to yield a just sense by assuming the usual errors normally made by scribes in copying texts. To attribute errors other than such to a copyist mechanically reproducing another's work, as Kantorowicz was forced to do, makes him appear to be a scapegoat, but if the work was not merely copied but recast, errors of other kinds were open to the redactor, It is possible to put a date to the redaction, for it seems to have been made after Edward came to the throne in 1272, as a reference to cases decided in the time of King Henry indicates. It follows, as Kantorowicz had surmised, that the treatise as we have it never came under Bracton's eye.

If we take the 200 *addiciones*, separate paragraphs once in the margin, and the independent paragraphs which I have been describing, awkwardly inserted in the text, we have some thousand or more separate paragraphs, and there are many others which were not so inserted but follow one another without connexion, separated by rubrics. The form of the treatise Bracton left at his death can only be conjectured, for his original is no longer extant, but he tells us on his first page that his book was written in the form of titles and paragraphs. These words are not unambiguous, but certainly one of the arrangements they aptly describe is that of Justinian's Digest, with which Bracton was clearly familiar. That work, it need hardly be said, is composed of some 400 titles, each dealing with a particular topic. Under each title there are a varying number of paragraphs, some long, some no more than a sentence in length. All are connected with the subject announced in the title, but are independent of one another in the sense that they do not form a continuous text. Depending on the topic treated, a title may have a hundred or more paragraphs or only one or two. The Digest is also divided into books, but the divisions between them are more or less arbitrary. The real unit is the title, which is also true of the *De Legibus*, where the division into books and chapters is clearly not part of Bracton's original scheme, but superimposed on another. The cross references in the treatise are not to books and chapters, but to titles, identified only by name, *De donationibus*, *De homagiis*, *De emptione et venditione*, and so on.

Its last editor considered the *De Legibus* to be in the form of independent titles or sections: he describes a title as a broad leading topic, under which were subsumed a series of paragraphs dealing with the sub-topics into which the matter fell. The most recent book on Bracton's text describes the treatise as a series of independent sections, of separate tractates dealing with particular topics, varying in length with the topic treated. The *De Legibus*, its author tells us, is made up of a number of separate entities, imperfectly ordered—an assembly of detached sections rather than an articulated and coherent whole. Both men seem to be describing a book very like the Digest.

A series of independent titles would have been a reasonable way for Bracton to have planned his treatise, especially those portions of it in which the matter could not be organized by presenting it in the order in which it would arise in an action, or by using the words of a writ or a charter on which to hang his exposition. From the outset a number of discrete topics would have been evident; to them new topics could be added as they occurred to him, for he could hardly have anticipated them all at the beginning. Nor could he have known at the beginning exactly what was to be said under each.

The words 'titles and paragraphs' have recently been taken to mean a short book in the form of a *summa*, on the model of the Institutes. The *De Legibus* is not in that form, but that, the author of this view tells us, is because Bracton later abandoned that scheme but forgot to alter the words that described it. There is no mistaking the meaning of the words, which can mean only a *summa* in the form of the Institutes, and Bracton must therefore have written a work of that kind. He soon began, however, to compile a number of separate tracts on various topics, independent of one another and each complete in itself. When for some reason he merged his two works, there were so many independent sections that the short *summa* was transformed completely, giving us a book composed of separate entities. It would be easier to believe, however, that the words 'titles and paragraphs' describe a work in separate titles, especially since that is the form the *De Legibus* has, and since there is no Institutional framework, nor anything else to suggest that Bracton ever contemplated or wrote a *summa* in that form. If we do not first define the words to mean a *summa*, we need not then explain why we do not have a book in that form.

A series of independent titles would also explain the many repetitions, and the presence of like matter in different parts of the work, for, as in the Digest, the same material would find an appropriate place under more than one head. And since titles sometimes overlapped, an observation might well be put into one in ignorance of the fact that, in more or less the same form, it was already present in another, or indeed, that a different or opposite view had been expressed elsewhere. Separate titles also seems the explanation for the often unintelligible introductions to sections, apparently written by the editor or redactor to supply some sort of continuity by linking a title with what had gone before. Phrases such as 'Inter alia placita coronae non est omittendum', and even the very frequent 'Dictum est supra . . . nunc autem dicendum est' serve the same purpose.

When we turn from titles to paragraphs, there is much to indicate that Bracton's titles contained a number of independent paragraphs, without rubrics, which would have made his book, in its original form, more like the Digest than now appears. Some titles evidently consisted of an initial exposition, to which supplementary paragraphs had been added over the years, as new matter came to Bracton's attention or as he worked over what he had already written. The title on dower, for example, seems at first to have been short, made up of brief answers to the obvious questions 'What is dower,' 'Who can constitute it,' 'When and where,' 'In what property'. In the course of time a good many separate paragraphs, supplementing the original exposition, accumulated at the end. Some still remain there, others were pieced into the portion first written. A number are in the middle of the sentence which now begins at the top of p. 269 and ends, many paragraphs later, on 271. In the same way, the title on seignorial jurisdiction seems originally to be composed of a single paragraph, to which two others, qualifying and explaining the first, were then added. The redactor later combined them into one, the joints being still visible. The title on usucapion is similar: there an explanatory gloss and a paragraph of illustrative matter were added. And so in the title on wreck, where the original paragraph is all but submerged by the additions. The titles on attornment, treasure trove, outlawry, abjuration, indictment, the *actio furti*, also consist of a number of separate paragraphs later awkwardly worked into what seems at first glance a continuous text. There are many similar instances.

Insertions such as these give the text a patchwork quality remarked by Maitland long ago, when he said that Bracton sometimes 'turns aside from the topic he was treating to discuss another'. He had noticed one of the many places where two originally consecutive sentences had been separated by the insertion of a supplementary paragraph, placed after the word it explained. Naturally enough, Bracton's additional paragraphs often explained, qualified, illustrated or supplemented what he had first written, and fitted most easily into the text at that point, though a series of such explanatory or illustrative paragraphs, thrust into a short sentence, expanded it enormously. Its last words, now far removed from what they had once followed, were thus left dangling at the end, preceded by an inserted paragraph with which they had no apparent connexion. A scribe might then omit them as superfluous, or make them the opening words of a new sentence. On the other hand, some titles still consist of a series of inconsecutive paragraphs, indicating that the redactor could not, or did not, work them into a continuous text. Rubrics were then supplied to indicate their different contents, for though such rubrics are clearly no part of Bracton's original, they appear in all the extant manuscripts and were thus in their common ancestor.

The inserted paragraphs I have been considering are, as I said earlier, indistinguishable from the *addiciones;* indeed their incorporation reminds one of nothing so much as an earlier reception of *addiciones.* A word about them may therefore not be out of place. A reader of any printed text of the *De Legibus* except the last will find it to contain many inconsecutive passages and abrupt transitions. Bracton seems often to turn aside from the topic he is considering to discuss another, and then, after a parenthetical aside, pick up the topic and continue it. An aside of that kind may appear in the middle of a sentence, separating its beginning from its end by many lines, even by a folio page. It was hard to believe that Bracton or anyone else would or could have written a book in that way, but the printed text had been taken directly from manuscripts, which were found to support it completely. But as Vinogradoff and Maitland discovered, in the earliest manuscripts these intrusive paragraphs appeared outside the text, in the margin or at the foot of the page. They were supplements to the text, additions to it, and since most were Bractonian, it seemed reasonable to suppose that after Bracton had finished his treatise he continued to work over it, returning to his book again and again to add new matter in its margins. His additional paragraphs had simply been thrust into the body of the text by later copyists, who incorporated them as best they could. Some were placed in the middle of sentences, others between sentences which had once been consecutive. Separate passages following one another in the margin had, on occasion, been mistaken for one, or one for two, and the two parts taken into the text at different points. Thus one of the reasons for the patchwork quality of the text, for its abrupt transitions and inconsecutive matter, was revealed.

Maitland took these additions to be Bracton's afterthoughts, as they seemed to be, but they cannot be so easily described. They are not, for instance, always later in time than the text, for passages which could not have been written before 1256, when Bracton put his book aside, and which must thus have been added to it at a late stage in its composition, when it was virtually complete, do not appear as *addiciones* but as integral parts of the text, while paragraphs which might well have been written earlier do appear as such. This leads us to think that the *addiciones* are not additions in that sense, and enables us to find an answer to a difficulty which baffled an eminent legal historian. If we assume that the archetype was not Bracton's original but was made by a scribe or redactor, why did he leave the *addiciones* in the margin instead of incorporating them, as later copyists were to do. This is an illusory question, for, in truth, it was he who put them there. They are typical Bractonian paragraphs, indistinguishable in language and form from the awkwardly inserted paragraphs which are not *addiciones*, those the redactor had taken into the text, or combined to form a text, except for the fact that, for one reason or another, they were not incorporated. Though to later copyists of the archetype this marginal matter seemed of uncertain authorship, to be taken or rejected as they thought fit, and if taken labelled 'addicio' as a warning to the reader, and to later scholars Bracton's afterthoughts, they were only those paragraphs in a title, written early or late, which the redactor had not been able to work into the text. To weave the paragraphs of a Digest title into a systematic exposition is a difficult, indeed an impossible task, and doubtless the same was true of a Bractonian title. No one but Bracton could have accomplished it successfully. The redactor, fortunately, did not undertake to rewrite, only to put together the material he found. He must often have come upon paragraphs he ought to have put in earlier, some which did not fit into the text, some which contradicted the text, some which, rightly or wrongly, seemed to him to fit more appropriately in other parts of the book, where like matter was considered. For example, a paragraph in the title on the king, in the portion on persons, made the point that no one may question his acts, much less contravene them. It was followed by another, which added that no one may pass on the king's charters so as to nullify them. That was thought to fall more appropriately in the section on charters, and was placed in the margin on that section, to be taken into the text when it was next copied. Such matter, together with passages inadvertently omitted in copying, and matter intended to remain in the margin, rubrics, for example, and the citations of the cases discussed in the text, all became *addiciones* when they were brought into the text at different places by different scribes or taken by some and rejected by others.

It is evident that we have Bracton's great book only in corrupt form, but many texts have come down to us in worse. What he wrote may still be recovered, with confidence, though not by simply accepting the manuscripts as they stand. If his manuscripts show Manilius, for example, writing nonsense about Roman astrology, composing defective verses, or using faulty Latin, we do not say that his long poem could not possibly be free of mistakes. We know that he did not ordinarily write nonsense, and proceed on the assumption that if nonsense appears it is not necessarily an indication of ineptitude. Certainly the emendations of textual critics do not always meet with universal acceptance, but they are not generally condemned as unwarranted attempts to arrest the judgment of incompetence which ought properly to fall on their author.

Maitland thought emendation in the English law portions unnecessary, in the Roman, improper. 'The future editor of

Bracton,' he wrote, 'will also have to consider the policy to be pursued in the matter of the romanesque passages. Will he endeavour to restore by conjectural emendation what ought to have been Bracton's meaning if Bracton had understood Azo and the Institutes? It is not for me to dictate, but I have ventured to suggest in the Introduction to this book that Bracton's knowledge of Roman law was by no means profound.' We now have another view of Bracton's knowledge, nor is the simple acceptance of the manuscripts any longer a reasonable way to approach either part of his text. Even the most determined defender of Maitland's position has had to make some small concessions, nor are we likely to see another book that makes so few or tries so hard to discredit Maitland's critics. By dint of constant repetition we may be tempted to believe that Bracton's book is a hopeless tangle, an incoherent draft, saved from oblivion only by the orderly *Fleta*, the last great monument of English legal science in the middle ages. But it is well to listen not only to H. G. Richardson and G. O. Sayles but to Maitland, who, if he was himself no Romanist, as he said more than once, and thus underestimated Bracton's competence in that field, did know a competent English jurist when he saw one. 'If we compare Bracton with his successors,' he wrote, 'he stands a head and shoulders taller than them all.' And he appears at a critical moment in the history of English law, when we most need to know what the rules were, for in a decade or two they would be lost beyond recall. He had a splendid plan and he followed it admirably. When we set our English legal literature beside that of continental Europe, it is not of Bracton that we need be ashamed. His is, as many have said, a great book worthy of careful study; indeed, it is now being studied by able men, some of them in this room. Its text, grossly and profusely corrupted by ignorance and carelessness, can yet be recovered, not by intuition or some elaborate hocus-pocus, but by close attention, an acquaintance with Bracton's usual mode of expression, some knowledge of English law in the first half of the thirteenth century, and, above all, by resisting the easy solution to all difficulties offered by the words 'Bracton was not impeccable'. Not every author has had to wait so long, but there is every reason to believe that at long last we shall soon be reading Bracton's book as he wrote it.

NOTE TO CHAPTER 7

When this lecture was given in Exeter on the 27th September 1968, my Introduction to the new edition of Bracton's *De Legibus* had not yet appeared. Now that it has become available,[1] there seems no need to document this paper, for the reader will find there, set out in more detail than would be possible here, the evidence on which its conclusions are based and the writings of those whose views are here briefly considered.

The view that Bracton first entered the royal service in 1239 is H. G. Richardson's (*Bracton: The Problem of his Text* (1965) at p.8). The article by C. A. F. Meekings is his 'Martin Pateshull and William Raleigh', in the *Bulletin of the Institute of Historical Research*, Vol. XXVI, p. 157, 1953. His valuable series of papers on individual thirteenth-century judges, scattered as they are in many publications, ought certainly to be collected into a volume. J. L. Barton's excellent 'Bracton as a Civilian', *Tulane Law Review*, Vol. XLII, p. 555, 1968, which reaches independently many of the conclusions here expressed, unfortunately appeared after my Introduction had finally left my hands. It is a pleasure to note it now. Those who deprecate the *De Legibus* and extol 'the orderly *Fleta*' are, of course, H. G. Richardson and G. O. Sayles, most recently in *Law and Legislation from Aethelberht to Magna Carta* (Edinburgh, 1966), at p. 79. They prefer to praise the copyist and abridger of another man's work rather than the author himself. The refrain 'Bracton was not impeccable', necessary if one is resolutely opposed to recognizing a redactor and convinced that the manuscripts, except in a few instances, give us Bracton's work as he wrote it, runs through Richardson's *Bracton*, noted above. It explains why so competent a critic, when there was so much to do, has done so little for the text of the *De Legibus*.

[1] Bracton, Henry de. *Bracton de legibus et consuetudinibus Angliae. Bracton on the Laws and Customs of England;* edited by George E. Woodbine; translated, with revisions and notes, by Samuel E. Thorne. Oxford University Press, 1968.

8

THE TEXT OF BRACTON'S *DE LEGIBUS ANGLIAE*

Bracton died in 1268, and next year will therefore mark the 700th anniversary of that event. His book was first put into print in 1569, so that the year following will mark its 400th anniversary. This is therefore an appropriate time to discuss the text of his great treatise, the principal authority on medieval English law. It presents many complex problems, some already considered by the learned John Selden in the middle of the seventeenth century, and no other English law book has been the subject of more books and articles or so much acrimonious debate. Since the treatise consists of the text proper plus a number of additional passages, much attention has been devoted to the addiciones and their authorship. Since Bracton often drew upon and quoted from Roman legal sources, which are not always accurately reproduced in his book, debate has long raged on the extent of his knowledge of Roman law, and connected with it, on the allied question of whether he or another is responsible for the text. In that discussion the names of Maitland, Vinogradoff, Woodbine, Hermann Kantorowicz, Fritz Schulz, Plucknett and Richardson figure prominently, a list which could easily be enlarged to include a dozen others.

I shall begin with the addiciones. In 1885 Vinogradoff discovered that the printed *De Legibus* contained passages which, though apparently integral parts of the text and marked off in no way in the printed editions, were interpolations [1]. They interrupted the sequence of thought, separated sentences which had clearly once followed one another, and in some cases appeared in the middle of sentences, splitting them in half, as though the author had inserted a long parenthetical remark. Resort to the manuscripts quickly confirmed that they were addiciones, supplementary matter, once in the margin, which had been awkwardly taken into the text. At least two hundred passages fell into this category. In one or two manuscripts most of them appear in the margin or at the foot of the page; in the others, some of the two hundred are in the text, some omitted. The same addicio might appear in a number of manuscripts or only in one of two. Those appearing in several, or many, were often found inserted at different places in the texts of each. In some manuscripts, though in the text, they were marked by the word " addicio " in the margin, indicating that some scribes had thought them supplements, not part of the text proper [2].

These additional passages consisted mainly of explanations, illustrations and qualifications of statements made in the text. Some, however, were supplementary and introduced new matter; some flatly contradicted the text. They were often no more than a sentence or two in length, but a number were long enough to fill half a page of the printed book and some were elaborate disquisitions extending to more than a folio. Some were obviously from Bracton's pen, and it seemed evident that after he had finished his treatise he continued to work over it, returning to it again and again to supplement it by additional material placed in its margins [3]. Others seemed to be the glosses or supplementary notes of others, for the existing manuscripts were all several generations removed from Bracton's original and during the intervening period possessors of the book had apparently made additions of their own. The much-discussed addicio de cartis, for example, contradicting as it did what Bracton had said more than once in other parts of his book, was thought by Vinogradoff and Maitland to be the work of a later

---

[1] *The text of Bracton,* « Law Quarterly Rev. », I, 189.
[2] MAITLAND, *Bracton's Note Book* (Cambridge, 1887) I, 27-8; BRACTON, *De Legibus* (ed. Woodbine, 1915-42) I, 92.
[3] BRACTON, *De Legibus,* I, 364; PLUCKNETT, *Early English Legal Literature* (Cambridge, 1958) 56; RICHARDSON, *Bracton: the problem of his text* (Selden Soc., 1965) 21, 22.

annotator[4]. Similarly a passage on the rights of villeins, which limited a broader statement in the text, seemed to them an attempt by some later lawyer to reconcile Bracton's assertion with the practice of his own time[5]. The problem facing an editor was therefore to separate such later work from Bracton's own[6]. In some cases the two were easily distinguished, for example, where reference was made in an addicio to an occurrence, or to a case heard, after Bracton's death, but that was possible in only very few instances. The language in which they were phrased proved of no help, for it failed to separate Bractonian from non-Bractonian addiciones[7]. All annotators apparently used the same vocabulary, a point which should be kept in mind. The editor therefore proceeded on the assumption that Bracton's own additions, having been in the common ancestor of all the manuscripts, would appear in a larger number of its descendants than those put into later copies, which would be transmitted only to those descending from them. To be clearly Bractonian, an addicio needed to be strongly supported by the manuscripts; if found in only few, or only in the descendants of a single manuscript, it was very likely to be the work of another. Similarly, Bracton's own additions, which had appeared very early in the life of the manuscripts, would not be likely to be still in the margin, for the normal career of an addicio was to begin in the margin and move rapidly into the body of the work; matter still in the margin was likely to be of more recent date. And finally, since the work had evidently grown in size, enlarged and developed by the glosses and supplementary notes of others, it seemed clear that the shorter redaction represented an older state of the text[8]. Manuscripts containing the fewest well-attested addiciones were the closest to Bracton's original, no longer extant, that is, to the text proper as he had left it at his death plus the supplementary passages he had himself added to it.

These assumptions were reasonable enough at the time, but as more was learned of Bracton's work it became clear that they were mistaken. Many addiciones found in only one or two manuscripts

---

[4] VINOGRADOFF in « Law Quart. Rev. », I, 199; *Bracton's Note Book*, I, 30; MAITLAND, *Bracton and Azo* (Selden Society, 1895) 65; BRACTON, *De Legibus*, I, 333.
[5] VINOGRADOFF in « Law Quart. Rev. », I, 197-8; *Bracton and Azo*, 71; POLLOCK & MAITLAND, *History of English Law* (2nd ed.), I, 416.
[6] POLLOCK & MAITLAND, I, 207; BRACTON, *De Legibus*, I, 93.
[7] BRACTON, *De Legibus*, I, 362-3.
[8] VINOGRADOFF in « Law Quart. Rev. », I, 193.

were undoubtedly Bractonian: among them were cases in which he had himself been the judge, cases touching churches of which he was rector, cases in which he had been plaintiff, cases marked on the plea rolls in his hand. Nor had they, though evidently in his original manuscript, ever been taken into the texts of its descendants. The manuscripts with many additions in the margins were not the latest but the earliest. The shorter redaction was not an early state of the text but the most recent. Instead of growing by the addition of glosses and supplementary notes, it was evident that the book had begun, almost from the first, to shrink in size, as scribes omitted matter in the margins of their exemplars and later readers deleted matter that was now outdated or of little value.

Historians had always thought that the addiciones, at least those they agreed to be Bractonian, were Bracton's afterthoughts. Maitland gave them that name, for as he said, they ought not to be called glosses since they were not attempts to explain a text thought to be in need of explanation. The best name we can give them, he said, is that noted against some of them in the manuscripts in which they have been taken into the text- they are addiciones, additions to his text made by Bracton after he had completed the draft of his book [9]. Now Bracton had completed his book, addiciones and all, by the end of 1256, for very little within it can be assigned a later date, and it fails to notice, either in the text or the addiciones, the important legal changes of the years immediately following [10]. It is a very long book, comprising three folios volumes of Latin text, and it certainly was not written in less than eight or ten years, if that quickly. We would expect, therefore, that matter coming from the years close to 1256 would appear in the margins as addiciones, for by that date the text must have been substantially complete. But the addiciones often consist of early material, while that which could not have been written before the year 1256 appears as an integral part of the text, present in every manuscript and having none of the characteristics of an addicio. For example, Bracton uses Richard of Cornwall's election to the Imperial throne to illustrate a doubtful event which might or might not occur [11],

---

[9] *Bracton and Azo*, 248.

[10] GÜTERBOCK, *Bracton and his relation to the Roman law* (trans. B. Coxe, Philadelphia, 1866) 26; RICHARDSON, *Studies in Bracton*, « Traditio », VI, 94, 100-1; *Bracton*, 10.

[11] *De Legibus*, II, 144.

but the condition « if earl Richard is made king of the Germans » is not one which would have come readily to mind before 26 January 1256, when William of Holland was killed and the throne became vacant, nor would it illustrate Bracton's point after 23 January 1257 when Richard's election took place [12]. Another such portion, in which the example given it that of a juryman who testifies to earl Richard's absence from a council of magnates in London, could not have been written earlier than a fortnight after Easter 1254 [13]. Thus we have matter which had certainly been inserted at a late stage in the preparation of the manuscript, which is, in a sense, an addition, appearing as an integral part of the text. This has been explained by assuming that in 1256 Bracton had various pieces of his treatise in his hand, some written long before, some recent, which he then fitted together [14]. We must keep in mind the possibility, however, that the text as we have it was constructed by another, who took into it material of whatever date which he found collected in Bracton's original.

II

The debate on Bracton's Romanism began in earnest with the appearance of *Bracton and Azo* in 1895. Maitland, who had examined the *De Legibus* to ascertain how dependant Bracton had been on Roman law, and the extent to which he had used it in his treatise, there announced two conclusions. The first, that Bracton owed only two substantial parts of his book to Roman law, both borrowed only to provide what his native sources failed to give him: the general jurisprudential introduction he thought a law book required, which fills folios 1-10, taken in the main from Azo's *summa* of the Institutes [15], and some generalities on obligations and actions, from the same source and from the Institutes itself, which fill some fifteen later folios, roughly folios 98-115 [16]. They were in effect Roman flourishes added to a work complete without them, to a book on English law based on English sources. The intervening portion of the text, that is, folios 11-98, were of an entirely

---

[12] GÜTERBOCK, 24-8.
[13] *De Legibus*, III, 337; GÜTERBOCK, 27 n.
[14] *Bracton and Azo*, 239; RICHARDSON in « Traditio », VI, 94-5, 96, 98, 99; *Bracton*, 62-3.
[15] *Bracton and Azo*, XX, XXI.
[16] *Ibid.*, XVI, XIX, XX, XXI.

different character: « He has pushed Azo's *summa* aside; he has Glanvill's treatise and the Note Book under his eye; he is no longer stumbling and blundering as he is in those first ten folios; he is writing about matters he understood, about law that he administers » [17]. And again, when he reached folio 11 « we can almost hear the " Laus Deo " that he uttered as he turned from alien matter that he did not well understand to the practical English law of feoffments that he administered. Here at length speaks the English justice » [18]. And so of the text after folio 115, when Bracton turned again to English matters: « now at last, all speculative questions being solved, he can turn to the procedure of the justices in eyre » [19]. And again, « He has turned aside from Azo and the Institutes and, having won his way to safe English ground, is writing fluently of real law » [20].

Maitland's introduction, with its insistence that the *De Legibus* was a book of English law founded on English materials, was intended to refute an erroneous statement by Sir Henry Maine, which today hardly seems to have needed refutation. He had said that Bracton « put off on his countrymen as a compendium of pure English law a treatise of which the entire form and a third of the contents were directly borrowed from the *Corpus Juris* » [21]. Maitland was concerned to show how little Bracton had borrowed. This helps to explain his conclusion, though it seems to have been based simply on inadequate knowledge. Many passages from the Roman books appear in folios 11-98, after Maitland thought Bracton had pushed them aside, and there are a great number of others in the remainder of the treatise. Maitland was, as he said more than once, no Romanist [22], and consequently failed to recognize the quotations from the Digest and other Roman sources embedded in Bracton's text. Ignorant of the extent to which Bracton had used Roman law, as everyone was, he consequently mistook his reasons for using it. The passages he analyzed were neither a display of virtuosity nor an ostentatious introduction to a treatise on English law. There would have been no treatise had Bracton not been a jurist with the

---

[17] *Ibid.*, xv.
[18] *Ibid.*, 134.
[19] *Ibid.*, 218.
[20] *Ibid.*, 194, 199.
[21] *Ibid.*, xiv, xxvi ff.
[22] *Ibid.*, xxxiii, 250; *The letters of F. W. Maitland* (Selden Soc., 1965) 165.

principles and distinctions of Roman jurisprudence firmly in mind [23], using them throughout his work, wherever they could be used, to reduce to order the results reached in the English courts, indeed, to fashion them, for the first time, into an articulated system of principles. Roman law supplied him not only with ideas about law generally, but with a number of concepts under which his English matter could be subsumed and rationalized, and a precise technical vocabulary, infinitely more subtle than the language of the plea rolls, with which it could be described and analyzed.

Maitland's second conclusion, reluctantly reached, was that his book showed Bracton to be an uninstructed Romanist, a beginner groping his way among foreign books and alien ideas, who frequently failed to understand his sources and often drew from them what was little better than nonsense [24]. This was based largely on his assumption that Bracton was seeking simply to reproduce the matter he had before him [25]. Departures from it therefore appeared as distortions or perversions of the texts he was using [26], though Bracton was not in fact copying without reflection, and a treatise on English law for English readers required some modifications of Roman material [27], some remodelling of its doctrines [28], some accommodation of Roman terms to comparable but not exactly similar English institutions [29]. It was therefore not altogether proper to place his work and Azo's side by side and draw the plausible but misleading conclusion that the differences were due to ignorance and misunderstanding. Nor when Bracton omitted portions of Azo's text, or failed to reproduce his more elaborate arguments, was there any need to assume that the matter was beyond his comprehension [30]: the *dissensiones dominorum,* proper in the work of an Italian jurist, were simply outside the scope of his book. And finally it must be recognized that Maitland saw mistakes where there were none [31], misunderstandings where none existed [32], and seems in general to

---

[23] VINOGRADOFF, *Collected Papers* (Oxford, 1928) I 237; WOODBINE in « Yale Law Jour », XXXI, 845 n.

[24] *Bracton and Azo,* XVIII, XXI-XXIII, 250.

[25] *Ibid.,* XVIII.

[26] *Ibid.,* 39, 49, 158, 159, 163, 170, 199.

[27] *Ibid.,* 152, 160, 172, 175, 205, 218.

[28] *Ibid.,* 175.

[29] *Ibid.,* 39, 49, 77, 78, 80, 154, 163, 179, 182, 185.

[30] *Ibid.,* 39, 41, 51, 55, 77, 91, 95, 109, 111, 119, 121, 156, 158, 159, 160, 170.

[31] *Ibid.,* 63, 75, 77, 93, 103, 151, 154-5, 160, 179.

[32] *Ibid.,* 51, 63, 71, 143, 147, 159, 163, 177, 182, 185.

have approached Bracton's book with less than his usual perceptiveness [33].

But though many of Bracton's errors were not errors at all, it is true that there were a number of defects — Maitland called them blunders — in the Roman law portions of his book. They were not sophisticated blunders, those a man who was not expert might make in constructing a doctrine out of the scattered and contradictory fragments of the *Digest,* where it is easy to overlook a relevant text or misinterpret it. They were mistakes of a much more elementary kind, gross enough to be made only by a beginner, one to whom the elements, even the ordinary words of Roman law, were new and strange [34]. Bracton was apparently capable of missing a simple point [35], of omitting or misreading words which left the passage he was copying meaningless [36], of failing to recognize and understand elementary legal terms and distinctions [37]. On the other hand, he did not always err, though Maitland considered that a fact hardly worth noting, since no special merit attached to a copyist who accurately reproduced what he had before him. He was clearly able to find his way in the sources, to reproduce accurately or summarize intelligently passages from the *Digest* and *Code* and from Azo's two *Summae* [38]. Thus he presents a puzzling mixture of competence and incompetence: able to handle a complex text and abstract it with evident comprehension, but at the same time capable of appalling blunders and mistakes of the most elementary kind.

This contradiction was made more evident when Woodbine, in a notable article written in 1922, showed Bracton using Roman sources intelligently and skillfully in folios 11-98 of his treatise [39]. He seemed there to draw upon them with great competence, quoting accurately from several titles of the *Digest,* bringing widely separated portions of the *Corpus Juris* into juxtaposition, and mak-

---

[33] *Ibid.,* 78: « And what could he make of *capitis deminutio?* »; 97: « That he should blunder over this matter is not unnatural, for what does English law know of the *hereditas iacens?* »; 143: « It is not improbable that the classical use of *obligatio* perplexes him. This word is only known to English practitioners as the word which describes a bond, a written and sealed confession of debt. How, then, can bonds arise *ex maleficio?* », 179.
[34] *Ibid.,* XVIII, XXIII.
[35] *Ibid.,* 33.
[36] *Ibid.,* 71, 97, 123, 150, 190, 208.
[37] *Ibid.,* 146-7, 177, 179.
[38] *Ibid.,* 109, 138, 156, 189, 190, 197-8, 210.
[39] G. E. WOODBINE, *The Roman elements in Bracton's De Adquirendo Rerum Dominio,* « Yale Law Journal », XXXI, 827.

ing frequent use of maxims and short passages, obviously quoted from memory. The Romanist that emerged from these pages differed remarkably from the man Maitland had described, but Woodbine cautiously confined his conclusions to the portions of the treatise he had examined, without disputing or rejecting those Maitland had drawn from its other portions. He found Maitland's judgment fully supported by the manuscripts and correct, as was his own, and thus all that could be said was that Bracton was sometimes in command of his sources, sometimes not. Any final judgment with respect to his attainments as a Romanist would have to await a detailed examination of the treatise as a whole [40]. He thus did not attempt to provide an answer to the nagging question of how the competent Romanist of folios 11-98 could elsewhere have committed the elementary blunders Maitland had noted. That answer was first offered by Hermann Kantorowicz in 1941 [41]. After reexamining the folios Maitland had analyzed, he advanced the thesis that the errors there found were not due to Bracton's ignorance but to the incompetence of his scribe. The defects were the result of accident, examples of the omissions and mistakes in copying normally made by scribes in reproducing texts. The correct readings lay just below the surface, like the true text of a letter copied by a typist unacquainted with the matter and unfamiliar with the technical terms used. By one who knew the subject, the garbled words and phrases could be put right at once. This was easier in Bracton's case than in some others, since he had drawn on a wide range of Roman, canonistic, theological and English sources, which could be used to correct omissions and free the text of the blunders the copyist had introduced [42]. The obvious objection, hitherto a serious stumbling block, that the manuscripts stood solidly behind the errors and misreadings, showing that they had appeared in their common ancestor, was met by asserting that their common ancestor had not been Bracton's original but an inaccurate copy made by the incompetent redactor of Bracton's work [43].

The thesis that the archetype had not been Bracton's manuscript but an inferior copy made after his death by an editor who had often failed to understand what Bracton had written, found a

---

[40] *Ibid.*, 847.
[41] *Bractonian Problems* (Glasgow, 1941).
[42] *Ibid.*, 40, 131.
[43] *Ibid.*, 36, 38.

sympathetic audience in those historians who had doubts about the validity of Maitland's low estimate of Bracton's Roman law learning [44]. But though attractive, there was much to be said against it. In a long review [45], Woodbine pointed out that it was based on only a few passages taken from a long work. The greater part of the treatise, that is, the portions dealing with English law, were well transmitted, and thus the redactor, though competent enough in copying nine-tenths of the work seemed to have been guilty of error only in one-tenth of it, that is, only in the portions where Roman law matter was used [46]. Also, it could hardly be denied that, prima facie at least, the manuscripts had all descended from Bracton's original, and thus the mistakes they all contained were presumably his, as Maitland had thought.. That assumption could be overturned, but not by simply assuming that Bracton had been a competent civilian, and then, since the text showed mistakes no competent civilian would be likely to make, alleging them to be the work of a redactor, for whose existence the only proof offered was the defects in the text [47]. Until evidence to the contrary was produced, it was preferable to believe that the manuscripts perpetuated Bracton's original, and to explain the faults, confined as they were to the small Roman law portions of his work, on the ground that, skilled as he was as an English jurist, he had not been an accomplished Romanist [48].

The difficulty lay in the fact that any conjectural emendation of a text assumes the competence of its author. We assume, for example, that Manilius was not likely to write nonsense about Roman astro-

---

[44] HOLDSWORTH in « English Historical Review », LVII, 502; PLUCKNETT, *The relation between Roman law and English common law*, « Univ. of Toronto Law Jour. », III, 24, 38; McILWAIN, *The problem of Bracton's text*, « Harvard Law Rev. », LVII, 227-9.

[45] « Yale Law Jour. », LII, 428.

[46] *Ibid.*, 430-1: « To prove his thesis that the entire text of Bracton, as we have it, is the work of a copyst, Dr. Kantorowicz would have at least to demonstrate that what he calls nonsense is to be found throughout the *De Legibus,* and to approximately the same degree in all portions. He cannot do this because, as is well known, the characteristic defects which he finds in some of the Roman law parts do not appear in that far larger portion on English law »; Mc ILWAIN in «Harvard Law Rev. », LVII, 229: « It is inconceivable that a copyist who was unable to do any better, on this purely mechanical side, than the redactor is supposed to have done in the civil law parts of the treatise, should ever have reached, in the course of producing a single book, the high standard of copying he must necessarily have obtained to have also been responsible for the English law portion. This is a serious difficulty which Dr. Kantorowicz never fully succeeds in explaining away ».

[47] WOODBINE in « Yale Law Jour. », LII, 439.

[48] *Ibid.*, 429, 430, 438.

logy, or to compose defective verses, or write faulty Latin, and thus if the text contains such matter there is every reason to emend it, even against the authority of the manuscripts. But if we are doubtful of his knowledge, or think he may well have written bad Latin or verses which fail to scan properly, it is otherwise, for emendation does not there restore what Manilius had presumably written but corrects and improves his text. Where Kantorowicz thought Bracton could not have made the grievous errors contained in the passages copied from Azo and the Institutes, and was therefore prepared to emend them, Maitland and Woodbine thought the manuscripts clearly indicated his lack of competence as a Romanist, and consequently that it would be a falsification if an editor brought his text into agreement with the sources he had apparently been unable to understand.

Kantorowicz was already dead when his book appeared in 1941. Woodbine's review, the last words he was to write on Bracton, appeared early in 1943. Later that same year, and in the years immediately following, a series of important papers by Fritz Schulz considerably enhanced Bracton's standing as a civilian [49]. They made it evident that he had been familiar not only with the Institutes and Azo's two *Summae,* which had long been known, but with Tancred's *Ordo justiciarius* and Raymond de Penafort's *Summa de casibus,* many passages from which, not before identified as such, were incorporated in his text. Ludwig Wahrmund had long ago drawn attention to the parallel passages in Bracton's introduction and the prefatory epistle to William of Drogheda's *Summa aurea,* and Bracton was now seen to have used that work more than once [50]. Tancred's *Summa de matrimonio* was also identified as one of his sources [51]. Far from being the uninstructed Romanist Maitland had described, gallantly grappling with the technicalities of Azo's *Summa* though unprepared by any instruction in first principles [52], Bracton could now be regarded as a civil lawyer who had received

---

[49] *Critical studies on Bracton's treatise,* « Law Quart. Rev. », LIX, 172; *A new approach to Bracton,* « Seminar », II, 41; *Bracton and Raymond de Pennafort,* « Law Quart. Rev. », LXI, 286; *Bracton as a computist,* « Traditio », III, 265; *Bracton on Kingship,* « English Hist. Rev. », LX, 136; and in *L'Europa e il diritto romano: Studi in memoria di Paolo Koschaker,* I, 23.

[50] RICHARDSON, *Azo, Drogheda and Bracton,* « English Hist. Rev. », LIX, 22.

[51] RICHARDSON, *Tancred, Raymond and Bracton,* « Eng. Hist. Rev. », LIX, 376.

[52] *Bracton and Azo* XXIII; POLLOCK & MAITLAND, *History of English Law* (2nd ed.) I, 208.

his formal training at a university, presumably Oxford [53]. As evidence of his knowledge and use of Roman and canon law texts accumulated, it became progressively more likely that it had not been Bracton who was responsible for the gross blunders which in places disfigured his book, but a scribe who had misread his exemplar. Kantorowicz's hypothesis that the archetype was not Bracton's original, but an inaccurate copy made after his death, now had something more to be said for it. Nor would a text transmitted through a corrupt archetype be a novelty. Nevertheless, the defects in the Roman law portions of his text, when contrasted with the excellence of the English law portions, continued to be an embarrassment. Miscopied words in his quotations from Raymond and Tancred, now added to those miscopied from Azo and the Institutes, seemed to show that though he had used a wide variety of sources he had not always understood them. Such blunders could not simply be disregarded and the manuscript evidence dismissed, and thus it was now said that though Bracton had evidently studied at a university, his studies had been interrupted [54], though trained, he was imperfectly trained [55], though he knew the Institutes and the text-books of Azo, Tancred and Raymond, his acquaintance with the *Digest* and *Code*, the mark of an accomplished jurist, was slight [56].

This was no more than what had often been said [57], but instead of the dozen quotations from the *Digest* and *Code* hitherto credited to him, Bracton's treatise has no fewer than five hundred extracts from those books, a count that does not include those contained in the passages Bracton took from intermediate sources such as Azo. They are not identified in the text, though they may once have had their proper citations by title, lex and paragraph in the margin, but are accurately reproduced, and, unless we assume that Bracton was quoting from memory, which was often the case, he clearly had those books at his side and knew how to use them. Further proof of his civil law training, if such is needed, appears clearly in the language in which he writes, even when his subject

---

[53] RICHARDSON in « Eng. Hist. Rev. », LIX, 40; *Studies in Bracton,* « Traditio », VI, 83; *Bracton: the problem of his text* (Selden Soc., 1965) 4, 10, 53, 83.

[54] RICHARDSON in « Eng. Hist. Rev. », LIX, 47.

[55] *Ibid.*; *Bracton,* 6, 53.

[56] RICHARDSON in « Traditio », VI, 70, 83, 84; *Bracton,* 6 n. 27, 66, n. 26.

[57] VINOGRADOFF, *Collected Papers,* I, 238-40; PLUCKNETT, *Early English Legal Literature* (Cambridge, 1958) 53.

is completely English. It is the unmistakable technical vocabulary of the schools, hardly to be acquired elsewhere.

Though in the absence of Bracton's original there could be no conclusive proof, it was becoming increasingly difficult to think that Bracton, who had often used Raymond's book without difficulty, had at one place failed to understand a simple passage on dower and made nonsense of it [58], or by writing ' facti ' for ' fati ' had so garbled the simple and elegant phrase he had taken from the Digest as to leave it meaningless [59], or by miscopying the word ' tuus' as ' Titii ' showed that he did not understand the long extract from Tancred he had copied into his book [60]. On the other hand, to set everything right at one blow, by assuming the existence of a redactor, an excellent copyist when the text was accurate but incompetent whenever it contained mistakes, was felt to be too easy a solution.

The latest and most violent proponent of that view is Mr. H. G. Richardson, whose book on Bracton's text appeared in 1965. In his opinion the manuscripts derive directly from Bracton's original [61]; there is no evidence that an inaccurate copy had ever intervened between it and the existing manuscripts. The mistakes they contain are Bracton's mistakes. The only way to his text is through the manuscripts, which show that he was quite capable of misunderstanding his sources and prove him the deplorable Romanist he was [62]. Those who would set them aside are simply creating an ideal text, freed from the supposed corruptions of the manuscripts, conforming only to their own conception of what Bracton should have written [63]. The redactor is nothing but an invention for shielding Bracton from the judgment which should properly fall upon him [64]. « It is not for me or for any other textual critic », he writes, « to disprove the existence of a redactor. It is the duty of the proponents of that notion to produce their evidence, evidence which can be found only in the existing manuscripts or contemporary records » [65].

---

[58] RICHARDSON, *Bracton*, 46-8; RICHARDSON and SAYLES, *Law and Legislation* (Edinburgh, 1966) 81.

[59] *De Legibus* (ed. Woodbine) II, 384; *Fleta*, I, ca. 31 (ed. Richardson and Sayles, Selden Soc., vol. 72, p. 80).

[60] RICHARDSON, *Bracton*, 40.

[61] *Bracton*, 69.

[62] « Traditio », VI, 96, 104; *Bracton*, 86, 89.

[63] *Bracton*, 39.

[64] *Bracton*, 44, 71.

[65] *Ibid.*, 42.

The evidence Richardson demands may be found in Bracton's text. Those engaged in the acrimonious debate on Bracton's Romanism have examined over and over again the so-called Roman portions of his treatise, the passages scattered throughout his book in which he drew upon or quoted from Roman law sources. Those amount in all to about one-tenth of the *De Legibus*. No attention has been paid by any of the participants to the remaining nine-tenths, the portion dealing with English law. That is largely because Bracton was an eminent English judge, expounding the law he himself administered, and it was consequently thought to present no problems [66]. But precisely the same defects are found there as in the Roman portion, and in greater numbers, all supported by the unanimous testimony of the manuscripts. There are the same erroneous words and phrases, obviously the mistakes of an incompetent scribe rather than those likely to have been made in the first instance by the author himself, who doubtless would not have written *animo* for *omnino, nolui* for *nolim, ut* for *utrum, Quod* for *Hodie, meus* for *medius, vinxit* for *iuvit, constitutiones* for *consuetudines,* and hundreds of others. In this portion the defects do constitute an argument for the existence of an incompetent copyist, for they can hardly be attributed to Bracton's ignorance or his indifferent understanding of the subject matter. The omissions the manuscripts all exhibit also support the conclusion that the archetype was a slipshod and erroneous copy made by an inattentive scribe. It thus seems likely that Bracton was competent in both fields and betrayed by his copyist in both.

Problems nevertheless remain. If, as seems probable, the archetype was prepared after Bracton's death by a scribe who failed to understand Bracton's disorderly manuscript, as Kantorowicz and Schulz supposed, we must ask why that archetype had its margins filled with Bracton's *addiciones,* that is, why he did nothing to incorporate, as later scribes were to do, the supplementary material standing in the margin of the original [67]. The answer seems to be that the *addiciones* in the margin were put there not by Bracton but by him.

If we examine the text proper of the treatise as it now stands, we find that independent paragraphs, sometimes several, have been

---

[66] *Ibid.,* 71, 86.
[67] PLUCKNETT, *Early English Legal Literature,* 56, 70.

thrust into the middle of sentences [68], or pieced into them by connective phrases [69], or placed between sentences which before had followed one another [70]. Paragraphs are often found in the wrong place, or in the wrong order, qualifying what has not yet been stated [71]; sometimes what had been a single paragraph has been divided in half and inserted at two different points [72]. A good deal of matter has been put together incorrectly, with disastrous results, leaving many portions of the text unintelligible [73]. That Bracton, or any rational man, could have written a book in this way is impossible to believe. No one could have begun a sentence on one page, considered several connected matters in a long parenthesis of several independent paragraphs running to more than two pages, and then written the words concluding the sentence on the third [74]. What this and other examples like it show is that the text is made up of paragraphs, once separate, which have been woven, not very successfully, into a more or less continuous whole. Maitland long ago remarked that Bracton often « turned aside » or was « led away » from the topic he was treating to discuss another [75]. What he had noticed was that the text was full of inconsecutive passages and abrupt transitions, which often make it more a mosaic of independent fragments than an orderly and systematic exposition [76]. It is very much as though there had been an earlier reception of addiciones, especially since the paragraphs of which I have been speaking, part of the text proper, are indistinguishable in form, content and language from those which are clearly addiciones.

A large part of Bracton's treatise seems therefore to have once existed in the form of separate paragraphs. He seems to have begun

---

[68] References are to the pages of my edition of Bracton (Cambridge Mass., 1968): II, 32, 33, 62, 68, n. 5, 73-4, 80, 94, 97, 114, 124, 125, n. 23, 130, 134, 142, n. 3, 143, n. 11, 150, 156, n. 5, 157, n. 5, etc.

[69] II, 21, n. 10, 52, 56, n. 16, 75, n. 3, 82-82, n. 6, 104, n. 4, 105, n. 3, 110, n. 17, 135, n. 3, 143, n. 14, 148, n. 5, 155, n. 11, 158, n. 2 etc.

[70] II, 36, 54, 58, 59, n. 8, 62, n. 3, 62, 63, 66, 101, 104, n. 2-105, n. 3, 109, 116-17, 138, 140, 142, 180-81, etc.

[71] II, 32, n. 3, 40, n. 17, 48, nn. 1-5, 62, nn. 8-10, 64, nn. 9-16, 67, n. 25, 68,

[72] II, 160, n. 5, 266, n. 17, 271, n. 8, 428, n. 9.

[73] II, 20, nn. 8, 11, 12, 36, 49, nn. 14-15, 16, 18, 26, 52, 56, 67, n. 24, 76, n. 5, 70, nn. 5, 7, 15-16, 72, n. 9, 75, n. 2, 79, nn. 5-12, 83, nn. 7-8, 85, nn. 1-2, 86, n. 2, 105, n. 3, 106, n. 2, 107, n. 11, 108, n. 1-110, n. 15, 110, n. 18-111 etc. nn. 2-3, 4-7, 85, 88, n. 5 89, nn. 18-19, 90, nn. 4, 5, 101, 104, 105, 106, nn. 3-5, 107, n. 20, 110, n. 10, 113, n. 6, 117, n. 9, 119, 125, nn. 16-17, 19-20 etc.

[74] II, 269-71.

[75] *Bracton and Azo*, 151, 197, 199; RICHARDSON, *Bracton*, 51.

[76] RICHARDSON, *Bracton*, 59, 60. 62.

his work by first choosing a number of discrete topics, each to be treated in a separate section, for example, homage, relief, marriage dower and so on. To his initial exposition of these subjects, long or short, he then seems to have added, over a period of many years, supplementary paragraphs, as new matter came to his attention, by reading or in some other way, or as he realized that qualifications or modifications were necessary. Depending on the topic, such paragraphs might be many or few. Most would be relevant to the subject being considered, but among them might well be some whose connexion was not apparent — passages which, on more careful consideration, would have been placed under another head. Some might repeat what had been written elsewhere, for his topics were not mutually exclusive and the same material would fall appropriately under more than one head. Then too, in a work so arranged it was easy to put a passage in one place without realizing that, in more or less the same words, it was already present in another. This explains the many repetitions in the treatise, often remarked, and the presence of like matter in different parts of it [77]. Some paragraphs contradicted what had first been written, for it is evident that Bracton, over the years, revised his views, often without taking the trouble to make the necessary changes in all parts of his large book [78]. It also contained paragraphs, entered at different times, which did not agree with each other: the text has many examples of contrary views, with no indication of which is preferable and no attempt to resolve the contradiction. After all, his book was a draft, never prepared for publication by him, only put into its present form after his death when he could no longer revise it [79].

Bracton may have intended to incorporate his paragraphs; certainly no one else could have woven them successfully into a coherent whole, a difficult task requiring extensive re-writing and recasting. That the redactor was not prepared to undertake, contenting himself with fitting the additional matter together or taking it into the text as best he could. Paragraphs written at a late date might thus be taken in, losing in that process any indication that they had once been additions; others, written earlier, might find no proper

---

[77] *Ibid.*, 51, 69.
[78] *Bracton's Note Book*, I, 36-7.
[79] II, 75, 160, 228, n. 6, 276, n. 23, 278, 290, n. 10, 355, 358, 441.

place in the text, especially when they contradicted it or modified it substantially [80]. These the redactor seems to have been unwilling to discard. They were Bracton's work, and he preserved them by copying them somewhere on the page, in the margin or at the foot. These are the addiciones of the archetype: matter the redactor came upon too late to work into the text he was constructing and then placed in the margin opposite where it ought to fall; matter he had omitted inadvertently and put in the same place; matter found under another head and removed to the margin of the section into which it seemed to fall more appropriately; and matter which was not closely enough connected to be easily inserted, or though connected was so contradictory that no place could be found for it.

The form the treatise had at Bracton's death can only be conjectured. Kantorowicz is clear that Bracton's original disappeared once the archetype had been made [81]. Richardson also believes that it was lost soon after the two primary copies from which, in his opinion, all the exant manuscripts descend, had been written [82]. Both agree that none of the existing manuscripts descends from it. Its mysterious disappearance is left unexplained, but it would be understandable if it had been superseded by a new work, arranged in a more acceptable way. That would also explain why a copy had intervened between Bracton's original and the extant manuscripts.

The form in which its sections were first cast seems to me to resemble that of a Digest title. In that work, the first lex, from Ulpian perhaps, which often provides an initial exposition of the subject, is followed by paragraphs from other jurists, some long, some short. Depending on the topic treated, there may be a hundred or more paragraphs or only one or two. All are connected with the subject announced in the title, but it would be no easy task to work them into a continuous text and the result, despite its form, would be awkward and disjointed, clearly revealing its origin. Proof is impossible, but Bracton has given us one indication of the form in which he wrote his treatise: « I, Henry de Bracton, » he writes, « to instruct the lesser judges if no one else, have turned my mind to the ancient judgments of just men, examining diligently, not without working long into the night watches, their decisions, consilia

---

[80] II, 367.
[81] *Bractonian Problems,* 36.
[82] *Bracton,* 37.

and responsa, and have collected whatever I found therein worthy of note into a summa, putting it in the form of titles and paragraphs, without prejudice to any better system, by the aid of writing to be preserved to posterity forever [83]. The words "titles and paragraphs" are not unambiguous, but certainly one of the arrangements they aptly describe is that of the Digest.

---

[83] II, 19.

9

GILBERT DE THORNTON'S *SUMMA DE LEGIBUS*

THREE hundred years ago, in 1647, John Selden wrote as a pendant to the text of *Fleta* a dissertation concerned in part at least with the problems raised by that anonymous and enigmatic tract.[1] In this prolix essay the *Summa de Legibus* of Gilbert de Thornton, chief justice of the king's bench in the late thirteenth century, emerged momentarily from oblivion to make a much belated first public appearance. Unnoticed and apparently unremarked since the days of Edward I, the work had found its way into Selden's possession and, being contemporary with *Fleta*, had come conveniently and usefully to hand for the purposes of his introduction. He quoted from it with perhaps less than his usual care, and in addition, since his copy was, so far as he knew, unique, and attention had not previously been drawn to Thornton's book, described the manuscript in some detail, supplying an account of its structure and external appearance. From an examination of the text itself he identified the *Summa* as an abridgement of Bracton and accurately indicated its place, if not its importance, among the Edwardian treatises that had followed in the waning Bractonian tradition. With so auspicious an introduction, especially in that great age of antiquarian enthusiasm, it is curious that the *Summa* should not at once have found both an editor and a printer, but it had come briefly into view only to disappear again. Certainly nothing more was heard of it for almost three centuries nor has the copy Selden had before him ever come to light.

[1] *Fleta seu Commentarius Juris Anglicani . . . subjungitur etiam Joannis Seldeni ad Fletam Dissertatio Historica* (London, 1647). There is no reason to doubt Selden's statement (p. 453) that he had had no hand in editing the text of *Fleta*: "Neque enim editio omnino mea est," and the bibliographical evidence, particularly the blank leaf at the end of the last text signature, supports his further remark that the text, including the mistakenly added *Fet Assavoir*, had already been printed when he was asked to write what would, under ordinary circumstances, have been an introduction. Nevertheless, the tract is usually known as Selden's *Fleta*. The *Dissertatio* has been printed several times, most recently (with some omissions) by D. Ogg, *Ioannis Seldeni ad Fletam Dissertatio* (Cambridge, 1925).

Selden's description of the manuscript and the excerpts from the *Summa* quoted in his *Dissertatio* provide an obvious touchstone by which the claims of any supposed Thornton manuscript may readily be tested. The very close correspondence between the manuscript once in Selden's hands and another presently in the Harvard law library leaves little doubt that Thornton's twice-lost work has again appeared, not in Selden's copy, which in all likelihood has been irretrievably lost, but in another. The evidence for this identification has been carefully set out in full by Professor Plucknett and need not be detailed here.[2] With the *Summa* again available, however, Selden's observations upon and conjectures about it may now be verified and the first steps taken toward clarifying the relationship between it and a manuscript in the library of Lincoln's Inn with which it is curiously and intricately allied.

Almost twenty years before the discovery of the Harvard copy, Professor Woodbine, already engaged in collating manuscripts for his great edition of Bracton, called the attention of legal scholars to a text in Lincoln's Inn which, though varying in several important respects from that described by Selden, seemed very likely to be a copy of Thornton's then still lost *Summa*.[3] The evidence adduced, if not sufficient for a final judgement *per verba de recto et ut de mero iure*, nevertheless was, at the least, persuasive enough to support a possessory verdict and more than adequate to avoid the imposition of an *in misericordia pro falso clamore*.[4] Before proceeding to an examination of it, however, the *incipit* of Selden's manuscript, as quoted in the *Dissertatio*, and that of the Harvard manuscript which agrees substantially with it, must first be set out.[5]

INSERT I

SELDEN	THORNTON
Incipit summa de Legibus et Consuetudinibus Angliae a Magistro Henrico de Bryctona composita tempore Henrici filii Regis Iohannis, quam quidem Summam Dominus	Incipit summa de legibus et consuetudinibus Anglie quam composuit Magister Henricus de Britonia tempore Henrici regis filii regis Johannis, quam quidem summam Dominus

[2] "The Harvard Manuscript of Thornton's Summa," in 51 *Harvard Law Review* (1938), at pp. 1038-56.

[3] "The Summa of Gilbert de Thornton," in 25 *Law Quarterly Review* (1909), at pp. 44-52.

[4] Sir F. Pollock in 25 *Law Quarterly Review*, at p. 52; P. H. Winfield, *The Chief Sources of English Legal History* (Cambridge, Mass., 1925), at p. 265; Ogg, *Ioannis Seldeni*, at p. xxii.

[5] *Fleta* (1647), at p. 459; Harvard law library MS. 77, fol. 1. Some changes have been made in the latter; an exact transcript is printed in 51 *Harvard Law Review*, at pp. 1044-5. In the excerpts printed in this study no words have been omitted. Mixed tenses, the result of the abbreviator's attempt to accommodate Bracton's language, phrased in the present, to the past, and other scribal departures have been corrected save where that was impossible without extensive alteration.

Gilbertus de Thornton tunc Capitalis Justitiarius domini Regis in Anglia secundum statuta et leges tunc usitatas, ad utilitatem posterorum diligenti studio postmodum abbreviavit sub compendio, anno regni regis Edwardi filii regis Henrici vicesimo. Et ipse idem dominus Gilbertus tempore illo scientia, bonitate et mansuetudine floruit eleganter.	Gilbertus de Thorntona cum capitalis justiciarius Domini regis Edwardi filii regis Henrici secundum leges Anglicanas in presencia usitatas ad comodum posteriorum abbreviavit. Anno regni regis Edwardi primi vicesimo. Et ipse idem Gilbertus tempore illo scientia, bonitate et mansuetudine floruit eleganter.

Evidently both look back to the time of composition and regard the twentieth year of Edward I (1292) as remote. It is "tempore illo" and Thornton, who died in office in 1295, was "tunc capitalis justiciarius." The scribe of the Harvard manuscript speaks unhesitatingly of "Edwardi primi" and presumably is writing in the reign of Edward II sometime after 1307.[6] Thornton, it seems clear from the concluding sentence of each, was already dead when these titles were being penned and obviously neither manuscript is his original. On the contrary, both are copies of a work composed earlier and somehow known to have been written by him. Thus the author's copy is still to be sought, and we must not be unprepared to find, in a manuscript that does not bear his name, Thornton's attempt to place within one book all the text of Bracton that seemed to him valuable, plus such additions and corrections as his learning suggested.

Selden's evidence for identifying his manuscript as a copy of Thornton's *Summa* was, of course, its *incipit*. The Lincoln's Inn manuscript, on the other hand, though like the *Summa* clearly a late thirteenth century abridgement of Bracton, contains neither title nor colophon and lacks completely any formal indication of authorship.[7] The importance of this at first sight insuperable objection, however, has been considerably minimized by the additional evidence Professor Woodbine brought forward. The manuscript's connexion with Gilbert de Thornton is undeniably close.[8] If it cannot be shown to have been actually in his hands, it clearly was written before his death and had

---

[6] 51 *Harvard Law Review*, at p. 1042. The first thirteen folios of the Harvard manuscript, however, are in a hand other than that responsible for the bulk of the volume and undoubtedly were written much, perhaps a century, later.

[7] It has the phrase usual in Bracton manuscripts: "ego talis animum erexi" (Linc. Inn MS. Hale 135, fol. 5); Selden's copy read "ego talis" (*Fleta* (1647), at p. 461); The Harvard manuscript reads "ego H," but attention must be called to the caution contained in the preceding note.

[8] Insert XIV (*infra*) notes that Margaret Strike had been the concubine of Stephen Sybry during the *whole* time he had been rector of the church at West Rasen. Stephen Sybry was among the witnesses to a deed transferring land in Caburne, Lincolnshire, to Gilbert de Thornton in 1289. Another document connects Thornton with the village of West Rasen, where he likewise held land. The evidence is set out in full in 25 *Law Quarterly Review*, at pp. 48-51 and restated in 51 *Harvard Law Review*, at pp. 1046-8.

been in the possession of his immediate family. Its fly-leaves record in memoranda form, as was not uncommon during the middle ages, some notes of financial transactions, in this case those of one Alan de Thornton, who seems almost certainly to have been Gilbert's son.[9] That the manuscript had come to him immediately upon his father's death is not unlikely since the notes concerning Alan begin the year after Gilbert's death. The text itself indicated that the manuscript was not merely a copy of Bracton, but whether it was Thornton's *Summa*, or in some way related to it, could not be ascertained in the absence of an undoubted example of that work. Thus the status of the Lincoln's Inn manuscript has long been unsettled: Professor Plucknett has indicated both his doubts and the divergences that seem to foreclose the claim made for it by Professor Woodbine. It is proposed here to fix its status with as much definiteness as the circumstances permit.

The general relationship between the manuscripts can best be illustrated by placing side by side the opening portions of their discussions of the writ of entry.[10]

INSERT II

LINCOLN	THORNTON
(1) Dictum est supra de causa possessionis que per assisam et recogniciones terminatur. Nunc autem dicendum est de causa proprietatis, que terminatur per iuratam ex testimonio et probatione eorum qui probare possunt de visu proprio et auditu, ubi quis seisinam suam propriam petierit vel antecessoris sui quam de voluntate ad terminum annorum vel vite dimissum fuerit, et que ad petentem post terminum reverti debet, et ubi locum non habet assisa nove disseisine, quia tenens contra voluntatem suam et iniuste non est disseisitus, nec etiam assisa mortis antecessoris, ubi alius habet terminum indeterminatum ut ad terminum vite et huiusmodi. Aliter forte esset si res aliqua dimissa fuisset ad terminum annorum, quamvis centum qui vitam hominis excedit, quo casu verus dominus habet ius, feodum, et liberum tenementum et firmarius habet usum et fructum. Et notandum quod iste dicciones ad terminum que preteriit generales sunt et terminare possunt plures casus speciales, et in narracione facti suppleri poterit quod minus dictum est in breve. Et istud breve de ingressu locum habet versus eos qui terram receperint ad terminum vite vel annorum et versus alios quoscumque possidentes qui originem traxerint de illis qui ad terminum	(1) Dictum est supra de causa possessionis que per assisam et recogniciones terminatur. Nunc autem dicendum est de causa proprietatis, que terminatur per iuratam ex testimonio et probatione eorum qui probare possunt de visu proprio et auditu, ubi quis seisinam suam propriam petierit vel antecessoris sui quam de voluntate ad terminum annorum vel vite dimissa fuerit, et que ad petentem post terminum reverti debet, et ubi locum non habet assisa nove disseisine, quia tenens contra voluntatem suam et iniuste non est disseisitus, nec etiam assisa mortis antecessoris, ubi alius habet terminum indeterminatum ut ad terminum vite et huiusmodi. Aliter forte esset si res aliqua dimissa fuisset ad terminum annorum, quamvis centum qui vitam hominis excedit, quo casu verus dominus habet ius, feodum, et liberum tenementum et firmarius habet usum et fructum. Et notandum quod iste dicciones ad terminum que preteriit generales sunt et terminare possunt plures casus speciales, et in narracione facti suppleri poterit quod minus dictum est in breve. Et istud autem breve de ingressu locum habet versus eos qui terram receperunt ad terminum vite vel annorum et versus quoscumque possidentes qui originem traxerunt de illis qui ad terminum

[9] The land held by Gilbert in Caburne in 1289 was apparently in the possession of Alan in 1311.

[10] Linc. Inn MS. Hale 135, fol. 78^v-79^v; Harvard law library MS. 77, fol. 70; Bracton, fol. 317^v-320^v.

receperint. Et similiter locum habet versus
eos qui feoffati   sunt per
illos qui rem transferre non possunt sine
consensu aliorum, licet aliquod ius habeant
transferendi, ut si canonicus sine assensu
episcopi vel capituli, uxor sine viro,
vir sine uxore, abbas sine capitulo,
celerarius sine abbate, et huiusmodi.
Assensus enim omnium quorum interest in
translatione facienda est requirendus.

(2) Non enim excedit istud breve tempus quod
de visu et auditu proprio probari non possit,
et currit istud breve temporibus modernis de
tempore coronacionis regis Henrici tertii et
de eodem tempore currit breve assise mortis
antecessoris, consanguinitatis et avi et ante
statutum regis Edwardi secundi locum tenere
solent huiusmodi brevia a tempore ultimi
reditus regis Johannis de Hibernia in Angle-
terra. Autem de recto quod licet terminari
non de visu proprio set alieno, sicut de visu
patris et auditu qui iniunxit filio, quo casu
oportet quod negocium terminetur per duellum
vel per magnam assisam. Huiusmodi vero limita-
ciones brevium plenius continentur in statutis
regis. In breve vero de recto locum habet
essonium de malo lecti et in breve de ingressu
locum non habet, nisi breve de ingressu versum
fuerit in breve de recto, quod antiquitus fieri
solet propter longissimum ingressum qui probari
non poterit per visum proprium alicuius vel
auditum set per alienum, et ubi agi oportet de
necessitate de mero iure per magnam assisam vel
per duellum. Et quando breve de ingressu versum
fuit in breve de recto, ubi petens omisit
narrare de ingressu et intencionem suam fundavit
super mero iure, merito habuit breve de ingressu
omnia que habet breve cuius naturam sequitur,
scilicet de recto, et hoc per narracionem, Et si
contingat quod per narracionem vertatur breve
de recto in breve de ingressu, desinit breve
naturam brevis de recto, set ista solebant fieri
per voluntatem tenentis et petentis et ex
permissione curie quod modo non est approbatum,
et merito, neque usitatum.

(3) In breve vero de ingressu quod regulariter
fundatur super iure possessorio non est semper
necesse quod petens loquatur de iure mero
nisi demonstrative, quia sepe firmarius vel
ille qui tenet ad vitam tantam terram
dimittit ad terminum et post terminum elapsum
ad ipsum reverti debet terra licet ius merum
non habuit. Si quis vero petat versus alium
terram ad terminum annorum vel vite dimissam
et tenens cartam de feoffamento ostendat quod
ipsum ius tangit, videtur quod super breve de
ingressu non est ulterius procedendum sed
recurratur ad breve de recto per quod ius
merum potest terminari.

(4) Constitutis igitur partibus in iudicio,
aut habet petens instrumentum probationis
adverse terminum testificans aut non habet.
Si autem nullum habuerit instrumentum de

---

receperunt. Et similiter locum habet versus
eos qui feoffati fuerint vel sunt per
illos qui rem transferre non possunt sine
consensu aliorum, licet aliquod ius habeant
transferendi, ut si canonicus sine assensu
episcopi vel capituli, uxor sine viro
et e converso, abbas sine capitulo,
                    et huiusmodi.
Assensus enim omnium quorum interest in
translatione facienda est requirendus.

(2)

Et currit istud breve de ingressu,

                                    morte
antecessoris, consanguinitate et de avo
a coronacionis Henrici regis.

(3) In breve vero de ingressu quod regulariter
fundatur super iure possessorio non est semper
necesse quod petens loquatur de iure mero
nisi demonstrative, quia sepe firmarius vel
ille qui tenet ad vitam tantam terram
dimittit ad terminum et post terminum elapsum
ad ipsum reverti debet terra licet ius merum
non habuit. Si quis vero petat versus alium
terram ad terminum annorum vel vite dimissam
et tenens cartam de feoffamento ostendat
secundum quosdam
          non est ulterius procedendum super
breve de ingressu sed curratur ad breve de
recto per quod ius merum potest determinari.

(4) Constitutis igitur partibus in iudicio
aut habet petens instrumentum probationis
adverse terminum testificans aut non habet.
Si autem nullum habuerit instrumentum de

termino, videtur quod tenens non habet necesse ei in aliquo respondere propter defectum probationis nisi sit quis qui sustineat quod de gratia iusticiariorum possit et debeat petenti subveniri per iuratam patrie, set cum cause cognitione, vel quia forte instrumenta probationis deperdita sunt, vel quia illa ad probationem suam faciendam ad manum non habuerit, vel sine difficultate habere non poterit, quo casu alius dies solet dari. Si autem instrumentum probationis protulerit de termino dimissione et ei contradicatur, probetur veritas instrumenti per testes et per patriam et recuperet petens si terminus lapsus fuerit. Si autem petens pro se nullam habeat probationem nisi simplex dictum et simplicem vocem de termino et dimissione, et tenens ex habundanti, licet ad hoc non teneatur, proferat cartam de feoffamento, breve cassari debet et tenens in seisina sua remanebit, quod quidem fieret licet petens instrumentum de termino habuerit ut supra paulo ante, set hic diversa opinio. Item dicere poterit firmarius qui tenet quod terminus non dum preteriit eo quod post primam concessionem prorogatus fuit terminus per aliud instrumentum quod incontinenti exhibeat. Item excipere poterit tenens quod terminus excedit tempus assise mortis antecessoris et huiusmodi. Item dicere poterit tenens quod non habet ingressum per talem de quo breve loquitur, immo per alium talem, et debet breve cassari quia non convenit veritati.

termino, videtur quod tenens non habet necesse ei in aliquo respondere propter defectum probationis nisi sit quis qui dicat quod de gratia iusticiariorum possit et debeat petenti subveniri per iuratam patrie, set cum cause cognitione, vel quia forte instrumenta probationis deperdita sunt, vel quia illa ad probationem suam faciendam ad manum non habuerit, vel sine difficultate habere non poterit, quo casu alius dies solet dari. Si autem instrumentum probationis protulerit de termino   et ei contradicatur, probetur veritas   per testes et per patriam et recuperet petens si terminus lapsus fuerit. Si autem petens nullam pro se habeat probationem nisi simplex dictum,
                   et
tenens ex habundanti, licet ad hoc non teneatur, proferat cartam de feoffamento, breve cassari solet, set hodie secus.

                       Item
dicere poterit firmarius qui tenet quod terminus non dum preteriit eo quod post primam concessionem prorogatus fuit terminus per illud instrumentum quod incontinenti exhibet. Item excipere poterit tenens quod terminus excedit tempus assise mortis antecessoris et huiusmodi. Item dicere poterit tenens quod non habet ingressum per talem de quo breve loquitur, immo per alium talem, et debet breve cassari quia non convenit veritati.

It will be seen at once that both manuscripts are post-Bractonian and attempt to incorporate statutory changes that occurred after his death. The "temporibus modernis" in paragraph 2 of the Lincoln's Inn manuscript is sometime after 1275 as the reference to Westminster I, ca. 39 indicates. Comparison with Bracton's text will show that the Lincoln's Inn manuscript severely abbreviates it by omitting Bracton's illustrative cases and writs, by eliminating elementary, obsolete, and unimportant matters, and by rephrasing in shortened form elements of his long and often repetitive exposition. A rigorously practical text is the result, which compresses into the extract printed above almost six folio pages of the vulgate and eight of Professor Woodbine's edition of the *De Legibus*. Thornton's *Summa* reduces Bracton's text even more drastically, yet curiously the omissions are the same. In other words, though its compiler did not reproduce as much of Bracton as does the Lincoln's Inn manuscript, he never selected any portion of Bracton that the author of the manuscript now in Lincoln's Inn had not also selected. That two abbreviators, working independently with manuscripts of Bracton's work, would always omit precisely the same portions in compiling their respective books, indeed precisely the same sentences out of a paragraph, seems very unlikely. That they would also, each by himself, abridge sections of that text into identically phrased summaries seems equally so.   It is difficult to resist the conclusion that the author of Thornton's *Summa* was working not with a full-length Bracton but with either the Lincoln's Inn manuscript or an abridged Bracton very like it.

The dependence of the *Summa* upon the Lincoln's Inn manuscript is not limited to particular sections of the two books but obtains throughout and may be illustrated by placing side by side almost any portion of their respective expositions.   To choose one at random, it may be seen in their discussions of intrusion, in which a folio of the printed *De Legibus* is condensed into a few lines.[11]

INSERT III

LINCOLN	THORNTON

Intrusio siquidem est ubi quis cui nullum ius competit, nec scintilla iuris, possessionem vacuam ingreditur que nec corpore nec animo possidetur, sicut hereditatem iacentem antequam adita fuerit ab herede, vel saltem a capitali domino ratione custodie vel escaete, vel si post mortem alicuius per finem factum vel per modum donacionis ubi successio locum sibi vendicare non possit, ponat quis se in seisinam antequam tenementum illud perveniat ad eum ad quem pervenire deberet. Et cum quis ita se intruserit et verum dominum rei venientem non admiserit, succurritur ei per breve casui suo conveniens, set non per disseisinam, eo quod vacua fuit seisina et non per verum dominum adita. Quia possessio aliquando ius parit et pro possessione presumitur de iure, ideo infra annum eiciat verus dominus intrusorem, vel versus eum perquirat per breve, quia de longiori tempore non respondebitur ad intrusionem. Et sunt quidam qui dicunt quod agi potest de intrusione quacumque ora infra duodecim annos.	Intrusio siquidem est ubi quis cui nullum ius competit, nec scintilla iuris, possessionem vacuam ingreditur que nec corpore nec animo possidetur, sicut hereditatem iacentem antequam adita fuerit ab herede, vel saltem a capitali domino ratione custodie vel eschaete, vel si post mortem alicuius per finem factum vel per modum donacionis ubi successio locum sibi vendicare non possit, ponat quis se in seisinam antequam tenementum illud perveniat ad eum ad quem venire debeat. Et cum quis se ita intruserit et verum dominum rei
	                non admiserit, succurritur ei per breve casui suo conveniens, set non per disseisinam, eo quod vacua fuit seisina et non per verum dominum adita. Quia possessio aliquando ius parit et pro possessione presumitur de iure, ideo infra annum eiciat verus dominus intrusorem, vel versus eum perquirat per breve, quia de longiori tempore non respondebitur ad intrusionem. Et sunt quidam qui dicunt quod agi potest de intrusione
	               infra duodecim annos.

It may be seen again, to better advantage, in their treatment of the writ of cosinage.[12]

INSERT IV

LINCOLN	THORNTON
Cum assisa mortis antecessoris infra certos gradus limitetur, et locum habeat de morte certarum personarum versus certas personas et ulterius non extenditur, ne semper ad ipsum ius per breve de recto recurratur de seisina que probari possit de proprio visu et auditu	Cum assisa mortis antecessoris infra certos gradus limitetur, et ulterius non extenditur, ne semper ad ipsum ius recurratur,

[11]Linc. Inn MS. Hale 135, fol. 49[v]; Harvard law library MS. 77, fol. 47[v]; Bracton, fol. 160-61.

[12]Linc. Inn MS. Hale 135, fol. 73[v]; Harvard law library MS. 77, fol. 66[v]; Bracton, fol. 281.

alicuius, in subsidium assise mortis antecessoris provisum est breve de consanguinitate,
et similiter breve de avo ad possessionem
terminandam super hiis de quibus possessor
obiit seisitus ut de feodo, ita quod non
oportet loqui de mero iure et ad evitandum
dubium eventum duelli et magne assise per
breve de recto, que quidem brevia locum habent
de certo tempore sicut breve mortis antecessoris et non ultra. Et cum loco mortis
antecessoris accipi debeant, merito sequi
debent in magna parte naturam illius assise,
ita quod locum non habent inter coniunctas
personas ascendendo usque ad fratrem triavi
et ulterius si tempus permittat, qui omnes
sic ascendendo recte dici possunt anteces-
sores ad modum assise mortis antecessoris, et
descendendo usque ad trinepotem et ulterius
si tempus permiserit, qui omnes recte dici
possunt consanguinei tam ascendentes quam
descendentes.

(2) Nec obstare debet quod dicitur quod breve
incipiens per *precipe* non fiet in preiudicium
curie domini capitalis prout in Magna Carta
continetur, quia si cui plures competant
acciones unam illarum quam voluerit eligere
poterit et ea experiri. Competunt enim alicui
assisa nove disseisine, mortis antecessoris,
breve de ingressu, et similiter breve de recto
uno et eodem tempore et sine preiudicio curie
domini capitalis agere poterit et incipere
per qualecumque breve voluerit. Si autem frater
tria vi, proavi, vel alterius antecessoris,
ante tempus in assisa mortis antecessoris concessum obierit, vel si avus vel alius
antecessor in recta linea ante illud tempus
obierit, locum non habet aliud breve quam
breve de recto.

---

provisum est breve de consanguinitate
et breve de avo et proavo ad possessionem
terminandam de hiis de quibus antecessor
obiit seisitus ut de feodo, ita quod non
oportet loqui de mero iure,

et habent locum ista brevia infra
certo tempore sicut breve mortis antecessoris.   Et cum loco mortis
antecessoris accipi debeant, merito sequi
debent in magna parte naturam illius assise,
ita quod locum non habeant inter coniunctas
personas ascendendo usque ad fratrem triavi
et ulterius si tempus permittat, qui omnes
sic ascendendo recte dici possunt anteces-
sores ad modum assise mortis antecessoris, et
descendendo usque ad trinepotem et ulterius
si tempus permiserit, qui omnes   dici
possunt consanguinei tam ascendentes quam
descendentes.

(2)

Si autem frater
triavi   vel ulterius
ante tempus in brevibus   concessum obierit,

locum non habet aliud breve quam
breve de recto.

As is true throughout its length, the Lincoln's Inn manuscript is closer
to Bracton's text, though it by no means simply reproduces it, and
Thornton's *Summa*, in turn, seems unmistakably derived from it, or
from a manuscript similar to it, independently of and without recourse
to the full text of the *De Legibus*, its ultimate ancestor.

The size of Bracton's book led to abridgements from the very first
and, in addition, the stream of legislation after 1272 made obsolete
larger and larger portions of his work. There are, consequently, abridgements and epitomes of all sorts.[13] Nevertheless, the hypothesis of another
revised and abridged Bracton, similar to the Lincoln's Inn manuscript,
upon which Thornton's *Summa* is dependent, may be discarded in the
light of a series of identical errors, difficult to suppose to be of independent
origin, which appears in both the manuscripts presently under examination. In the two excerpts printed immediately above, the words
"alias nisi inter" or an equivalent are required to save the sentence

---

[13] *Bracton* (ed. G. E. Woodbine, New Haven, 1915), at pp. 22-4.

"locum non habent inter [alias nisi inter] coniunctas personas" from unintelligibility. A similar slip appears in a section dealing with the limitation of the writ of right in which the period established by Westminster I, ca. 39 is set out.[14]

INSERT V

LINCOLN	THORNTON
Nam ex tenera seisina et momentanea sine usu et expletiis non competit actio super proprietate set tamen assisa de seisina propria vel aliena, et qui assisam omiserit et ad breve de recto processerit omnino amittet sine recuperacione. Item fiat mencio de tempore regis certi et de tempore pacis et de aliis substancialibus quia breve de recto sicut alia brevia infra certum tempus limitatur. Nunc loquendum est de limitacione. Et sciendum quod tempore Henrici regis tertii filii regis Johannis se extendidit tempus in breve de recto usque ad tempus Henrici regis primi filii Conquestoris, et tunc oportet narrare de seisina antecessoris de tempore regis predicti et de anno et die quo predictus rex fuit vivus et mortuus vel petens cecidit ab accione [eo quod toto tempore predicti regis fuit guerra excepto ultimo anno vite sue.] Et illud tempus tenuit usque ad statutum de Merton editum tempore regis predicti Henrici tertii et tunc abbreviatum fuit tempus usque ad tempus regis Henrici secundi filii Imperatricis, et illud tempus se tenuit usque ad statutum regis Edwardi secundi, et tunc abbreviatum fuit tempus usque ad tempus regis Ricardi. Et est ratio limitacionis quia ultra tempus centum annorum non poterit quis aliquid probare, licet ius habeat in re, cum nullus aliquid probare possit ultra tempus illud ex quo loqui non poterit de visu suo proprio vel de visu patris sui qui ei iniunxit quod testis esset si inde audiret loqui. Et unde si quis loqueretur de tam longissimo tempore amittere posset propter defectum probationis. Et fit mencio de tempore certi regis quia si numquam tempore talis regis fuit antecessor in seisina, quamvis tempore alterius, amittere potest tenens per errorem ac si antecessor suus numquam inde esset in seisina.	Nam ex tenera seisina et momentanea sine usu et expletiis non competit actio super proprietate set tamen assisa de seisina propria vel aliena, et qui assisam omiserit et ad breve de recto processerit omnino amittet sine recuperacione. Item fiat mencio de tempore regis certi et de tempore pacis et de aliis substancialibus. Et quia breve de recto infra certum tempus limitatur, nunc loquendum est de limitacione. Et sciendum quod tempore Henrici regis tertii filii regis Johannis se extendebat tempus in breve de recto usque ad tempus Henrici regis primi filii Conquestoris, et tunc oportuit narrare de seisina antecessoris de tempore regis predicti et de anno et die quo predictus rex fuit vivus et mortuus vel petens cecidit ab accione, eo quod toto tempore predicti regis fuit guerra excepto ultimo anno vite sue. Et illud tempus tenuit usque ad statutum de Merton editum tempore predicti Henrici regis tertii et tunc abbreviatum fuit tempus usque ad tempus regis Henrici secundi filii Imperatricis, et illud tenuit usque ad statutum regis Edwardi secundi, et tunc abbreviatum fuit tempus usque ad tempus regis Ricardi. Et est ratio limitacionis quia ultra tempus centum annorum non poterit quis aliquid probare, licet ius habeat in re. **Et fit** mencio certi regis quia si numquam tempore talis regis fuit antecessor in seisina, quamvis tempore alterius, amittere potest tenens per errorem ac si antecessor suus numquam esset inde seisitus.

Though for small portions of text on the same subject the legal writers of the thirteenth century show little difference of style or expression, the close similarity in the phrasing of the post-Bractonian portions may be remarked. It will be noted as well that both manuscripts regard the Edward whom after ages called the Confessor as the first Edward, and that consequently for both the king usually known as

---

[14] Linc. Inn MS. Hale 135, fol. 97; Harvard law library MS. 77, fol. 82; Bracton, fol. 373. In the Linc. Inn MS. the portion in brackets is marginal.

"Edwardus filius Henrici" is "Edwardus secundus": a usage not of great frequency.[15]   Likewise, both use the word "tenens" in the last lines of the passage: an obvious error for "petens."   To this example of identical error may be added a third contained in a section that abridges one of the less practical and more oratorical portions of Bracton's book.[16]

INSERT VI

LINCOLN	THORNTON
Debet enim iudex per examinacionem de dubiis facere certum, de credulitate veritatem, de ignorancia noticiam, de ignoto notorium. Item consistit veritas iudicii in iusta sentencie prolacione et iusta et diligenti execucione, ut in Deuteronomio capitulo sexto decimo *Iuste quod iustum est persequeris ut vivas et possideas terram quam dominus Deus daturus est tibi.* Et in secundo libro Paralipomenon capitulo xix ubi dicitur *Videte quid faciatis, non enim hominis exercetis iudicium set Dei, et illud idem quod iudicaveritis in vos redundabit. Sit timor domini vobiscum, et cum diligencia cuncta facite. Non est apud Deum iniquitas nec personarum acceptio, nec cupiditas munerum* que excecant oculos sapientum et pervertunt verba iustorum, ut legitur in Ecclesiastico xx capitulo *Exennia et dona excecant oculos iudicum.* Et qui munera dixit omne genus munerum intellexit. Munus scilicet a manu quale est res que donatur. Munus a lingua quale est blandiens et adulatoria supplicatio, laudem celebre preconium, vane glorie symphonia. Item munus ab obsequio, quale est servicium impensum et acceptum, pro quo extorquetur iudicii rectitudo. Item nec minus munus a sanguine vocari meretur, ut cum pro sanguinis linea recti iudicii linea recurvatur. In hoc enim tangit sanguis sanguinem. Hec profecto genera munerum sordidorum nomine nuncupantur et lex humana gravem penam infligit iudici corupto per sordes, id est per munera sordida, ut si iudex pacificatur cum litigore ad tertiam partem litis ut Codice *ad legem milit. repet.* 1. *omnes,* ubi dicitur *omnes cognitores et iudices a pecuniis manus abstineant, neque alienum iurgium putent suam predam. Est enim privatarum quoque litium* cognitor idemque mercator statutam legibus cogetur subire iacturam. Iactura sive pena erit quod id quod recipit restituat in quadruplum ut codice C. eodem 1. ult. in fine, quia ibi tenentur in quadruplum sive tempore administracionis aliquid receperint sive post, quocumque titulo vel quocumque velamento, ut si finxerint intervenisse titulum donacionis vel vendicionis.	Debet enim iudex per examinacionem de dubiis facere certum, de credulitate veritatem, de ignorancia noticiam, de ignoto notorium. Item consistit veritas iudicii in iusta sentencie prolacione et iusta et diligenti execucione, ut dicitur in libro Paralipomenon *non enim hominis exercetis iudicium set Dei, et illud idem quod vos iudicaveritis in vos redundabit. Sit timor domini vobiscum, et cum diligencia cuncta facite. Non est apud Deum iniquitas nec personarum acceptio, nec cupiditas munerum* que excecant oculos sapientum et pervertunt verba iustorum. Et qui munera dixit omne genus munerum intellexit. Munus scilicet a manu quale est res que donatur. Munus a lingua quale est blandiens supplicatio, munus ab obsequio quale est servicium impensum et acceptum, munus a sanguine, ut cum pro sanguine linea recti iudicii recurvatur. Lex autem gravem penam infligit iudici corupto per munera sordida, ut C. *ad legem milit.* 1. *omnes,* ubi dicitur *omnes cognitores et iudices a pecuniis manus abstineant ne alienum iurgium putent suam predam.* Pena iudicum coruptorum per munera erit quod ea quod receperint restituant in quadruplum.

---

[15]Similarly *supra*, p. 117, insert II; *infra* pp. 125-8, inserts IX, X, XII and p. 132, n. 42. 25 *Law Quarterly Review*, at p. 47, n. 1; 51 *Harvard Law Review*, at p. 1051 (V).

[16]Linc. Inn MS. Hale 135, fol. 31; Harvard law library MS. 77, fol. 30^v^; Bracton, fol. 106^v^.

The Lincoln's Inn manuscript here misquotes a reference to the *Codex Justiniani:* the citation is properly (as Selden pointed out) to Cod. 9.27.3, *ad legem Iuliam repetundarum.* Though Thornton's *Summa* contains perfectly adequate citations to Roman law, it will be noticed that it reproduces the same error, and the manuscript once in Selden's hands here (just as in its use of "Edwardus secundus") is in agreement.[17]

The extant Bracton manuscripts are at least three generations removed from their original and most reflect additions and interim changes such as those contained in the manuscripts before us. To eliminate the possibility that Thornton's *Summa* derives its text from one of these, rather than from the Lincoln's Inn manuscript, two sections for which full collations are available are added to those printed above. Comparison will indicate that the excerpts differ from both the printed Bracton texts and from the variant readings that appear. The agreement between them, on the other hand, is complete in almost every particular.[18]

INSERT VII

LINCOLN	THORNTON
(1) Item secundum quosdam datur exceptio contra iusticiarium si aliqua ratione habeatur suspectus timore, odio vel amore, vel si fuerit consanguineus petentis, heres vel subditus, parens vel amicus sive affinis, familiaris vel commensalis, consiliarius vel narrator et huiusmodi. (2) Sed non video qualiter debeat recusari, quia si male iudicaverit ex certa sciencia litem suam facit et tenebitur ad restitucionem dampnorum cum de hoc per superiorem fuerit convictus. Si autem per impericiam non sic. (3) Sed quia utilius est	(1) Item datur exceptio contra iusticiarium secundum quosdam si aliqua ratione habeatur suspectus timore, odio vel amore, vel si fuerit consanguineus petentis, heres vel subditus, parens vel amicus sive affinis, familiaris vel commensalis, consiliarius vel narrator et huiusmodi. (2) Sed non video qualiter debeat recusari, quia si male iudicaverit ex certa sciencia litem suam facit et tenebitur ad restitucionem dampnorum cum de hoc per superiorem fuerit convictus. Si autem per impericiam non sic. (3) Sed quia utilius est

[17] *Fleta* (1647), at p. 463. Note that the useless expansions "peculiar to the Lincoln's Inn manuscript" which "introduce a meaningless tautology" (51 *Harvard Law Review,* at p. 1050 [II]) are in fact reproduced from Bracton. Professor Woodbine's conjecture (25 *Law Quarterly Review,* at p. 46) that Selden abbreviated the passage quoted in his *Dissertatio* seems to be groundless. "Pacificatur" is a blunder for "paciscatur" and the "lex humana" is, of course, the Roman law. Cf. H. Kantorowicz, *Bractonian Problems* (Glasgow, 1941), at p. 62 and F. Schulz, "Bracton on Kingship" in 60 *English Historical Review* (1945), p. 166.

[18] Linc. Inn MS. Hale 135, fol. 106; Harvard law library MS. 77, fol. 87^v; Bracton, fol. 411^v; 1 *Bracton* (ed. Woodbine), at p. 160. Dr. Fritz Schulz ("A New Approach to Bracton," in 2 *Seminar* (1944), at pp. 41-50) has recently commented on the first portion of this passage as it appears in Bracton and I have distributed the section into his numbered paragraphs to facilitate comparison. It will be noted that the author of the Lincoln's Inn manuscript has cleverly abbreviated the text by incorporating the *causae suspicionis,* placed elsewhere by Bracton, into the first lines of his exposition. The troublesome "inimicus tenentis" of the *De Legibus,* undoubtedly an interpolation, is omitted, and though the haphazard order remains a difficulty, it is helped by reading "heres" rather than "homo." In §2 "video" seems not out of place in the argument

in tempore occurrere quam post causam
vulneratam remedium querere, idio amoveatur
suspectus et substituatur non suspectus, cum
nichil gravius detur alicui quam si detur ei
quis ad iudicandum qui dampnificare intendit.
Et valde inutile est sub iusticiario litigare
suspecto quia sepius tristissimus sortitur
eventus.

(4) In fine notandum de iurisdiccione maiorum
et minorum et unde dominus papa in spiritualibus super omnes ordinariam habet iurisdiccionem, item rex in regno ordinarium habet
iurisdiccionem in temporalibus, et pares non
habent neque superiores. Et sunt qui sub eis
ordinariam habent   in multis,
set non ita meram sicut papa vel rex. Item
sicut a papa poterit quis habere iurisdiccionem delegatam in spiritualibus, ita
poterit quis a rege in temporalibus, sicut
iusticiarii maiores et minores et illi qui
sunt quasi iusticiarii videlicet quibus rex
concesserit iurisdiccionem et libertates
pertinentes ad coronam. Et debet unusquisque
iudex estimare an sua sit iurisdiccio vel
non, ne falcem ponat in messam alienam.

in tempore occurrere quam post causam
vulneratam remedium querere, ideo amoveatur
suspectus et substituatur non suspectus, cum
nichil gravius detur alicui quam si detur ei
quis ad iudicandum qui dampnificare intendit.
Et valde inutile est sub iudice litigare
suspecto quia sepius sortitur tristissimus
eventus.

(4) In fine notandum de iurisdiccione maiorum
et minorum et unde dominus papa in spiritualibus super omnes iurisdiccionem habet ordinariam, item rex in regno ordinariam habet
iurisdiccionem in temporalibus, et pares non
habent neque superiores. Et sunt qui sub eis
habent iurisdiccionem ordinariam in multis,
set non ita meram sicut papa vel rex. Item
sicut a papa poterit quis habere iurisdiccionem delegatam in spiritualibus, ita
poterit quis a rege in temporalibus, sicut
iusticiarii maiores et minores et illi qui
sunt quasi iusticiarii videlicet quibus rex
concessit iurisdiccionem et libertatem
pertinentem ad coronam. Et debet unusquisque
iudex estimare an sua sit iurisdiccio vel
non, ne falcem ponat in messam alienam.

The second example for which a full collation of the Bracton manuscripts
has been made is the famous *addicio de cartis*.[19]

Insert VIII

LINCOLN

Factum regis nec cartam potest quis iudicare
ita quod irritetur. Set dicere poterit quis
quod rex iusticiam fecerit, et bene, et si hoc,
quod fecerit voluntatem suam et ita imponere
ei quod iniuriam emendet, ne incidant rex et
iusticiarii in iudicium viventis Dei propter
iniuriam. Rex enim habet superiorem, Deum et
legem per quos regnat. Item curiam suam.
comites et barones, quia comites dicuntur
quasi socii regis, et qui socium habet, habet
magistrum. Et ideo si rex fuerit sine freno
erit sine lege, debent ei frenum apponere
nisi ipsimet fuerint cum rege sine freno; et
tunc clamabunt subditi et dicent *Domine Jesu,
in chamo et freno maxillas eorum constringe.*

THORNTON

Factum regis nec cartam potest quis iudicare
ita quod irritetur. Set dicere poterit quis ,
quod rex iusticiam fecerit, et bene, et si hoc,
quod fecerit voluntatem suam et ita imponere
     quod iniuriam emendet, ne incidant rex et
iusticiarii in iudicium viventis Dei propter
iniuriam. Rex enim habet superiorem, Deum et
legem per quos regnat. Item curiam suam
comites et barones, quia comites dicuntur
     socii regis, et qui socium habet, magistrum
habet. Et ideo si rex fuerit sine freno
erit sine lege, debent ei frenum apponere
nisi ipsimet fuerint cum rege sine freno; et
tunc clamabunt subditi et dicent *Domine Jesu,
in chamo et freno maxillas eorum constringe.*

"secundum quosdam—Sed non video—Sed quia utilius" and "qualiter" is better than
Dr. Schulz's emended "quod" found in but one Bracton manuscript. In §3 "ad iudicandum," of course, is correct. The words "tristissimus eventus" which appear in
both manuscripts, but are found in no other, may be taken as a further illustration of
the close connexion subsisting between them.

[19]Linc. Inn. MS. Hale 135, fol. 19; Harvard law library MS. 77, fol. 20; Bracton,
fol. 34; 1 *Bracton* (ed. Woodbine), at p. 124. This passage has also been remarked
upon by Dr. Schulz ("Bracton on Kingship," pp. 136-76, esp. pp. 173-5). Thornton's
text and that from which it is derived seem superior to that usually found in Bracton.
Difficulties remain: the singular "superiorem" is troublesome and, though Bracton
elsewhere correlates "lex" and "frenum" (fol. 107^v), "et" or "id est" seem preferable

Ad quos dominus: *Vocabo super eos gentem robustam, longinquam et ignotam, cuius linguam ignorabunt, que destruet eos et evellet radices eorum de terra, et a talibus iudicabuntur, quia subditos noluerunt iuste iudicare.* Et ligatis eorum pedibus et manibus mittentur in caminum ignis et tenebras exteriores.

Ad quos dominus: *Vocabo super eos gentem robustam, longinquam et ignotam, cuius linguam ignorabunt, que destruet eos et evellet radices eorum de terra, et a talibus iudicabuntur, quia subditos noluerunt iuste iudicare.* Et ligatis eorum manibus et pedibus mittentur in chaminum ignis et tenebras exteriores.

Immediately back of Thornton's *Summa* as Selden knew it and as we have it in the Harvard manuscript, then, lies not Bracton's full text but the abridged, revised, and supplemented text of the Lincoln's Inn manuscript.

Attention may now be turned temporarily from the text to the internal arrangement of the manuscripts. Selden's copy, with which the Harvard copy is in agreement, was divided into eight books, each containing a varying number of chapters. Professor Plucknett has provided a list of these which is reproduced in the appendix. The Lincoln's Inn manuscript, on the other hand, is divided into *centenae* and at first glance bears no resemblance either to Selden's or to the Harvard manuscript. This obvious divergence presents a stumbling block the importance of which must not be overestimated, for in fact the texts follow each other exactly, even in the curiously composite eighth book.[20] As the excerpts already printed indicate, the *Summa* is an abridgement abridged, and consequently its compiler often was able to compress two or more *centenae* of his model into one chapter. For example, Centena II, 7-10 were combined into Liber II, xi and Centena II, 73-75 into Liber IV, xiii. Less often he divided a long section of his exemplar into two or more smaller portions: for example, Centena II, 32 became Liber III, vii-ix, just as Centena III, 52 became Liber VIII, ix-xiii. There are 253 *centenae* in the model and 202 chapters in the *Summa:* in by far the greatest number of cases, as the comparative table in the appendix shows, chapters of the *Summa* correlate completely with the *centenae* of the Lincoln's Inn manuscript.[21]

The division of the *Summa* into books presents a more difficult problem. Though a blank is left in the Lincoln's Inn manuscript on folio 35[v], and it is at that point that Liber III of the *Summa* begins,

---

to "erit." Nevertheless, both manuscripts agree in that apparently unique reading. A third fully collated passage may be found in 1 *Bracton* at p. 136, where the variant readings of the Lincoln's Inn manuscript (there designated LE) are noticed. It will be observed that the differences between it and the other manuscripts collated are many.

[20]25 *Law Quarterly Review*, at pp. 47-8.

[21]The correspondences in the table printed *infra* are plain. A further word may be added in connexion with two books of the *Summa* in which the correlations are not immediately obvious: in Liber IV: Centena II, 89-96 (first half) = Liber IV, xxiv; II, 96 (second half) = IV, xxv; II, 97 = IV, xxvi. In Liber VII: Centena III, 37 (first

this seems no more than coincidental.[22] Especially since at the points
that correspond to the beginnings of the other books of the *Summa*
there are no such indications. It is likely that the division into eight
books, common among Bracton manuscripts, was taken from one of
them: perhaps from the copy Thornton must have used to fill a gap in
his exemplar. The *Summa* ends its Liber V, vi (*De nocumentis iniuriosis*)
on folio 61 with the same non-Bractonian words that conclude the
Lincoln's Inn manuscript's Centena III, 2 (*De nocumentis iniuriosis*) on
its folio 68ᵛ. The *Summa* then proceeds to V, vii (*De presentacione
ecclesiarum*) on folio 61, to V, viii (*De brevi quare impedit*) on folio 62ᵛ,
and to V, ix (*De assisa mortis antecessoris*) on folio 62ᵛ. In the Lincoln's
Inn manuscript, however, the last words of *De nocumentis iniuriosis* are
followed immediately by a centena beginning "Premortuorum ut videri"
(folio 68ᵛ) and numbered III, 3. Thus it omits a section which appears
in the *Summa* at V, vii-viii and in the first part of ix, for the words
"premortuorum ut videri" occur in the middle of V, ix and are the first
words of the first line on folio 63ᵛ. From that point the manuscripts
resume their correspondence. The gap in the Lincoln's Inn manuscript
does not result from loss, but is found in several manuscripts of Bracton,
all of which doubtless stem from a faulty common ancestor.[23] A manuscript other than the Lincoln's Inn manuscript therefore was used by
Thornton for this portion of his work (folios 61-63). It was perhaps
from this that he adopted the more usual and useful division into chapters and books, though this must, of course, remain conjectural. That
he used it to supply portions of text other than the two and a half
chapters omitted in the Lincoln's Inn manuscript seems very unlikely.

II

Both the Lincoln's Inn manuscript and Thornton's *Summa* were
written after 1275, the date of the first Statute of Westminster. Indeed
both were written after 1285, the date of Westminster II, as the reference
to *De donis* in the following excerpt indicates.[24]

---

part) = VII, i; III, 37 (last part) and 38 (first part) = VII, ii; III, 38 (second part)
= VII, iii; III, 38 (last part) and 39 (first part) = VII, iv; III, 39 (second part) = VII,
v; III, 39 (third part) = VII, vi; III, 39 (last part) = VII, vii; III, 40 (first part) =
VII, viii; III, 40 (second part) = VII, ix; III, 40 (third part) = VII, x; III, 40 (last
part) = VII, xi; III, 41 (first part) = VII, xii; III, 41 (last part) = VII, xiii; III,
42 = VII, xiv.

[22]25 *Law Quarterly Review*, at p. 45.

[23]1 *Bracton* (ed. Woodbine), at pp. 64 ff. The manuscripts are his ML, LT, CF,
and LA.

[24]Linc. Inn MS. Hale 135, fol. 13; Harvard law library MS. 77, fol. 14; Bracton,
fol. 17ᵛ-18. The author of the Lincoln's Inn manuscript refers to 1284 (12 Edw. I) as
past (*infra* p. 20, insert XIV *in fine*): certainly he is writing after 1285.

INSERT IX

LINCOLN

Et ubi quis feoffatus fuerit de aliqua terra tenenda sibi et heredibus suis de corpore suo procreandis, quam cito tales habuerit, secundum legem ante statutum regis Edwardi secundi editum, potuit alium feoffare, quia cum habuit liberum tenementum, ius, et feodum, licet artatum maxime in illo casu ubi huius-modi heredes speciales antecessorem super-vixerint, quo casu reversio ad donatorem nulla, nec ipsi heredes petere possunt per succes-sionem contra factum eorum quibus succedunt, nec dici potest quod huiusmodi heredes cuncti cum antecessoribus sint feoffati. Et videtur aliquibus quod huiusmodi feoffati in prima donacione, antequam huiusmodi heredes certos habuerint, habent feodum licet talliatum, adeo bene sicut simpliciter feoffatus. Habet feodum generale quod quidem feodum coartatum sufficit ad dotis peticionem, quod esse non solet secundum quosdam.

THORNTON

ut ubi quis feoffatus fuerit de aliqua terra tenenda sibi et heredibus suis de corpore suo legittime procreatis, quam cito tales habuerit, secundum legem ante statutum regis Edwardi secundi editum, potuit alium feoffare, quia cum habuit liberum tenementum, ius, et feodum, licet artatum maxime in illo casu ubi huius-modi heredes speciales antecessorem super-vixerint, quo casu ad donatorem reversio nulla, nec ipsi heredes petere possunt per succes-sionem contra factum eorum quibus succedunt, nec dici potest quod huiusmodi heredes cuncti cum antecessoribus sint feoffati. Et videtur aliquibus quod huiusmodi feoffati in prima donacione, antequam huiusmodi heredes certos habuerint, habent feodum licet talliatum, adeo bene sicut simpliciter feoffatus. Habet feodum generale quod quidem feodum coartatum sufficit ad dotis peticionem secundum quosdam.

Another reference to the legislation of 1285, this time to Westminster II, ca. 25, is contained in a section that follows closely after that quoted above.[25]

INSERT X

LINCOLN

Item fieri possunt donaciones sub modo et adiecta condicione ut si dicat quis, *do tali tantam terram ut det michi tantum* vel *ut inveniat michi necessaria* et ubi distinguendum est si mencio fiat in contractu quod accipiens et heredes sui invenire debent tradenti neces-saria de tenemento dato, ita quod tenementum oneratum sit et persona obligata, vel quod mencio non fiat de quo tenemento invenire debeant necessaria, ita quod accipiens et heredes sui obligantur tantum. Et similiter considerandum est si tradens condicionem talem apposuit in principio contractus quod nisi accipiens invenerit necessaria quod tradens licite possit ingredi terram illam et retinere, quod si fecerit et questio inde habeatur, in principio inquirendum erit utrum accipiens invenerit tradenti necessaria sua sufficienter et secundum hoc iudicare. Et si necessaria inventa non fuerint et tradens se ponere non possit in seisinam, competit ei actio versus accipientem quod teneat quod convenit; vel si tenementum translatum fuerjt ad alium, competit ei repeticio per breve de

THORNTON

Item fieri possunt donaciones sub modo et adiecta condicione ut si dicat quis, *do tali tantam terram ut det michi tantum* vel *ut inveniat michi necessaria* et ubi distinguendum est si mencio fiat in contractu quod accipiens et heredes sui invenire debent tradenti neces-saria de tenemento dato, ita quod tenementum oneratum sit et persona obligata, vel quod mencio non fiat de quo tenemento invenire debeant necessaria, ita quod accipiens et heredes sui obligantur tantum. Et similiter considerandum est si tradens condicionem talem apposuit in principio contractus quod nisi accipiens invenerit necessaria quod tradens licite possit ingredi terram illam et retinere, quod si fecerit et questio inde habeatur, in principio inquirendum erit utrum accipiens invenerit tradenti necessaria sua sufficienter et secundum hoc iudicare. Et si necessaria inventa non fuerint et tradens se ponere non possit in seisinam, competit ei actio versus accipientem quod teneat quod convenit; vel si tenementum translatum fuerit ad alium, competit ei repeticio per breve de

---

[25]Linc. Inn MS. Hale 135, fol. 13-13^v; Harvard law library MS. **77**, fol. 14-14^v; Bracton, fol. 18-18^v; *infra* p. 132, n. 42.

ingressu in quod non habet ingressum nisi per talem cui ipsement dimisit ad terminum que preteriit et cetera. Si tenementum concessum fuit quamdiu necessaria fuerint inventa, vel forte competit ei actio per breve nove disseisine de libero tenemento per statutum Edwardi regis secundi ad similitudinem corodii et bene teneret assisa si necessaria ita essent certa, sicut est corodium.

      Item aliquando datur terra alicui habenda et tenenda sibi et heredibus suis, vel cui dare vel assignare in vita vel in morte legare voluerit, set modernis temporibus non valet huiusmodi legatum nisi fuerit de tenemento in burgis vel villis privilegatis et ubi tenementa pro catallis accipiuntur et in aliquibus antiquis dominicis domini regis per consuetudinem manerii. Est   quedam donacio omnino sub modo de quatuor generibus contractuum innominatorum, scilicet, *do ut des*, ut si dicatur, *do tibi digestum ut des michi codicem;* ut si dicam *do ut facias*, id est, *do tibi codicem ut facias michi scribi digestum;* vel si dicam *facio ut des*, id est, *facio tibi domum ut des michi centum;* vel si dicam *facio ut facias*, id est, *facio tibi aulam ut tu facias michi cameram.* Iste donaciones consistunt sub modo et obligant contrahentes.

ingressu in quod non habet ingressum nisi per talem cui ipsemet dimisit ad terminum que preteriit et cetera. Si tenementum concessum fuit quamdiu necessaria fuerint inventa, vel forte competit ei actio per breve nove disseisine de libero tenemento ad similitudinem corodii per statutum regis Edwardi secundi et bene teneret assisa si necessaria ita essent certa, sicut corodium. Et revera tradens potest distringere tenementum datum quousque accipiens invenerit sibi necessaria. Et si accipiens dimiserit terram iacere incultam, ita quod tradens non potest invenire districcionem racionabilem et sufficientem per biennium, competit ei repeticio et hoc per statutum regis Edwardi secundi. Item aliquando datur terra alicui habenda et tenenda sibi et heredibus suis, vel cui dare vel assignare in vita vel in morte legare voluerit, set modernis temporibus non valet huiusmodi legatum nisi fuerit de tenemento in burgis vel villis privilegatis et ubi tenementa pro catallis accipiuntur et in aliquibus dominicis domini regis per consuetudinem manerii. Est autem quedam donacio omnino sub modo de quatuor generibus contractuus innominatorum, scilicet, *do ut des, facio ut facias, facio ut des, des ut facio* (!).

               Iste donaciones consistunt sub modo et obligant contrahentes.

In neither manuscript is there any indication that these references are interpolations or written in a hand other than the normal one in which the body of the manuscript appears.

It will be noticed that the *Summa* adds a reference to Gloucester ca. 4, which does not appear in its exemplar. Though Thornton for the most part was content to abridge the Lincoln's Inn manuscript, and the excerpts so far printed illustrate the skill in compression that enabled him to reduce its size to a considerable extent, on not a few occasions he supplemented it. These additional portions are always small and generally are concerned with the new remedies or penalties provided by the legislation of Edward I. Another supplemented portion is that concerned with the fourcher of essoins by parceners and tenants in common prohibited by Westminster I, ca. 43.[26]

---

[26]Linc. Inn MS. Hale 135, fol. 86^v; Harvard law library MS. 77, fol. 75^v; Bracton, fol. 341^v. It will be noted that the Lincoln's Inn manuscript reproduces Bracton's exposition, labelling it "ante statutum," yet does not supply the new rule.

INSERT XI

LINCOLN

Sunt enim plures tenentes aliquando in uno brevi qui tenent in communi simul et pro indiviso, vel separatim et pro diviso, partita inter coheredes hereditate. Et unde ante statutum　　　　　tenentes pro indiviso quilibet eorum unicum habuit essonium uno die vel diversis et unusquisque se essoniaverit et plura non habebunt antequam simul compareant, licet illi qui primo fuerint essoniati sepius compareant, quia semper diem habebunt quousque omnia simul comparuerint.

Dicitur autem quod ad omnem aparicionem non sequitur essonium quia sic fieret dilaciones immortales. Si autem unus moriatur ex pluribus tenentibus in communi sine herede de se, cadit breve.

THORNTON

Sunt enim plures tenentes aliquando in uno brevi qui tenent in communi simul et pro indiviso, vel separatim　　pro diviso, partita inter coheredes hereditate. Et unde ante statutum regis Edwardi tenentes pro indiviso quilibet eorum habuit unicum essonium uno die vel diversis donec unusquisque se essoniaverit et plura non habebunt antequam simul compareant, licet illi qui primo fuerint essoniati sepius compareant, quia semper diem habuerint quousque simul comparuerint. Hodie per statutum Westmonasterii editum anno regni regis Edwardi tertio provisum est quod huiusmodi tenentes non habeant nisi unicum essonium et ad unum diem et non plura essonia.

Si autem unus moriatur ex pluribus tenentibus in communi sine herede de se, cadit breve.

A passage dealing with the punishment for rape provided by Westminster II, ca. 34, provides a third expanded portion.[27]

INSERT XII

LINCOLN

(1) Et est raptus virginis quoddam crimen quod femina imponit alicui de quo se dicit se esse violenter oppressam contra pacem regis, pro convicto sequitur

amisio membrorum, ut sit membrum pro membro, quia virgo cum corrumpitur membrum amittit... (2) Olim quidem corruptores virginitatis et castitatis et eorum fautores, cum nec tales ab homicidii crimine vacui essent, maxime cum virginitas et castitas restitui non possunt, ultimo puniebantur supplicio. Modernis temporibus aliter observatur, quia pro corruptione virginis amittuntur membra cum amissione bonorum et exheredacione. Et de aliis oppressoribus sequitur gravis pena corporalis, set tamen sine amissione membrorum . . . (3) Item dicere poterit quod adhuc virgo est, et quo casu secundum quosdam probetur veritas per aspectum corporis per quatuor legales feminas

THORNTON

(1) Et est raptus virginis quoddam crimen quod femina imponit alicui de quo se dicit violenter esse oppressam contra pacem regis, et convictus per statuta regis Edwardi secundi amittet vitam et membra. Ante illud statutum editum convictus amittit membra tantum ut sit membrum pro membro, quia virgo cum corrumpitur membrum amittit . . . (2) Corruptores virginitatis et castitatis et eorum fautores, cum　　tales ab homicidii crimine vacui non sunt,　　cum virginitas et castitas restitui non possunt, ultimo puniuntur supplicio

cum amissione bonorum et exheredacione.

(3) Item dicere poterit quod adhuc virgo est, et quo casu secundum quosdam probetur veritas per aspectum corporis per iiii legales feminas

---

[27]Linc. Inn MS. Hale 135, fol. 46; Harvard law library MS. 77, fol. 44-44^v; Bracton, fol. 147. Kantorowicz, (*Bractonian Problems*, at pp. 46-7) has commented on §2 and there is a replication by Professor G. E. Woodbine in 52 *Yale Law Journal* (1943), at p. 435. The excerpts printed above permit us to supply an important part of the sentence, omitted both in the Bracton manuscripts and in the printed editions of the *De Legibus*, and to eliminate the interpolated "suspendebantur," clearly erroneous, which appears in its stead in the 1569 and later editions. The words "ultimo puniebantur supplicio" may be Thornton's, but they are also eminently Bractonian: fol.

iuratas. Que quidem si dicant ipsam esse
virginem, recedat appellatus quietus et femina
custodiatur. Si autem invenerint ipsam
corruptam, inquiratur veritas per patriam,
postquam appellatus se super patriam posuerit,
utrum inde   culpabilis nec ne, sed talis
processus non est in usu temporibus modernis . . .
(4) Set modo in huiusmodi fiunt dispensationes,
scilicet quod ipsi
                    raptores accipiunt
violatas in matrimonium non de lege set de
permissione sancte ecclesie et regis.

iuratas. Que quidem si dicant ipsam esse
virginem, recedat appellatus quietus et femina
custodiatur. Si autem invenerint ipsam esse
corruptam, inquiratur veritas per patriam,
postquam appellatus se super patriam posuerit,
utrum inde sit culpabilis nec ne, sed talis
processus non est in usu temporibus modernis . . .
(4) Hodie autem per statuta regis convictus
habebit ultimum supplicium tantum. Et ante
illa statuta edita raptores accipiebant
violatas in matrimonium non de lege set de
permissione   ecclesie et regis. (5) Qui
monialem a domo sua abduxerit, licet monialis
consenserit, puniatur per prisonam trium
annorum et satisfaciat domui a qua abducta
fuerit competenti et nichilominus redimatur
ad voluntatem regis, et hoc per statutum regis
Edwardi secundi.

A fourth and last illustration is afforded by Westminster II, ca. 3, which allowed a wife to be received after the default of her husband.[28]

INSERT XIII

LINCOLN	THORNTON
Si vero vir et uxor implacitentur quilibet eorum suum habebit essonium simul vel vicissim, tum propter unitatem iuris tum propter unitatem sanguinis, cum sint una caro vir et uxor. Et unde si unus illorum defaltam fecerit, ambo produnt per defaltam	Si vero vir et uxor implacitentur quilibet eorum suum habebit essonium simul vel vicissim tum propter unitatem iuris tum propter unitatem sanguinis, cum sint una caro vir et uxor. Et tunc si unus eorum defaltam fecerit, ambo produnt per defaltam, nisi mulier venerit ante iudicium et petat quod defalta quam vir suus fecit non sit ei preiudicabilis, et tunc admittetur uxor ad defendendum ius suum, et hoc per statutum regis Edwardi filii regis Henrici.
quod non est inter particepes, ius commune participum recipit divisionem. Ius viri et uxoris de re uxoria nullam, et maxime cum res sit propria uxoris et non viri, cum ad virum non pertineat nisi tantum custodia racione uxoris. Si sutem plures . . .	Si autem plures . . .

That the Lincoln's Inn manuscript deals with rape as of the period directly prior to 1285 and reproduces Bracton unaffected by Westminster II, ca. 3, does not mean that it was written before that date. Its author included some of the changes necessitated by that statute and did away with much of Bracton's text that had been made obsolete by it. We must not expect to find every alteration noted and every out-dated

119[v]: "ultimum inducit supplicium"; fol. 155: "ultimum inducunt supplicium." It is curious that both learned guesses at the proper position of the verb missing in the sentence should turn out to be incorrect. The excerpts set out the punishment for rape both directly before and directly after 1285: it will not escape notice that §5 of the *Summa* contains the concluding words, quoted without alteration, of Westminster II, ca. 34.

[28]Linc. Inn MS. Hale 135, fol. 86[v]; Harvard law library MS. 77, fol. 75[v]; Bracton, fol. 341[v]-342.

portion expunged.[29] A parallel may be found in *Britton*, which includes a reference to *Quia emptores.* (1290) but fails in places to make the changes required by *De donis*, enacted five years before.[30] The Lincoln's Inn manuscript, written after 1285, clearly antedates the *Summa* which, in turn, apparently was not written after 1290, since a careful examination of the portions that might be expected to reflect *Quia emptores* reveals no revision. Both then fall into the period 1285-90: the *Summa* presumably into the latter half of it. The twentieth year of Edward I (1291-2), the date given in the *incipit*, nevertheless may well be correct. Certainly the *Summa* reflects the changes after Westminster II with more fidelity than does the Lincoln's Inn manuscript and it gives every indication of having been written when the effects and implications of that statute had become clearer than they could possibly have been in 1285.[31]

III

As Professor Plucknett has pointed out, in the light of its provenance it seems reasonable to suppose that the Lincoln's Inn manuscript may once have belonged to Gilbert de Thornton, but that, of course, does not mean that he was therefore the author of it.[32] With this we may agree, but if he is not, Thornton's contribution to legal science, apart from his judgements, must be limited to an admittedly skilful abridgement of that manuscript plus some occasional, supplementary observations concerning the effect of the legislation of Edward I. There is, however, evidence that Thornton was the author of the Lincoln's Inn manuscript, much of which already has been brought forward by Professor Woodbine.[33] The most impressive part of that evidence is the inclusion, as the only illustrative case in the manuscript, of the case of Margareta Strike, in all probability drawn from Thornton's own knowledge of the persons involved.[34]

---

[29]For example, neither manuscript includes the limitation put upon grantors by the statute *De viris religiosis* (1279).

[30]1 *Britton* (ed. F. M. Nichols, Oxford, 1865), at pp. xviii, 236-8.

[31]The Lincoln's Inn manuscript (fol. 114) does not allow a second husband curtesy in land entailed to the wife "[secundum quosdam] quia statim post mortem uxoris succedere debent heredes in feoffamento comprehensi, vel si defecerint, ad feoffatorem spectat reversio." This right was especially withdrawn from the second husband by *De donis* and the *Summa* (fol. 92^v), though it makes no mention of the statute, omits the words in brackets. See 1 *Britton* (ed. Nichols), at p. 289, n.

[32]51 *Harvard Law Review*, at p. 1046.

[33]25 *Law Quarterly Review*, at pp. 48 *et seq.*

[34]Linc. Inn MS. Hale 135, fol. 109; Harvard law library MS. 77, fol. 89-89^v; not in Bracton. The remarks in 51 *Harvard Law Review*, at p. 1047, n. 28, based on Professor Woodbine's text, may be disregarded. The abridged form of the passage in the *Summa*

INSERT XIV

LINCOLN	THORNTON
Quia sunt quidam presbyteri et rectores ecclesiarum qui antequam constituti fuerunt in sacris ordinibus affidaverunt mulieres et illas cognoverunt et que sunt eorum uxores secundum Deum et quod quidem factum probari possit. Et postea huiusmodi presbyteri et rectores, salutis sue immemores, de facto sacros ordines recipiunt et se gerunt quasi rectores et presbyteri, et uxores suas proprias tenent ut concubinas et redempciones pro eis faciunt ordinariis, et per omnia et per omnes reputantur pro rectoribus et presbyteris qui in veritate sunt uxorati. Et post mortem huiusmodi presbyterorum et rectorum filii eorum bastardi se ponunt forte in hereditatem, ita quod non possunt eici, et cum recti heredes per breve hereditatem suam petierint in curia regis allegantes se esse filios et heredes mortuorum et cum contra eos fuerit replicatum quod sunt bastardi eo quod matres eorum numquam in facie ecclesie fuerunt disponsate, set quod tente fuerunt per omnes et per omnia publice pro concubinis rectorum et presbyterorum et pro talibus cognite in ecclesia publice et non pro uxoribus. Quo casu fieri poterit inquisicio in curia regis utrum tales cognite extiterint pro concubinis sive pro uxoribus, sine preiudicio ecclesie, et unusquisque vero iudicari debet secundum quod a vulgo reputatur et non secundum quod est in veritate.	Quia sunt quidam presbyteri et rectores ecclesiarum qui antequam constituti sunt in sacris ordinibus affidaverunt mulieres et illas cognoverunt et que sunt eorum uxores apud Deum et quod quidem factum probari possit. Et postea huiusmodi presbyteri et rectores, salutis sue immemores, de facto sacros ordines suscipiunt et se gerunt quasi rectores et presbyteri, et uxores suas tenent ut concubinas et redempciones faciunt pro eis ordinariis, et per omnia et per omnes reputantur rectores et presbyteri qui in veritate sunt uxorati. Et post mortem huiusmodi rectorum et presbyterorum filii eorum bastardi se ponunt in hereditatem, ita quod non possunt eici, et cum recti heredes per breve hereditatem suam petierint in curia regis versus eos dicantes se esse heredes mortuorum et replicatum fuerit contra eos quod sunt bastardi eo quod matres eorum numquam in facie ecclesie fuerunt disponsate, set quod tente fuerunt per omnia et per omnes pro concubinis rectorum et presbyterorum et pro talibus cognite in ecclesia et non pro uxoribus, quo casu poterit fieri inquisicio in curia regis utrum tales cognite extiterint pro concubinis sive pro uxoribus, sine preiudicio ecclesie, et unusquisque iudicari debet quod a vulgo reputatur et non secundum quod est in veritate.
Per huiusmodi vero cogniciones ad curiam christianitatis missas sepe contingit quod bastardi heredantur et concubine rectorum et presbyterorum dotes suas recuperant, ut contingit de Margareta Strike, concubina Stephani Sybri toto tempore suo rectoris ecclesie de West Rasen in comitatu Lincolnie, que dotem suam recuperavit in banco circa annum decimum vel duodecimum regis Edwardi filii regis Henrici. In casu vero ubi inquisicio bastardie mittitur ad curiam christianitatis procedendum est . . .	Per huiusmodi cogniciones ad curiam christianitatis missas sepe contingit quod bastardi heredantur et concubine presbyterorum et rectorum dotes suas recuperant, ut contingit de Margareta Styrke, concubina Stephani Sybry toto tempore suo rectoris ecclesie de Westrasen in comitatu Lincolnie, que dotem suam recuperavit in Banco circa annum decimum regis Edwardi filii regis Henrici. In casu vero ubi inquisicio bastardie mittitur ad curiam christianitatis procedendum est . . .

The close connexion between Stephen Sybry, the village of West Rasen, and Thornton has been traced by Professor Woodbine and retold by Professor Plucknett: thus it need not be again detailed. The *Summa*, in which it is likewise the sole illustrative case, merely copies the Lincoln's Inn manuscript, abridging it in the usual way and with the same characteristic method exhibited in the excerpts printed above. In the light of this, the case supports only the position that Thornton was the author

is characteristic: the relation between it and its exemplar is the same here as throughout both works. No more precise knowledge as to the date of the case on the part of the author of the Harvard manuscript can be implied: cf. 51 *Harvard Law Review*, at p. 1047.

of the Lincoln's Inn manuscript, and it must remain a possibility, perfectly consonant with the known facts, that it alone is Thornton's work and the *Summa* an abridgement after Thornton's death by another hand. But assuming, as perhaps we must, that Thornton wrote the *Summa* that bears his name, that he wrote the Lincoln's Inn manuscript as well is the only reasonable explanation for the fact that both include the case of Margareta Strike. Some small, additional scraps of proof may be adduced to show that the same hand lies back of both. The notation "hic opino," marginal in the Lincoln's Inn manuscript, is made part of the text of the *Summa*.[35] Further, the author of the Lincoln's Inn manuscript, as we have seen, used the form "Edwardus secundus" for Edward I, and this usage was several times carried over into the *Summa*. This is not in itself of value, but in several instances Thornton, writing a supplementary passage not taken from his exemplar, used the same form.[36]

The question that cannot now be answered with definiteness is why Thornton, possessing an adequate *summa* of Bracton, into the margins of which could have been entered whatever notes of altered procedure and *novel ley* he wished, nevertheless proceeded to prepare another. It is not impossible, as Selden believed, that this was done at the direction of Edward I:[37] "Sed abunde satis mihi ex ante allatis probatur regnante *Edwardo* primo opus ipsum conscriptum fuisse; adeoque ex eis esse quae jussu *Edwardi* primi, sicut & *Thorntonii* Summa, & compendium *Britton* dictum, a jurisconsultis celebrioribus componebantur." And finally, it may not be merely coincidence that Chief Justice Prisot's remark in 1457, as emended by Selden, refers to the year 1287.[38]

IV

In this last section a rapid survey will be attempted of Selden's observations on Thornton's *Summa*. Apparently Selden gave only a few days to the writing of his *Dissertatio* and only part of that time, naturally, could have been devoted to a reading of the *Summa*. In

---

[35]Linc. Inn MS. Hale 135, fol. 97[v]; Harvard law library MS. 77, fol. 82.

[36]*Supra*, p.126,insert X and p.128,insert XII §5.

[37]*Fleta* (1647), at p. 547; also p. 461: "Jussu autem Regio aut non sine Regis auspiciis conscriptum esse hoc *Thorntonii* opus par est ut credamus ex eo quod in annalibus juris nostri habetur *Edwardum* illum tum leges moresque Regni in scripta redigere universos voluisse, tum libros aliquot alios, praeter notissimum illum *Britton* dictum, opera Jurisprudentiorum qui sub ei floruere eam in rem confecisse idque veluti suos." T. F. T. Plucknett, *A Concise History of the Common Law* (London, 1940), at p. 236.

[38]Y. B. 35 Hen. VI, 42, pl. 2, *in fine*.

addition, the copy in his possession was incomplete and badly mutilated. That his judgements about it, therefore, were not always correct is understandable.   Clearly, if his manuscript was similar, as it must have been, to the copy of the *Summa* presently in the Harvard law library, his statement that Thornton's purpose was to elucidate the law of Bracton's time rather than his own, evidences at best only a slight acquaintance with the work.[39]   His remark was, of course, the result of not realizing that Thornton was already dead when the *incipit* was written,[40] and thus that the word "tunc" in the sentence "juxta statuta et leges *tunc* usitatas" referred to Thornton's time, then already in the past, rather than to Bracton's.   Likewise, a more careful examination would have led Selden to repudiate his belief that Thornton made no reference to the statutes passed in the period between Bracton's death and the date of the compilation of the *Summa*.[41]   And similarly, it would have saved him from regarding a passage using "Edwardus secundus" (usual for Edward I throughout) as a gloss, inserted later.[42]   There are other slips,[43] but nevertheless Selden was correct in his general appraisal of the work: "Neque Epitomator solum sed etiam subinde est interpres egregius *Thorntonius* et expositor."[44]   The *Summa* reflects the changes that had taken place after Bracton's death, revealing them in its additions and not less clearly, in its omissions.   Behind its "secundum quosdams" the doubts and difficulties that faced a commentator on

---

[39]*Fleta* (1647), at pp. 459-60, 545.   This necessitates some alterations in the final paragraph of 51 *Harvard Law Review*, at p. 1049.

[40]He twice regarded it as contemporary: *Fleta* (1647), at p. 457 and again at p. 545: "in *Gilberti Thorntonii* quem ante diximus exemplari veteri de autoris tempore."   The Harvard manuscript's "in presencia" avoids the ambiguous "tunc."

[41]*Fleta* (1647), at p. 460.

[42]*Ibid.*, at p. 545; 25 *Law Quarterly Review*, at p. 47, n. 1; 51 *Harvard Law Review*, at p. 1051(V).   Selden quoted a passage from his manuscript which I have compared with the Lincoln's Inn (fol. 11^v) and the Harvard (fol. 10^v) manuscripts, "dari [*L.* Item dari] non poterunt aliter [*L.* alicui; *H.* alicui; *Br.* alicui] singulari personae res quae sunt spiritualibus annexae, sicut corrodia ex abbathiis [*L.* abbatiis; *H.* abbatibus; *Br.* abbatiis] & domibus religiosis percipienda & huiusmodi in quibus nullus vendicare sibi [*L.* sibi vendicare; *H.* sibi vendicare; *Br.* vindicare sibi] poterit liberum tenementum, *temporis retroactis*.   *Sed hodie per statutum regis Edwardi secundi fiat breve de corrodio subtracto sicut de libero tenemento*."   The italicized portion is omitted in both the Lincoln's Inn and Harvard manuscripts and, of course, in Bracton.   Thus, if Selden's quotation is correct, his copy differed from them in this respect, though both include a reference to the statute (Westminster I, ca. 25) a folio or two further on: *supra* p. 16, insert X.   Selden goes on to say, "Ita citatur statutum *Edwardi* secundi, cum manifestum sit *Thorntonium*, ut ostensum superius est, sub *Edwardo* primo scripsisse, etiam & obiisse.   Adeoque ita scribere ille nequibat."

[43]"Ego talis animum *induxi*" is obviously an error: *Fleta* (1647), at p. 461.

[44]*Ibid.*, at p. 463.

English law in the late thirteenth century are clearly visible : nor are these concerned merely with *minutiae*. Like *Fleta* and *Britton*, the *Summa* seems to be the work of a man more familiar with and at home in the years immediately prior to *De donis*.[45] Thornton was created chief justice in 1290, but fourteen years before he already was engaged in judicial work and doubtless the period prior to 1285 saw his apprenticeship and by far the greater part of his professional life.[46] Thus his *Summa* bridges to some extent the narrow gap between the *De Legibus* and the earliest Year Books, presenting with detailed clarity the alterations of the first great statute of Westminster and the effects of its provisions upon the rules of the common law. Of necessity, this study has been concerned with *termini a quo* and *ad quem*, correspondences and differences, but enough has been printed to indicate that the *Summa* is neither uninteresting nor unimportant. A presentation and discussion of its treatment of some post-Bractonian difficulties it is hoped will follow shortly.

---

[45]For example, note his fumbling efforts to accommodate the new concept of an estate in fee tail to the existing corpus of real property law: Harvard law library MS. 77, fol. 13-14; *cf.* Plucknett, *A Concise History of the Common Law*, at pp. 492-8.

[46]G. O. Sayles, 1 *Select Cases in the Court of King's Bench* (London, Selden Society, 1936), at p. lvii.

APPENDIX

Lincoln		Thornton			Lincoln		Thornton	
Centena I		*Liber I*			*Centena I*		*Liber I*	
1	5a	[i]	1a		78	20b	xlii	21b
2	5a	[ii]	1a		79	21a	xliii	22a
7	5a	[iii]	1b		80	21b	xliv	22b
13	6a	[iv]	2a		81	22a	xlv	23a
14	6a	[v]	2b		82	22b	xlvi	23a
16	6a	[vi]	2b		83	22b	xlvii	23a
17	6a	[vii]	2b		84	23b	xlviii	24a
18	6b	[viii]	3a		85	23b	—[1]	24b
19	6b	[ix]	3a		86	23b	xlix	24b
20	6b	[x]	3a		87	24a	l	24b
21	6b	[xi]	3a		88	24a	li	25a
25	7a	[xii]	4a		89	24a	lii	25a
34	8a	[xiii]	5a		90	24b	liii	25a
36	8a	[xiv]	5b		91	25a	liv	26a
38	9a	[xv]	6b		92	25a	lv	26a
39	9a	[xvi]	7a		93	26a	[lvi]	26b
40	9b	[xvii]	7b		94	26b	lvii	27a
44	10b	[xviii]	9a		95	26b	lviii	27a
45	11a	[xix]	9b					
—	12a	[xx]	12b				*Liber II*	
49	12b	[xxi]	13b					
50	13a	xxii	14a		96	26b	i	27a
51	13b	xxiii	14b		97	27a	ii	27b
54	14a	xxiv	15a		98	27a	iii	27b
55	14b	xxv	15b		100	28a	iv	28a
57	15a	xxvi	16a					
58	15b	xxvii	16b				*Centena II*	
60	16b	xxviii	17a					
61	16b	xxix	17b		1	28b	v	28b
62	16b	xxx	17b		2	29a	vi	29a
63	17a	xxxi	18a		3	29a	vii	29a
64	17a	xxxii	18a		4	30a	viii	29b
65	17b	xxxiii	18b		5	30b	ix	29b
66	17b	xxxiv	18b		6	30b	x	30a
67	18a	xxxv	19a		7	31a	xi	30b
68	18a	xxxvi	19a		11	31b	xii	30b
69	18b	xxxvii	19a		12	31b	xiii	31a
70	18b	xxxviii	19b		13	32a	xiv	31a
72	19a	xxxix	20a		14	32b	xv	31a
73	19a	xl	20a		15	32b	xvi	31b
76	20a	xli	21a		17	34a	xvii	32a

[1]See 51 *Harvard Law Review*, at p. 1053.

Lincoln		Thornton	
Centena II		*Liber II*	
20	34b	xviii	32b
21	35b	xix	33b
		Liber III	
22	36a	i	34a
23	36b	ii	34b
24	36b	iii	34b
26	37a	iv	35a
27	37b	v	35b
31	38b	vi	36a
32	39a	vii	36b
—	39a	viii	37a
—	40a	ix	37b
33	40b	x	38a
34	40b	xi	38a
[fol. missing]²		xii	39a
37	41b	xiii	39b
39	41b	xiv	40a
—	41b	xv	40a
40	42a	xvi	40b
42	43a	xvii	41b
43	43b	xviii	42a
44	44b	xix	42b
45	45a	xx	43a
—	45b	xxi	43a
46	45b	xxii	43b
47	45b	xxiii	43b
48	45b	xxiv	43b
49	46a	xxv	43b
—	46a	xxvi	44a
52	47a	xxvii	44b
53	47a	xxviii	44b
54	47a	xxix	44b
58	47Aa³	xxx	45b
59	47Ab	xxi	46a
		Liber IV	
61	48a	i	46b
62	49b	ii	47b
63	50a	iii	47b

Lincoln		Thornton	
Centena II		*Liber IV*	
64	50a	iv	47b
65	50b	v	48a
66	51b	vi	48b
67	51b	vii	48b
68	52a	viii	49a
69	52b	ix	49a
70	53a	x	49b
71	53b	xi	50a
72	54a	xii	50a
73	54a	xiii	50b
76	55a	xiv	51a
—	55a	xv	51a
77	56a	xvi	52a
—	56b	xvii	52a
79	56b	xviii	52a
80	57a	xix	52b
81	57b	xx	53a
82	58b	xxi	53b
83	60a	xxii	54b
84	60b	xxiii	55a
89	62b	xxiv	56b
—	64a	xxv	58a
97	64b	xxvi	58a
		Liber V	
98	65a	i	58b
—	66a	ii	59a
100	66b	iii	59b
Centena III			
1	67a	iv	59b
—	67a	v	60a
2	67b	vi	60b
[omitted]⁴		vii	61b
[omitted]		viii	62b
3 [in part]	68b	ix	62b
—	70b	ix (bis)	64b
7	71a	x	65a
9	72a	xi	65b
10	73a	xii	66a

²An unnumbered folio missing: it undoubtedly contained centenae 35 and 36.

³The early hand that numbered the folios omitted this, numbering the one preceding it 47 and that following it 48.

⁴*Supra* p. 124.

Lincoln		Thornton	
Centena III		*Liber V*	
11	73b	xiii	66b
12	74b	xiv	67a
13	74b	xv	67b
—	75b	xvi	67b
14	78b	xvii	70a
15	79b	xviii	70a
		Liber VI	
16	81a	i	71a
17	81b	ii	71b
—	82a	iii	72a
—	82a	iv	72a
18	84a	v	73b
—	84b	vi	74a
20	85a	vii	74b
21	86a	viii	75a
22	87b	ix	76a
23	88b	x	76b
25	91a	xi	78a
26	91b	xii	78b
27	92a	xiii	79a
28	93b	xiv	79b
29	94a	xv	80a
30	94a	xvi	80a
33	97a	xvii	81b
34	97b	xviii	82a
—	98b	xix	82b
—	99b	xx	83a
36	100b	xxi	84a
		Liber VII[5]	
37	103a	i	85b

Lincoln		Thornton	
Centena III		*Liber VII*	
—	103b	ii	85b
—	104a	iii	86a
—	105a	iv	86b
—	106a	v	87a
—	106b	vi	87b
—	107a	vii	88b
40	109a	viii	89b
—	109b	ix	89b
—	110b	x	90b
—	111a	xi	90b
41	112a	xii	91a
—	113b	xiii	92a
42	114a	xiv	92b
43	116a	xv	93b
		Liber VIII	
[44][6]	117a	i	94b
45	118b	ii	95a
46	120b	iii	96b
47	121b	iv	97a
48	123b	v	98b
49	125a	vi	99a
50	127a	vii	100b
—	127b	viii	100b
52	130a	ix	101b
—	130a	x	102a
—	131a	xi	102b
—	131a	xii	102b
—	132a	xiii	103a
53	133a	xiv	103b
Explicit	133b	*Explicit*	104a

[5] *Supra* p. 123, n. 21.
[6] Though the centena begins here its number is omitted.

10

THE EARLY HISTORY OF THE

INNS OF COURT

WITH SPECIAL REFERENCE TO GRAY'S INN

It is a rash American who proposes to speak to English lawyers about the Inns of Court and a particularly foolhardy lecturer who undertakes to lecture to the members of Gray's Inn on the history of their Inn. Like a dog walking on its hind legs, the wonder is not that it is done well but that it is done at all! My only excuse is a long interest in the history of legal education and the possession of a theory which — so far as I know — is held by no one except myself. As an enthusiast, I am naturally anxious to put it before you. My unorthodox approach requires me first to say a word about the law terms. As you know, the law terms were necessarily situated in those portions of the year which remained available for legal business after certain days and seasons had, for one reason or another, been excluded. The excluded days, all holy days, were numerous, and a cluster of such days falling close together naturally made the whole period between them impracticable. Two large excluded seasons were those periods during which the Church had forbidden the taking of certain types of oaths — that is, from Advent to the octave of Epiphany and from Septuagesima to the quindene of Easter. The third excluded season was due to the harvest. Lawyers, jurors and litigants alike could not leave their estates during harvest nor during the period of stock-taking, rent collecting and accounting which centred on Michaelmas. In practice this ruled out August and September. The combined effect of all this was to leave four main periods during which fairly continuous legal business was possible and these periods became the law terms. Michaelmas necessarily began some few days after that feast and had to end before Advent. The Advent break was prolonged by the cluster of great feasts following Christmas — St. Stephen, St. John the Evangelist, Holy Innocents, St. Thomas the Martyr, Circumcision and Epiphany — and lasted until the octave of Epiphany, which coincides with St. Hilary. Hilary is thus the earliest practicable date for resuming business, but the duration of that term depended upon the divagations of Septuagesima, which might fall as early as January 19th or as late as February 22nd.

Septuagesima to the quindene of Easter is excluded, as I have said, and thus Easter term starts on the quindene. In the long stretch from the quindene of Easter to harvest-tide there is clearly a break caused by the cluster of great feasts of Ascension, Whit-suntide, Trinity and Corpus Christi. The octave of Trinity is therefore the first normally practicable date for resuming business, which had to be suspended again at harvest time. Thus, for four short periods of several weeks at a time, legal business was possible and lawyers came together in Westminster. It was, of course, possible, for them to live with friends or relatives, or to find rooms somewhere in London — perhaps in the dingy and often dangerous travellers' inns which lined the Strand. That is doubtless what that litigants themselves, their witnesses, the jurors and others who came to London but infrequently, did. Lawyers, however, and others directly connected with the courts in some official capacity, came without fail four times a year. For them it was easier, cheaper, safer and more comfortable to band them-selves together and rent a house, hire a cook and a manciple, engage a servant or two, and be assured of a bed and a reasonable dinner. This was their equivalent of the town house, maintained only by the wealthy, ecclesiastics or lay.

An establishment of this kind was thus a combined club, business office and hotel. It was not a school. By 1350, perhaps earlier, there must have been a number of them. It is without doubt true that the Temple was already a residence of lawyers at that time, as Chaucer's famous lines indicate. In 1355 a judge, his words preserved for us in the Year Books, refers to the apprentices in their hostels. Clifford's Inn is mentioned in a record of 1404 and it doubtless was older than that.

When the surviving records of Lincoln's Inn open in 1422, they picture a settled society with a number of distinguished and elderly members, some of whom must have been connected with it for forty years. Nor is there any reason to doubt the truth of Christopher Yelverton's remark in 1589, in his speech entitled "The Farewell that I made at Gray's Inn at my departure from thence, when I was chosen serjeant, Michaelmas 1589," in the course of which he acknowledged himself "deeply and infinitely indebted unto this house for the singular and exceeding favours that I and mine ancestors have received in it, for 200 years ago at the least have some of them lived here," which fixes the date as 1389.

It is true that the fourteenth century does not provide us with many such references, but that is because it is only in the fifteenth that the Inns became something more than lodging houses and that men began to take pride in belonging to them. In the fourteenth century, before they were differentiated into Inns of Court and Inns of Chancery, or greater Inns and lesser, they were neither large nor elaborate nor wealthy.

Not built for the purpose but rented, they consisted of a small hall for dining, which became a common room after dinner — the only room having a fire and reasonable lighting ; a kitchen, a garden, a small number of sparsely furnished, unheated chambers, each holding two or three men, and forty men in term time would be a large number for such an Inn ; many were much smaller ; Chaucer's manciple provided for thirty in some converted buildings of the recently abandoned Temple; the members themselves generally came from the same part of the country — county ties were stronger in those days — they all knew one another, or if not, each other's families. Not infrequently they were related, either directly or by marriage. Sons, following their fathers in the profession, were introduced and continued the connection. But with the end of term all dispersed to their homes. The house or Inn must then have taken on the appearance of a resort hotel in the off-season.

Finance particularly and the running of a quiet, orderly and respectable house were the main concerns of such an establishment. Thus it is the Treasurer who occupied the place of importance, not a President, Provost, Principal, Warden or Master. The officers of Lincoln's Inn in the early fifteenth century are the Treasurer, the Pensioner, the Marshal, the Collector of fuel money, the auditors of accounts, and the collector of chapel money. The yearly meetings of these men were wholly concerned with the payments or pensions of the members, with auditing accounts, with debts due to the Inn and sums owed by it to bakers, brewers and servants. The records of Lincoln's Inn show this still to be true in the first years of the fifteenth century.

The official Inn business for one entire year is the following: " Memorandum, that it is ordained that no person of the fellowship be behind of his dues due within the fellowship, that is, of his commons, that it pass not 14 days ; and if he be behind over 14 days that he be estranged from the fellowship till he pay. And also that no man be behind of his pension over a year upon the same penalty. And that the steward warn all those that be behind of their commons over 14 days out of commons, unless he will undertake for them that be so behind himself.' '

Each year the members were bound anew as sureties for one another, as guarantors, that they and their fellows would discharge their dues and other payments to the society. The number of times a member might, while being in London, be away from commons without paying was strictly regulated, for even such small losses were important. The task of making both ends meet was not an easy one — to pay the yearly upkeep of a house that was full for only a few short months, to find the wages of servants who were at work only for a small portion of the year for which they were paid, without making the dues and charges prohibitive, was a troublesome business, the subject of many an anxious meeting. One of the reasons why the more progressive of the Inns turned themselves into schools for young men may have been economic: the need of every club for additional members and more dues and the desire to utilise more fully a building, empty for long periods, whose yearly rent had nevertheless to be paid. But that this was not the sole reason is quite evident.

Let me turn briefly to the universities. The medieval universities came into being throughout western Europe in the twelfth and thirteenth centuries; in England, Oxford had already established its reputation as a seat of learning by 1250. In the universities, students attended to hear the lectures given by eminent teachers in the schools. These began early in the morning and finished at dusk, in the cold, comfortless, straw-strewn rooms. The course was a very long one and many did not stay it. Those who did were faced at the end by a series of searching oral examinations, which stressed not only memory but facility in exposition and disputation. The hardships and difficulties, both physical and mental, the cost of maintaining oneself over a long period, did not, however, put students off. They scraped and borrowed to come to the university, where many lived half-starved in bitter poverty. For those who pursued the long course to its end and obtained their degrees, the way was open to advancement, particularly in the Church, but also in the royal administration, the courts, the diplomatic service, in the schools themselves as teachers, or in the entourage of some great lord or churchman.

The life, as I have said, was severe, but the students liked it. It was wild, free and entirely uncontrolled. Some came as men, some as boys of fifteen or sixteen, some as children of twelve, but all looked after themselves and did as they wanted. The university offered them nothing but lectures, to which they went if they pleased. They found their own lodging, often in the garrets of the little town. Their time was their own, to work if they so pleased, or to talk, gamble and drink, to reel hilariously home at dawn through the squalid streets.

The students liked their life, but no one else did. Certainly not the townspeople, nor the students' parents, nor the teachers, nor possibly the more bookish and domesticated of the students themselves. So, almost from the origin of the university, there were attempts to get them out of their lonely lodgings into boarding-houses. Boarding-houses were cheaper, they could live four or five to a room and have meals in common — the salt meat, salt fish, beer and bread of a medieval English winter. These were run by respectable and trustworthy men, who lived in the same house and kept their eye on their charges. It was to their care that thoughtful parents entrusted their sons ; it was they who safe-guarded the students' funds, advanced their pocket money, and paid their university fees out of the sum provided for the term's expenses by parents. It was they who formulated the rules of their respective houses — the hour at which the young men were to be in their rooms, their conduct within the hall and outside it, and other such matters. These boarding-houses had nothing to do with teaching ; the students simply lodged there and went off in the morning to the schools. They were simply a sensible means of controlling and supervising such youths and of keeping those so inclined from the wilder excesses.

Quite apart from these halls, were the colleges. These were endowed establishments, subsidised by ecclesiastics, royal adminis-trators, noble ladies, local guilds, kings or lords. What moved such persons to found colleges, what persuaded them to provide a little money and the rents of a bit of land (for gifts were small in the thirteenth and early fourteenth centuries) it is impossible to say — perhaps the sensible recognition of a need ; perhaps a spark of imagination ; more likely, in that religious age, the security of having a few young clerics obliged to say each day in perpetuity a Mass for the founder's soul and the satisfaction of having provided for the training up of an unending series of young men dedicated to the furtherance of God's work.

The money given provided first a building — not an ambitious affair, but one generally built as cheaply as possible, containing nothing more than the bare necessities of a medieval community. A kitchen, a large room or hall in which meals were taken, a series of separate rooms for the fellows, a set of rooms for the master, and a chapel, for master and fellows were, as were all members of the university, clerks in orders. The remaining money, invested in land, served to support the small community, a master and eight or perhaps ten fellows — young clerics of promise who had passed their first degree and were continuing at the university for higher ones. Their fellowships enabled them to live simply and frugally until their degrees were attained ; then they departed for service in the Church or State as opportunity offered, leaving their places to be filled again by a similar group.

No beginner, or as we would say today, no undergraduate student was housed in the medieval colleges, nor did the master or the fellows teach, but in the second half of the fourteenth century a transformation began to take place. The colleges began to admit boys and young men who paid for the privilege ; at first a few, then larger numbers, the increase requiring the erection of second courts and additional quadrangles. The master and the young fellow-scholars now began to feed and house their charges, and to supervise their behaviour, as the keepers of the halls had done, but more important than that, they began to teach them Instead of being students only, they began to instruct, and before long their teaching was as important as the lectures in the schools.

The university still consisted of those who gave the traditional lectures ; it conducted examinations and gave degrees. But, apart from that, the colleges did all. The earlier boarding-houses or halls-of-residence were either absorbed into existing colleges, as their owners sold up their no longer prosperous businesses, or organised into new ones, bearing the names of the new founders who supplied the money necessary to convert to the collegiate pattern. The day of the old hall, run along medieval lines, was over, as was that of the old college. The future lay with the new creation — and colleges subsequently founded all adopted the new arrangement.

Fellows of colleges who at first had had no duties except their studies and their prayers, now found themselves playing the role of teacher, and new fellows came on to the foundation on the understanding that they were to spend a portion, often a large portion, of their time in instruction. This individualised teaching within the college was greatly superior to the old lectures — at least for those who were not mature scholars, and college teaching, rather than university lectures, now became the attraction of university life.

The change, once well started, went on like the growth of a snowball ; with the increase in numbers the colleges became the beneficiaries of increasingly large incomes ; they were able to attract superior men as master and fellows. Superior students were anxious to be admitted to such colleges in order to be taught by such men, and the congregation of such students in one place made it easy for them to learn from each other, to sharpen their wits on their fellows. The reputation borne by the college was based upon the quality and the achievements of the men who had attended it, who were advertisements of its excellence, so to speak ; and this led others to seek entrance in order to follow along the same road. Those who achieved success—and more often, perhaps, those who did not — looked back with affection and loyalty to the house where they had lived in the years of their young manhood, leaving it, when they could, a farm or a manor, a lease of land or a piece of plate, further to enrich and advance it. And so the process was repeated. The spacious days of master's lodges and great halls, tastefully decorated, of expensive new buildings designed by eminent architects, were at hand. Progress of this kind was not to be continuous, there were ups and downs ahead, but it was steady throughout the period with which we are here concerned.

The university, on the other hand, was poor — no one left it money ; it was too impersonal for that. It had just enough to pay its few professorships, to keep up the buildings of the schools, where the relics of the old lectures still went on. The right to examine and confer degrees it still retained, but everything else had passed to the colleges. By Elizabethan times, if not earlier, each had become a university in miniature.

If we ask ourselves why the fellows of the old colleges took on the troubles involved in the care of feeding and general supervision of an increasingly large group of young men, and the heavy duty of instructing them, it is not easy to provide an answer. The college endowments were sufficient to provide for the master and fellows without any undergraduates at all. Under the new system they could, perhaps, look forward to some increase in comfort, some increase in stipend or dividend, the satisfaction of being a fellow of a larger, wealthier, more powerful college, but it seems clear that the additional work was undertaken out of no mere hope of personal gain. They were moved primarily by the sensible recognition of a need ; by the sorry spectacle of wasted years of unsupervised study, by the conviction that the old methods of formal instruction were antiquated and wrong. The expansion of the colleges and the growth of college teaching mark a profound change in educational practice and signal the first large step away from the long medieval tradition.

This same sort of transformation took place in legal education at about the same time. Indeed, the revolution in educational thought was sweeping not only through England, but through the Continent. At Paris, Bologna and all the medieval universities, boarding-houses were transformed into colleges; at Paris, for example, they were endowed, given much the same start in property, and almost exactly the same statutes and constitutions. They did not, it is true, flourish there. By 1550, when the Oxford and Cambridge colleges were dwarfing the university, those in Paris were dead, but they had taken form under the same stimulus that set the English colleges going as teaching institutions.

In the fourteenth century, as I have indicated, the Inns in Holborn and elsewhere in the suburbs of London in which lawyers congregated had nothing in common with colleges. Yet by 1550 the four great Inns could be justly described as " the third university of England " and the teaching of law as their essential characteristic and main preoccupation. The status they had then achieved has coloured all attempts to discover their origins. " It has been conjectured with great probability," Sir William Holdsworth writes, " that we must seek the germs of the Inns of Court in a body of masters of the faculty of law, giving lectures and instructing their pupils in law, and when satisfied with the proficiency of their pupils, admitting them to the order of masters by calling them to the Bar."

But it is much more likely that at the Inns, just as at the colleges of Oxford and Cambridge, teaching duties were only slowly grafted on to older institutions in which they had originally played no part. The steps by which Inns for lawyers were transformed into teaching institutions are far from clear — no clearer, indeed, than those by which the colleges displaced the university as the prime source of teaching. Of the four great Inns, only the Lincoln's Inn records survive for the fifteenth century, and they begin only in 1422. But there, and perhaps elsewhere, the process of change had begun not long before.

At Michaelmas, 1422, there were thirty young men *in status pupillari* at Lincoln's Inn. This number was the intake over the preceding three years — six in 1420, ten in 1421, fourteen in 1422. When we compare these numbers with those taken in yearly from that time on — a constantly increasing number — we may perhaps take it that we are not far from the point at which the admission of young men had begun. It may even be said that the Society's move in 1422 from its former to its new quarters in Chancery Lane, to a large property rented from the Bishop of Chichester, was made to provide lodging for the students it had begun to enrol and those it expected to enrol in the future. This is conjecture, but it is clear that in the years immediately following 1422 the procedures for educating these young men were first being worked out ; in other words, that a system of legal education had not from the first been provided for in the Inn.

When the colleges undertook the housing, supervision and teaching of students, burdens they had not formerly borne were cast upon their masters and fellows. That was also true at Lincoln's Inn. We know very little of the willingness of individual masters and fellows to assume these burdens, but at the Inn, except for a few enthusiasts — " visionaries " they probably were called by the older members who were convinced the system would never work —they were not assumed without protest.

Among the early entries in the Lincoln's Inn Black Book, almost all relating to the payment of dues and the collection of money, we find in 1428 an ordinance by the Society to the effect that residents of the City of London and of Middlesex, who were members of the Society, must pay commons for the period from the vigil of Christmas to the morrow of Epiphany ; that is, for the two weeks of vacation before the opening of Hilary term ; for two weeks in Lent — that is to say, the two weeks of vacation before the opening of Easter term ; and for three weeks in Autumn, the last before the octave of Michaelmas, that is, the three weeks of vacation immediately preceding the beginning of Michaelmas term. Now, dues were payable throughout the year, of course, but commons only in term time. They must now be paid for these weeks which was a step calculated to bring those who had to pay them into the Inn during those vacation weeks. The only members of the Society concerned were London residents, who presumably had no estates to supervise or country rents to collect. At any rate, those nearby were more likely to be coerced into attendance than those farther off, in Norfolk or Yorkshire, who, in view of the time and expense of getting to London, could not be coerced except under a heavier penalty.

The object of the exercise was left unexpressed, but there can be no doubt that the ordinance was intended to secure the attendance of fellows as teachers. Those seven weeks were already becoming known as the learning vacations and all those in the status of students were compelled to keep them. I think I am not far wrong in assuming that the Inn had embarked upon supervised instruction, that its members, like the fellows of a college, were now to be responsible for the teaching of the young men, that the burden had fallen upon those few forward-looking men who had initiated the new system, and that help from others, who were unlikely to attend voluntarily, was badly needed.

How a legal education was secured in the period preceding it is most difficult to say, despite the efforts of several generations of legal historians. Some small tracts, evidently used for teaching purposes, have survived from the late thirteenth century — the 1260s and 70s — and have recently been described by Professor Plucknett in his book " Early English Legal Literature." They consist of stock cases, perhaps a hundred of them, stated very briefly and doubtless put by the instructor to his class year after year, and their stock answers. There are a number of one-sentence rules of law — maxims — to be committed to memory. The great statutes of Magna Carta, Merton, Marlborough, Westminster I, Gloucester and Westminster II had also to be learned by heart, as had a great number of writs. Who the teachers were is unknown, though they were quite clearly not the most eminent men of the profession. Where their instruction was given is likewise unknown, though London is the most likely place, and it is not impossible that the halls of Inns were used by such teachers during the vacations. The student probably was expected to spend much time in court during term, observing and listening ; we know that a place, called colloquially " the crib " was set aside for law students in the Court of Common Pleas in the early fourteenth century, and that a difficult point was sometimes explained for the instruction of the young gentlemen in the crib by one of the Justices. But at best, from the complex manoeuvring of the serjeants and their rapid-fire exchanges of technicalities, preserved for us in the Year Books, a young student could expect to learn no more than from the technical lectures at the university. What was needed was something more individualised and more supervised, something a bit more up to date than the old stock cases, supplied by men who were themselves not far removed from the elementary questions that troubled the novice — most of all, an opportunity to talk and argue among themselves and with others already trained but not yet eminent, not yet so absorbed by their practice that time could not be spared for the explanation of difficult points, or too busy or too distinguished to take part in a moot. Where could this be supplied better or more easily than at an Inn or, *mutatis mutandis,* at a college?

But to return to the developments at Lincoln's Inn. The ordinance requiring attendance during the learning vacations by those resident in London apparently was not of itself sufficient. In 1436, a few years later, we find nineteen of the younger fellows of the Inn covenanting with and promising each other, under penalty, to continue in residence during some or all of the vacations for the next several years. The agreements take this form: "Davers will continue a month every Lent and a month every harvest this three years next coming." "Hayworth has promised to continue every Christmas and a month in every Lent and a month in every harvest this three years now next coming." "Wode has promised in like form as the said Hayworth has done." "Gainsford has promised to continue every vacation this three years next coming so that his father assent thereto." "And hereto," the clerk has added, "his father assented, the 9th day of November."

These nineteen commitments can be nothing but spontaneous undertakings, voluntarily entered into, to be present during the learning vacations "to sustain the burden of learning at the Inn." Though entered in the official record, they are clearly private agreements ; and if these nineteen, none of whom lived regularly in London, so bound themselves to each other, we may assume that their attendance was not already required by Inn statute. These undertakings can represent nothing but the resolution of a group of enthusiastic and willing young men — able young men as their later careers indicate — to make the system of legal education at Lincoln's Inn work. Their efforts seem to have been successful, for in 1442 it was enacted by the governors that every person who shall hereafter be admitted to the society, that is, those who shall come in as fellows or those who graduate from clerk or student to the status of fellow, shall continue, for the three years next after his admission, for two weeks before the opening of Hilary term, for three before the opening of Easter term, and for three before the opening of Michaelmas term. All those already admitted who had not already continued during the vacations for three years were now required to do so.

The system had now taken its final form. Like the new fellows of a college who came on to the foundation on the understanding that they were to spend a portion of their time in instructing others, the young men who had finished their nine vacations at the Inn, and been made fellows, had to take on the instruction of those just beginning, and serve at that task for nine further vacations. There was no further need of volunteers ; the system had become a formal part of the life of the Inn, its requirements applicable to all. Young fellows of one, two or three years' standing now supervised the exercises of those in their first, second or third year of elementary instruction, putting them cases, presiding at their moots, joining with them in grand moots before the benchers, explaining difficulties and discussing questionable points. We still know much too little of what took place during the learning vacations, but the presence at the Inn of thirty or more keen young men in the quiet weeks preceding the opening of term must have made all the difference to the students.

If we ask now, as we did before, why the fellows sacrificed their vacations and undertook the additional burden of teaching, I think the answer must be the same as that given earlier. For a fellow of an Inn the chance of personal gain was even more remote than for the fellow of a college. Both were moved by the sensible recognition of a need and by the conviction that the old methods of formal instruction were antiquated and wrong. Both college teaching and Inn teaching are aspects of the same profound transformation that was altering the ancient educational tradition throughout western Europe.

Requiring the presence of its fellows at the learning vacations was not the only step taken by the Inns to further the education of its young men. The weeks prior to Michaelmas and Easter terms, that is, the Autumn and Lent vacations, were the times of the readings. At Lincoln's Inn by the middle of the fifteenth century these were lectures given by men senior to the newly-elected fellows of three years' standing, that is, senior to the men who had been at the Inn for six years, first as students and then as fellows, and who then had attended eighteen learning vacations.

The Readers were men who had been at the Inn for at least nine or ten years. Their readings or lectures, at first four a week for four weeks, later three a week for three weeks, were always on statutes, and always until the sixteenth century on the old statutes, that is, the statutes prior to Edward III, on which so much of English law rested. These were taken in order, so that successive Readers covered the chapters of Magna Carta, Merton, Marlborough, Westminster I, Gloucester, Westminster II and the rest. The chapters varied in importance, of course, and in the amount that could profitably be said about them. Thus a typical series — this is one from the Inner Temple — would run as follows: Autumn 1491, Westminster II, cc.1-2 ; Lent 1492, cc.3-5 ; Autumn, cc.6-11 ; Lent 1493, cc.12-14 ; Autumn, cc.15-22, and so on.

Westminster II concluded, the next statute in the series would be begun and, the entire cycle completed, it would begin over again with Magna Carta. In the late fifteenth century the whole cycle lasted about ten or twelve years, but it had not always taken that long.

The great change in legal education came in Lincoln's Inn in 1442, though it was already in the air twenty years before, and several preliminary steps had already been taken. It was in that year, as I have said, that the Inn first instituted its requirement of nine further vacations to be kept by those just made fellows. Readings had been given at the Inn before 1442, but they were perfunctory affairs, expounding in a few lectures many chapters of a statute, perhaps all the forty or fifty chapters of a long statute. In the years immediately before the middle of the century, however, the readings began to become elaborate and learned works. The chapters of statutes were not merely explained in a few lines, but taken as points of departure for complete and detailed examinations of the subjects with which they dealt. Thus a reading on Westminster II, ca.1, *De donis*, becomes a long and elaborate account of the fee tail and all its intracacies, requiring eight lectures, an hour a day for eight days. A reading on Westminster II, ca.25, becomes an elaborate examination of the assise of novel disseisin in all its manifold aspects ; one on Merton, ca.1, a full account of dower, and so on. Where in 1430 the whole long cycle of statutes might have been completed in four or five years, by the middle of the century ten or twelve years were needed.

To prepare such lectures was no longer a simple job but the work of many weeks, and it is about that time that the giving of a reading became a prerequisite for admission to the Bench of the Inn. A reading was not required, as the nine supplementary vacations were, nor was every fellow anxious or able to give one, but a way was offered to those who aspired to the Benchers' table. More than that, it was only from the ranks of Readers that serjeants were chosen, and becoming a serjeant was essential for one who thought hopefully of the Bench.

Thus the Inns became modernised teaching institutions, the places as tutors being filled by the younger men, those of Readers or lecturers by the older. Lincoln's Inn, and doubtless the others, had been completely organised along instructional lines by the middle fifteenth century — so long ago that the Elizabethan antiquarians who investigated their histories could think of them only in terms of schools. But not all Inns moved with the times. The four which *had* could already be distinguished from the others in 1468, as Fortescue in fact distinguished them. It was to the greater Inns that the young men who aspired to the Bar naturally flocked. As with the colleges, superior instruction attracted superior students, superior men made the competition keen and standards high, and when they went to the Bar advertised the excellence of their training. The lesser Inns, like the Oxford and Cambridge halls, had to accommodate themselves to the new as best they could, or perish. Some disappeared, others took their places as preparatory schools for the greater Inns, still others resigned themselves to the status of boarding-houses, very like what they had had in the fourteenth century. Though in 1409 William Skrene had been made serjeant from Clifford's Inn, he was the last to come from an Inn other than the four great ones. And it must have been not long afterwards that a call to the Bar of any one of them became the equivalent of a general admission to practice. After 1450 the position and wealth of the four large Inns began to show itself in new buildings and new halls. As in the colleges, the bare and utilitarian medieval rooms now seemed small and mean, money was available, and an increasing demand for chambers had to be met.

The time had not yet come when the great of the realm would be pleased to dine splendidly with the Benchers — and present a piece of plate as a remembrance of their visit — but the Inns had attained a magnificence hardly surpassed by the most prosperous city company. To be a fellow had become a sign of distinction, and after 1450, though seldom before, tombstones began to bear the proud addition " of Gray's Inn " or " of the Temple " — not only those in nearby churches, St. Andrew's, Holborn, St. Dunstan's in the West, or St. Bride's, Fleet Street, but those in far-distant parishes of England.

The four great Inns had clearly overshadowed the others in something less than sixty years and were going forward steadily and rapidly. Progress was not always to continue at that pace, nor was the future to be without setbacks. The admirable and elaborate system, the reason for their success, which provided knowledge through endless arguments over cases, moots and grand moots, first readings and second readings, and ensured the necessary and constant supervision of the work of the young by the older and of the older by the old, though wholly suited to education by way of the ear, was made obsolete almost overnight by the printing press. But that takes us to the sixteenth century, and I must now turn to what I know of the history of this Inn.

I have no dramatic surprises to offer you and nothing that I have to say of the history of Gray's Inn concerns it in the four-teenth century, for I take it that a legal Inn was already in existence at this place in 1350 or thereabouts. What I have found in the course of a dozen years spent in turning over legal manu-scripts are the names and something of the careers of some of the men who were fellows of this society in the fifteenth century — a period for which neither admission registers nor Inn records of any kind survive. There is much still to be done along the lines I have been following, and since an examination of the legal manuscripts in the libraries and great houses of the century is beyond the endurance of any one man, it is my hope that what I have to say tonight will encourage others to carry on this fascinating and not very difficult pursuit.

I began with a reading on the Statute of Westminster II, ca.25, contained in a manuscript collection of miscellaneous legal materials preserved in the University Library at Cambridge. It is anonymous, bearing neither the name of the Reader, the Inn at which it was given, nor the year in which it was delivered. Earlier in the volume, however, there appears the note in law-French: " See below in this book, the reading of old Spelman on Westminster II, ca.25 " — a cross-reference applicable only to the reading I had examined. That note was clearly in the hand of Walter Atwell of Gray's Inn, the compiler of the volume, who had written his name and Inn on the flyleaf, and who had copied the reading into his book in July, 1516, as his memorandum on its last page said. The reading, then, was earlier than 1516 and given by one Spelman. Now a contemporary of Atwell's at Gray's Inn was John Spelman, later one of the Justices of the King's Bench, who had been Reader in Lent, 1514, his name as Reader in that term having been duly entered in the Pension Book. John Spelman thus seemed likely to be the author of the reading, though it seemed strange that Atwell should call one a few years older than himself " old " Spelman.

Further examination of the reading soon revealed that Spelman's views had been disputed by several members of his audience, whose names were supplied. This was the usual proce-dure, for a reading was not merely a set lecture. It was that in part, but the Reader's exposition could be, and often was, interrupted by disagreement from the floor, the resulting interchange between the Reader and his disputant — often an eminent lawyer — frequently being the most interesting as well as the most instructive part of the proceedings. The first of the disputants was one Wangford. No one of that name was listed in the Inn records, but one William Wangford had been called to become serjeant-at-law in 1453, with seven others, including Thomas Littleton of the Inner Temple, the author of the *Tenures,* and it seemed likely that he was the man who had spoken at Spelman's reading. This Wangford, however, was dead before 1459, when his will was probated in Rochester Consistory Court, and thus Spelman's reading could not have been given after that date. A second disputant was one Needham, identified as John Needham, also called to be serjeant in 1453, with Wangford, and a Justice of the Common Pleas by 1457. But Needham was not described as a judge in the reading and thus Spelman must have read before 1457 — indeed, before 1453, since Wangford and Needham, both serjeants-at-law in that year, were not so described. In 1453 John Spelman had not yet been born, and thus the reading had been given by another Spelman, one differentiated by Atwell as " old " Spelman, that is, John's father Henry, whose connection with Gray's Inn is clear since he was one of the feoffees to whom Reginald Grey transferred the manor of Portpole, commonly called Gray's Inn, in 1456. A third disputant in Spelman's reading was one Heaton, readily identified as Richard Heaton, another of the feoffees of the Inn in 1456.

Thus I had rescued four fellows of the Inn: Wangford and Needham, probably already Benchers in the 1440s ; and Spelman and Heaton, Benchers in the 1450s — certainly before 1456. Armed with these names, other Benchers and fellows, long lost to the Inn, were gradually brought to light. Wangford's name appears as disputant in a number of readings. Now that he was identified as a fellow of this Inn, they must all, of course, appear in Gray's Inn readings. In one — a British Museum manuscript — he appears with one Robert Joyce ; in other readings in the same volume Joyce appears with Gilbert Haltoft. Now Haltoft, in turn, appears (in a reading preserved in the Cambridge University Library) with two other men, Alexander Anne and John Markham. And Alexander Anne appears this time in a reading that bears its author's name — Walter Moyle — with Richard Hungate. These must all be Gray's Inn men ; and that the links in the chain were secure was established independently by an entry in the London letter-books, which records the fact that Thomas Coventry, an orphan, was sent by direction of the Mayor and Aldermen on the 17th June, 1432, to Gray's Inn to be instructed under the care of Richard Hungate.

Thus we have Richard Hungate, known to be of Gray's Inn in 1432, and from other records known to have been engaged in legal practice in the 1420s, and Alexander Anne, his contemporary, Common Serjeant of London in 1424, Recorder in 1436. Both these men, who died in the same year, 1439, were born before 1400 and must have been students at the Inn before the century was more than a few years old. Then John Markham, called Serjeant in 1438, a Justice of the Common Pleas in 1445 ; Walter Moyle, Common Serjeant of London in 1441, serjeant-at-law, 1443, and a Judge of the King's Bench in 1454 ; and Gilbert Haltoft, Baron of the Exchequer in 1447.

Working with the names of these nine men, a dozen others were recalled from oblivion, though not without some difficulty : William Yelverton, serjeant in 1438, later a judge of the Common Pleas ; Thomas Billing, serjeant in 1453, whose connection with the Society is confirmed independently by a remark in one of the Paston letters ; William Laken, serjeant with Billing in 1453, and a judge of the Common Pleas in 1462 ; Thomas Urswick, Common Serjeant of London, 1453, Recorder, 1454, and Chief Baron of the Exchequer in 1471 ; John Clark, Baron of the Exchequer 1460 ; Robert Molyneux, Common Serjeant of London 1469, and his father Thomas, a Bencher in 1456 and doubtless much earlier ; Miles Metcalf, Recorder of York 1477, Justice of the Duchy of Lancaster 1483 ; Thomas Brigges, serjeant-at-law 1478 ; William Hussey, serjeant-at-law in the same year, Chief Justice of the King's Bench, 1481 ; Thomas Roger, serjeant in the same year ; and Richard Jay and John Fineux, both serjeants in 1485.

To these something over a second dozen was added, and I shall not bore you by reciting their names, though I may say that Edmund Dudley, of the notorious team of Empson and Dudley, Henry VII's financial agents and advisers, was a fellow of this Inn until he was beheaded by Henry VIII in the first year of his reign. Both Dudley's readings still survive, and learned readings they are. His reading in Lent 1496 was attended by two eminent Gray's Inn men — Thomas Brian, then Chief Justice of the Common Pleas, and John Fineux, then Chief Justice of the King's Bench.

Taken all together, only a small portion of the men who so long ago studied, argued and dined in this place have been identified. Nevertheless, some interesting figures now emerge. In 1453, of the seven called to be serjeants, four were from Gray's Inn and one from each of the other Inns. In 1463, the next call, of the eight three were from Gray's Inn, two each from the Inner and Middle Temples and one from Lincoln's Inn. In 1478, the next call, of the seven there were two each from Gray's Inn, Lincoln's Inn and the Inner Temple and one from the Middle Temple. In 1495, the next call, of the nine there were three from Lincoln's Inn, two each from Gray's Inn and the others. This was the first time in half a century that Gray's Inn had had fewer men than any one of the others. Throughout the entire century more men from Gray's Inn were called to be serjeants than from any other, and, by the same token, more Gray's Inn men were raised to the Bench. From the fifteenth century manuscripts of Gray's Inn provenance that survive — as many as those of the other three put together — it seems evident that during that century it was the largest and most prominent of the Inns. Only towards the end of the century did the others begin to become serious rivals.

It may well be that the revolution in legal education to which I have referred first took place here, some time around the year 1400. Certainly the Inn flourished mightily soon after that date, attracting men of aptitude and brillance who went on to occupy high office. Their contemporaries at Lincoln's Inn, for example, with one or two exceptions, were in no way comparable. If so, it was here that the system of teaching took form which saved England from the reception of Roman Law that threatened it in the sixteenth century and ensured the survival of the Common Law and its eventual transplantation to my own country and to the others that had not yet begun to appear on the maps. If that is so — and as an impartial and completely unprejudiced investigator I believe it to be so — that was an achievement of the first magnitude and one of which the members of this Inn can be very proud.

11

THE EQUITY OF A STATUTE AND HEYDON'S CASE

Much as the author of *The Mirror of Justices,* dissatisfied with the reforms of Edward I, appealed to legal history in the form of a fabricated, pre-Conquest system of law vastly superior to the one under which he lived, and Sir Edward Coke, urged by the conflict of Crown and Parliament, found support for his political theories in the books of an earlier age, so the authors of recent articles upon statutory interpretation make haste to buttress their own convictions by the production of historical precedent. Mr. James M. Landis, anxious to have grammatical interpretation give way to functional construction, regards the doctrine of the equity of a statute as one

"Enabling judges to distill from a statute its basic purpose . . . [and] to slough off the archaisms in their own legal structure. Even general legislation could thus be made to yield a meaning for law beyond its expressed operative effect. The class of situations to which the statutory remedy was expressly made applicable were but illustrative of other analogous cases that deserved to be governed by the same principle. The extension of one remedy beyond its recognized common law area by the statute justified judges in giving another remedy the same expansive effect."[1]

Mr. W. Ivor Jennings[2] and Mr. D. J. Llewelyn Davies[3] likewise see

---

[1] *Statutes and the Sources of Law* in HARVARD LEGAL ESSAYS (1934) 213, 216, 235 n.8, citing Y. B. 3 Hen. VI, Mich. 18 (1425); Y. B. 20 & 21 Edw. I, 42 (1292); Y. B. 17 & 18 Edw. III, 516 (1343-4); Le Warde v. Wullesthorpe, Y. B. 17 Edw. III, 142 (1342-3); Plenty v. Gold & Talbot, Y. B. 13 Rich. II, 9 (1389-90); Abbot of Croyland v. de Veer, Y. B. 17 & 18 Edw. III, 472 (1343-4); 2 Inst. 110, 241, 346. The only case in which the principle of equitable interpretation may properly be found is the first, which illustrates in a modest way Plowden's revolutionizing idea that "when the words of a Statute enact one Thing, they enact all other Things which are in a like degree" by extending to administrators the statute of 9 EDW. III, c. 3 which provided that in an action of debt against executors he who comes first by distress shall answer.

[2] *Courts and Administrative Law* (1936) 49 Harv. L. Rev. 426, 435: "It is now almost platitudinous to remark that the common law rules of interpretation are fundamentally inconsistent. The older rule, laid down by Plowden and Coke, was that a statute must be interpreted in the light of the evils that it was intended to remedy. This rule was derived from the practice of judges who themselves drafted the statutes. But eighteenth century judges applied entirely different rules. In the first place they were more accustomed to the interpretation

in "the theory of interpretation accepted by Plowden, Coke, and Blackstone" that the aim of the judge in the seventeenth century must have been to give full effect to the purposes of the enactment, and find little in the rules of interpretation in *Heydon's Case* but anticipations, in more pedantic language, of the modern theory that behind the formal fiat of the statute lies an emphatically asserted end which the appropriate exercise of judicial power will permit courts to advance. This theory of freedom of interpretation is certainly based largely upon mediaeval precedents and the extent to which they justify it is an interesting subject for investigation: it is that to which we turn here.

The interpretation of statutes in its modern sense is a latecomer to English law: it must be obvious that so long as the law maker is his own interpreter the problem of a technique of interpretation does not arise. Only when he is forced to delegate the function of interpretation to a different person does the matter become urgent. The extension or contraction of a statute's words in the light of the legislator's actual intention, known to the judge in fact, or in the light of the judges' own intention when they themselves drew it, is a very different thing from the extension or contraction of its words under a doctrine of equitable interpretation. In the first case there is no interpretation at all: the words of the provision are little more than a faint and distant echo of a very real and well understood intention, and it is in its light that the judge gives or withholds a remedy; the words may seem to expand, contract, or disappear completely, but in fact they have played no part in the result. It is only after the middle of the fourteenth century, when judges find themselves no longer able to draw either upon the actual intention of the legislator or upon the royal dispensing power, that they are forced to construct a body of rules of statutory interpretation:[4] a document, and no longer the verbal explanations

---

of deeds . . .   These eighteenth century rules were created without express overruling of the rule in *Heydon's Case* . . .   But the normal practice of the nineteenth century was to follow the rules of the eighteenth century. A statute was to be interpreted by what it said, not by what it was intended to do; and if there was any doubt it was to be interpreted in such a way as not to interfere with common law rights."

[3] *The Interpretation of Statutes in the Light of Their Policy by the English Courts* (1935) 35 Col. L. Rev. 519. Mr. Lauterpacht, *Some Observations on Preparatory Work in the Interpretation of Treaties* (1935) 48 Harv. L. Rev. 549, 560, finds in the first and second rules laid down in Heydon's Case permission to admit extrinsic evidence in the interpretation of statutes.

[4] Richardson and Sayles, *The Early Statutes* (1934) 50 L. Q. Rev. 201, 540, 562. PLUCKNETT, STATUTES AND THEIR INTERPRETATION IN THE FIRST HALF OF THE FOURTEENTH CENTURY (1922) 55-56: "The lateness of this development is largely due to the close union of powers which rendered it at first unnecessary, while even later the courts were so willing to refer disputed points to the council or parliament

of one man to another, becomes the sole basis for the judge's action, and if the facts do not fall within the statute's precise words, then perhaps it may be possible to resort to some doctrine of equitable interpretation which, on its face, can mean nothing unless by its side there exist the contrary view of strict interpretation from which it is distinguished. Just how far equitable interpretation will permit the judge to expand the express words of a statute we shall see later, but it seems clear that a doctrine of equitable interpretation does not appear until early in the fifteenth century, after, as we should expect, the doctrine of strict interpretation from which it relieves, and which itself first takes form late in the preceding century, has made its rigors felt. Therefore, in so far as they antedate the complete differentiation of courts and *curia,* and certainly in so far as they antedate any formulation of a rule of strict interpretation, the Year Book cases cited by Mr. Landis in support of his contention (which we have quoted above) anticipate a doctrine of later growth and are concerned neither with equitable interpretation nor, in fact, with what we understand as interpretation at all. They represent a method of handling statutes that has been impossible since the middle of the fourteenth century: one in which the words of the statute play (if any) a minor part—and they certainly cannot be considered characteristic of English law except in its first and partly undifferentiated phase which already is drawing toward a close when Shareshulle, J., says in 1346, "Nous ne poms prendre lestatut plus avant qe les paroles en ycele ne parle," we cannot take the statute further than the words of it say.[5]

Professor Plucknett's conclusions are general,[6] but his gaze is

---

that they would not feel the need for extending their technical equipment. One cannot expect a very highly developed science of interpretation until the courts are conscious of their isolation; when no outside help is to be expected from the legislature or the executive, and when the Judges no longer take so much part in the functions of government other than judicature, then the courts will have to accept statutes as the commands of an authority exernal to themselves whose will is known to them only as expressed in the written word."

[5] Waghan v. Anon., Y. B. 20 Edw. III, 2, 198. The first sign of this new tendency may be seen in Scrope's speech in 1312 (Balsham v. atte Street, Y. B. 5 Edw. II, 2, 46): "We ought not to understand the statute otherwise than it says; but the statute says nothing save in the case where the tenant is about to lose by default, but the tenant here is not losing by default but by failure to prosecute a summons against a warrantor." Toward the end of the reign of Edward III this policy becomes embodied in a short phrase—*Privilegia statuti sunt stricti juris.* Le Warde v. Wullesthorpe, Y. B. 17 Edw. III, 142 (1342-3); Sybeling *et al.* v. Mussendene *et al.*, Y. B. 17 & 18 Edw. III, 446 (1343). Plucknett, *op. cit. supra* note 4, 82-90, 164-69.

[6] *Op. cit. supra* note 4, 168, §4: "Toward the end of our period, however, circumstances compelled the courts to set bounds to their activities. The rapid fixation of the Common Law necessarily involved the resignation of considerable power by the courts; nor was this resignation altogether voluntary, for the growing separation of the courts from the King's immediate personal sphere will

fixed upon interpretation in only one of its senses: that of extending a statute to include a situation not expressly provided for by its
words, and he finds during Edward III's reign a noticeable tendency
to read statutes more strictly. But strict interpretation is a double-
edged device, as Plowden well recognized, and of its use in its
second sense—that of strict adherence to the words of a statute so
as to permit no exceptions out of its general words—we can find no
evidence. Prior to the reign of Edward III the court frequently
restricted the scope of a statute by excepting particular cases from
its operation,[7] and it is likewise true that it long remains possible
for the court to read sound common law policy into loose statutory
generalizations in much the way that had been done by Hengham
and Bereford—without extended comment and unencumbered by a
theory of equitable interpretation. In 1356 there is an interesting
example of this process. The Countess of Athol had taken cattle
to agistment in her park; the defendant broke into the park and
reclaimed his cattle without agreement to pay for their pasture.
This was, of course, a simple trespass for which the Countess might
recover damages, but action was brought instead under the Statute
of Westminster I, c. 20, which had been made to punish deer
stealing but phrased unfortunately to include trespassers in parks
generally—"de mefesurs de parks"—and under its provisions the
trespasser might be liable not only to pay damages but to imprisonment for the term of three years.[8]

Burton (for the Countess) prayed judgment under the statute and
also that the defendant be sent to prison for three years. *Thorpe, J.*—
This statute was not made to apply except where a man hunted in the
park. *Burton*—It seems that it does, for it speaks of misfeasors in parks
generally and it has been found that he broke our park, etc. *Thorpe, J.*

sufficiently explain the diffidence of the new school of Judges who could no
longer draw upon the vast reserve of power at the disposal of the King's personal entourage . . . the remoter Common Law courts confined themselves to
the old law. Inevitably they adopted the same attitude toward the new, that is,
the statute law, and soon they reached the maxim, *statuta sunt stricti juris.*"
Note that all the cases cited to illustrate growing strictness of interpretation under
Edward III (pp. 87-90) are concerned only with refusals to extend, not to limit,
the words of the statute.

[7] Plucknett, *op. cit. supra* note 4, 57-65.

[8] "Purueu est de mefesurs de ˙parkes & de viuers ke, si nul soit ateint par
seute le pleintif, soient agardes bones & hautes amendes soulum la manere del
trespas, & eint la prison de iij anz & de ilokes soient reinz a la volunte le rey, sil
ad dount estre issient reint; & trouesse bone seurete ke mes ne les face; e sil ne
ad dount estre reint apres la prison de iij anz trouesse meme la seurete; e sil ne
puise trouer la seurete, forsiurge le reaume; & si nul de ceo rette, soit futif &
nen eit terre ne˙ tenement suffisand par quei il puise estre iustice, si tost com le
roy auera ceo troue par bone enqueste soit demande de cunte en cunte; & sil ne
vient soit vtlage." The text in the Statutes of the Realm (i. 32) is from a manuscript later than that from which the text we quote is taken. SELECT PLEAS OF THE
FOREST (Selden Society, 1901) cxxi.

—You will not have such judgment from us. And *Willoughby*, J., awarded that she receive [only] damages.[9]

In 1396 it was held that the Statute of Westminster II, c. 49, which provided that no one "receive any church, nor advowson of a church, land not tenement in fee, by gift, nor by purchase, nor to farm, nor by champerty, nor otherwise, so long as the thing is in plea before us" did not apply to one who had bargained his land before the writ was brought against him and delivered seisin after the land was in plea.[10] Similarly in 1422, despite the clear words of the Statute of Marlborough, c. 4, which made it a serious trespass, it was held possible to drive beasts distrained in one county to another county when the land upon which the distress was taken was held of a manor in the second county.[11] And likewise in Littleton's *Tenures*, written shortly before his death in 1481, although the Statute of Gloucester, c. 1, made it clear that the disseisee should recover damages in a writ of entry upon novel disseisin against him that was found tenant after the disseisor, if the disseisor had made a deed of feoffment to B, C, and D, but livery of seisin to B and C only, after the death of B and C the disseisee could not recover damages from D, if D had not been at the livery, had not consented to it, nor taken the profits.[12] This process of imposing limitations upon statutes too widely drawn is nowhere in the Year Books dignified by the title of equitable interpretation: it rests rather upon a "construction reasonablement."[13] The general words of the statute are quietly set aside without inquiry into

---

[9] Y. B. 30 Edw. III, Mich. 6, 2 Inst., 199. The most obvious cases of exceptions out of the statute are those in which the statute, though generally phrased, is not interpreted to include infants, married women, and persons *non compos mentis*. So despite the general words of WESTMINSTER II, c. 25, if an infant named disseisor in an assize vouches a record and fails, he will not be imprisoned. Y. B. 36 Edw. III, Mich. (1362). FITZHERBERT, ABRIDGEMENT, *Assize*, 443; BROOKE, ABRIDGEMENT *Assize*, 460. And likewise, a married woman will not be imprisoned. Y. B. 11 Hen. IV, Hil. 28 (1410).

[10] Y. B. 19 Rich. II, Mich. Bellewe, LES ANS DU ROY RICHARD II, *Champertie* 1; Fitzherbert, *Champerty*, 15 Y. B. 9 Hen. VII, Hil. 12 (1494); Brooke, *Champertie*, 9. See also: Y. B. 21 Hen. VII, Hil. 28 (1506); Brooke, *Fees & Extortion*, 6.

[11] Y. B. 1 Hen. VI (Selden Society, 1933) 30. The exception out of the statute had been made much earlier: Fourneux v. Prior of Blythe, Y. B. 14 Edw. III, 88. *Cf.* Y. B. 33 & 35 Edw. I, 252, where the difficulty due to the manor extending into two counties was avoided by taking issue on the maliciousness of the driving. Plucknett, *op. cit. supra* note 4, 62 n.1.

[12] LITT. §685. *Cf.* Coke's comment: "Here it appeareth, that acts of parliament are to be so construed, as no man that is innocent, or free from injurie or wrong, be by a literall construction punished or endamaged: and therefore in this case, albeit the letter of the statute is generally to give damages against him that is found tenant, and the case that *Littleton* here putteth, D being survivor, is consequently found tenant of the land; yet because he waived the estate, and never agreed to the feoffment, nor tooke any profits, he shall not be charged with the dammages."

[13] Y. B. 4 Hen. VII, Trin. 6 (1489).

the nature of statutes, the sovereignty of Parliament, or the supremacy of a controlling common law, and simply upon the dictate of legal reasonableness. Plowden, in the sixteenth century, looks upon this doctrine "in which the sages of the law have qualified the rigor of the word according to reason" as one in which they "have ever been guided by the intent of the legislature," but there is little talk in the Year Books of intention, and less of an "equity that diminishes the letter according to its discretion."[14] To call the process a doctrine is to give it form it did not have; so too, to justify departures from the statute's words by resort to the intention of the legislature or to a theory of equitable interpretation, indeed to justify them at all, would have seemed quite unnecessary to judges of the fifteenth and sixteenth centuries. Their great preoccupation was to apply the best law they knew as courageously as they could. It is true that the best law was perhaps too often synonymous with the common law, but they were not entirely mistaken in regarding the common law as the expression of human reason in a great body of doctrine, nor is their anticipatory acceptance of the view of Sir John Davies that "the customary law of England, which we doe likewise call *ius commune,* as comming neerest to the lawe of Nature, which is the root and touchstone of all good lawes, and which also is *ius non scriptum,* and written onley in the memory of man . . . doth far excell our written lawes, namely our statutes or acts of Parliament," altogether misplaced.[15] It must be emphasized, however, that Coke's political and juridical difficulties are still definitely in the future.

But the reverse of the medal yields a very different picture. There can be no doubt that the reign of Edward III shows a strong

---

14 Stradling v. Morgan, Plowd. 199, 205 (1560). Eyston v. Studd, Plowd. 465 (1574). Thomas Ashe, ΕΠΙΕΙΚΕΙΑ (1609) devotes the largest chapter (pp. 172-209) in his small volume to a tabulation of the cases "ou, & en queux statutes le generality des paroles serra restraine par construction fait per equite, & exposition fait sur iceux encounter la lettre & les paroles mesmes," but no mention of this equity can be found in the Year Book cases he cites. He, like Plowden, reads the early cases in the light of Renaissance theories of natural law. *Cf.* Plowden's remarks (at 204, 205) upon the case cited *supra* note 12: "The interpretation is founded upon the Intent of the Makers of the Act, and upon good Reason. And yet it seems contrary to the Text, which says generally that *the Disseisee shall recover Damages against him that is found Tenant after the Disseisor.* And: Littleton says that in the said Case he is found Tenant after the Disseisor, and yet the Disseisee shall not recover Damages against him but it was the Intent of the Legislature that made him say so. And that their Intent was so, he gathered from Reason, for Reason would never suffer him to pay damages to the Disseisee, where he never assented to the Wrong done to the Disseisee, and never received nor intended to receive any Profits of his Land." (I take this opportunity to express my gratitude to Professor Eldon R. James, Librarian of the Harvard Law School Library, for permission kindly afforded me to examine Ashe's rare volume.)

15 LE PRIMER REPORT DES CASES ET MATTERS EN LEY (1628). MCILWAIN, THE GROWTH OF POLITICAL THOUGHT IN THE WEST (1932) 365.

tendency to limit severely the words of a statute and to refuse to extend them beyond their plain, grammatical meaning. Thus administrators were barred by the action given to executors by the Statute of Westminster II, c. 23,[16] and though Bereford in an earlier reign had held that the Statute of Marlborough, c. 9, applied equally to a release whereby the lord had surrendered a portion of the services,[17] this sensible interpretation did not persist into the next reign for one of the reasons assigned for ousting a tenant from the benefit of the statute was that he was pleading a release, while the statute said only feoffment.[18] The unprinted Year Books of Edward III and Richard II make definite statement hazardous, and there is at least one case in 1389 which permitted an action of detinue *de racionabili parte* against two executors, one of whom appeared, to proceed against that one alone by virtue of the statute of 9 Edw. III, stat. 1, c. 3, which mentions expressly only actions of debt,[19] but signs are not wanting to indicate the continuance of strict interpretation during the period. The matter becomes especially clear with the appearance of the doctrine of' *l'equite de la statut* in the early fifteenth century.[20] It soon must have become evident in practice that a refusal to extend the words of a statute led frequently to injustice when applied to legislative acts drawn with the lack of attention to exact meaning and careful phraseology exhibited by the statutes of the time, and in the light of what we have said above of the judges' willingness to except cases out of the statute, it perhaps is difficult to understand their corresponding unwillingness to extend legislation beyond its exact words. That they are unwilling cannot be denied for, as we shall see below, the appearance of the doctrine of equitable interpretation is itself strong evidence of the existence of a vigorous policy of strict interpretation. Statutes are to be taken as they stand; though they may be restricted in scope without comment, any extension, however slight, must be justified by reference to a definite doctrine of interpretation. But these methods of dealing with statutes are not inconsistent: the general attitude during the later Year Book period is one of jealousy for the common law which was not to be modified by statute more than could be avoided. Statutes will be held to do no more than they literally say in changing or adding

---

[16] Administrators of Wedergrave v. Prior of St. John, Y. B. 18 & 19 Edw. III, 532, Y. B. 19 Edw. III, 12. Plucknett, *op. cit. supra* note 4, 88 n.2.

[17] Attemulle v. Saunderville, Y. B. 6 & 7 Edw. II, 11.

[18] Y. B. 11 & 12 Edw. III, 62-4 (1337).

[19] Plenty v. Gold & Talbot, Y. B. 13 Rich. II (Ames Foundation) 9. Y. B. 24 Edw. III, Mich. 16 (1350).

[20] Y. B. 12 Hen. IV, Pasch. 5 (1411).

to common law rules, and on the other hand, common law policy will be read into statutes to restrict general words that change common law principles too violently.[21] The two seemingly opposite views of the nature of a statute—one requiring strict adherence to its words, the other permitting the words to be disregarded—are both based upon the feeling that common law ought not to be changed, a policy that develops during the reign of Edward III, and that may be observed dominating the action of the court during the entire later Year Book period along three parallel lines of force: increasing strictness in interpreting statutes beyond their literal meaning;[22] no change in the free policy of an earlier day permitting cases to be excepted out of the statute's general words;[23] increasing strictness in the application of common law rules.[24] With the appearance of the Chancery as a separate court in the years just before the middle of the fourteenth century, the common law courts had been left to confine themselves to the old law, and they inevitably adopted a respectful attitude toward it which is well illustrated by the remark of Hilary, J., in 1342, "We will not and *cannot* change ancient usages."[25] That this attitude should be reflected in their treatment of statutes is not surprising.

---

[21] Where a statute clearly superseded common law there was frank acknowledgement. It was recognized that a statute was a modification of the law of the land which henceforth courts would apply: it extended the common law and had the same validity as the common law. But by the side of this recognition there exists the necessity of fitting into a symmetrical and coherent body of closely-knit common law, statutes straightforwardly changing a portion of the law but affecting other portions in unexpected ways. We find this process profusely illustrated in the later Year Books: see Y. B. 9 Hen. VI, Pasch. 5 (1429) and it finds expression in Coke's phrases: "The surest construction of a statute is by the rule and reason of the common law;" "To know what the common law was before the making of any statute . . . is the very lock and key to set open the windows of the statute." As Mr. Allen points out in LAW IN THE MAKING (2d ed. 1930) 268, this principle is an essential guiding rule without which the continuity of legal development would have been gravely imperilled. Dean Pound indicates (*op. cit. infra* note 39) that the principle conduces to a narrow and jealous interpretation but we may believe this was not apparent to the lawyers of the time. A recent writer (PICKTHORN, EARLY TUDOR GOVERNMENT: HENRY VII (1934) 55) states that the mediaeval idea of the supremacy of law is an idea of which it is hardly too much to say that before the sixteenth century it was all there was in England in the way of a constitution, that during the seventeenth it was most of what there was, and during the eighteenth the best of what there was. Though this must be taken subject to certain reservations, it is not further from the truth than a statement as strikingly expressed as it is should be. Certainly the theory of fundamental law does not become weaker after the sixteenth century: it grows in force and becomes explicit in Coke's identification of the law of reason and the common law. With its growth we can expect increasing veneration of the common law and a not too cordial welcome for statutes that restrict or nullify it.

[22] See *infra* notes 26-32, 34-38.

[23] See *supra* notes 9-12.

[24] PLUCKNETT, *op. cit. supra* note 4, 124-127.

[25] Y. B. 16 Edw. III, 1, 90. Y. B. 19 Edw. III, 12: "*Hilary, J.*—Ceo no poms faire saunz estatut."

For the late fourteenth and early fifteenth centuries, then, we may postulate rigorous adherence to common law usage and strict interpretation of statute, and we likewise may take the appearance of the doctrine of the statute's equity as an admission of the impossibility of these two rules when used in conjunction. With the acceptance of the new doctrine the very strict reading of a statute may be modified to admit something beyond that which its words expressly provide, or in other words, statutory changes may be extended *de similibus ad similia.* Just how different this doctrine is from that visioned by Mr. Landis, the essence of which he can describe as "the recognition by judges that behind the formal fiat of the statute lay an aim that challenged their sympathetic attention, and that the appropriate exercise of judicial power permitted courts to advance ends so emphatically asserted" we must now see.

The strict, literal meaning of a statute may be extended, but only slightly extended, through use of the doctrine of the statute's equity. The statute of 1 Hen. V, c. 3, provided an action against forgers of false deeds "by which the titles and possessions of others be disturbed." In 1426 it was held that the action lay against one who had forged a deed which disturbed the defendant's title to a reversion but did not affect his possession since he had not entered. In the words of Martin, J., "although the statute speaks of one disturbed in possession and title nevertheless, by its equity, he will be aided by the statute," and this was the opinion of the whole court.[26] The action of waste is given by the Statute of Gloucester, c. 5, against tenants by the curtesy, for life, for years or in dower; it was necessary to resort to the equity of the statute to hold it applicable to one who is tenant for but half a year,[27] or for twenty weeks.[28] Westminster II, c. 3, gives the action of *cui in vita* to a wife whose husband has alienated her heritage during coverture: the statute read "after the death of her husband," but by the equity a woman whose husband was still alive but whose marriage had been dissolved by divorce was permitted the action.[29] An action was given by Westminster II, c. 11, against a jailer who lets out of his prison one committed to his custody for arrears of account, by its equity it is regarded as permitting an action against the jailer if a person committed in condemnation of debt is released.[30] The statute of 4 Edw. III, c. 7, gave an action of trespass *de bonis asportatis* to ex-

---

[26] Y. B. 4 Hen. VI, Trin. 4; Fitzherbert, *Forger de faux faits*, 1; Y. B. 15 Edw. IV, Pasch. 5 (1476); Brooke, *Forger de Faits*, 14.
[27] Brooke, *General Brief* 15; LITT. §67. 2 INST. 302.
[28] Plowd., 467.
[29] Y. B. 14 Hen. VII, Hil. 7 (1499).
[30] Y. B. 15 Edw. IV, Hil. 8, at 20.

ecutors, administrators were included by the equity.[31] The act of
13 Rich. II, c. 17, gives receipt for feint pleading, by its equity receipt for feint defending may be had.[32] These extensions of the
statute's words are simple and reasonable. They mention legislative intent only in passing, and it is promptly resolved into and
equated with reason. Surely they recognize nothing behind the
formal fiat of the statute but its patent inability to provide properly
for the case in hand. Halting extensions such as these offer little
more support for the broad doctrine enunciated by Plowden—
"When the words of a Statute enact one Thing, they enact all other
Things which are in a like degree"—than do the cases cited by Coke
in support of his own theory that "the Common Law will control
Acts of Parliament and sometimes adjudge them to be utterly
void."[33] But though they do not support the theory in its large
sense, they may seem to support it in some measure, and therefore
it is necessary to refer to the cases that militate sharply against it.

As Mr. Landis recognizes, definite principles as to the circumstances which would justify extending statutes beyond the scope of
their language did not evolve. Rather there. was simply the urge
to do equity by permitting the judge to handle the statute according to his customary process of juridical logic. But there are traces
of a very definite theory as to the circumstances in which a statute
will *not* be extended. There is an interesting exchange in 1499.

> *Kingsmill*— . . . Where a statute abridges the common law nothing
> will be taken by its equity. This statute abridges the law . . . *Con-
> ingsby*—On the contrary, this statute is made to eliminate delays . . .
> for it enlarges the common law . . . and if so, should be taken largely,
> and cases in the same mischief included by the equity. But if a statute
> abridges the common law or is penal, there nothing will be taken by
> the equity.[34]

The report is a long and instructive one and both serjeants and
judges seem agreed upon the statement that a statute which
abridges the common law or is penal will not be extended beyond
its words by equitable interpretation, though upon the question of
whether or not the particular statute under consideration fell within
either of these classes there was violent disagreement. There are
many formulations of this rule in the cases. In 1479 there is an
interesting case upon the voucher to warranty of the husband's heir

---

[31] Y. B. 3 Hen. VI, Mich. 18 (1425); Y. B. 11 Hen. IV, Hil. 20 (1410); Y. B.
14 Hen. VII, Hil. 2 (1499); *ibid.*, Hil. 7 (1499).

[32] Plowd., 53.

[33] Plucknett, *Bonham's Case and Judicial Review* (1926) 40 Harv. L. Rev. 30;
McILWAIN, THE HIGH COURT OF PARLIAMENT (1910) 286 *ff.*

[34] Y. B. 14 Hen. VII, Hil. 7.

by the alienee under Westminster II, c. 40. Under the old law,[35] the alienee could vouch the husband's heir to warranty and then the action would demur until the heir was of age—usually a considerable period, the alienee retaining the land in the interim. The statute removed a great hardship by enacting that in such case the widow shall receive seisin at once, and "let the purchaser (who ought not to have been ignorant that he was buying the right of another) tarry until the vouchee is of age." The question arose as to whether the statute applied only to the first purchaser who bought direct from the husband or to all subsequent purchasers. William Huse, who was appointed chief justice of the King's Bench three years later, allowed himself the following remarks:

". . . it was adjudged (in an earlier case) that he (the subsequent purchaser) is out of the case of the statute, for the statute is *caveat emptor,* which does not extend, for the statute restrains the common law and will be taken *stricti juris.*"[36]

And in 1506, Rede, J., spoke to the same effect:

"No equity can be taken of statutes in abridgment of the common law; forcible entry is given by the statute for land but will not extend to rent, for forcible entry for rent cannot be taken by the equity because the statute is in abridgment of the common law. *Et issint clere opinion des Justices.*"[37]

There are not a few cases that state this rule,[38] and under it, only those statutes in affirmance of the common law, or in other words, statutes that embody the already existing common law rule, and those which extend an existing common law remedy, may be used (as a case might be) as the basis for analogy. Nothing could be further than this from Mr. Landis' view of the equity of a statute, and the instances cited likewise must give pause to those who adhere to Dean Pound's widely-accepted view that the doctrine that statutes in derogation of the common law are to be strictly construed is a product of late eighteenth-century thought.[39] Dean

---

[35] PLUCKNETT, STATUTES AND THEIR INTERPRETATION (1922) 59.

[36] Y. B. 18 Edw. VI, Mich. 18 (1479). Andrew Ognel's Case, 4 Rep. 50a. 2 INST. 455.

[37] Y. B. 21 Hen. VII, Hil. 28.

[38] Y. B. 7 Hen. VI, Mich. 16 (1429). Y. B. 11 Hen. VI, Trin. 23. Y. B. 5 Edw. IV (Long Quinto) 62 (1466). Y. B. 5 Hen. VII, Mich. 11 (1490). Y. B. 7 Hen. VII, Pasch. 2 (1492). Y. B. 14 Hen. VII, Hil. 2 (1499). In the unpaged appendix to Ashe's EPIEIKEIA which consists of cases reported by Dalison, J., and Serjeant Bendloe "queux concerne lexposition descun statutes per Equitie" many cases similar to those mentioned above are printed.

[39] We print Mr. Landis' (*op. cit. supra* note 1, 235) note 11 to orientate the reader. "The doctrine that statutes in derogation of the common law are to be strictly construed was a product of late eighteenth-century thought. Its first

Pound finds that Plowden and Coke do not require and are no warrant for a doctrine of judicial antipathy toward legislation, and the interpretation of these authorities as establishing a presumption of legislative intent not to interfere with the common law a nineteenth century one. But the line between antipathy and refusal to extend is not a wide one, especially when we remember the drastic limitation and narrow compass of statutes denied equitable interpretation.

There is no clear distinction in the Year Books between statutes in derogation of the common law and penal statutes: statutes which take away some right a litigant might have had at common law frequently are considered penal. But with respect to statutes that are penal in our use of the word there is complete agreement that such statutes will not be extended by equity. Thus, a statute which inflicts a penalty upon malefactors in parks will not extend to malefactors in forests,[40] and one that makes it penal for the sheriff to lease his county will not be extended to him if he leases but part of his county.[41] An excellent, if drastic, example of this rigorous doctrine in action may be seen in the early sixteenth century, thirty-five years before *Heydon's Case*. The statute of 37 Hen. VIII, c. 8, took the benefit of clergy from one who stole any horse; the statute of 1 Edw. VI, c. 12, enacted that those who were attainted of stealing *horses* should not have their clergy, but that in all other cases of felony, attainted persons should have their clergy. The second statute was regarded as abrogating the first, and he who had stolen but one horse was permitted his clergy. The matter was settled by the passage of the act of 2 Edw. VI, c. 33, which ousted of his clergy he who had stolen one horse only.[42]

There can have been but little sympathy for logic-chopping interpretation of this kind and an effort is made a few years later, in the Hilary term of 1553, to escape its rigors. Though all the judges

announcement seems to have been in Ash v. Abdy, 3 Swanst. 664, decided in 1678 but not reported until 1819; in America it found its first expression in Brown v. Barry, 3 Dall. 365 (U. S. 1797). See Pound, *Common Law and Legislation* (1908) 21 Harv. L. Rev. 383, 400. Professor Allen attempts to date the attitude back to the origins of common law. See ALLEN, LAW IN THE MAKING (2d ed. 1930) 268 n.2. The spirit as distinguished from the letter of its foundation, cannot, however, be regarded as dominating judicial thinking until the period indicated by Dean Pound."

[40] Y. B. 21 Hen. VII, Pasch. 8 (1506).

[41] Y. B. 20 Hen. VII, Mich. 22; Y. B. 21 Hen. VII, Mich. 45 (1506). Y. B. 14 Hen. VII, Hil. 2: "*Hody*, C. B.— . . . for I have never seen anything taken by the equity of a penal statute . . . *Brian*—Nothing will be taken by the equity of the statute for two reasons: one, because it is penal, and nothing is taken by the equity, as Hody says, secondly, because statutes which give attaints never are extended by equity . . ." Other judges spoke to the same effect.

[42] Plowd., 467.

agreed that the statute "should not be taken by equity, for it is a penal statute" yet it was argued by Coke that

"by the statute of 25 Edw. III it is declared that if a servant kill his master it is treason. And in 19 Hen. VI [Mich. 102] one was arraigned upon an indictment for killing the wife of his master, and he confessed, and there it came in question whether he should be drawn or hanged only, whereupon it is to be seen whether it be treason or not, and there it was adjudged, by the advice of all the justices of the one Bench and the other [in the Exchequer Chamber] that he should be drawn and hanged, because it was treason; and there it is not taken within the equity of the statute, which speaks only of killing his master, but it is rather within the words of the statute, for master and mistress are the same thing in effect. So that there the taking it to be treason is a declaration of the words of the statute rather than an equitable construction of it."[43]

The matter was further expounded by Hales, J., in a manner suspiciously reminiscent of the *interpretatio declarativa* of the civilians.

"The plural number contains in itself the singular number and more. And therefore the statute of 1 Henry V, c. 3 recites 'that whereas some people do of late use to forge divers false deeds and muniments, etc.,' therefore it ordains that the party thereby grieved shall have his suit in that case, etc., here the statute speaks of false deeds in the plural number, yet if a man forge one deed, he shall be punished by the statute. So the statute of 5 Rich. II, c. 7 ordains, 'that none shall make entry into any lands and tenements, except in case where entry is given by law,' yet if a man enters into one tenement, he shall be punished notwithstanding the statute is in the plural number."

No further mention of the matter can be found and therefore we may not know how this theory was received. But it is clear that no modern theory of statutory interpretation is in the minds of the justices. If it is matter for doubt and debate whether the statute should be extended by equity from the singular to the plural number and *vice versa,* how much more doubtful must we feel of a statement that "situations to which the statutory remedy was expressly made applicable were but illustrative of other analogous cases that deserve to be governed by the same principle?"

We come finally to the celebrated rules in *Heydon's Case.*[44]

---

[43] Partridge v. Strange and Croker, Plowd., 77, 86.

[44] 3 Rep. 7a: "It was resolved by the Barons of the Exchequer that for the sure and true interpretation of all statutes in general (be they penal or beneficial, restrictive or enlarging of the Common Law) four things are to be discussed and considered: 1st, What was the Common Law before the making of the Act; 2nd, What was the mischief and defect for which the Common Law did not provide; 3rd, What remedy the Parliament hath resolved and appointed to cure the disease of the commonwealth; and 4th, The true reason of the remedy; and then the office of all the judges is always to make such construction as shall suppress

They are not new—Plowden had anticipated them years earlier—but in the light of the tyrannically strict theory of interpretation we have sketched above they are revealed in their true light. They represent an effort to substitute *Sinnauslegung* for the mechanical *Wortauslegung* that was current judicial theory. They are phrased in very wide terms, and on their face may seem to envisage the idyllic picture they are said to describe. But that picture is brought by the words only to a modern mind. Their kernel lies in the fourth rule—"the true reason of the remedy"—the purpose of the remedy—the *Sinn* of the remedy. The rules cannot be taken anachronistically as an early effort to inculcate in judges a view that the statute revealed an attitude that the appropriate exercise of judicial power permitted courts to advance. Courts had not yet reached the stage of looking beyond a statute's *words*. Two hundred and fifty years will elapse before Baron Parke enunciates his golden rule of statutory interpretation, narrow as it is.[45] The resolutions in *Heydon's Case* are instead much closer to what courts were groping toward by means of the equity of the statute: an understanding of the *ratio legis* rather than the *ratio verborum,* an effort to make the interpretation of statutes, whether they be phrased in the singular or plural, something more than merely a grammatical exercise. The words, and not their sense, had heretofore absorbed complete attention: *Heydon's Case* points toward another side, and gives a rule of thumb for illuminating the words by reference to that which they are to do. The choice is not the modern one between what a statute said and what a statute intended to do, but rather between what it said in abstract, *in vacuo,* so to speak, and what it intended to do. It is needless, as Professor Plucknett has pointed out in another connection, to pretend that it is easy to think in these unfamiliar dimensions, and it may be urged that the distinction put forward here is a distinction without a difference. Nevertheless we think it one of much importance and one too frequently overlooked.

Let us turn to the case itself. The statute of 31 Hen. VIII, c. 13, as quoted by Coke, provided that "if any abbot, etc., or other re-

---

the mischief and advance the remedy, and to suppress subtle inventions and evasions for continuance of the mischief, and *pro privato commodo,* and to add force and life to the cure and remedy according to the true intent of the makers of the Act *pro bono publico.*"

[45] Becke v. Smith, 2 M. & W. 191, 195 (1836): "It is a very useful rule in the construction of a statute to adhere to the ordinary meaning of the words used, and to the grammatical construction, unless that is at variance with the intention of the Legislature to be collected from the statute itself, or leads to any manifest absurdity or repugnance, in which case the language may be varied or modified so as to avoid such inconvenience, but no further."

ligious and ecclesiastical house or place . . . make any lease or grant for life, or for term of years, of any manors, messuages, lands, etc., and in the which any estate or interest for life, year or years . . . then had his being or continuance . . . every such lease shall be utterly void." It would be difficult to find an act whose purpose is as evident as that of this Suppression Act of 1539. This *ratio legis,* if no other, was known to all, even to the common lawyers, and likewise it was common knowledge that the monasteries were evading the provisions of the act wherever possible. The Abbot of Dieulacres caused blank forms to be prepared, sealed with the convent seal, on which (when the Commissioners were out of the way) leases were subsequently made out, much to the benefit of his own family. The manor of Rialton was leased by the prior of Bodmin Priory to his brother for ninety-nine years. The monks of Newenham by means of a disused seal (the real one having been removed by the Commissioners) could grant leases long after the dissolution.[46] Yet there was great doubt, in Coke's words, "whether a copyhold estate . . . at the will of the lord, according to the custom of the said manor, should in judgment of law be called an estate and interest for lives, within the said general words and meaning of the said act." Though Coke does not give the debates, we may assume that they centered around the fact that the statute clearly abridged the common law, and as such was to be strictly construed, for before the statute religious and ecclesiastical persons might have made leases for as many years as they pleased, and also about the nice problem of whether a copyhold estate fell within the statute's provisions. For although a copyholder had in judgment of law but an estate at will, yet custom had so established and fixed his estate that he possessed many advantages, and for most practical purposes he was owner of an estate, subject only to services analogous to the services due from a great deal of other land.[47] It was not a violent extension to provide, as did the Barons, that "when an act of Parliament is generally made for the good of the weal public, and no prejudice can accrue by reason of alteration of any interest, service, tenure or custom of the manor, there many times copyhold and customary estates are within the general purview of such acts." If in the course of the case they took occasion to lay down rules of statutory interpretation, we may be sure that these rules are not completely unconnected with the case in

---

[46] Baskerville, *The Dispossessed Religious After the Suppression of the Monasteries* in ESSAYS IN HISTORY PRESENTED TO R. L. POOLE (1927) 436, 447-48.

[47] 3 Holdsworth, HISTORY OF ENGLISH LAW (1923) 206-13; 7 *id.* at 296-312. Y. B. 13 Rich. II (Ames Foundation) xxxiv-xliii.

hand: that of a restrictive statute viewed in the light of a very clear and apparent *ratio legis*. That they thought it necessary to recite these very wide rules is itself an interesting commentary upon the strict rule of interpretation we have spoken of above at length.

Prior to *Heydon's Case* we find no effort to extend statutes (except those in affirmation of an already existing common law rule) beyond their literal word content in the light of what they were intended to do. *Heydon's Case* itself extends a statute only slightly, and that in view of an apparent and exceptionally clear *ratio legis*. After the case we similarly can find no insistence upon purpose distinguished from words: the meaning of the statute continues to be gathered from its words as they stand, and the process of interpretation is confined to the grammatical or literal meaning of the text. This may be due to the fact that what the Barons were saying was something little different from Baron Parke's rule. It took many years before their successors finally achieved it, and when they did, the conception of the separation of powers had changed both it and that to which it applied, but there is a steady and continuous growth that must not be lost from view. It is a pleasant picture Mr. Davies draws of eighteenth century judges interpreting deeds, but it is not necessary to posit them to explain the change from the earlier rules of interpretation laid down by Plowden and Coke. There is always the possibility that there was no change and that the old rules were also the new.

12

SOVEREIGNTY AND THE CONFLICT OF LAWS

Much has been written on the history of the conflict of laws, or, as it is known on the Continent, on the history of private international law, but in a very real sense the subject is the product of, and first makes its appearance in, the sixteenth century. Though traditionally it is said to have had its origin in the ancient world, and to have flourished in thirteenth and four-teenth century Italy and France, the appearance of the idea of sovereignty marks not a stage in its development, as is usually believed, but the beginning of it. Nevertheless, since everything must have a history, a history stretching back into antiquity has been provided for it. The same is true of the subject of statutory interpretation, as that is understood in England and in the United States, and, indeed, the two subjects are more closely connected than is sometimes realized. It was only in the sixteenth century that statutes began to occupy in England a position roughly com-parable to that which they hold today. It was then that judges first became conscious that in restricting the words of an act in the interests of justice, or in extending them to include equally deserving but unmentioned cases, they were performing something more than an incidental, routine function of judicial administra-tion. As parliament slowly became the sovereign, the task of the judge slowly became that of merely determining what parliament had said and applying it. This was a change that did not take place at once, but the steadily increasing necessity for reconciling the words of acts of parliament and the simple administration of justice between party and party had, by the sixteenth century, set judicial practice off sharply from that which had preceded it. The juridical and constitutional questions latent in the application of statute law were not as yet acute, but they were becoming sufficiently manifest to transform the courts' treatment of legisla-tion into a practice to which the term « interpretation » is pro-perly applicable, and it is in no sense accidental that the word is first commonly used in the sixteenth century to describe the judicial handling of statutes. It was at that time that the first treatises on statutory interpretation appeared.

So with the conflict of laws. That law is the articulation of the will of a legal sovereign is a conception that begins to appear on the European continent at the end of the middle ages. Law is no longer simply justice, nor is it solely the duty of a judge to do justice between the persons who appear before him, by applying the law that seems best under the circumstances. He must reconcile justice in the individual case with the fact that the law of a foreign state can have no effect within the state in which he acts. It is at once evident that to solve all questions by the law of the forum is unreasonable and unjust. On the other hand, a judge is empowered, as the officer of a state, to apply only the law of that state. It therefore only then became necessary to create the subject we know as the conflict of laws, for if the law of the forum and the foreign law involved were in agreement, no difficulties were raised. Nor is it in any sense an accident that the first treatises on the subject then appear.

The English parallel is a most instructive one, and to make my point clear I must first present that.

In England, prior to the sixteenth century, it was quite clear that all statutes did not bind all persons within its borders. Citizens of London, tenants on the ancient demesne of the crown, residents of Ireland, strangers and aliens, were often said not to be bound by parliamentary acts. On the other hand, some statutes clearly did bind them. Whether a statute did or did not bind those on the ancient demesne of the crown, for example, depended solely upon considerations of private law: if the statute took away the rights of those resident there, or in other words, if it led to an unjust result, it was said not to extend to ancient demesne; other statutes, if they led to no injustice, were said to extend to such persons. What was here controlling was the specific content of the enactment in question. Of course, more general theories occasionally made their appearance. For example, that a particular act of parliament did not apply in ancient demesne was once in the fifteenth century accounted for on the ground that tenants there were not parties to the making of the statute. But though this was clearly true, they were bound by other acts, to which they had not been parties, nor is to certain that if they had been represented in the parliament, as citizens of London were, that every general statute enacted there would have bound them. Abstract thinking about statutes did not play an important role in the cases, for in most instances discussion was restricted simply to the specific content of the enactment in question, and its effect upon the customary rights of those in ancient demesne, without reference to any general theory of statutes and their application. That the privileges of the tenant would be infringed, or the lord disinherited, was itself sufficient reason for holding an action unavailable in ancient demesne, and the problem presented by a statutory remedy was not distinguished by contemporaries from that raised when a common law action was held to be inapplicable. The infrequent appearance of theory makes it impossible to regard it as anything more than an occasional, ad hoc explanation for results that could be secured without its aid, and the inadequacy of the theories put forward indicates that private law considerations, those of *meum* and *tuum*, were actually controlling. The attention of judges was directed primarily to the simple administration of justice between party and party. Thus if a statute led to a legally reasonable result it extended to ancient demesne; if it infringed rights or produced injustice there, it did not. Under such circumstances, the difficulties involved in denying application of a statute which included no exemption of ancient demesne did not arise. That tenants there were not bound by some general statutes did not disturb the lawyers of the fifteenth century, whose thoughts moved wholly within the frame of private law, and they thus felt themselves under no obligation to provide an adequate solution of problems that still lay in the future. Nor do the cases themselves exhibit any effort to regard their rulings as « exceptions out » of statutes made by judges, to draw a distinction between the words of an act and the intention of its makers, or to reconcile in other ways the fact that ancient demesne was unaffected by some statutes and the maxim « everyone is bound by an act of parliament ».

With the appearance of a more modern attitude toward statutes in the sixteenth century, a change may be detected in the judicial approach to legislation. It was now admitted that express words in a statute can bind ancient demesne, but that all acts of parliament bound it was not yet understood, for whether a general statute might have that same effect remained doubtful.

The distinction between general and express statutes, which stressed not the content but the form of the enactment, marks an unmistakable departure from the approach customary earlier, but it was itself transitional. A more tenable position was advanced in the middle sixteenth century- « by generall wordes in a statute, pryvate mens interestes be not taken awaie, notwthstandinge that which is commenlye sayde, that everye man ys partie & privie to an acte of Parlemente». Thus, an act phrased in general terms will not destroy private rights in ancient demesne, but the language used leaves it doubtful whether ancient demesne was was bound by the act and excepted from its operation, or whether the statute did not extend to it. To contemporaries such a distinction, if not unintelligibile, was unnecessary, and was not made. But it was becoming difficult to deny that all statutes, regardless of their effect or the form in which they were drawn, bound ancient demesne, and thus is became correspondingly evident that « pryvate mens interestes » were protected there, not because general statutes did not extend to it, nor because residents there were unrepresented in parliament, but solely through judicial « exceptions out » of statutes.

Whether courts may exempt a particular area or a definite class of persons from the operation of an act of parliament was a question that had not arisen earlier, nor had discussions concerned with it appeared in the reports. No judge or serjeant had regarded the non-extension of an act to ancient demesne as an « exception out » of the statute, accomplished through the exercise of judicial discretion, for to say that ancient demesne was bound by an enactment but saved from its operation is a refinement, superfluous in a private law scheme, for which no contemporary support can be found, indeed, as been pointed out, explanations were sought in other quarters. But as the necessity arises of reconciling the attainment of a just result in a particular instance with new political and juridical principles, that distinction is adopted. Though judges had not looked to an « exposition » or « construction » of the act, made in the light of reason or general convenience, to account for the fact that some statutory provisions were not available against tenants on the ancient demesne of the crown, yet, as the sanction behind parliamentary enactments is stressed and the doctrine that « everyone is bound by an act of parliament » makes its way, that approach becomes common. As

the fact gradually becomes clear that all parliamentary enactments bound ancient demesne, residents of Ireland, citizens of
London, and strangers and aliens, there was a corresponding alteration in the distinction between general and express statutes.
First stated objectively- such persons are not bound by general
statutes- it was then modified in the light of growing parliamentary sovereignty into the narrower, transitional rule that general
words in an act do not destroy private rights, and finally assumed
its modern form, in the phrasing of which the completed change
in emphasis is apparent: statutes which encroach upon private
rights must be cautiously regarded by judges and general words
therein strictly construed.

This development has its exact parallel in the medieval law of
Italy and France. It was often said that the statutes of a commune do not extend to strangers, and the majority of the post-
Glossators and canonists refused to make such persons subject to
all the laws of the territory in which they happened to be. They
were, however, bound by some of its statutes, and thus there, as
in England, the distinction was made on the grounds of justice.
Whether a local statute did or did not bind a stranger from another commune depended upon whether its application led to a
just result or to an unjust one. The specific content of the enactment was controlling, and there was, in fact, no need for a general
theory of statutes, though such theories occasionally appeared.
It was said, for example, that each person is governed by the
laws of the community to which he belongs, not those of the place
in which he is temporarily resident, but such theories must not
be thought to be the basis upon which the decisions rested, for
they were inadequate and only partial explanations of results
reached on private law grounds alone. Only in the sixteenth century, with the development of territorial sovereignty, do all
strangers become subject to the laws of the city in which they are,
and only then does it become impossible to say that the acts of
a territorial sovereign do not extend to them. If they were to be
saved from the operation of local law, especially where, when
applied to them, it led to an unjust result, they had now to be
excepted by a judicial interpretation of the act. This power of
judges to except persons out of the operation of an act was
itself to be progressively curtailed, as I shall show in a moment.

To return once again to my English parallel- in the fourteenth

century an enactment might be radically supplement by reading
into it provisions that were wholly judicial in origin, yet for such
actions judges did not feel it necessary to offer apologies, nor
do explanations of any sort appear. Alterations of this kind
were not regarded as interferences with legislative power, and
thus *ultra vires* acts to be explained only in the light of a broad
judicial discretion, but instead as an integral and in no way
exceptional part of the judges' task, which had for its objects
the reaching of legally sound results and the proper administration of justice between litigants. If the words of an act supplied
a remedy for one complex of facts but did not provide for a
comparable situation that deserved equal treatment, no difficulty
was experienced in achieving justice by permitting the same result
in the analogous case. To describe this process in terms of
conflicting legislative and judicial authority, or, in other words,
to visualize it as an illustration of the power of the judiciary to
supplement legislative fiat, is to conceive it in modern and therefore anachronistic form. It was simply a facet of the administration of justice and reflects nothing more than the familar medieval
definition of equity and the maxim *de similibus idem est iudicium*.
Under such circumstances, definite principles indicative of the
factors that must be present for an unmentioned situation to
be remedied by a statute did not evolve. If a useful result could
be reached, a case might be brought within an act that had not
dealt with it in express terms. It is sometimes said that analogous
cases are not to be taken by the equity of penal statutes, or that
statutes in derogation of common right, or those that restrained
or abridged the common law, were to be taken strictly, but such
remarks must not be given undue prominence, for the decisions
in fact turned only on the answer to these questions: Is the
case in the same mischief as that for which the statute was provided? Is the result a legally reasonable and beneficial one? That a
statute was penal or abridged the common law did not mean
that it must necessarily be denied extension. These categories
supplied a useful rule of thumb, and the cases in which extension
was denied undoubtedly fell within them, but an act must be
taken strictly only when a liberal application led to an undesirable
result. This absence of rules is characteristic of the judicial approach to legislation in a private law scheme.

In the sixteenth century, when the words of parliamentary

acts begin to take on the appearance of sovereign commands and were no longer to be handled in essentially the same manner as common law rules, explanations became necessary for the extension of an act to analogous cases. Such may be made in the light of a controlling *Equitas*, « which is no part of the law but a moral virtue which corrects the law ». Or if the statutes confirm the common law they may be extended just as the common law itself may be. Statutes which broaden a common law remedy may, by the same token, be further extended. Where the common law had not dealt with a situation at all, the « reason » of the statute might unaided serve to extend it to similar but unmentioned cases, since « ratio legis est anima legis ».

As acts of parliament take on the attributes of modern legislation, the intention of the legislator must grow in importance and take the place of the equity, conjectured purpose, or reason that had controlled earlier. It is in the middle years of the sixteenth century that the intention of the makers begins to form the justification for extending a statute beyond its words. The phrase « the cases which are in the same mischief as those which are remedied by the statute are taken by the equity of that statute », and other variations of the maxim *ubi eadem est ratio ibi idem jus*, then gave way to another- « for everything that is within the intent of the makers of the act, although it be not within the letter, is as strongly within the act as that which is within the letter and intent also ». The words, « the intention of the makers » did not immediately lead to results contrary to, or more limited than, those that had been reached earlier by « equity » or by reliance on the general purpose of the act or the ratio legis. Indeed, they were all methods for reaching the same end. But legislative intent narrows progressively in scope and becomes less clearly identified with the « advancement of truth » or the « conservation of tranquillity, peace and concord » as the the seventeenth century advances, and by the eighteenth we have reached the rule that parliament having spoken only of specific things and specific situations, all others were *casus omissi* within the maxim *casus omissus habetur pro omisso*. As parliament became the sovereign and the duty of the judge was recognized to be merely to determine what parliament has said and to apply it, omitted particulars could no longer be supplied, since that would amount to a usurpation of, or encroachment upon, the power of the legislature. This was a view of the judicial function that differed fundamentally from that which had prevailed earlier.

I have been concerned with the extension of statutes to analogous cases. I now turn to the converse operation of imposing limitations upon them. Prior to the sixteenth century in England there was no difficulty in disregarding an enactment which, though reasonable and practicable in general, led to injustice in a particular instance. Despite the words of the act, the situation presented for decision was said to be simply « extra casum statuti ». The attention of the English judges of the period was directed primarily to the attainment of a practical and legally sound result and, administering justice as they did wholly within the ambit of private law, they were in no way troubled by the difficulties that would subsequently be raised. No principle of jurisprudence or political theory that might serve as an explanation for the disregard of the words of a parliamentary enactment was offered, nor did the reporters note these cases as especially important or distinguish them in any other way from the other adjudications of *meum* and *tuum* they set down in their books.

The growing sanction back of parliamentary enactments that appears in the sixteenth century may be seen both in the more complex explanations used to account for the restriction of statutory words and in the recognition of judicial « interpretation », which is understood in a very wide sense as the power to bring acts of parliament into the fullest possible accord with substantial justice. Thus it may be said straightforwardly that « those that are out of the mischief of a statute are likewise out of the compass of the statute » ; that a statute must be taken « contrary to its words » or « against the text » to avoid injustice; and that statutes are to be read in the light of convenience and reason, or, in other words, so understood that neither injustice nor absurdity ensues. A distinction was often drawn, as well, between the words of an act and its « meaning », « reason » or « sense ». It as also possible to justify restrictive construction by reference to the intention of the makers, behind which lie the presumptions that the legislature acts according to reason and does not intend harsh or harmful results. These concepts permitted a good deal of freedom, but by the opening of the seventeenth century it could no longer be easily said that a case presented for decision did not fall within the intent of the makers of the act, for by that time the facile and frequently drawn distinctions between words and meaning and words and intention had become less common. It became more and more necessary as the century advanced to adhere to the plain language of an enactment, even though the result was an unjust one. That it was such was now no longer the fault of the judge, for his task was simply to apply what the legal sovereign had enacted. As I remarked before, this was a view of the judicial function that differed fundamentally from that which had prevailed earlier.

Now in fourteenth century Italy, just as judges were at liberty to extend or restrict the words of an enactment in order to obtain a just result, so they were able to apply the law of a foreign commune. Neither of these operations was regarded as anything more than an incidental, routine function of judicial administration. Consequently, the problems such actions would later raise, when the doctrine of territorial sovereignty had established itself, were not as yet troublesome. If a contract had been drawn at Pisa and was sued on in Perugia, it was only just that its validity be judged by the law of the place where it had been made. If such a contract did not meet the requirements necessary in Perugia, but had been properly drawn under Pisan law, it was eminently reasonable that Pisan law should be applied. At a late date this would be regarded as giving the law of Pisa extraterritorial effect, but in the fourteenth century, in the absence of any necessity for reconciling the simple administration of justice between party and party with any theory of territorial sovereignty, that was not yet so. Put in other words, the judicial function had not yet been confined to applying the law of the judge's state only, but was still essentially that of doing justice under the circumstances. Discussion was restricted simply to the specific content of the foreign enactment and whether its application or that of local law was preferable, thus raising no issues of conflicts of law. It is true that glosses dealing with the application of foreign law were usually hung on the lex Cunctos populos, the famous initial text of the Codex, but that was not always so nor must any special significance be attached to it. The glosses were written from a point of view so different from that of private international law- using that term in the sense it has had since the sixteenth century- and in a spirit so alien to it, that it is only in the reflected light of a later age that they appear to be writings on the conflict of laws at all. So with the theories-theories classifying statutes into personal and real, odious and beneficial, affirmative and negative, were numerous, and were to have a long history, but they were inadequate and not in any sense controlling, being essentially ad hoc explanations for results secured without their aid. Working wholly within a private law scheme, it was on principles of what is right and just that Bartolus established his rules, which have lasted from his day to our own despite the advent of territorial sovereignty and a complete change in outlook. The results they achieved directly had later to be obtained through a doctrine of comity, then by one of vested rights, but the essential rules remained. Let me put them before you.

Contracts: a contract is governed, both as to its form and its intrinsic validity, by the law of the place where it was made; but in all that has to do with performance it is governed by the place of performance. *Wrongs*: torts and crimes are governed by the lex loci delicti, except where a foreigner may plead ignorance of an unusual local law. *Wills*: wills are governed as to their form by the law of the place where the instrument was made; as to testamentary capacity by the lex domicilii. A will good by the proper law passes property everywhere, even in a place by the law of which the will is not valid. Conversely, a will not valid by the proper law passes the inheritance nowhere, even in a place to the law of which the will conforms. *Property*: the regulation of property is according to the law of the situs; this law applies to and determines the validity of any attempted transfer of the property made in another place. *Judgments*: ordinary foreign judgments are freely executed upon property within the state. Penal judgments, however, are not executed in another state, though they run against property alone. If the judgment has affected the status of the guilty party, that status remains though he go into another place. *Procedure*: all matters of form of action and procedure are governed by the law of the forum. With regard to statutes- statutes regulating the form of an act, or giving power to an officer, cannot operate beyond the territory. An act done in conformity with the statute within the territory, however, is valid outside as well as within it. Statutes regulating dealings with real property apply only to property within the territory; but as to such property they apply to dealings outside as well as within the territory. Statutes regulating the capacity or status of persons are governed by the personal law; those that are beneficial follow the citizen wherever he goes, but those that are odious apply within the state only.

By the sixteenth century, the theory of territorial sovereignty had established itself, and it was the work of the jurists of the Netherlands to apply that doctrine to the conflict of laws. Ulric Huber, the author of the brief treatise « De conflictu legum » published in the seventeenth century, is, at least for English and American lawyers, the great name in the Dutch school. He was a positivist who stated fearlessly what he believed to be the law. He saw that the recognition and enforcement of foreign law depended upon the assent of the state called upon to recognize or enforce the alleged right. A foreign law could have no effect ipso jure outside the territory of the state whose law it was; it had to be recognized or accepted, that is, incorporated, by the law of the forum. His view was stated in three self-evident axioms, which are, first: that the laws of a state apply within its territory and bind all those subject thereto, but do not bind them beyond its limits; second, that all persons within the limits of a territory, whether they live there permanently or temporarily, are deemed to be subject to its laws; third, that sovereigns will so act by way of comity that rights within a territory will be recognized as having their effect everywhere, in so far as the power or law of another state or its citizens are not prejudiced thereby. Thus, as Huber explains, the law of conflicts of law must be derived not merely from the civil law but from the needs and tacit consent of nations, since, though the laws of one nation cannot directly have force in another, nevertheless nothing could be more inconvenient for commerce and general international practice than to invalidate elsewhere what is valid by the law of the country in which the transaction took place.

Though there had been anticipations of it for almost a century, this was a complete change in theory. In practical result, however, the change was not great. In an earlier day it had been said that for some purposes citizens of Pisa were not bound by the law of Perugia when they were temporarily resident there. That was no longer true under the territorial theory, for all persons within the territory were bound. But strangers temporarily resident were « excepted out » of statutes by judicial discretion if it was unjust to hold them to some unusual local law. Similarly, for some purposes the law of Pisa had been regarded as effective with relation to citizens of Pisa when they were outside its territory. Under Huber's theory that could no longer be said, but a Pisan statute regulating status or capacity, for example, would be given effect in another city when a citizen of Pisa was concerned on grounds of comity.

Huber's theory departed from that of an earlier time by dealing with statutes as a group, without regard to their content. Nor could they any longer be treated on a purely private law plane, for it was now necessary to reconcile justice in individual cases with political theory, with the idea of territorial sovereignty- a reconciliation to be achieved through the idea of comity. The law of a state can, by reason of its own inherent force, have no extra-territorial operation, but it may be recognized as applicable by the courts of the state in which the action is brought.

This was also the position adopted by Joseph Story in his great work on the conflict of laws, published in 1834, the influence of which in England and in the United States can scarcely be overestimated. « Before entering upon any examination of the various heads which a treatise upon the Conflict of Laws will naturally embrace », he said, « it seems necessary to advert to a few general maxims or axioms which constitute the basis upon which all reasonings on the subject must necessarily rest; and without the express or tacit admission of which it will be found impossible to arrive at any principles to govern the conduct of nations, or to regulate the due administration of justice ».

« The first and most important general maxim or proposition is that which has been already adverted to, that every nation possesses an exclusive sovereignty and jurisdiction within its own territory. The direct consequence of this rule is, that the laws of every state affect and bind directly all property, whether real or personal, within its territory, and all persons who are resident within it, whether natural-born subjects or aliens, and also all contracts made and acts done within it. A state may, therefore, regulate the manner and circumstances under which property, whether real or personal or in action, shall be held, transmitted, bequeathed or transferred; the condition, capacity and status of all persons within it; the validity of contracts and other acts done within it; the resulting rights and duties growing out of these contracts or acts, and the remedies and modes of administering justice in all cases calling for the interposition of its tribunals to protect, vindicate, and secure the wholesome agency of its own laws within its own domains».

« Another maxim or proposition is, that no state or nation can by its laws directly affect or bind property out of its own territory, or bind persons not resident therein, whether they are natural-born subjects or others. This is a natural consequence of the first proposition, for it would be wholly incompatible with the equality and exclusiveness of the sovereignty of all nations, that any one nation should be at liberty to regulate either persons or things within another's territory ».

« Every nation has a right to bind its own subiects by its own laws in every other place, but the obligatory force of such laws cannot extend beyond its own territories. And if such laws are incompatible with the laws of the country where they reside, or interfere with the duties which they owe to the country where they reside, it will be disregarded by the latter. Whatever may be the obligatory force of such laws upon such persons if they should return to their native country, they can have none in other nations where they reside. They may give rise to personal relations between the sovereign and subjects, to be enforced in his own domains; but they do not rightfully extend to other nations. Nor, indeed, is there, strictly speaking, any difference in this respect whether such laws concern the persons or the property of native subjects. A state has just as much intrinsic right, and no more, to give to its own laws an extraterritorial force as to the property of its subjects situated abroad as it has in relation to the persons of its subjects domiciled abroad- that is, as sovereign laws they have no obligation or power over either. When, therefore, we speak of the right of a state to bind its own native subjects everywhere, we speak only of its own claim and exercise of sovereignty over them, and not of its right to compel or require obedience to such laws on the part of other nations. On the contrary, every nation has an exclusive right to regulate persons and things within its own territory according to its own sovereign will and polity ».

« From these two maxims or propositions there flows a third, and that is, that whatever force and obligation the laws of one country have in another depends solely upon the laws and municipal regulations of the latter, that is to say, upon its own proper jurisprudence and polity, and upon its own express or tacit consent ».

Thus the laws of a country operate proprio vigore only within the limits of its own territory. Whatever extraterritorial power they have results from their voluntary recognition, on grounds of comity, by other states or countries.

These maxims did not alter the Bartolist rules that I set out a moment ago, though they explained them in a new way. Nor were they changed when, toward the end of the nineteenth century, the continued curtailment of judicial discretion and the limitations placed upon the judicial function by a strict theory of separation of powers made the idea of comity no longer acceptable. In England the classic exposition of this point of view is to be found in the work of Dicey, first published in 1896. Starting with the proposition that nothing can be law unless it is part of the municipal law of the country in which it is applied, he rejected the doctrine of comity first, because it promotes the idea that the recognition of foreign law depends upon judicial discretion; second, because it confuses the law which will be enforced, that is, the national law, with the reason for adopting a specific rule of national law. The excision of comity from the doctrines of Huber and Story left only the concept of vested rights. In Dicey's words, « The nature of a right acquired under the law of any country must be determined in accordance with the law under which the right is acquired. The basis of a plaintiff's claim is that he possesses some right. When, therefore, he applies to an English court to enforce a right acquired in France, he must show that at the moment of bringing his action he possesses a right that is actually acquired under French law. English law does not apply to transaction occurring out of England, nor does French law apply in the English courts. Hence the foundation of the claim is that the plaintiff wishes to enforce a right that has accrued to him in France. Whether such a right actually exists is a matter of fact depending upon the law of France and upon the circumstances of his case ».

In the United States this conception was followed by Beale, in both the Restatement of the Law of Conflict of Laws and in his Treatise, which constitute the most influential reformulation of the subject matter since Story's Commentaries. « Although the law to be applied to the solution of the conflict of laws is the territorial law » he says, « this does not mean the law by which such rights as those brought in question would be created within the territory. To impose a national law within territorial limits does not decree the application of that law to all the cases there arising. The national law which is applied is that portion of the national law which deals with the solution of conflicts. If by the national law the validity of a contract depends upon the law of the place where the contract was made, then that law is applied in order to determine the validity of a contract made abroad- not because the foreign law has any force in the nation, nor because of any constraint exercised by an international principle, but because the national law determines the question by the lex loci contractus. The provisions of that law having been proved as a fact, the question is solved by the national law, the foreign factor in the solution being present as mere fact- one of the facts upon which the decision is to be based ».

The vested rights theory, currently the accepted American view, having put aside any notion of comity, is closer to the fourteenth century than to the seventeenth. Indeed, the American law of private international law is closer than any other modern system to the law developed by the statutists. As Beale has pointed out, in both medieval Italy and in the United States today the ordinary law is a common law, prevailing throughout the whole territory, each state having the power to modify it by local statute. Beale himself translated the writings of Bartolus on the conflict of laws into English, and through that, and through the references in his Treatise, the work of Bartolus has become widely known to a public ordinarily ignorant of medieval law. I can do no better than end my paper with Beale's words, « While Bartolus's doctrines were fortified by the writings of his predecessors as well as by the texts of the Corpus Juris, he found in those sources only the germs of the general principles that he formulated. To him is due the entire credit for discovering and stating a body of principle on the conflict of laws which has been adopted by all civilized countries and will still repay the most careful study ».

13

ENGLISH LAW AND THE RENAISSANCE

I have chosen for the title of my paper today the precise title of Maitland's famous Rede Lecture delivered in Cambridge 60 years ago. Its thesis, as you will remember, was a simple one: that in the second quarter of the 16th century the continuity of English law was seriously endangered by a threatened reception of Roman law. Now I must say at once that in my view that thesis is completely mistaken. I do not mean that it is exaggerated, that there was a threat of reception the gravity of which Maitland over-estimated, but simply that there was no threat at all. Maitland's essay is such an attractive one, its words have so often been repeated (sometimes with and sometimes without qualification) by the most eminent, that any historian must hesitate to contradict it. When so many distinguished men have admired the Emperor's new clothes, one who sees only nakedness must look and look again. Even then he cannot be sure that it is not a deficiency of his own to which he is calling attention. Still, if we are to understand the history of English law in the 16th century, that marvelously persuasive study in historical atmospherics must first be re-examined and re-assessed.

Writing at the beginning of the modern study of English legal history, indeed himself the first begetter of that discipline, Maitland was unduly influenced, perhaps unavoidably so, by writings from a country in which the history of law had long been a well-established and respected subject. Unable to draw upon much else, it was to the impressive German literature that he had perforce to turn, and that it should leave no impress upon him in that heyday of German scholarship was manifestly impossible. It is to Stintzing and Schröder that his interest in the question of a reception may be directly traced, and it is essentially their outline, constructed abroad out of foreign materials, into which he fitted, with masterly skill, what little English evidence he could muster.

It would indeed be very curious if at the very moment when an unmistakable nationalistic note was being sounded, when Henry VIII, with Cromwell's help, and the tacit approval of a majority of his people, was establishing himself as an English *imperator in regno suo*, when the usurped authority of the bishop of Rome was being cast off under the guise of restoring traditional English liberties, that a movement should be under way to substitute an alien system of law for the native variety. As one searches unsuccessfully for evidence of Roman infiltration, or for indications of preparations for its eventual welcome, Maitland's remarkable tour de force is seen to rest solely upon but one definite statement — the well-known one put into the mouth of Reginald Pole by his secretary, Thomas Starkey.

Starkey's *Dialogue* was written between 1536 and 1538, but from the day the manuscript was presented to Henry VIII until 1878, when it was first put into print, it seems to have gone quite unnoticed. Neither in the obvious political and legal literature of the three and a half centuries that followed its composition, nor in a fair sample of the less obvious, have I been able to find a reference to it; nor have its two editors been more fortunate. In this uninfluential work, Pole's remarks on the subject of law, if indeed they are his and not Starkey's, occupy no more than a page or two. They open with a vehement and well-deserved attack on the common law. It is confused, uncertain, full of delays which cause suits to be long in decision. Process, therefore, should be made more summary. Similarly, both statutes and the reports of cases are over-many and should be reduced to manageable size by the wisdom of some politic and wise men. Furthermore, they are written in this barbarous tongue of old French, a great blot upon us, which should be removed by putting them into our mother tongue, or, preferably, into Latin. All this is straightforward enough, and no more than will be said by Francis Bacon a century later. But, his enthusiasm rising, Pole goes on to add that all these defects might be cured at once could the heads of our country be induced to receive the civil law of the Romans as the common law of England.

Now a good case can be made for the introduction into sixteenth century England of the Roman law of the Bartolists, which already was dealing competently with problems the common law would not solve before the eighteenth century. But it was not this body of doctrine, already elaborated to meet the needs of a society such as England was soon to become, that Pole and Starkey had in mind. Elegant classical scholars and academic lawyers, their Roman law was not the practical law of the Italian courts, soon to cross the Alps into Germany and be adopted there, but the new Roman law of the humanists, whose aim it was to restore the clear light of classical jurisprudence freed from the crabbed commentaries in outrageous Latin that misinterpreted and obscured it.

With this in mind, Pole's proposal, I think, falls into proper perspective. It was no reasoned plan, no practical project, but an idea thrown out in conversation by a Renaissance humanist, more at home in university circles in Padua than in the Italian or English courts, who had been moved to enthusiasm, as so many of his colleagues were, by the rediscovery of ' the veray cyvyle law, the most auncient and nobil monument of the Romaynys prudence and pollycy ', then just emerging from the medieval glosses and commentaries that had so long hidden it from view. In that age, much was expected from the Roman law revealed in its true classical purity. Pole went so far as to equate it with the law of nature itself. But as the first flush of enthusiasm died away, pure antiquity, though its attractions were many, was found to supply something less than a complete answer to the ever more complex legal problems that pressed for solution. Pole's speech has been regarded as one of the questionings of established institutions characteristic of the liberal minds of the day, but that is to say too much for it. It takes its place beside those equally extravagant and impractical remarks of Rabelais, Lorenzo Valla, Ulrich Zazius, and the others, themselves but the legal division in a violent attack on the Middle Ages in general, carried on with exuberance on many fronts and taking many forms, from the *Epistolae Obscurorum Virorum* and *The Praise of Folly* to the Reformation itself.

Whether the reception of Roman law in England was possible or not remains an academic question. The Pole of the *Dialogue* thought it could be brought to pass quickly, and in view of all that Henry did bring about, it seems likely that this too could have been accomplished. But the idea of a reception seems never to have appeared in official circles nor to have had the slightest government support. It was never talked about, never urged, never considered. Indeed, what evidence has come to light since Maitland's essay points in an opposite direction: that the substitution of Roman law for its own, was very far from the thoughts of a government that found its support in English legal history, and continually justified its acts by references to it. The suggestion does not appear again in Pole's books, or in the five stout volumes of his collected correspondence. No scheme for a general reception manifested itself when he returned to England in Mary's reign, to become a power in the state. Starkey's other writings likewise are silent on this subject, nor were the words he attributed to Pole ever, to my knowledge, echoed by another Englishman. It is, of course, possible that further evidence may alter this conclusion, but it seems clearly true now that but one statement in favor of a general reception of Roman law in England can be adduced, and that a by no means seriously put forward or deliberately considered one.

It is interesting to compare these unique remarks with those of Richard Morison contained in a short tract presented to Henry VIII sometime shortly before the year 1540. Morison, who wrote readily in Greek and Latin, was another of the young humanists who had been at Wolsey's college at Oxford with Starkey, and, like him, had later enjoyed Pole's hospitality in Padua. His tract follows almost exactly Pole's suggestions, but only so far as they deal with the *reform* of English law; it does not go on, as Pole had, to urge the reception of another system. As I have said, Starkey's *Dialogue* remained unprinted for 350 years. Morison's tract remains unprinted still among the Royal manuscripts, which must be my excuse for quoting a portion of it here.

'It may please your majesty's most gracious lordship to understand that my desire hath been to attempt if the common laws of this your realm that now be unwritten might be written; that now be dispersed and uncertain might be gathered together and made certain; that now be in no tongue might be reduced into the Latin tongue; which thing, if it might be accomplished, as with your grace's help I am fully persuaded it may be, me thinketh there could be nothing devised more expedient, profitable and necessary for your commonwealth '.

He goes on to say, ' This art to write laws that be unwritten; to digest them in order that be confounded and uncertain; to bring them into the Latin tongue that be in no tongue; some will say is impossible. But this thing, though it be hard, as all noble things be, yet is it not impossible. The laws which we now call civil, before the Emperor Justinian's time were as much dispersed and as far out of order as ours be. To prove that it is not impossible I have drawn a rude plat in the Latin tongue of the tenures of land and of services that your subjects, being tenants, by the common laws of this your realm owe unto their lords, which is the greatest and hardest piece of all your laws for that the matter thereof differeth from all other laws '. Here ends Morison's *Discourse touching the Reformation of the Laws of England*, but Morison's *Tenures*, in Ciceronian Latin and written in an elegant Italian hand, is still extant. It is a small book, of English not Roman law, which would have pleased Hotman no more than Littleton's *Tenures* did. I may add that it would have pleased Coke still less and that its value to a common lawyer would have been of the smallest.

Morison's tract was essentially the New Learning's attack on the common law, the sort of criticism to which it was particularly vulnerable. What Pole had said about its hateful language was undeniably true. Morison's observation that good letters and the law seldom if ever appeared together in the same person, perhaps equally so, though Thomas More is an obvious exception and there were others. Evidently the problem was a serious one, for another attack, contemporary and along the same lines, lies back of the documents printed in Waterhous's commentary on Fortescue, which set out either contemplated changes in the curriculum of the Inns of Court or a plan for a new foundation to take their place. The improvements suggested are notably humanistic: the true pronunciation of the French language is to be introduced; moots are to be argued in good Latin and good French. Three days of each week, during both term and vacation, one of excellent knowledge of the Latin and Greek tongues is to read some orator, or book of rhetoric, openly to all the company, for the knowledge of both the said languages. In the mean vacations, after two years passed, instead of moots there are to be daily declamations in Latin, though to this last the happy proviso is added, ' that none of the company shall be bound to be at this '. But as nothing was done officially to encourage Morison's project, so nothing came of these plans, though the king himself seems to have been interested in them. What we already know from the literature of the law itself is confirmed by the references to ' puling Littletonians ' in the Parnassus plays, the savage satire of Ruggles' *Ignoramus*, the countless references in Elizabethan and Jacobean pamphlets and plays. The common lawyers persisted in their barbaric French and dog Latin and these crudities, which cut them off from humane letters, continued to draw the fire of the University wits. This was, to be sure, annoying and irritating, but hardly seriously destructive, for the reforms themselves were never effectively pressed. As with medicine, there long continued to be much noisy discontent with law. All that we need note here is that the cry was reform, not reception, in the years before the middle of the sixteenth century which Maitland described as critical.

Maitland's conjecture that the proposed Court of Conservators of the Common Weal, projected in 1534, was one more Romanist plot proved baseless once the draft act was read, for it expressly provided that the law and procedure of the new court were to be those of the common law. His view of the Statute of Proclamations of 1539 as a *lex regia*, conferring upon the crown the power of wide legislation without the concurrence of parliament, has likewise been abandoned. Whatever may have been the bill's form when it left Cromwell's hand, in the four years it took to pass the two houses of even that most tractable of parliaments, it must have met opposition that was determined and prolonged. Certainly it emerged with carefully drawn safeguards, and in the end gave the crown no greater powers than it already possessed.

A word must be said of the number of graduates of foreign universities, tainted by contact with Roman law abroad, whom Maitland found intruding themselves into government posts, and whom he suspected of preparing the pathway for a reception. Is it not much more likely that we have here but another example of a common phenomenon? In periods of crisis and rapid transition, it is the enthusiastic young liberals, tired of the old and in revolt against it, who are called upon. In the England of 1533 they were apt to be Grecians or jurists trained in the *mos gallicus*. All were men who had embraced the new learning and put off the traditionalism of the past. All were young; all wore the signs of their emancipation openly; and all were equally in demand by governments committed to substantial changes. If the sixteenth century liberals, as was often said, had read Marsilius and Machiavelli, their twentieth century counterparts had read Marx, but neither group was prejudiced by this reading. Indeed, of the Tudor men (to say nothing of their modern analogues) it may well be true that their familiarity with this literature, rather than any facility in Greek letters or Roman law, prompted their appointments. Enough of the details of their careers in government posts have been painfully assembled to make evident how few found their Greek or their Roman law of use. Even those few doctors of the civil law who were absorbed into the Chancery or the Court of Requests, into the Council of the North or the Council of the Marches — appointments to which their legal training might be thought material — soon found that these administrative courts afforded little if any scope for the application of what Roman law they knew.

'But might not these courts', Maitland asked, after quoting Brunner's account of the developments in Germany, 'courts not tied and bound by ancient formalism, do the romanizing work that was done in Germany by the Reichskammergericht?'. This is a skilfully framed rhetorical question, harder to answer than to ask, committing the questioner to nothing, but leaving an impression which a Year Book reporter would have expressed in the words 'quasi diceret, sic'. Much has been done on these courts since Maitland's day, and the answer we may now give is that they might indeed, but they did not, nor is there the slightest evidence that they tried or had the least interest in trying. When, in 1538, Rowland Lee wrote to Cromwell from the Council of the Marches, which was then endeavoring to control the considerable unrest in Wales, that 'if we should do nothing but as the common law will, these things so far out of order will never be redressed', he was stating an obvious truth, one being proved daily in the Star Chamber, the Privy Council, and in the other agencies that were making good the common law's defects, which were many. It is only Maitland's suspicion that an active Romanist lurked behind every D.C.L. that makes him here see Lee contrasting English and Roman law and stressing the advantages of the latter. It was this same Lee who, two years later in 1540, writing to Cromwell of the deaths of William Sulyard, who had read at Lincoln's Inn, and John Porte who had been a reader at the Inner Temple, said he must have equally learned men in their place for none other is of any help.

Now, the Year Books. Their cessation in 1535, at the moment when the Henrician terror was at its height, Maitland regarded as dramatically appropriate, but it is only the coincidence of dates that is striking and nothing more. The last printed Year Book is indeed that for the 27th year of Henry VIII, but there are no printed Year Books for the first 11 years of his reign, for the 15th to the 17th years, or from the 20th to the 25th. With the introduction of written pleadings, these guides for serjeants pleading orally in court became obsolete. After 1535, as before, there was no absence of reports, but what was wanted was something more informative than the arguments between judge and counsel leading to the formulation of an issue. Reports in Year Book form for the missing years of Henry VIII's reign and for the years after 1535 exist unprinted in manuscript. The future lay with reports in another form.

One final criticism, and that somewhat more fundamental than the others. The real defect of Maitland's essay seems to me to lie in the illusory question asked, the unreal terms in which the problem is set and dealt with. As in the endless nineteenth-century debates over those familiar absolutes, socialism and individualism, Roman and English law seem for Maitland to be simply two bodies of abstract thought, two competing ideologies, subsisting in a detached and purely intellectual world. If we judge from the essay alone, neither has any connection with actual practice or with results reached in courts. Both compete for dominance, but like Good and Evil, Roman law surely being evil, their battle is waged high aloft in the heaven Jhering reserved for pure concepts. In Maitland's words, the problem was this: ' How was it and why was it that in an age when so many creeds were crumbling and all knowledge was being transfigured, one body of doctrine, and a body that concerns us all, remained intact? '. His answer is phrased in the same terms: the Inns of Court had so toughened and hardened the traditional body of English law that it was able to resist attack successfully.

Now law is not simply a creed, or a body of doctrine like the comprehensive system of scholastic philosophy, to be swept away or supplanted on humanistic or intellectual grounds alone. It is, like them, an intellectual structure, but unlike them, one intimately connected with practical life and tested by practical standards. Law, like medicine, cannot fall victim, as abstract theological and philosophical systems may, to sudden changes in mere intellectual fashion, for it finds its justification independently in its success in dealing with the problems life presents to it. Only when it is unsuccessful in the practical sphere, when its rules lead to results contrary to, or different from, what is required or expected, does the way open for reform or reception. These follow upon failure, or what is the same thing, new needs with which the law does not, or can not, cope. Thus any realistic estimate of the seriousness of a threatened reception cannot rest upon a changed climate of opinion alone, but most go beyond it to an examination of defects at home and advantages abroad. This Maitland's essay never attempts. In failing to come to grips with the question on its merits, it seems to me to leave itself open to a charge of inconclusiveness, just as do the writings of the German historians of the late nineteenth century, who saw the reception of Roman law in Germany as simply the triumph of rationalism, the substitution of scientific for pre-scientific legal thinking. In Maitland's essay there is nothing of the progressive reorganization of 16th century society along new lines. Nothing of the economic effects of the dissolution of the monasteries, of the commercialization of land, enclosures, the agrarian revolution, of expanding trade, both domestic and overseas, of the new mobility of population, or of the rise of an indeterminate middle class. Yet it is precisely these movements that might have made a reception possible. If there was no reception, as we know there was none, it was not because of the four Inns of Court and a medieval system of moots and readings, but because English law found solutions within itself for the very serious and threatening problems raised by these movements. In the rise of these problems and in the methods devised for dealing with them lies the real story of English law in the Renaissance.

14

TUDOR SOCIAL TRANSFORMATION AND

LEGAL CHANGE

The century 1540-1640 in England was a period of profound change, almost universally regarded as the dividing line between the old and the new. At a point half-way in that hundred-year span the educated Englishman's mind and world were still more than half medieval; at its end they were more than half modern. Recent work in fifteenth century agrarian history and investigations into fifteenth century commerce and trade have blurred the black and white of any abrupt transition from feudal to capitalist England by emphasizing the non-feudal elements already at work in medieval society and heralding its disintegration. In the same way, studies in eighteenth century social stratification and commercial and agricultural organization have made clear how distant the society of that age still was from the industrial and finance capitalism of our own day. Thus exaggerated and excessively sharp lines have been softened and the extravagant claims sometimes still made for the period sensibly reduced. Nevertheless, it remains true that in the years between 1540 and 1640 disruptive and creative forces accelerated the normal process of change to a degree that makes the century, unless we except our own, the most conspicuous example of rapid and many-sided transformation in English history.

Revealed equally well whether one looks at religion or science, politics or economics, literature, music, medicine or architecture, the changes took place against a background of continuity, with the clash and fusion of old and new on every side. Accurate scientific observation did not drive astrology at once and *in toto* out of the medical treatises, nor did medieval ideas on the supremacy of law disappear in the face of growing parliamentary sovereignty. Rather both subsisted side by side, incompatible and essentially irreconcilable, waiting, in the case of one, further emancipation from tradition, or in the case of parliament, a resolution dictated by the turn of future events. So in the subject with which I am particularly concerned here: the dilution of a preponderantly agricultural economy by the infiltration of commercial capital occurred only slowly, nor was the transition from a feudal to a bourgeois or embryonic-capitalist society accomplished everywhere or at once. If in London and the home counties the changes were marked and disagreeable, in Cornwall, the North, and the marches of Wales, life continued much as it had in the days of Edward III.

Contrary to the circumscribed opportunities of his no less acquisitive predecessors, there was no limit to the variety of financial adventures open to the Tudor merchant. A man of mixed enterprise, his economic activities never were confined to ventures of a particular type nor specialized within a limited range. Patents and monopolies, loans secured by mortgages or penal bonds, the purchase and sale of goods of whatever description if a suitable profit might reasonably be anticipated, the financing of slaving voyages or piratical expeditions; nothing out of which wealth might accrue escaped his eye. But the means of profit brought most frequently to hand by the exigencies of the age, with its rising prices and consequent depreciation of fixed incomes, was land. Here the merchant was joined by the enterprising yeoman who had amassed capital, whether by land or sheep farming, by lawyers who like Coke, Popham, Ellesmere and Walmesley had made money in the law, by distinguished civil servants and crown officials of varying descriptions, and by others—all representatives of much the same indeterminate middle class. Just as their fathers had prospered on monastery lands at the dissolution, this bourgeoisie fattened on the lands of the ancient aristocracy, heirs of great but frozen wealth, with properties dispersed in a dozen different counties, who found themselves caught in the price spiral incumbered by the dead weight of huge and passive estates, long leases, static dues, fixed freehold and copyhold rents, and the great disadvantage of what had now become wasteful and irrational methods of estate management.

The method of the new agricultural capitalists was to work the land as a commercial undertaking, to watch costs and yields, to charge an economic rather than a customary rent, to keep careful accounts, to shrink from neither grasping chicanery nor evasion, and to take at all times a realistic view of the cash nexus. Given a knowledge of the ropes, a manor could be refloated as easily as a mill. To the purchaser with the capital and capacity to undertake it, modernization was as profitable as it was unpopular with his tenants. Customary payments dwindling, the new landlord could get rid of unprofitable copyholders and small freeholders by buying them up, or as more often happened, by twisting manorial custom, screwing up admission fines to unreachable sums, litigating fanciful flaws in title until the limited assets of his tenant were exhausted, or if these failed, by threats, duress, or intimidation. If the pressure of the price rise could be avoided only if leases were granted for periods of not more than seven years, there were a variety of unscrupulous means by which holders of longer leases, for life or for several lives, could be discouraged and ousted. If there were common lands, these might be usurped and brought into cultivation. The records of the Star Chamber bear witness to hundreds of such cases and the despairing outcries of the villagers in their answers to charges of riot and the casting down of enclosures. They plead ancient rights of common, immemorial rights of grazing for their cattle, and resent bitterly the rapacity of the new rack-renting landlords, merchants and lawyers from London, men of business and speculators, who have taken the place of the old feudal landlords. Into this hated but rapidly rising class fell, as well, those noble landlords who moved with the times, for such peers, living on the profits and rents of commercial farming, are indistinguishable from the merchant or trader—all equally products of capitalist transformation.

The first response to this landslide, accurately diagnosed to be responsible to no minor degree for the ever-present threat of serious social dislocation that hung over the Tudor age, was repression. In 1535, Thomas Cromwell contemplated an act 'that no merchant shall purchase more than £40 lands by the year'; in 1552 it was Edward VI's belief 'that this country can bear no merchant to have more land than £100'; in 1559 Lord Burghley proposed to set at a convenient figure a legal maximum to the real property merchants and traders might buy; in 1576 the future acquisition of land by clothiers was limited to twenty acres. But if the peer, his wealth locked up in frozen assets, preferred to keep the *parvenu* in his place, the latter, unfortunately, had the money which the former was at his wits' end to obtain. Indeed, stronger objections came from the gentry: those who had established themselves earlier and were not averse to having the door selfishly closed to others who now sought to follow along the same promising path. General legislation on this focal point never materialized, and by the end of our hundred-year span opposition to the unpleasant, grasping, crude, land-grabbing gentry, the exploiting and rack-renting lord of the manor, was becoming limited to parliamentary acts curbing his more violent interferences with tradition. He remained, of course, an apt subject for the satire of dramatists and the sermons of country clergy, but already the words were changing from 'grasping' to 'thrifty' and from 'rapacious' to 'enterprising', foreshadowing his transformation into the altogether admired, solid and sober country gentleman of the eighteenth century.

If the Tudor agricultural capitalist farmed his lands, as those generally did who came to the gentry from the class of smaller yeomen, he could sell his produce in a rising market. If he dealt in land as a commercial speculation, he could count on reselling at a profit to newer recruits, fresh from trade, anxious to vary the risks of commerce by the decorous stability of what was regarded as a gilt-edge investment. What better use for money so gained by profitable sales of produce or through shrewd speculative enterprise than the purchase of larger manors and broader acres? By 1620 if not earlier, it was difficult to find a prominent London merchant or lawyer who was not also a constant dealer in land. Coke owned at his death ninety-nine manors, but twice that number had passed through his hands. The same is true of countless others. The land market was most active in the home counties, where prices rose rapidly and length of tenure was short, reflecting the spectacular growth of London and the profits that lay in supplying its inhabitants, but what was true of the forty miles about London was only slightly less true of the environs of other growing cities, for example, Bristol. Elsewhere, though the passage of land from owner to owner was slower, manors moved with a tempo unknown in the middle ages.

Some members of this species, which was later to be the admiration of the world, survived and prospered; others struck no permanent roots. Since land often was in no way distinguished from other business enterprises by a class in which agricultural, commercial, and industrial interests were inextricably intertwined, it was equally and readily subject to the ebb and flow of business fortune. Reached by recognisance, statute merchant, and statute staple, mortgaged, re-mortgaged or liquidated as reverses required or as more lucrative opportunities elsewhere were offered, property floated from hand to hand, coming to rest at intervals only again to resume its wanderings as financial embarrassment, bankruptcy, or the promise of larger profits called the turn. Of 2,500 manors in seven counties whose owners can be traced, 33 per-cent were sold between 1560 and 1600; 36 per-cent between 1601 and 1640. Of 600 manors in Hertfordshire and Surrey, close enough to London to feel the wash of the whirlpool, 40 per-cent changed hands in the same periods. Of the gentry who had purchased land in Bedfordshire by 1620, two-thirds were said to have sold out by 1668, and the remark that half the properties in conservative Staffordshire had changed hands in sixty years does not appear too implausible.

Other crises set the wheel spinning at an even faster rate. Between 1558 and 1633 crown lands to the value of £2,250,000 (much of the total after 1605, to satisfy the government's deficit spending of the war years) were sold, largely to syndicates of London financiers, who bought in substantial blocks, subdivided, and resold, partly to subsidiary rings of middlemen, partly to the public. Thus political conditions combined with economic to erode the upper strata of the social pyramid—the crown and the peerage —and to increase the amount of property that passed into new hands.

Since land was an instrument of social prestige and political power, its mobilization had other effects, and the shifting center of gravity in the State, to which rather more attention has been paid by historians, affords an opportunity to view the leveling process from another side. Of 135 peers in the House of Lords in 1640, over half had obtained their titles since 1603: the creation by the Stuarts of a new nobility through the sale of titles to knights and esquires with an income from land of £1000 a year was nothing beyond a simple recognition of economic realities. Such translations obscure the picture, but peers so recruited from the gentry, though they sometimes bore ancient names, had neither the wealth, power, nor prestige of those who earlier had sat in their seats. The landslide had turned the upper ranges of English society from a precipitous mountain chain to an undulating high table land, on which variations in altitude were recognizable but, compared with the tremendous peaks of an earlier age, small. The richer gentry had the income of Earls and in 1628 it was quite properly observed that the Commons could buy the House of Lords three times over. Clearly the substantial gentry entrenched in the Commons, commanding most of the land and therefore most of the wealth of an England still largely agricultural, held the keys to what seemed the indefinite future in its hands. Nor would this be altered in essentials until the factories and the long industrial streets came to modify the face of England and transmute one world of privilege into another.

If the repercussions of the 1540-1640 redistribution of landed property were many and of profound importance in English history, I touch upon them only to illustrate the extent to which land had been transferred from crown and peerage to a gentry closely allied with, in fact indistinguishable from, the merchant class. The flow of commercial capital into land, which rationalized estate management, likewise modernized portions of the law of real property. Such changes seldom took the form of sharp reversals of earlier rules, but a shift in emphasis, a choice of alternatives, a heightened importance given to a case formerly ignored, the sudden blossoming of a doctrine barely hinted at earlier, the broader construction of statutory words, mark the transformation well enough.

Security, for example, was a matter of the greatest concern to purchasers, who feared most the remote or dormant title, brought forward without warning, against which the law left them helpless. These fears were well founded, for financially pinched sellers did not scruple to defraud the business men and speculators, ruthless bargainers determined to force acceptance of the lowest prices, who were insinuating themselves into the land. The common law did not require disclosure of defects in title and afforded no means for destroying outstanding claims. Rather, in true medieval fashion, it preserved indefinitely the rights of heirs and remaindermen and protected latent titles against purchasers of every kind. In the interests of security legal ingenuity sanctioned by the judiciary developed the common recovery, at best a bare-faced fraud since there was no possibility of recompense from the common vouchee, but a fraud to which the courts resolutely closed their eyes, thus depriving heirs in tail, by an obvious fiction, of their inheritances.

A questionable antiquity was given the device by alleging as its origin a singularly obscure case of 1472, though the common recovery itself did not become usual until almost a century later. *De donis* had enacted expressly that a fine was no bar to the issue in tail and a statute of 1536, dealing with the general subject of fines, did not repeal it. Nevertheless, a strained judicial interpretation of the act declared it to be a bar and set a five-year statute of limitations running against remaindermen and reversioners which barred their rights absolutely and finally. Though it made the fine 'a piece of firm ground in the midst of shifting quicksands', this reading of the statute was implausible enough to raise questions, but it was quickly confirmed in 1540. Since the fee tail, a fully recognized and legal estate, now could be barred by fine or recovery, efforts were made to create estates tail that could not be so upset, a legitimate aim for an owner seeking to establish a landed family. But judges, more concerned with the fact that 'titles would be wholly uncertain' and the plight of a prospective purchaser of property so encumbered than with the owner's aspirations, found all such devices void. They continued to emphasize the destructible nature of estates in tail until the end of the seventeenth century, when they became willing to accept the work of conveyancers creating entails impossible to break—a reversal closely tied in with the diversion of commercial money from land to industry in the eighteenth century and the re-establishment of a large-landed aristocracy.

Among the more conspicuous signs of agricultural backwardness in 1550 was the lease for lives, most frequently found on the estates of the aristocracy, which had been granted when falling, not rising, prices had been the great landholder's problem and fixed rents for long terms were an insurance. Manors whose lands were held on long leases at low rentals attracted the Tudor speculator prepared to modernize, whose profit was measured by the difference between the improved and old rents. Short-term leases were the standard answer to the price rise, and as they became common the position of the tenant for years improved considerably. Precarious in an earlier age that had regarded land as the permanent and normal economic basis for the family and had distrusted the termor, who more often than not was a money-lender evading the law against usury, the entreprenurial activity of the termor was so far condoned that freeholders, envying the means given him for recovering his term, secured the same advantages to themselves by the fictitious demise in the action of ejectment.

English land law was organized about the concept of seisin: neither possession nor ownership but a combination of both. To have seisin one must enter upon land and stay there, though the seisin so acquired might or might not be superior to another's older and better seisin. A conception peculiar to the middle ages, it was unsatisfactory in an age when property moved rapidly and in which buyers dealt in land they had never seen and did not expect to occupy. The growth of the concept of title, only hinted at before Elizabethan times, is reflected in the new importance given title-deeds, originally simply memoranda of livery of seisin. Actions for their recovery became frequent and their simple deposit was held in 1673 to effect a valid mortgage. In the light of this separation of title from possession, seisin was equated with the latter. Livery of seisin—an actual, complete, and public change in the occupancy of land—declined into mere form as title was transferred by bargain and sale or by lease and release. At these and other points, often technical and small but not unimportant as harbingers of the future, transformation was slowly taking place.

To the speculating Elizabethan purchaser buying to improve and sell, or to hold subject to the reconversion of his capital into enterprises of other kinds, there was much that seemed antiquated in the English law of real property. To the Elizabethan merchant acquiring two or three thousand acres with the intention of establishing a landed family of significance in the county, the law of real property, a product of the heroic age of feudalism when the nexus between lord and tenant had been not merely economic, but military, social, and psychological, was an outrage. Though he might buy knowing nothing of, and caring less about, his lord paramount, in legal contemplation his land was held of a superior in the feudal pyramid and, if held by knight service, a tenure more likely than any other, was subject to substantial burdens surviving from the feudal age. The most severe of these, wardship and marriage, took effect at the tenant's death, seriously limiting the estate passed on to his heir and interfering to a prominent degree with his dynastic pretensions. For centuries intermittent skirmishes had been fought against the feudal incidents, tenants in every age having been anxious to transmit their lands free of their burden. The Statute of Uses, four years before our period begins, had closed off the most useful evasory device. But in the second half of the sixteenth century the hundred-year war began in earnest. Fought through the Elizabethan and Jacobean courts, its battles enshrined in case after case in the black-letter reports, the long struggle was technical in the extreme and left as its monument a mass of subtlety and misdirected ingenuity whose effect on our property law was considerable and greatly to its detriment.

Since the principle that lay at the root of both prerogative and simple wardship was that it attached to one who entered as heir of the deceased tenant, the problem was to enable the heir to succeed to the land by some means other than inheritance. The rule in *Shelley's* case fixed the character of heirs upon persons whom conveyancers had represented to be purchasers, but this was a simple and obvious device, easily penetrated. At the bidding of their clients, lawyers resorted to progressively elaborate and increasingly technical schemes, some to take effect *inter vivos* others only at death, to make heirs purchasers, even at a number of removes from the donor. The contingent remainder, which makes its first appearance in Elizabeth's reign, is a product of this effort, as are shifting and springing uses: all directed toward the same end. Since there were other ingenious means of solving the problem, the long term of years, 99 years or 999 years, unknown in the middle ages, comes into prominence: not being an estate of inheritance, the feudal incidents did not attach to it. The running battle of wits may be traced in the books, but efforts to transmit land free of its medieval dues and incidents were doomed to failure when carried on within the traditional law of real property, itself painfully forged for the governance of a feudal society in which those very dues and incidents were of major importance. Casuistical alterations in detail accomplished something, but more often raised frightening problems of other kinds, notably the perpetuity, like the others a problem first grappled with in the Elizabethan age. The courts moving slowly from case to case met the question always as one of *meum et tuum,* for if sixteenth century landholders as tenants felt the feudal incidents intolerable, as lords they were anxious not to be deprived unjustly of rights guaranteed them by law. Pressure was less ambiguous and more readily felt in Parliament. The incidents of tenure were abolished in 1660, unfortunately without the concomitant abolition of the tortured law of real property to which they had given rise, a law that was to confound judges for two centuries and disprove the maxim *cessat causa, cessat effectus.*

The slow emergence of contract from tort and the halting development of assumpsit in a strikingly active commercial society pose problems for the sociological jurist and have led historians into alternate misconceptions. To some, familiar with the extent to which business economy pervaded contemporary life, the needs of commerce in the sixteenth century were served in the local courts. But it can be nothing more than unlikely that yokels in the country were the beneficiaries of a commercial law, developed locally, while the large-scale trade of Elizabethan London or Bristol made do with the rudimentary contractual concepts of the common law. Other historians have postponed the emergence of developed commercial activity in England until *Slade's* case, or at least until *Strangborough v. Warner* (1588) in an effort to balance the equation by manipulating its other variable. But there can be little doubt that the turbulent business activity of the sixteenth century took place, as might be expected, within inherited forms. The ubiquitous bond, the recognisance, the statute merchant, and the statute staple, all were medieval and all had their origins in the simple relationship of debtor and creditor.

I need not expand on the familiar bond under seal, usually drawn to twice the amount due and defeasible by payment of half face value, nor on the action of debt that was used to enforce it. A creditor could avoid the necessity of having to bring an action of debt by having his debtor appear before a superior court, or more frequently before a clerk in the offices of the chancery of exchequer, and there enter into a recognisance, duly enrolled, whereby he acknowledged the indebtedness and submitted to immediate execution upon non-payment. His position was the same as if he had been successfully sued upon a writ of debt. The Statute of Merchants of 1285 set up registries in a number of towns before whom the creditor might have his debtor appear and acknowledge the debt. If this form of assurance was adopted, rather more drastic remedies were available on default. The debtor was forthwith committed to prison; during his first three months there he had facilities for selling his chattels and lands to satisfy the debt, but if he failed to do so, all his chattels then were given to the creditor, to be sold and deducted from the amount due. If this was insufficient, all his lands were transferred to the creditor until the remainder of the debt was discharged out of their issues. The Statute of Staples of 1353 provided much the same method of acknowledgment, but before the Mayor of any Staple town, and similarly direct methods of collection. It seems to have been intended only for Merchant-Staplers, but the general public nevertheless continued to use it until the statute of 1532 confined it to Staplers and created for others the 'recognisance in the nature of a statute staple' entered into before the chief justices of either bench or the recorder of London.

Situations later recognized as within the sphere of the normal contract relation were dealt with in the sixteenth century and later by means of these devices. Defeasible bonds, statutes merchant or statutes staple, served the purposes of the unilateral contract. *A* bound himself in a bond of £1200 to *B* and *C* defeasible on his paying each of Richard Hooker's four daughters £100 at her full age. *A* bound himself in the sum of £20 to deliver certain goods at Boston, Lincolnshire. *A* bound himself on a bond defeasible on his rebuilding a tenement, barn, and watermill. *A* bound himself in a bond of £100 to *B*, it to be of no effect if *B* did not cure him of the pox. The same instruments also served the purposes of the bilateral contract. *A* gave his bond of £500 to the purchaser of his land defeasible on his making the buyer a sufficient estate prior to a fixed date; in return *B* gave his bond of £500 defeasible on payment of the purchase price. *A* agreed to sell goods at £800 payable the 15th of August; *B* agreed to buy. But these preliminary negotiations were further assured by the exchange of £1000 bonds: *A's* to remain in full force until he transferred the goods; *B's* until payment was made. *A* agreed to marry *B's* daughter, *B* to make an estate to *A*, the daughter, and the heirs of their bodies. Here likewise, final arrangements took the form of an exchange of defeasible bonds. The same results could be achieved by the recognition of reciprocal statutes merchant or staple containing similar defeasances, transactions already common in the fifteenth century.

It is a tempting hypothesis that the cases that came before the common law courts during the sixteenth century, out of which the action of assumpsit grew, were those in which the preliminary bargain had not been followed by the exchange of assurances, either because of the insignificance of the sums involved or the inexperience

of the parties. The cases which together comprise the traditional
history of contracts have an unmistakable flavor of unsophistication
and leave the impression that Tudor commercial activity was confined to the dealings of petty traders bargaining for twenty quarters
of wheat or for the payment of a £5 debt. In such cases a false
prominence is given the wager of law, a survival from the middle
ages when men and transactions were local and known to all, but
which had long been obviated in transactions of importance by the
bond or statutory recognisance. The hypothesis is best supported
by the marriage settlements that play their part in the evolution of
the informal contract. Transactions such as these were by no means
new: lands, often of immense value, and money had for centuries
been assured by parents on the marriage couple, using the standard
procedures of bonds and counter-bonds, simultaneous fines, or feoffments on condition. No instruments are more common in family
archives. The settlements litigated in the common law courts of the
sixteenth and seventeenth centuries, on the other hand, seem without exception to be concerned only with small estates and to mirror
only unsophisticated suitors and their parents acting in the absence
of legal, or even of reasonably informed, advice.

A law of contracts that lags behind the growth of commercial
activity presents an awkward stumbling block to the acceptance of
a theory of roughly concomitant social and legal change, but in fact
the lag is illusory. Commercial transactions were handled by means
of self-executing, medieval forms ingeniously adapted to post-
medieval enterprises. Consequently the run of commercial cases by-
passed the common law courts, for defences to a bond under seal
or to an execution sued on a statutory recognisance had of necessity
to be heard in chancery. If relief could not be had there, a seventeenth century chancery reporter noted, 'men would do that by
covenant which now they do by bond'. Under such conditions, contract doctrine remained undeveloped and inadequate: Blackstone's
treatment of contracts does not quite fill one chapter, and that is
hidden in a volume devoted to property and conveyancing; Lord
Mansfield looked for contract theory to Pothier, chancery practices,
mercantile usages, and natural law. Only later to come into its own,
the law of contracts then was provided with a history; if prior to
the late eighteenth century the informal contract was not the form
commercial agreements took, that history cannot fail to be confused,
disappointing, and economically anachronistic.

I pass over the well-worn subject of the sixteenth century legitimation of interest, though it aptly illustrates the title of this paper, and mention only in passing the series of Tudor bankruptcy statutes and acts against fraudulent conveyances that constitute direct legal responses to growing commercial sophistication. The connection between social change and precedent is not quite that clear.

Medieval political and legal thought reflect essentially a society not yet complicated by problems beyond *meum et tuum* and secure in an ethic, accepted by all, based upon the solid bedrock of undifferentiated and universal belief. Under such conditions, the hypothesis that justice provided the ultimate touchstone of human behaviour, and was an ascertainable absolute to be recognized by reason in every case with immediately apprehended confidence, was not an untenable one. If reason worked well enough in an essentially static society, or one in which the rate of change was slow, the sixteenth century found it not altogether an advantage to be ruled by a judge's intuitive feeling for what was right. In the first year of our hundred-year period it was pointed out that 'our law ys infynyte and without ordur or end. Ther ys no stabyl grounde therin nor sure stay, but everye one that can coloure reson makyth a stope to the best law that ys before tyme devysed. There is no stabyl ground in our commyn law to leyne unto and the jugys are not bounden, as a rule, but aftur theyr owne lyberty they have authoritye to juge as the cyrcumstance of the cause doth them move.' Those engaged in trade, whether of lands or goods, would be particularly interested in what Max Weber called 'the calculability of chances', preferring prediction to ethical imperatives no longer either clearly enunciated or unambiguous. Francis Bacon's experience in chancery, the court to which most commercial cases came, led him to insist that certainty was the primary necessity of law, nor is he here to be contrasted with Coke, who substantially delimited the 'reason' of the middle ages when he recognized that 'causes which concern the life or inheritance or goods or fortunes of subjects are not to be decided by natural reason, but by the artificial reason and judgment of the law'. If in 1502 Bracton's (and Justinian's) well-known adage *'non exemplis, sed rationibus adjudicandum est'* could still be cited with approval, by 1602 precedent, a word which appears first in 1557, was becoming a small but recognizable part of judicial technique. Still far from Lord Mansfield, and farther from the industrialized nineteenth century's insistence on predictability, it is nevertheless difficult to escape the fact that rudimentary but none the less real principles of certainty and of the consistency of decision were coming into use.

This already over-long paper may be aptly brought to a close by four quotations which seem to me to raise a fundamental question —the separation of law from ethics. In 1370: *'Nam licet in rescripto principis exprimatur, ut judex recusari non possit, nihilominus ex justa causa poterit recusari. Recusatio enim species est defensionis, quam, cum sit de jure naturae, princeps in suo rescripto etiam expresse tollere nequit. Manifestum est, quod cum voluntas principis ab aequitate, justitia et ratione deviet, non est lex.'* In 1503: *'si le roy granta a une home destre justice de peas licet ipsemet sit pars, cest grant est void.'* In 1606: 'One cannot be judge in his own case, and it appears in our books that in many cases the common law will control acts of parliament and adjudge them to be utterly void'. In 1765: 'if an act of parliament gives a man power to try all causes that arise within his manor of Dale, yet if a cause should arise in which he himself is party, the act is construed not to extend to that, because it is unreasonable that any man should determine his own quarrel. Yet if we should conceive it possible for the parliament to enact that he should try as well his own causes as those of other persons, there is no court that has power to defeat the legislature when couched in such evident and express words as leave no doubt whether it was the intent of the legislature or no'.

15

ST. GERMAIN'S *DOCTOR AND STUDENT*

T. Germain's *Doctor and Student* is a most important book for the historian of English law and, as Sir Paul Vinogradoff has shown, for scholars tracing the influx of Continental ideas into fifteenth- and early sixteenth-century England.[1] These dialogues, coming as they did at the close of the period during which the Court of Chancery had been presided over by ecclesiastical chancellors, and at the beginning of the period when its development was to be guided by the common lawyers, enabled the new chancellors to understand and apply the principles which their predecessors had applied, and must have been seized upon by the profession with avidity. Its numerous editions testify to its popularity and success, and from its first appearance in English, in 1530, to the close of the sixteenth century it seems to have been even more in demand than that most important and valuable work, Littleton's *Tenures*.

Although the two dialogues comprising the work have been printed together since 1543 as one complete volume, and had been so printed before that time save for separate title-pages and tables, it must be borne in mind that originally they were issued neither simultaneously nor in the same language. The first dialogue was printed in Latin in 1523 by John Rastell, but no known copy of that printing exists.[2] It was reissued in 1528 by the same printer, in an edition showing two different

[1] 'Reason and Conscience in Sixteenth Century Jurisprudence', *Law Quart. Rev.* xxiv, p. 373. Also see Holdsworth, *History of English Law*, v, p. 266.
[2] P. H. Winfield, *Sources of English Legal History*, p. 323.

title-pages.[1] But this dialogue was quickly overshadowed by the appearance of the second dialogue, which was written and printed in English, and of a ' translation ' of the first dialogue into the same language.

The second dialogue, curiously enough, was the first to appear in English. It was written in English, rather than in Latin or French, ' for the profyte of the multytude ' and printed by Peter Treveris ' in the yere of our lorde god 1530 the 24th day of Novembre '. It continues, as must be patent to any reader, the Latin rather than the English first dialogue. This is the first printing of the second dialogue, and in it there is no reference to an existing first dialogue in English. There are, to be sure, references to the first dialogue, but these are to the Latin first dialogue, and in many cases they are meaningless unless so construed. Peter Treveris reissued this second dialogue ' with newe addycyons ' in 1531. This was almost a word for word reprint of the previous edition with new matter, duly labelled ' addycyon ' to show its novelty, inserted at several places in the text. But in this edition all references to the ' first dialogue ' are carefully changed to the ' first dialogue in Latin ', although other departures from the text of 1530 are few. In other words, references which were perfectly plain in the closing months of 1530 have become ambiguous in 1531, and it seems likely that this was due to the appearance of Wyer's earlier undated edition of the first *Dyaloge in Englysshe* in the interim.

I think, therefore, that Wyer's earlier issue must be dated 1531 rather than 1530, and the conjecture is further strengthened by comparing the volume with one of the three dated books bearing Wyer's ' Norwich ' colophon. St. Bernard's *Golden Pystle* is dated 1531, and in both volumes the same ' Secretary ' type is used, both show the large lower-case *w* and *v*, both use the same black-letter type where the ' Secretary ' will not answer,

[1] J. H. Beale, *Bibliography of Early English Law Books*, p. 169.

and both use the same letters of Wyer's incomplete set of grotesque-faced woodcut initial letters. Mr. H. R. Plomer, working with only two of the three books mentioned above, came to the conclusion that the Wyer was the earliest of the dialogues in English, and his dating seems to be followed by most bibliographers, but I think the explanation he gives clearly insufficient.[1]

Wyer reissued this dialogue in an edition which, unfortunately, is also undated, but which had been published by 1532 and most probably by the end of 1531. It must not be supposed, however, that this later edition is a reprint of the earlier. It is entitled *The Fyrste dyaloge in Englysshe with newe addycons* and is a very different book indeed. There are some two hundred changes (excluding those of spelling and punctuation) and even a hurried comparison will show that the earlier edition has undergone a most searching and rigorous revision. The later edition shows a surer acquaintance with the subject-matter and seems to have been written by one who felt himself less hampered by the Latin original, for, although neither of Wyer's editions is in any sense a translation of the Latin dialogue, the later differs more widely than the earlier from it, and where the earlier is most stilted the fault may almost always be laid to a too strict rendering of the Latin.[2] St. Germain himself is said to have been the translator of the first dialogue, but comparison seems to show a different hand, and it is at least possible that the success of the English second dialogue in Treveris's edition led Wyer or some one connected with him to undertake a rapid translation of the first dialogue for publication and sale, which translation was later extensively revised by St. Germain.

[1] H. R. Plomer, *Robert Wyer*, p. 5.
[2] For the major differences between the Latin and English dialogues Prof. Vinogradoff's article (*op. cit., sup.*) is most helpful. It also appears in his *Collected Papers*, ii, p. 190.

The approximate date of Wyer's later edition may be fixed as before or after 1531 by comparing it with the text of Redman's edition of that year. It is probable that Redman used the later Wyer text, so that Wyer's two editions were published in 1531, making the *Doctor and Student* a very much sought-after book indeed. I have, unfortunately, not been able to see a copy of the 1531 Redman edition.[1]

In 1532 Redman reissued both dialogues, and this is the earliest printing of both dialogues in one volume that I have seen. Both dialogues appear in their revised form, although they still retain their separate title-pages and tables. The text has reached its final form and remains the same (mistakes and all) down to Tottel's edition of 1593, in which several of the more obvious printer's errors were corrected, and that text, imperfect as it is, reappears in every edition I have been able to examine.[2] In Myddylton's edition of 1543 (and perhaps in Wyer's edition of 1542) the second title-page has been abandoned and the two tables merged, and in that form the dialogues are reprinted over and over again. In 1751 a treatise called *The newe addicions* is added;[3] in 1815 two of the controversial tracts written about the time of the dialogue's first appearance form an appendix.

[1] Both the S.T.C. and Prof. Beale's *Bibliography* list only the Bodleian copy.

[2] There seems to be no complete list of the editions, although there are several partial compilations. I list only those editions including both dialogues : 1531, 1532, 1542, 1543, 1554 (2), 1569, 1575, 1580 (2), 1593, 1598, 1604, 1607, 1609, 1613, 1623, 1638, 1660, 1668, 1671, 1673, 1687, 1709, 1721, 1746, 1751, 1761, 1787, 1815, 1874, 1886.

[3] Two editions of this treatise were printed in 1531, but it must not be thought that it contains the ' addycyons ' which were added, as shown above, to both the first and second dialogue in that year. Several bibliographies give that impression, but the treatise is concerned with an entirely different question and seems to be merely an essay by St. Germain in a subject which he later treated in his *Treatyse concernynge the diuision betwene the spirytualtie and temporaltie*, which was probably published in 1532.

A thorough survey of the editions and a critical examination of the text is necessary. Successive generations of printers have done little toward making an understandable text. It is hoped that a new edition will soon make its appearance, so that St. Germain's *Doctor and Student* may again fill its important place in the history of English legal institutions. A reissue of the Latin first dialogue, whose third and last appearance was in 1604, with adequate reference to its Continental sources, would also fill an important gap in a most interesting subject. We await another Maitland who will turn the eyes of legal scholars not so much toward our unprinted as toward our printed sources.

1530

The secūde ǁ dyaloge in Englysshe bytwene ǁ a doctour of dyvynytye and ǁ a Student in the lawes of ǁ Englande. ǁ
Title in border 26 (Beale).
Signatures: unsigned eight; B–I in eights; K–S in eights; T ten.
Pagination: T.-p.+ii–cxlvii+(5).
Colophon: ☾ Impryntyd at London in Southwarke by ǁ Peter Treuerys In the yere of our lorde god ǁ M.v.C.XXX. the xxiiii day of Nouembre. ǁ

1531

☾ Hereafter fo-ǁloweth a Dyaloge in Englysshe / ǁ bytwyxt a Doctoure of Dyuynyte / ǁ and a Student in the Lawes of ǁ Englande : of the groundes ǁ of the sayd Lawes and ǁ of Conscyence / ǁ (McK. 57.)
Signatures: unsigned four; b–i in fours; k–r in fours; s in six.
Pagination: T.-p.+(1)+iii–l+(24).

Colophon : ❧ Imprynted || by me Robert Wyer / dwellynge || in seynt Martyns parysshe || in the felde / besyde Cha-|| ryngcrosse / in the Bys||shop of Norwyche || Rentes.||

s6–McK 57.

s6 verso. ❧ And these bokes be for to sell at || the sygne of seynt Johñ Euange||lyste in seynt Martyns parys-||she besyde Charyngcrosse. || (McK. 67a.)

The fyrste dya-||loge in Englys||she / with newe addycyons. || (McK. 57.)

Signatures : unsigned one ; a three ; b–i in fours, k–n in fours.

Pagination : T.-p. +ii–lxxviii +(2).

Colophon : ❧ Imprynted by me Robert Wyer || dwellynge at the sygne of saynt || John Euangelyste, in saynt || Martyns parysshe / besyde || Charyngcrosse, in the Bys-||shop of norwych rentes. || (McK. 68, 69.)

The secunde dya||logue ĩ englysshe || wyth new addy-|| cyons, || ❧ here after folowyth the secũde dya||logue in Englysshe bytwene a doctour || of dyuynytye and a Student in || the lawes of Englande / || newly correctyd and || Emprentyd. || with new || addicions. || Jesus, || (within ornaments.

Signatures : unsigned one ; a seven ; B–I in eights ; K–U in eights ; X in eight ; Y six.

Pagination : T.-p. +ii–cxlvi +(6).

Colophon : ❧ Impryntyd at London in Southwarke by || Peter Treueris. || 1531 ||.

16

FITZHERBERT'S *ABRIDGEMENT*

The abridgments of the Year Books constitute a large and interesting class of document of which the foremost representative is the *Graunde Abridgement* of Sir Anthony Fitzherbert.[1] The work falls properly within the scope of Year Book research, and the work of successive Year Book editors has thrown a good deal of light upon its contents,[2] but still both the materials from which it was compiled and the method of compilation remain largely unknown. It is with this latter problem that we concern ourselves here; more particularly, with the reconstruction of Fitzherbert's original manuscript text by a strictly bibliographical examination of its printed form. That this will aid in the discovery of the sources of the *Abridgement* seems clear; one of the strongest bits of evidence Maitland adduced to prove Fitzherbert's use of the British Museum manuscript numbered Add. 12,269 was the order in which cases from that manuscript appeared in the *Abridgement*,[3] and in a similar manner, the peculiar order of Year Book cases may point toward corresponding, peculiarly arranged, Year Book manuscripts. This assumes, of course, that Fitzherbert was not entirely dependent upon the work of earlier compilers and that he followed some rational plan in entering his cases—assumptions difficult to make in the absence of definite information as to his use of Statham and the earlier abridgments, and in view of the fact that the *Abridgement* was compiled for his own use, without an eye toward publication, and that therefore its only true criterion of arrangement

---

[1] Its worth has frequently been appraised: Holdsworth, *History of English Law,* ii, 544, 545; Plucknett, *A Concise History of the Common Law,* 194-5. For a bibliographical account, see: Cowley, *A Bibliography of Abridgments, Digests, etc. of English Law,* xlv,xlviii, but *cf.* my review, *Columbia Law Review,* xxxii, 1275. The best discussion of the earlier abridgments is found in Professor Winfield's paper *Abridgments of the Year Books* in *Harvard Law Review,* xxxvii, 214, reprinted in his *Chief Sources of English Legal History,* 200-251.

[2] The Year Books edited by Pike in the Rolls Series and all those published by the Selden Society and the Ames Foundation contain concordances of the Year Book and Fitzherbert's *Abridgement.* Editors have frequently discussed the work in their introductions: *30-31 Edw. I (Rolls Ser.)* xxi, xxii; *12-13 Edw. III (Rolls Ser.)* xxix-xxxii; *13-14 Edw. III (Rolls Ser.)* xlv-xlvi; *20 Edw. III (2)* [*Rolls Ser.*] li-lix, lxxxi-lxxxii; *2-3 Edw. II (Selden Soc.)* ix-x; *4 Edw. II (Selden Soc. vol. 26)* xxix-xxxvi; *4 Edw. II (Selden Soc. vol. 42)* xxxii; *13 Rich. II (Ames Foundation)* xx-xxii.

[3] Maitland, *Bracton's Note Book,* i, 119.

must have been one of personal convenience.[4] But a careful study of the text
seems to support the theory that, if Fitzherbert worked through the materials
pretty much as they lay at his hand without any further attempt at harmoni-
zation,[5] he nevertheless worked through them systematically, with the result that
the cases fall into the definite arrangement we detail below. At the outset, however, it must be noted that the very nature of Fitzherbert's work militates against
exactness. Nothing would be more natural than for the abridger to place an
isolated case of interest in the first available blank space beneath a title, in the
margin near a similar case, or on an inserted sheet, regardless of whether or not
it marred a systematic plan. And, too, in view of what we know of Year Book
manuscripts, Fitzherbert frequently must have come upon fuller reports supplying additional cases for a term he had already abridged. That these were entered
as he came upon them, without regard for their fellows, seems probable; an
example may be seen in the cases from similar terms of 34 and 35 Henry VI
which appear in both groups A and C below. Thus we must be prepared to find
a number of so-called abnormal entries, but examination has proved them to be
not numerous enough to obscure the regular recurrence of identical blocks of
cases under each title. Mr. G. J. Turner's investigation led him to believe that
chronological arrangement was entirely absent,[6] and Professor Winfield's analysis
of some ten of the largest titles sorted out of the tangle nothing more definite than
a system subject to many exceptions and qualifications, and complicated by the
appearance of cases from the reign of Edward III at any imaginable point.[7] Our
own analysis has led to a somewhat different conclusion.

A good many of the cases under each title fall into the following five groups,
which generally follow each other. In the instances in which they do not, the
interruption is due to part of the series of Edward III cases, of which more will
be said below. It is the opinion of the writer that these five groups form the
basis of the *Abridgement,* and that most if not all of the other material it now
includes was added later from a separately compiled work. Whether Fitzherbert
was the author of that work it is impossible to say; indeed, it is not improbable
that he was entirely unconnected with the abridgment bearing his name.[8]

A—Henry VI (1422-1461), 1-39, omitting 5, 6, 12, 13, 16, 17, 23, 24, 25, 29.

B—Edward IV (1461-1483), 1-22, omitting 14, 15, 16, 18, 19, 20.

C—Richard III (1483-1485), 1-2; Henry VII (1485-1509), 1-9; Henry VI
(1422-1461), 18, 21, 34, 35, 36; Henry V (1413-1422), 1, 2, 5, 9; Henry
IV (1399-1413), 2, 3, 8, 9, 7, 11, 12, 13, 14.

---

[4] That this criterion was not that of contemporary lawyers is evidenced by the appearance of the *Tabula libri magni abbreviamenti librorum legum Anglorum* in 1517/8, a year
after the *Abridgement* itself. Cowley, *op. cit. sup.*, xlvii; Winfield, *Chief Sources of English Legal History*, 229, 231.

[5] Winfield, *op. cit. sup.*, 229-30.

[6] *Y.B. 4 Edw. II (Selden Society vol. 26)* xxix ff.

[7] Winfield, *op. cit. sup.*, 229-30.

[8] The earliest edition does not bear Fitzherbert's name or give any indication of alleged
authorship. Fitzherbert's name first appears in the edition of 1565, twenty-seven years after
his death. *Plucknett, op. cit. sup.*, 194.

D—Edward III (1326-1377), 38-50, 41 appearing both in its normal position and after 44.

E—Richard II (1377-1399), 2, 5, 6, 7, 11, 12, 13.

TABLE A

	A	B	C	D	E
Age	14-17	18	19-24	25-43	44
Avowrie	1-29	30-42	43-61	62-84	85-89
Ayde	47-53 57-84	85-94	95-105	106-118	119-127
Barre	1-80	81-121	122-192	193-226	227-244
Briefe	1-142	143-184	185-239 482-497	498-629	630-649
Coron	1-24	25-45	46-89	90-106	107-110
Dower	1-10	11-16	17-33	34-53	54-55
Essoin	89-117	118-121	122-142	143-157	158-161
Estoppel	14-59	60-80	81-108	2-13; 109-119; 197-209	210-213
Executours	1-26	27-39	40-60	61-72	75
Garde	50-61	62-66	67-86	89-104	105-106
Garrantie	1-4	5	6-8	9-19	-
Judgment	1-46	47-53	54-74	75-107	108
Monstrauns	73-98	99-109	110-131	132-156	156-165
Quare Impedit ...	74-96	97-101	102-123	124-142	143-144
Resceit	48-66	67-71	72-84	85-93	94-99
Trespass	16-93	94-144	14-15; 145-180	181-205	206-210
Viewe	1-23	24-28	29-46	47-62	63-67
Voucher	28-41	42-43	44-54	55-79	80-84
Waste	33-51	52	53-64	65-96	97-99

Group E is always followed by cases from the reign of Edward III, starting with the sixteenth year and arranged in the following series:

16, 17, 18, 19, 11, 12, 13, 14, 15, 31, 32, 30, 21, 14, 15, 12, 13, 19, 20, 22, 23, 24, 25, 27, 28, 7, 8, 9, 10, 4, 5, 6, 1, 2, 3, Eyre of Nottingham, Eyre of Northampton, Eyre of Derby, and Liber Assisarum.

Of course each year is not represented in each title, but the series is recognizable in each. Thus entries 109-218 in the title *Judgment* appear in this order: 16, 17, 18, 19, 11, 13, 15, 31, 32, 30, 21, 14, 12, 13, 19, 20, 22, 24, 27, 28, 7, 8, 9, 10, 4, 3, Liber Assisarum. And *Dower* 56-120 in this: 16, 18, 19, 11, 13, 15, 1, 3, Eyre of Northampton, Liber Assisarum, 15, 31, 21, 12, 13, 6, 19, 22, 24, 28, 7, 8, 9, 10, 4, 5, 6. This series, however, does not occur in one group, but is scattered throughout each title.

TABLE B

Age 1-13; 45-75; 80-118	Garde 1; 15-49; 107-116
Avowrie 90-177	Garrantie 20-68
Ayde 1-46; 54-56; 128-158	Judgment 109-218
Barre 245-307	Monstrauns ...1-33; 46-72; 166-179
Briefe 240-481; 650-775	Quare Impedit.1-42; 49-73; 145-161
Coron 111-226	Resceit 1-47; 100-146
Dower 56-120	Trespass 1-8; 211-232
Essoin 1-70; 162-173	Viewe 68-135
Estoppel 120-196; 214-249	Voucher 1-27; 85-207
Executours ...76-100	Waste 1-32; 100-109

It seems clear that these Edward III cases were inserted later; in fact, the compiler, or printer, was not always careful to insert them at the end of a group.[9] The peculiar order seems to be due to the incorrect refolding of the sheets of another book. There can be little doubt that an abridgment of Edward III cases was made by Fitzherbert or another, and incorporated into the volume we know as the *Graunde Abridgement*; that this was one method of compiling an abridgment we know.[10]

The Edward II cases form an interesting group, and we incline toward the belief that they form part of the original work. Their order is broken by cases from the reign of Henry VII later than those included in group *C*, by late Henry V and Henry IV cases, by cases from the regnal years 31-38 Edward III, by cases from the end of Richard II's reign, and by Henry III cases from *Bracton's Note Book*.[11] The Edward II cases follow a regular chronological order, but the

---

[9] See especially *Ayde, Briefe, Estoppel.*

[10] Harvard Law School Library MS. Dunn 41 consists of two separate abridgments which have been taken apart and fitted together again into one alphabet. Professor Plucknett has alluded to this: *Concise History,* 193-95; *Y.B. 13 Rich. II (Ames Foundation)* xxi. A description of the MS. can be found in Winfield, *op. cit. sup.,* 206, n.

[11] The Henry III cases throw an interesting light upon Fitzherbert's use of *Bracton's Note Book.* In the cases in which it is possible to notice, *i.e.* in those titles which contain more than one entry from the reign of Henry III, the entries follow the order of the *Note Book* and appear in an uninterrupted group. *Age,* 148-9; *Assize,* 425-39; *Attaint,* 72-75; *Avowrie,* 242-3; *Bastardy,* 29-30; *Briefe,* 877-82; *Comen,* 25-6; *Darrein Presentment,* 22-3; *Devise,* 25-6; *Dower,* 179-203; *Droyt,* 55-66; *Essoin,* 186-96; *Garde,* 139-52; *Garraunt des chartres,* 25-7; *Mesne,* 75-78; *Mortdancestor,* 51-5; *Partition,* 18-9; *Prerogative,* 25-7; *Prescription,* 56-64; *Prohibition,* 13-30; *Proses,* 209-10; *Quare Impedit,* 182-4; *Recovere en value,* 25-7; *Viewe,* 144-5, 173-5; *Villeinage,* 42-3; *Voucher,* 273-83; *Waste,* 129-42.

intervening cases seem to possess very little systematic arrangement. That they may have been gathered from reports of single regnal years and entered as Fitzherbert came upon them seems not unlikely. It seems clear that they do not form part of the groups noticed above. We hope shortly to be able to substantiate our theory by reference to definite manuscript sources of the *Abridgement*; until that time, the question must be regarded as a purely bibliographical one.

17

SIR EDWARD COKE, 1552-1952

I AM conscious of the honour I have today of inaugura-
ting what I hope will be a long and distinguished series
of annual lectures under the auspices of the Selden Society.
My invitation is doubly gratifying, for it allows me to acknowledge publicly, to a Society that has never before permitted itself to be so addressed, the guidance and help I
have had from its many publications—volumes edited with
devotion and scrupulous care, that have done so much to
advance the knowledge of the history of English law. I
know I do not speak here only for myself, but for many
others, not only professed legal historians but historians of
all kinds, and lawyers, both academic and professional.

I need hardly remind you that in advancing the knowledge of English legal history, the Society has advanced as
well the history of many other laws beyond the seas. American law does not begin in 1607, or 1620, or 1776. It begins
when English law begins, and its sources are precisely those
the Selden Society is engaged in publishing. The Year Books
lie back of our law as they do of yours, and the slow evolution of the ideas by which Englishmen regulated their
legal relationships with one another is as important and
interesting on the other side of the Atlantic as it is on this.
So it is with the man we honour today. Edward Coke never
crossed the Channel, to say nothing of the ocean, but a
partial set of his Reports travelled over on the *Mayflower* and
until well into the nineteenth century *Coke on Littleton* was a
book every lawyer knew. Some of his doctrines and ideas,
as you know, have taken firmer root abroad than they have
at home, and more American than English law can be
traced back to his books and no further. Thus I speak of

him without embarrassment and with no sense of trespassing upon another's preserve. If he was born and died a British subject, he has since achieved dual nationality.

We meet this afternoon to pay our respects, on the 400th anniversary of his birth, to an extraordinarily able lawyer, a great judge, and a remarkable parliamentary leader. He was, as well, an unpleasant, hard, grasping, arrogant, and thoroughly difficult man, of whom his widow, after thirty-six years of married life, could write, not without more than sufficient cause, 'We shall never see his like again, praises be to God.'[1] Born in 1552, he did not die until 1634, and thus his long lifetime spans the reigns of Edward VI, Philip and Mary, Elizabeth, James, and almost half that of Charles. During these important and critical years, he held many high judicial offices: Solicitor-General in 1592, at the age of forty; Attorney-General in 1594—a post he occupied for twelve years, leaving it in 1606 to become Chief Justice of the Common Pleas—and finally, in 1613, Chief Justice of the King's Bench. In 1616 he was dismissed from office after several direct clashes with the King and his well-known struggle with Lord Ellesmere, the Lord Chancellor, over the independence of Chancery. Five years later, at the age of sixty, he began a new career in parliament that was to bear great fruit in the Petition of Right and not to end until he was seventy-six.

Coke presents, if not an attractive, certainly an interesting and important figure to the biographer. A long and turbulent life not lacking in public and private dramatic incidents, that range from his brutal prosecution of Raleigh to the kidnapping with force of his own daughter, and to an interview with King James in which 'his majesty fell into that high indignation as the like was never known in him, looking and speaking fiercely, with bended fist offering to strike him, the which the Lord Coke perceiving, fell flat on all four'. A hand in every important law-suit for more than forty years in a period when far-reaching questions of private and public law were before the courts. A leader of the parliamentary opposition in the critical parliaments of the 1620's. The author of many books, including the massive *Coke on Littleton* and three other large Institutes, which together comprise the first comprehensive statement of the common law since Bracton. An astute business man interested in trading ventures, the Virginia Company, and extensively involved in land speculation, who made a very substantial fortune in a variety of Elizabethan and Jacobean ways. A man who knew everyone of importance and to whom everyone came for legal advice. But the very wideness of his interests is overwhelming and the many complex affairs in which he was engaged defeat comprehensive treatment. The biographer almost immediately finds himself caught up in problems of the largest scope. The history of Chancery, the constitutional conflicts of the sixteenth and seventeenth centuries, the doctrines of the common law in a period of great and rapid change, the lives, correspondence and affairs of numberless contemporaries. To take but one of Coke's books, it is no small matter to assess *Coke on Littleton*, and if we are to make an estimate of Coke as a lawyer and legal scholar, there remain, after that, the thirteen volumes of his Reports. It is not at all surprising that of the several biographies announced in the last thirty years by scholars, none has yet appeared, nor that the existing ones are inadequate. This afternoon I can do no more than touch upon one side of this many-sided man and show you something of his legal work. Maitland remarked, long ago, that 'Coke's books are the great dividing line, and we are hardly out of the middle ages until he has dogmatised its results'. What I should like to illustrate is this process of dogmatisation.

It is a commonplace to say that the sixteenth century was a period of profound change. In Vinogradoff's words, 'it marks one of those critical epochs in history when all the possessions of mankind seem to be thrown into the crucible and cast into new shapes; when men feel the soil under their feet giving way'.[2] The words medieval and modern are admittedly inexact; they must be carefully qualified and restrictively hedged about; yet there is much that makes the sixteenth century the dividing line between the old world and the new. It is enough to mention, in addition to the Renaissance and the Reformation, the economic effects of the dissolution of the monasteries, the commercialisation of land, enclosures, the agrarian revolution, expanding trade, both domestic and overseas, the new mobility of population, and the rise of the gentry. The medieval world was indeed dissolving and reshaping into another. Not completely, of course. Change must of necessity take place against a background of continuity. But the clash and fusion of the old and the new are visible equally well whether one looks at religion or science, politics or economics, literature, music, medicine or architecture. We have not reached an age of industrial capitalism, nor is it yet time for the Duke of Wellington's magisterial pronouncement on railways, 'I see no reason to suppose that these machines will ever force themselves into general use', but England under James and Charles had more in common with the nineteenth century than with the fifteenth. If the educated Englishman's mind and world had been, twenty-five years before Coke was born, still more than half medieval, in 1634, when he died, they were more than half modern.

This transformation was not hidden from contemporaries. New men, new manners, new morality—no word appears more frequently in the plays and sermons, the tracts and pamphlets, of Elizabethan and Jacobean days. And just as the citizen in gild or City company, or the clothier or farmer in the country, met problems that had not burdened his grandfather, so Tudor and Stuart judges faced legal problems that had never troubled the judges of Henry VII's reign or Henry VIII's. As Bacon described them, these were 'the cases of modern experience that are fled from those that were adjudged and ruled in former times'. In the Chancery and in the Privy Council they were recognised for what they were, but if we turn to the common law reports, particularly to the pages of Coke's Reports, nothing will be found there that labels itself 'new'. On the contrary, the impression is one of almost unrelieved medievalism. The cases cited most frequently are those decided by judges, long in their graves, who knew not Shakespeare, Jonson and Donne, but Wyclif, Chaucer and Lydgate, and every doctrine there set forth bears, prominently displayed, the stamp of approval of the ancient sages of the law. The casual reader, even the learned reader, may be misled, but it would be a mistake to think that courts were doing no more than reproducing rules formulated in the fourteenth century for the governance of a feudal society. Occasionally the sages' stamp is authentic and the article genuine, which is, more often than not, a pity. Given a new lease on life, it will nonetheless eventually find its way to the lumber room to be thrown out in the course of some general house-cleaning. But very often the stamp is bogus, like the counterfeit seals sold at Robert Buck's shop in Elizabethan London— the Great Seal, twenty shillings; the Lord Admiral's, fifteen.[3] What we have then is a skilful Elizabethan reproduction. They are not always easy to discover, for the materials are old and Coke was frequently an excellent craftsman, quite familiar with medieval tools, whose good pieces confounded contemporaries as they continue to confound legal historians today. But by patient analysis the past may be disentangled from the present and they may be isolated for what they are. As a rule of thumb it is well to remember that sentences beginning 'For it is an ancient maxim of the common law', followed by one of Coke's spurious Latin maxims, which he could manufacture to fit any occasion and provide with an air of authentic antiquity, are apt to introduce a new departure. Sentences such as 'And by these differences and reasons you will better understand your books', or 'And so the doubts and diversities in the books well resolved', likewise indicate new law. If I may formulate a theorem of my own, I advance this—the longer the list of authorities reconciled, the greater the divergence from the cases cited.

Such re-workings of old materials cannot often be spectacular. Frequently the new points that emerge are not only small, but technical, and the extent to which transformation has taken place becomes clear only when many such changes are seen as a whole. But something of the methods employed may be seen in the famous case of *Darcy* v. *Allein*, the Case of the Monopolies, decided in 44 Eliz., 1602.[4]

The granting of monopolies to private individuals was one of the most characteristic features and one of the scandals of Elizabethan life. Gentlemen in attendance upon the Queen and public officials of many kinds who held positions in the various offices of state, were paid at rates, fixed in medieval times, that had long become inadequate. There is a story of Dr. Valentine Dale, who was appointed ambassador to France at a salary of a pound a day. He pretended to be overcome with gratitude; he could not spend, he said, above nineteen shillings daily, and he would be able to send home the remaining shilling for the support of his wife and family. A pound a day, £365 a year, was, however, a substantial salary compared with many. In 1610, that of the Chief Justice of the King's Bench, Sir Thomas Fleming, was £238 6s. 8d.; that of the Chief Justice of the Common Pleas, Sir Edward Coke, £201 19s. 2d. The other justices of both benches received £148 6s. 8d.[5] Christopher Hatton, when he was Vice-Chamberlain, drew the sum of £66 13s. 4d. yearly—a sum absurdly inadequate to the establishment he was compelled to keep.[6]

To meet the legitimate demands of men who were doing then the work now entrusted to the Home Office, the Board of Trade, the Departments of Customs and Inland Revenue, the Foreign Office, and others, the Tudors developed the patent of monopoly. In the absence of adequate state funds, their salaries, pensions, and rewards were to be taken from the public. In return, they were charged with seeing that the public was safeguarded and protected against exploitation. If poor soap or impure salt or bad glass was being put on the market, as they often were, the device of granting to an official by patent a monopoly for the making of soap, salt or glass, with power to license, at a price, and supervise those engaged in the actual manufacture, seemed to solve at one stroke the questions of his salary, the protection of the public, and the control of irresponsible industry. The system, however, was open to abuses of the gravest kind. Men soon found themselves bedevilled by patentees, or, more often, by their unscrupulous deputies or those who had purchased the patent outright, whose functions of searching, sealing, measuring, weighing, registering, or licensing were completely subordinated to money-making. Questions were raised in Parliament as early as 1571, and again in 1597. In 1601 the subject was thoroughly debated and forty of the most obnoxious patents revoked by proclamation. *Darcy* v. *Allein* was heard in 1602. The Statute of Monopolies was to come twenty-two years later.

The Queen had granted by patent to Edward Darcy, a groom in the privy chamber, authority to have the sole making of playing cards within the realm for twenty-one years; he, his servants, factors, and deputies to enjoy the whole trade. His patent was infringed by the defendant. In the suit that followed, the court held the patent void for two reasons: it was a monopoly and against the common law, and secondly, being a monopoly, it was against divers acts of parliament. It is against the common law for several reasons. All trades which prevent idleness, the bane of the commonwealth, and put men to labour, are profitable for the commonwealth, and therefore the grant to the plaintiff to have a trade in his hand alone is against the common law and the benefit and liberty of the subject. Granting the sole trade to one man is not only a damage and a prejudice to those who exercise the same trade, but also to all other subjects, for the end of all monopolies is the private gain of the patentee. The monopoly tends to the impoverishment of divers artificers and others, who before, by their labour, had maintained themselves and their families, and who now will of necessity be constrained to live in idleness and beggary. And finally, every man's trade maintains his life, therefore he ought not to be deprived or dispossessed of it.

Now these are good Elizabethan reasons for holding monopolies bad, and we may well sympathise with them, but what support can be found in the past for this point of view about a device that had not been a problem in the middle ages? Much is brought forward, including a chapter in Fortescue's *De Laudibus Legum Anglie*, a writ out of the Register, cases in the reigns of Edward III and Henry IV, a passage in the Old Testament, and one from Justinian's Institutes, but they are hardly convincing precedents. They form a disappointing collection, not at all characteristic of Coke's remarkable ability to find the answers to present discontents in the past. We may take them to show how little persuasion Coke and his colleagues needed and also how new the problem was, for what is being enunciated is Elizabethan law, disguised, as legal innovations usually are, in the clothes of the past.

A glimpse of the real Coke emerges in the second half of the case. The patent, being a monopoly, was held to be against divers acts of parliament. Several were cited, but reliance was placed in Magna Carta (1225), ca. 29, which says, 'No freeman shall be deprived of his free tenement or liberties or free customs but by the lawful judgment of his peers and by the law of the land.' 'So,' Coke says, 'if grant be made to any man to have the sole making of playing cards, or the sole dealing with any other trade, that grant is against the freedom and liberty of the subject, that before did or might have used that trade, and consequently against this Charter.' 'Generally,' he concludes, 'all monopolies are against this great Charter because they are against the freedom and liberty of the subject and against the law of the land.' I need hardly point out that 'liberties' in Magna Carta is the equivalent of 'immunities and franchises' and that ideas about free trade were Elizabethan ideas, not those of the barons petitioning King John. Yet reading that document through the most unhistorical of eyes, Coke

found them there. He has often been regarded as the pro-
tector and defender of the traditional rights of Englishmen.
With that judgment we may safely agree, adding only that
many of them were his own invention.

This is an example of Coke's method when the past
offered no rule. A rather different problem was raised when
the past provided a rule he did not intend to follow. This
was the situation presented in the Case of the Tailors of
Ipswich.[7] The gild of tailors had been established in Ipswich for two hundred years. It had been incorporated by
the King, and its charter and by-laws ratified by the justices as required by the statute of 19 Henry VII. One of
its by-laws provided that no person should exercise the
trade of tailor in Ipswich until he had presented himself to
the Master and Wardens of the society and proved to their
satisfaction that he had served seven years as an apprentice.
He would then be admitted by them as a sufficient work-
man. If he exercised his trade without first being admitted,
he was subject to a fine. The defendant did exercise his
trade without going through the prescribed formalities and
was sued by the gild for the fine. In Henry VII's day, and
Henry VIII's, this would have been quickly and easily
decided in the plaintiff's favour. The defendant would
have found little to say for himself and would have gotten
little sympathy from the court. Many cases make this clear.

But by the early seventeenth century, the social, financial, territorial and political foundations of the medieval
gild system had been seriously undermined. It had once
been an instrument used by the local authorities for regulating economic activity, and had served a useful purpose.
But the integration of national life, the widening of markets,
the mobility of population, had transformed gilds from
regulatory bodies which concerned themselves with the
quality of goods, fair dealing and high standards, into what
were, more often than not, combinations in restraint of
trade. As in *Darcy* v. *Allein*, the real reason behind the decision, which held the by-law contrary to both common law

and statute law, is set out clearly. By-laws such as the one involved here, Coke says, are frequently a means of extortion for drawing money from workmen, either by delay or some other subtle device, or of oppression of young tradesmen by the old and rich of the same trade, not permitting them to work in their trade freely. To some gilds it was useless to present one's self, despite complete qualifications, for by one pretext or another permission to enter into trade in the town was bound to be denied.

This is true enough, but what of the precedents? They were quietly ignored—a frequent occurrence in Coke's writings and one that makes them so misleading as a guide to the law of the middle ages. Instead it is announced in a resounding sentence that no man can be prohibited from working in a lawful trade and that 'this is and always has been the common law'. If so, doubtless many cases might be brought forward out of Coke's magnificent store in support, but only two are cited, neither of any great value. He goes on to say that a gild cannot regulate a trade or restrain anyone from working at one. In this outrageously unhistorical statement several centuries of gild life are brushed aside as though they had never existed. Clearly we have left the fifteenth century behind, broken completely with the past, yet out of isolated remarks in fourteenth-century cases, and by ignoring others, Coke somehow managed to give this seventeenth-century view a semblance of historical support. So in his next point. In the middle ages the gild had supervised production, and seen to it that goods were well produced and that a man practising an art was skilful at it. It is not the past but the future that is implicit in Coke's remark that anyone may practise an art, for if he who takes work upon himself is unskilful, his ignorance is a sufficient punishment for him. He will get no clients. And if he spoils work, an action on the case lies against him.

Thus in a new age ancient precedents became valueless and were ignored, and others, even Magna Carta itself, took on meanings they had never had before. This is as it should be. Law must grow through the re-interpretation of the past, for only in such ways do judges and lawyers solve the paradox that law must be stable yet must never stand still. It is fortunate that Coke was not a better historian than he was, just as it is fortunate that the Noys and Hakewills, who went rummaging in the Tower intent upon parliamentary precedents, and who took only what they required from the parliament rolls of preceding centuries, were not over-particular about historical accuracy. Despite his intense concern with history, this most unhistorically-minded of men was no scholar, but a tremendously busy practising lawyer and judge. Coke did not try to rid his mind of the assumptions and presuppositions of his own age, and by an effort of will throw himself back into the fourteenth century, or re-think the thoughts of his predecessors on the Bench or the draftsmen of Magna Carta. He was always the Elizabethan, filled with the ideas of his own time and honestly convinced that they had always been current, even in the old days when the ancient Britons, as he believed, had talked Greek. Had he been more fastidious in his use of evidence, or spoken less resoundingly with what Hazlitt and Keats called 'the gusto of the Elizabethan voice', or ever stopped to consider that he might be wrong, he could never have accomplished the impossible task of reconciling the medieval and the modern. Though his work confounds the legal historian, its value can hardly be overestimated.

When his age spoke unequivocally to him, the fact that Coke read the Year Books as a Tudor, not as a medieval lawyer, and could draw a modern and progressive doctrine out of obsolescent technicalities to his own satisfaction and to that of his contemporaries, was an advantage, and in this lay his real strength. When it did not, the presuppositions of his own times, which he never put aside, were a decided disadvantage and led to added complexities. Here we may wish that he had understood our ancient law better, had realised the parts of it that were outdated and obsolete, and permitted them to perish with the age that had given them birth. To do this one must be a master, and though it is often said that Coke was a master of our medieval law, we will understand him better if we take the word 'master' to mean much what it does when we say Svengali was Trilby's master. I shall illustrate this and then be done, but first I must take you back for a moment to the fourteenth century.

When seisin is the basis of property law, if one thing is evident it is that a man who has been disseised is not an owner out of possession. We may talk of ownership and possession, but our medieval lawyer predecessors knew only seisin, which was a mixture of both. A disseisee simply and obviously has no seisin. He has a right of entry, and by entering he can recover his seisin, but until he has done that he has no seisin and can transfer none. If he attempts to transfer his land to another, the grantee will get no seisin and therefore nothing. If he gives or sells his claim to seisin, what then? The assignee will get nothing, for such a claim was valueless in the hands of any but the disseisee himself. The assignee, as one who has never had seisin, cannot enter upon the disseisor. If he does so, he can be ejected by force or by an assize of novel disseisin. He cannot bring an action of entry sur disseisin, for that assumes that he had once had seisin, which is clearly untrue. So too, in a writ of right, he must count on his own seisin or that of an ancestor. It is thus perfectly clear that an assignment by the disseisee of his right of entry gave nothing to the assignee. The rule follows directly from the concept of seisin and the writs for recovering seisin. Exactly the same result follows when A grants an estate for life to B, reserving a right of re-entry for default in services or in the payment of rent. The life tenant has seisin. The grantor, having once had seisin, may re-enter for default or bring an action to recover his seisin. The assignee of his right of entry can do neither.

If we open Coke's books, it is obvious at a glance that this simple state of affairs has long been forgotten. Despite the change in emphasis, a fourteenth-century lawyer might have recognised the rule, but certainly Coke's explanation for it would have seemed to him fantastically far-fetched. 'It is a maxim of the common law', Coke says, that no rights of entry or re-entry can be granted over. They are personal and non-assignable. The reason thereof is for the avoiding of maintenance and the stirring up of suits.[8] 'And here', he goes on to say, 'we may observe the great wisdom and policy of the sages and founders of our law, who have provided that no right nor thing in action shall be granted or assigned to strangers, for that would be the occasion of multiplying of contentions and suits, and of great oppression to the people.'[9] This was a reinterpretation of the past. As in the cases I dealt with earlier, Coke saw the old decisions as examples of a doctrine they did not contain and explained them in terms that made contemporary sense. But where *Darcy* v. *Allein* and the *Ipswich Tailors Case* looked toward the future and had a liberating effect, this was to have an unfortunate influence on English law for two centuries.

Let us look now at a right of re-entry for default reserved on a lease for life. As I have said, in the fourteenth century only the grantor could recover on default the seisin to which he had a claim. He had once had seisin, had given it on condition to the life tenant, and could recover it. Writs were framed for the recovery of seisins, and if a man had once had seisin, whether by purchase or by descent, it was proper that he should regain it. But if he had never gotten it, as the assignee of a right of entry or re-entry never had, the system did not protect him. Now, what if the grantor, having reserved a right of re-entry, transferred his reversion to a stranger? Seisin of the seigniory passed, with its right to wardship and escheat[10]; seisin of the services passed, with power to distrain and avow.[11] But what of the right of re-entry? Clearly the grantee of the seigniory, though he had gotten seisin of land in service, had not gotten seisin of land in demesne. This the grantor had once had, but he had given it to the life tenant, who still retained it. Having never had that, the assignee could not now claim it, for he had no former seisin on which to base his case. The grantor, on the other hand, having once had seisin, could still assert it. Thus we reach an anomaly. The only man who can assert the right of re-entry is the man who no longer has the slightest interest in the land. This is the rule laid down in Littleton's book.[12]

'If a man letteth land', Littleton says, 'to another for term of life, rendering to the lessor and his heirs a certain rent, and for default of payment a re-entry, and if afterwards the lessor granteth the reversion of the land to another in fee and the tenant for life attorn, if the rent be behind, the grantee of the reversion may distrain for the rent, but he may not enter into the land and oust the tenant, as the lessor might do, or his heirs. But if the lessor be allowed to enter and oust the tenant, then he would be remitted to his former estate, which he should not be since he has parted with it. Therefore the entry is taken away for ever.' Thus since the grantee cannot enter, having no defence to an assize of novel disseisin, and it would be unfair for the grantor to enter, the life tenant is simply relieved from any possible forfeiture for default.

How does Coke explain this case? 'Here', he says, 'Littleton illustrates one of the maxims of the common law, and the reason thereof is that if anything in entry or re-entry could be granted over, then pretended titles might be granted to great men whereby right might be trodden down and the weak oppressed, which the common law forbids.'[13] I draw your attention particularly to the word 'titles'.

As I have said, in the fourteenth century, when seisin is the basis of property law, a disseisee could recover the land of which he had been disseised not because he was in fact the owner, but because he had once had and was entitled to seisin. That is the only fact he must allege and prove. After 1500, it first became possible to recover land without alleging a seisin inherited or obtained, by the action of ejectment, essentially a personal action of trespass used fictitiously for trying titles. Before Coke was born it was well on its way toward displacing the real actions. In his own day, as Coke himself said, 'all titles of lands are for the greater part tried in actions of ejectment'.[14] But the old cases had said nothing of titles to land, only that a disseisee, until he had regained seisin, could not transfer it. To Coke and his contemporaries, who no longer thought in such terms, what they now said was that a man who had title, but not possession, could not transfer his title to another until he had regained possession. Once the fourteenth-century decisions were seen in this false light, a new problem that had not troubled the middle ages was posed, and thus a new answer was needed. Why had the ancient sages of the law held that one who has title but not possession cannot transfer his title to another until he has regained possession? As Coke pondered this illusory question, the only possible answer, as you will agree, was that the wisdom of the founders of the law had considered the transfer maintenance.

If Coke had understood our medieval law as Maitland understood it, or as our Literary Director understands it, these old cases, left behind from a previous stage of history, might well have been allowed to disappear with the vanishing concept of seisin itself. With them should have gone many others, preserved out of an almost superstitious reverence for the Year Books and the pages of Littleton's *Tenures*. But this is to expect too much from both the seventeenth century and from Coke. If we, as Englishmen and Americans, are indebted to him for an unhistorical but profoundly influential commentary on Magna Carta, and for much fundamental constitutional law not completely supported by the sources, we must be content to accept as well other examples of the past seen through unhistorical eyes. To the extent, and it is not small, that Coke's Institutes and Coke's Reports are modern and forward-looking books, we are deeply indebted to him. What English law would be without those volumes it is difficult to imagine. Indeed, when I consider all the judges England has had, I can think of no other whose absence would have had more serious effects on the course of English law than that of Edward Coke. A man of numerous faults, many of which I have conveniently forgotten on his birthday, he nevertheless fills a uniquely important place in English history and in the history of English law. The Selden Society must be congratulated on not permitting his anniversary to pass without recalling him to mind. It has been a great pleasure for me to say a word in his memory today.

NOTES

[1] B. M. Harl. MS. 7193, fol. 16.

[2] 24 L.Q.R. 373; *Collected Papers*, II, 190.

[3] C. J. Sisson, *Thomas Lodge and other Elizabethans* (1933), p. 498.

[4] 11 Rep. 84^v. D. O. Wagner, 'Coke and the rise of economic liberalism', *Ec. Hist. Rev.*, VI, 35 (1935).

[5] B. M. Harl. MS. 1857, fol. 9.

[6] E. St. J. Brooks, *Sir Christopher Hatton* (1946), p. 220.

[7] 11 Rep. 53.

[8] Co. Litt. 214.

[9] Co. Litt. 379.

[10] Litt. §579.

[11] Co. Litt. 310-11.

[12] Litt. §347.

[13] Co. Litt. 214.

[14] 5 Rep. 105^v.

18

PRAEMUNIRE AND SIR EDWARD COKE

THE DRAMATIC EVENTS of the last day of Hilary term, 1616, which concluded the long conflict between the court of chancery and the courts of common law[1] and led directly to the removal of Sir Edward Coke from his post as chief justice of the King's Bench,[2] have long been known. Though Francis Bacon was not present, his letter to James supplies the main outlines,[3] and the records of the Privy Council the substance,[4] of the proceedings. Two documents in the Ellesmere papers, however, bring us a step closer to the incident. They are résumés of the evidence of eyewitnesses, and appear to be the briefs from which the Solicitor-General made his oral presentation to the Council. Coke's words are set forth verbatim, and the names of those who were to substantiate them duly listed. The text is taken from EL 5971. EL 5973 is less complete, but some extracts from it have been placed in the notes.[5]

On the 13th day of ffebruary beeing the last day of Hillary Terme 13 Jacobi Regis two bills of inditements of praemunire were preferred to the grand jurie, beeing 19 persons, then appearing att the Kings Benche barre. The one of the bills preferred by Richard Glanvile, the other by William Allen.

The court presently tooke knowledge of them both. And the Lord Coke sayed secrettlie to the judges Wee must seeme to knowe nothing of this matter. And afterwardes his Lordship did openlie proteste that hee did not knowe the matter.[6]

The jurie having hadd theise bills but a verie short tyme by them to consider of, did not in their discretions holde yt fitt to finde them on a sudden, but conceyving the matter to bee waightie, and the case

[1] W. S. Holdsworth, *A History of English Law* (London, 1922), I, 459–65.

[2] *Ibid.*, V, 440.

[3] *Works*, ed. Spedding (London), XII (1869), 246–54.

[4] *Acts of the Privy Council, 1615–1616* (London, 1925), pp. 644–48.

[5] The capitalization has not been retained, but punctuation has been followed. The few obvious abbreviations have been expanded.

[6] To bee prooved by Robert Wolsley. Mr. Tothill did informe the woordes the Lord Coke spake secrettly to the judges."

a rare and leading case, desired they might have further tyme to consider of them. And that sithence the busines concerned the Kings service they desired allso (thoughe att their owne charges) that some of his Majesty's learned counsell might bee acquainted with the matter that so the said counsell might the better advise and directe them in their proceedinges. But this my Lord Coke denyed them, his Lordship then saying the case was so cleere as they needed not once to goe from the barre.[7]

Afterwards, the Lord Coke perceyving the jurie were resolved not to finde either of the sayd bills, his Lordship stoode upp, on his feete, and lifting upp his handes, sayed to the jurie, Why maisters? Have not they who informe for the King shewed unto you coppyes of the proceedinges in the chauncerie? And have they not made oathe that the same are true? Yes answered the fforeman, and sayed his Lordship then further, Is there not a judgment in the case? And is there not an oathe for the King? What would you more? Yes, againe was answere made, Your Lordship is rightly informed of bothe. There is an oathe indeed but yt is againste men of knowen honestye and creditte, and made by such a one as is reported to have neither honesty nor creditt, but knowen rather to bee a cheator and a coziner and therfore to such a one wee may not give creditt, especially hee beeing a partie that sweares in his owne case. And for the judgment, my Lorde, wee are not yet satisfied that the judgment was duely gotten, ffor judgmentes duely obteyned ought to bee obteyned in the terme tyme, and wee never yett knewe a terme in the middest of December, which is the tyme when his judgment was gotten. How know you that, sirra, (sayed my Lord Coke). Why, my Lorde, for the tyme wee finde yt so layed downe in the inditement ytselfe, for the woordes are theise, *vizt.*, that the judgment was gotten on the 22th of December, 4 of the Kinge.[8]

Att the juries first comming to the barre, the Lord Coke did grace the jurie with many good woordes, saying they were honest men, and a verie sufficient and substantiall jurie, and willed and advised them to deliver their consciences cheerfully and boldly, and not to feare the face of anyman, so long as they weere to speake for the Kinge, as

[7] "To bee prooved by George Parker, by Nicholas Bragg, Ryton, ffrancis Smithe. And by the examinacions of some of the jurie themselves remayning with Mr. Attorney."

[8] "To bee prooved by the jurie and by Robert Wolsley."

in this case they were. And Justice Dodderidge used some speeche to the like effect.[9]

The jurie was called to the barre 3 tymes, and at their second coming to the barre, the Lord Coke sayed unto the jurie, that yf they would not finde the bills hee would committ them. And that hee woulde sitt by yt, and not depa[r]te, untill the busines were done. And therfore willed them to goe togeither againe the third tyme. And att their beeing togeither the third tyme in a private roome conferring touching those inditements, [blank] Cotes, one qf the tippstaffs attending that court did goe into the sayd roome to the jurie, and to encourage them to finde the inditementes sayed unto them, Now,[10] maisters, you may goe on boldly and feare nothing for now newes is brought for certein that this great man is deade.[11]

But att the juries thirde retorne to the barre, when his Lordship sawe that they were fully resolved not to finde the bills, the foreman telling his Lordship that they were not satisfied in the evidence, and therfore that 17 of the 19 were agreed to retorne an *ignoramus*, his Lordship then sayed openly, that hee did not like such jurours that did use to meet in alehouses for dispatche of businesses that concerned the Kings service, swearing that their hadde been juggling, and that they hadd been tampered with, and badd them looke to themselves, and protested hee thought they hadd been instructed before hand, and that they were varlettes and knaves. And then willed Allen and Glanvile to prepare themselves against the next terme, saying that then hee would have a more sufficient jurie, and would have the evidence given openly att the barre.[12]

The same day upon a mocion made in the Kings Bench between Goodwyn and Gouldsmithe concerning a judgment in that court, the Lord Coke sayed openlie to the lawyers att the barre, Maisters,

[9] "To be prooved by William Nelson, and the later parte of the article prooved by George Parker, Robert ffrithe, and Ryton, et al."

[10] EL 5973: "The Lord Coke was angrye they staid soe long and badd them feare nothing, the lord Chaunncellor was dead."

[11] "To bee prooved by Robert ffrithe and Robert Wolsley and George Parker."

[12] "To be prooved by [Richard] Kelway, George Parker, Robert ffrithe, and Johnson and Bragg and Thomas Woode." EL 5973 adds: "Nota that upon lord Coke's threatening wordes one of the jury formerly agreed with the rest fell from them. And that Levesey being the fourth that spake, saying he found the billes, Lord Coke said, I thinke theise billes wilbe found anan."

looke to yt and take yt for a warninge that whosoever shall sett his hande to a bill into any Englishe court after a judgment att lawe wee will perclose him from the barre, for ever speaking more in this court. I give you a faire warning to preserve you from a greater mischiefe.[13] Wee must looke aboute, or the common lawe of England will bee overthrowen. And sayed further that hee thought the judges shoulde have little to doe att the assises in their circuites by reason the light of the lawe was like to bee obscured. And therupon sithence this matter now mooved was after judgment, willed the partie to preferre an inditement of praemunire.[14]

The court of Kings Benche did sitt untill almost two of the clocke, and that for the space of a full hower they satt still without hearing any other cause or mocion (all other busines of the court beeing dispatched) wherupon some of the judges told his Lordship that the day was more then spent, and that for their parte they coulde not sitt any longer with him, and therupon his Lordship verie discontentedly rose and went away with them.[15]

Theise thinges weere thus handeled in the Kings Benche the laste day of the terme when the Lorde Chancelor was supposed to bee deade or past all hope of recoverye.

[13] EL 5973 adds: "Some must be made an example and on whome it lighteth it will fall heavy."

[14] "To be prooved by Wolsley, Skynner, and ffrithe." EL 5973 adds: "Nota the Lord Coke said the judges of that court were the superintendents of the realm."

[15] "To bee prooved by Woolsley and 100 more."

19

COURTS OF RECORD AND SIR EDWARD COKE

THE middle ages rarely replaced one institution with another. New responsibilities and growing intelligence gave rise almost imperceptibly to new organizations, which for centuries might overlap and compete with the old before they finally superseded them. Thus after the introduction of the practice, late in the twelfth century, of regularly enrolling court proceedings, older methods for ascertaining what had occurred at a session of a court did not disappear; indeed the suggestion that the rolls might substitute completely for, and make unnecessary resort to, the older practice of oral record would have impressed contemporaries not at all. In Normandy, the author of a long and important book of Norman law, the *Grand Coutumier de Normandie,* though writing late in the second quarter of the thirteenth century, will find it not impossible to discuss in detail the rules as to the manner in which what had happened in a court on a previous occasion may be proved without making the smallest reference to the rolls upon which the events presumably were recorded.[1] And similarly in England, when plea rolls are still new, it is primarily to the justices before whom the pleas had been heard, their memories aided now by their rolls, or if the proceedings had occurred during the session of an eyre, aided by the record of the county,[2] or, if needs be, by the original recognitors of an assize,[3] that litigants, who continue to put themselves

---

[1]Viollet, "Les coutumiers de Normandie" in *Histoire littéraire de la France* (1906), vol. XXXIII, pp. 153-4; Delisle, *Mémoire sur les anciennes collections de jugements de l'Echiquier de Normandie* (Paris, 1864), at p. 257, n. 2; Besnier, *La Coutume de Normandie* (Paris, 1935), at pp. 116-9.

[2]Glanvill, *De Legibus,* lib. viii, c. 5. In 1207 (*Curia Regis Rolls,* v, p. 50) to prove a fine levied in the county, since almost all the judges before whom it had been done were dead ("eo quod fere omnes justiciarii obierunt") the sheriff was ordered to seek the record of the county. In 1211 (*C.R.R.,* vi, p. 135) two justices in eyre, John Grey, bishop of Norwich, and Walter de Crepping, "veniunt et recordantur". One of the parties "hoc audito, non vult contradicere recordo curie" but proceeds to show the case could not have ended as the justices record. Since it did not seem to the court that the record of the two justices was sufficient, "preceptum est quod vicecomes faciat venire coram domino rege xii milites de comitatu ad faciendum simul cum justiciariis recordum illud".

[3]*C.R.R.,* iii, p. 45 ("ponit se super rotulos anni primi regni regis Ricardi et super recognitores de eadem assisa"). In 1211 (*C.R.R.,* vi, p. 162) the question whether an assize had been brought "tempore regis Henrici patris coram Ricardo de Luci tunc capitali justiciario" is settled by an inquest which is to report "utrum assisa capta fuit sicut dictum est necne". The sheriff is instructed to inquire "si quis sit superstes qui fuit recongnitor in assisa illa".

upon the *recordum curie* and to vouch the justices to warranty, appeal.[4] The justices, in turn, "record", and this record, which may be oral or by writ, takes the form of a deposition: a narrative statement of facts based apparently upon the deponents' experiences and their recollection of them; frequently, it is but a simple reply to the question put.[5]   Though there is every reason to believe that the justices had consulted their rolls, there is no mention of rolls as such, for, though we bear in mind that the distinction between official and private documents is largely a fruitless one when applied to judicial records at this early date, we nevertheless may say that in the early thirteenth century the written rolls of decisions might be distinguished only with difficulty from the private memoranda of the justice, with which a litigant or another court, desirous of being apprized of a past judicial event, could have little direct concern.[6]   Just as before rolls were kept, the testimony of the judge before whom the matter had been pleaded, if, of course, he were still alive,[7] remained the most effective

---

[4]*C.R.R.*, i, p. 418; ii, pp. 15, 41, 210; iv, pp. 210, 264, 306; v, p. 49; vi, pp. 23, 308, 327; Maitland, *Bracton's Note Book*, ii, at p. 79.   The existence of rolls is reflected in the pleas of litigants who put themselves upon the "justiciarios et rotulos" or seek the "recordum curie et rotulorum".   *C.R.R.*, i, pp. 57, 177; iii, pp. 168, 170; iv, p. 36; D. M. Stenton, *Rolls of the Justices in Eyre* (Selden Society), nos. 142, 412, 928.   But "rolls" is used in no technical sense.   D. M. Stenton, *The Earliest Lincolnshire Assize Rolls* (Lincoln Record Society), at p. xxii.   For this period Professor Woodbine's statement in his edition of Glanvill (p. 241) that in the king's courts, with their written records, it was customary to vouch the rolls, must be taken with caution.

[5]*C.R.R.*, ii, p. 265; v, p. 173; ii, p. 19; vi, p. 354.

[6]There are many rolls which differ from one another in substance and verbal form.   *C.R.R.*, iii, pp. 301, 334; Bracton, *De Legibus*, f. 352b; Maitland, *Bracton's Note Book*, i, at p. 66; *English Historical Review* (1924), vol. XXXIX, p. 268; *Y.B. 5 Edw. II* (ed. Bolland, Selden Society), at pp. xi-xviii.   In the late thirteenth and in the fourteenth century it was still customary to allow a judge to retain his rolls until his death, and it was frequently years afterwards before his executors or his clerk were told to return his records.   Sayles, *Select Cases in the King's Bench of Edward I* (Selden Society), at pp. cxvi-cxxii; cliv-clxx; Stenton, *Rolls of the Justices in Eyre*, at pp. xix-xx.   Certainly in 1194 plea rolls are held in less esteem and regarded as serving more temporary purposes than the great rolls of the exchequer, for litigants make payments to have cases entered on the pipe roll both where the case is before itinerant justices, and where it is before the central court at Westminster.   *Pipe Roll 5 Rich. I*, at p. 29; *6 Rich. I*, at p. 163.   *Cf.* Richardson, "An Early Fine" in 48 *Law Quarterly Review* (1932), at p. 415.

[7]Glanvill, *De Legibus*, lib. viii, c. 8: if the judges before whom a fine had been levied could not remember it (or if they were dead) the court would act as though none had been levied.   This is, of course, prior to the introduction of the device of the "foot".   In 1203 a litigant at Northampton referred to a case heard "in the court of the lord king in the time of king Henry before Sir H. archbishop of Canterbury,

way of establishing the fact. Thus at Lincoln in 1202, when it was uncertain what had happened in two earlier suits before Geoffrey fitz Peter, it is to him that reference is made, not to his roll.[8] And at Westminster, where pressure of increasing litigation tended to make an appeal to the record of the court, whose intimate connexion with the exchequer should be noted, a simple reference to a roll,[9] when Ellis de Bello Campo and Constance, his wife, alleged that Guy de Fukeworth had lost a suit "in curia domini regis coram justiciariis suis apud Westmonasterium . . . scilicet coram Simone de Pateshulle, E. de Faucumberge, J. de Gesting [et] Waltero de Crepping", and this was denied, the fact was determined not by reference to a roll but by summoning the justices "qui tunc fuerunt justiciarii" who came and recorded ("venerunt et recordati fuerunt") what had occurred before them.[10] This must be due in part to the smallness of staff and contiguity of offices of the *curia,* in part to the continuance of a practice universal in the absence of rolls, but we must note that a written record made at the time of the event did not have a special sanctity in the popular view, and that this is especially true of written rolls that were brief and informal, and made to serve primarily as memoranda of

---

then dean of York, and before Osbert fitz Hervey and master Godfrey de Insula, who are alive, and before other justices who are dead. And he thereupon vouches the king's court and the aforesaid justices to warranty." In 1214 (*C.R.R.,* vii, p. 66), the defendant in an assize of *darrein presentment* claimed that the plaintiff's father had unsuccessfully urged the same suit "tempore regis Ricardi" before itinerant justices and again "coram justiciariis apud Westmonasterium". The defendant "de recordo curie dicit quod, si justiciarii presentes essent, inde poneret se super eos, set omnes obuerunt [*sic*]".

[8]*The Earliest Lincolnshire Assize Rolls,* nos. 263, 922; *Select Civil Pleas* (Selden Society), no. 231.

[9]Though we should not, perhaps, stress the words of litigants reflected through the clerk too strongly, of the four cases in the printed curia regis rolls in which the litigant places himself simply on the rolls, two concern the rolls of the bench. *C.R.R.,* i, p. 402 ("ponit se super rotulos curie domini regis de Westmonasterio"), p. 408 ("vocat ad warantum rotulos de Westmonasterio"). *Cf.* the method of vouching exchequer rolls: *C.R.R.,* ii, p. 299 ("vocavit rotulos magni scaccarii") ; Assize Roll no. 362, m. 8, printed in *Transactions of the Royal Historical Society* (ser. 4), vol. V, p. 61; ("ponit se super rotulos de scaccario"). For exchequer administrative expedients which were multiplying rapidly toward the close of the twelfth century to produce the highly organized system of the thirteenth, see: Richardson, "William of Ely, the King's Treasurer" in *Transactions of the Royal Historical Society* (ser 4), vol XV, p. 54; Mills, "Experiments in Exchequer Procedure" in *ibid.,* vol. VIII, p. 151.

[10]*C.R.R.,* vii, p. 213. Similarly two years earlier, in 1212, Pateshulle, Fauconberg, and Pointon are summoned "et venerunt coram justiciariis et recordantur". *C.R.R.,* vi, pp. 308, 354.

the appointment of attorneys, essoins, and assignment of days. The roll could well be brief, for as we have indicated, it did not yet comprise the record which the court when required could furnish fully and completely. The tremendous growth and consolidation of administrative technique during the reign of Henry III, and the similar expansion of the common law, clearly visible in a comparison between the treatise that goes under the name of Glanvill and Bracton's huge but unfinished work, will effect very substantial changes in the rolls and in the method of bearing record, but it will be many years before traces of earlier practice completely disappear.

Though the cases in *Bracton's Note Book* do not give an entirely accurate picture of the normal and usual entries upon a plea roll of the reign of Henry III,[11] it is safe to say that the general form of enrollment varies considerably from that found upon the rolls of Richard and John. The entries are longer and reflect a deliberate attempt to put on the roll not simply a brief narrative of the proceedings, but all the essential details of the suit. This, of course, is but another example of the growth of administrative technique in the governmental machine, for throughout the century new records, or new divisions in already existing records, make their appearance and betray corresponding changes in the methods or in the organization of many departments, made without doubt to facilitate administration.[12] Yet we must look beyond this general departmentalization and improvement in method to explain the expansion of plea roll entries satisfactorily, though here, as in the exchequer and chancery reforms, the increasing volume of business forms a common underlying cause. The rapid multiplication of writs made it necessary to discriminate between forms of action, and as the technical body of common law grew under the hands of Henry's professional judges—Stephen Segrave, Martin Pateshulle, William Raleigh, Henry of Bath, Roger Thurkelby, and Gilbert of Preston—the necessary facts in each suit became more and more numerous. Similarly, the growth of pleading, for example the use of the *exceptio* in the possessory assizes, drew new facts into the record.

---

[11]The *Note Book*, of course, consists of cases which interested Bracton and were copied for him from the plea rolls into the collection of loose quires which Vinogradoff named the Note Book. An examination of the cases marked by Bracton on the rolls, not separated from their context, indicates that longer and fuller entries frequently were selected. Stenton, *Rolls of the Justices in Eyre; Placitorum Abbreviatio*, at pp. 101 *ff*.

[12]E. F. Jacob, "England: Henry III" in *Cambridge Mediaeval History* (1929), vol. VI, p. 273; R. F. Treharne, *The Baronial Plan of Reform, 1258-1263* (Manchester, 1932), pp. 18-30; 37-47; Jenkinson and Formoy, *Select Cases in the Exchequer of Pleas* (Selden Society, 1932).

But of more importance is the growth of appellate procedure which made the process of bearing record to a superior court tremendously more frequent. No adequate account of the history of this procedure has yet been written: we may see its germ in the 1178 reservation of difficult problems for the consideration of the king and his wiser men,[13] and by the reign of Edward I development is well advanced, and records are no longer transferred from one court to another only with difficulty and only at the initiative of the court itself. A party to an action may purchase a writ in the form of a *venire facias* calling upon the judges or the treasurer and chamberlains of the treasury to send into court any transcript from the rolls upon which he proposed to rely in support of his case. Whether this came from the justices or from the treasury, it is quite evidently a simple copy of the proper entry on the roll, even to the inclusion of the marginal venue.[14] At some intermediate time, perhaps during the first quarter of the thirteenth century, it must have become increasingly apparent that reliance upon memory, aided by the brief memorandum on the roll, was no longer practical, and judges must have come more and more to rely instead upon what they found entered in their roll, and to insist that the case be entered in sufficient detail to permit them this complete reliance.[15] Each judge had his own roll, kept for him

---

[13]*Benedict of Peterborough* (Rolls Series), vol. I, at p. 207; Sayles, *op. cit.,* at p. xxv.

[14]How soon plea rolls were deposited in the treasury we cannot say. At Michaelmas, 1257, a general injunction, which has often been quoted, was issued to the barons of the exchequer ordering them to inquire into whose custody had come the records of Henry III's time of eyres, common bench, and king's bench, and to get them deposited in the treasury; henceforward, the judges were always to return their records there. *L.T.R. Memoranda Roll,* no. 33 (42 Hen. III), m.8, printed by Sayles, *Select Cases in the King's Bench,* at p. cliv. But even after this order there is great dilatoriness and laxity in placing rolls under official custody. Sayles, *op. cit.,* at pp. cxvi-cxxii, cliv-clxx, and note Professor Sayles's remark that judges were permitted to keep their rolls as if they were their personal property (at p. cxvii) which throws light upon n. 6, *supra.*

[15]The record of the king's courts was incontrovertible, and when that record became simply what was entered on the roll, the roll acquired similar incontrovertibility. This must be understood to be unconnected with any theory of the *testamentum regis* (Brunner, "Das Gerichtszeugnis und die fränkische Königsurkunde" in *Abhandlungen zur Rechtsgeschichte* (Weimar, 1931), vol. I, at pp. 434, 440; *Die Entstehung der Schwurgerichte* (Berlin, 1872), at p. 50; *Forschungen zur Geschichte des deutschen und französischen Rechtes* (Halle, 1916), at p. 290) to which Mr. Lapsley has recently directed attention. Lapsley, "The Court, Record and Roll of the County" in 51 *Law Quarterly Review* (1935), at p. 319. *Cf.* Thorne, "Notes on Courts of Record in England" in 40 *West Virginia Law Quarterly* (1934); above, 61ff. We can leave to Occam's razor the theory (Plucknett, *A Concise History of the Common*

by a clerk—a survival of earlier days when the record was the deposition made by the justices, each aided by his personal memoranda—but since personal rolls can and do vary,[16] and since the record is rapidly becoming simply what is entered on the roll, Bracton tells us that in case of variance the court is to be guided by what appears in the principal roll (*primum rotulum*), the roll of the protonotary.[17] In 1279 there is an indication that the justices in eyre likewise kept a principal roll, for they explain their failure to send a record of a plea to the court *coram rege* by the absence of William of Saham who, they say, at that time kept the principal (*primum*) roll, and word is then sent William that he have the record before the king's bench a fortnight after Hilary.[18] In these principal rolls we may observe the rolls of *placita* assuming their new character as official records of the court and losing their earlier status as judges' memoranda; they are the ancestors of the single roll of the early fourteenth-century bench.[19]

For most purposes, then, the entry on the roll will be the court's record, and though judges still appear in person and record,[20] litigants no longer vouch the court to warranty or put themselves upon the *recordum curie,* but place themselves forthrightly upon the rolls or "super recordum rotulorum"; indeed record and roll have become, at least in the mouths of litigants, synonymous. We may hazard the opinion that the change takes place early in Henry's reign, after the justices of John's have passed out of active service, though based as they are upon the selected cases in *Bracton's Note Book* and on the words of litigants entered on the rolls by clerks, our results must be regarded as largely provisional.[21] More im-

---

Law (ed. 2, Rochester, 1936) that the rolls become indisputable through domesday book and exchequer example. We have dealt elsewhere with the question of the king's power to record (*Y.B. 11-12 Edw. III* (Rolls Series), at p. xxxiii; *Y.B. 12-13 Edw. III* (Rolls Series), at pp. 97-101, 183) and with that of the transformation of a simple transcript into an incontrovertible record by the great seal (*Y.B. 6-7 Edw. II* (Selden Society), at pp. xxv-xxvii) : see Thorne, *op. cit.,* at p. 68, n. 24.

[16]*C.R.R.,* iii, pp. 301, 334; *B.N.B.,* ii, at pp. 62, 124; iii, at pp. 364, 397-8.

[17]*De Legibus,* f. 352b. In 1222 in the bench, the roll of William of York, which the annotator of *Bracton's Note Book* (Bracton) calls the principal roll, equals the testimony of the others. *B.N.B.,* ii, at p. 124.

[18]Sayles, *Select Cases in the King's Bench of Edward I,* at p. 51.

[19]For the reign of Edward II and later there are but two rolls: the rex roll and that of the chief justice. *Y.B. 5 Edw. II* (Selden Society, 1916), at pp. xi-xviii; *Y.B. 6 Edw. II* (ed. Vinogradoff and Ehrlich, Selden Society), at p. xxiv. In the reign of Edward III the rex roll is about one-tenth as complete as the roll of the chief justice. *Y.B. 16 Edw. III* (Rolls Series), at pp. xxv-xxix.

[20]Sayles, *op. cit.,* at pp. 7, 169.

[21]Voucher of justices to warranty or voucher of justices and rolls: *B.N.B.,* ii,

portant is the appearance of the distinction between "matter of record" and "matter in pays" or matter which lies in the cognizance of the country and therefore can be established by the verdict of jurors. Now that the judges' *recordum* is no longer a statement of recollected facts, similar to that of the county court and comparable to the *recordatio vel recognitio* of the constitutions of Clarendon and of the smallest inquest, but an entry on a roll, it is felt that it may not be gainsaid by the country, and that events determined before the justices may not be established in any way other than by examination of the roll.[22] This differs quite widely from the procedure of the twelfth century as we have indicated it above.

The complete equation of record and roll led lawyers to exhibit much uneasiness about what appeared there, it being well understood that judgment would be on the basis of what had been enrolled. Lawyers had no access to the rolls,[23] and since in the course of the hearing they might advance, withdraw, or modify their pleas, they were anxious to have their final, and not an intermediate, provisional plea (put forward to draw their opponent's fire and perhaps to afford a glimpse of the strength of his case) entered and thus made into an unalterable part of the record.[24] They seek to draw a distinction, therefore, between record and roll in a way very reminiscent of the older practice we have sketched above.[25] A century later the question of amending the roll to correspond with the

---

at p. 69 (1219), at p. 257 (1220), iii, at p. 364 (1220), at p. 552 (1226), at p. 721 (1219); Record equated with roll: *B.N.B.*, ii, at p. 480 (1231), at p. 524 (1232), iii, at p. 154 (1235), at p. 552 (1226); Simple voucher of rolls: *B.N.B.*, ii, at p. 450 (1231), at p. 638 (1234), iii, at p. 678 (1232), iii, at p. 65 (1224), at p. 289 (1239/40). From these cases we may date the changes roughly early in the second quarter of the thirteenth century. *Cf.* ii, at p. 79 (1220): "inventum est in rotulis *et* curia domini Regis recordatur." In 1200, five years after feet of fines began to be preserved in the treasury, a litigant will so far remember the prior procedure as to vouch both the justices and the foot to warranty ("vocat justiciarios ad warantiam et pedem cirographi qui est in thesauro"). *C.R.R.*, i, p. 208. Twenty-four years later (*B.N.B.*, iii, at p. 26) the practice will have changed ("vocavit pedem cirographi ad warantum").

[22]*B.N.B.*, iii, at p. 415; *cf.* ii, at p. 550; iii, at p. 664; Sayles, *op. cit.*, at pp. 11, 19, 50, 97-8; *Y.B. 9 Edw. II* (Selden Society), at p. 42.

[23]This must be taken subject to some exceptions: transcripts were made by the clerks, for in no other way could entries be duplicated in private archives. Sayles, *op. cit.*, at pp. lxxxvii-lxxxviii. Entries appear likewise in the printed Year Books, due perhaps to the cordial relation between clerk and compiler.

[24]Holdsworth, *History of English Law* (1923), vol. III, at pp. 636 *ff.*; Plucknett, *Concise History of the Common Law* (ed. 2, 1936), at pp. 355-9.

[25]*Y.B. 16 Edw. III* (Rolls Series) 2, at p. 133 ("ceo quest ore entre en roulle ne put neynt estre dit recorde; par quei, Sire, nous prioms qe vous voillez recorder la chose tiel com il fut").

record (by which is meant the proceedings as they actually occurred) will be a serious one to which many folios in the Year Books will be devoted, and the mechanical identification of record and roll will give rise to transparent fictions such as that enunciated by William Cheyne, chief justice of the king's bench: "Car tout le premier term le record n'est pas en le roll, mes en nous justices, et le roll n'est, meme le term que le jugement est done, forsque notre remembrance."[26]   Echoes of an earlier practice remain, however, at least as late as the fourteenth century.[27]   In 1334 an inquest had been taken at *nisi prius* "et nota qen le recorde ny ad pas mencion fait que enquys fut des damages".   Willoughby, however, who had taken the inquest and was now one of the judges sitting in the bench, "recorda de bouche" that the jury had assessed damages.[28]   In 1313 the judges refused to seal a bill of exceptions as required by the Statute of Westminster II, c. 31, but offered instead the testimony of the whole court ("testmoygniance de tote la courte") which is nothing more or less than what would have been the record of the court, though we observe that it is no longer so called.[29]   But instances of this sort become less frequent, and it may be said that roll and record soon are completely synonymous, so much so, indeed, that in the *Termes de la Ley* record is defined as a writing on a parchment roll, and courts of record distinguished from others by simple reference to a parchment roll.

In the twelfth century the question of the incontestability of a court's record must be quite clearly distinguished from that of written rolls.   As early as the *Leis Willelme* and the *Leges Henrici,* long before the introduction of court rolls, it seems clear that the king's court has record, or in other words, that its testimony to all that had been done before it is conclusive; other courts' accounts of their own proceedings, on the contrary, may be impeached by witnesses who had been present at the trial.[30] We may hazard the opinion that this privilege of the king's court is connected with the procedure of an age when both plaintiff and defendant must make their cases formally in statements bristling with words of court, in which a variation would be fatal, for both the *Leis Willelme* and Glanvill discuss record in relation to the procedure of denying or adding

---

[26]*Y.B. 7 Hen. VI, Pasch. 22,* at p. 30; *Y.B. 7 Hen. VI, Mich. 24,* at p. 15.

[27]*Rotuli Parl.,* vol. I, at p. 84; *Y.B. 17-18 Edw. III* (Rolls Series), at pp. 555-6, 564.

[28]*Y.B. 18-19 Edw. III* (Rolls Series), at p. 299.

[29]*Y.B. 6 & 7 Edw. II* (Eyre of Kent) 1, at pp. 175-6; *cf.* Plucknett, *Statutes and their Interpretation in the Fourteenth Century* (Cambridge, 1922), at p. 68.

[30]*Leis Willelme,* c. 24; *Leg. Henr.,* c. 31, §4, c. 49, §4; Glanvill, *De Legibus,* lib. viii, c. 9; *C.R.R.,* ii, p. 260.

to what one has said in court.[31]   With the spread of the administrative practices of the king's court, or with the employment of a practice which other courts, as well as those of the king, found useful, we find records of enrolled proceedings in other courts, in particular the county court. But here as at first in the royal courts, the rolls did not substitute for the *recordum,* or statement of recollected facts, nor did the appearance of a roll affect in the slightest degree the recognized status of the county court as one which distinctly did not enjoy the privilege of incontrovertible record.   This is a point of considerable importance which has not been sufficiently emphasized by the participants in a recent controversy on the record of the county court.[32]   The county plea roll was neither a wholly public or wholly private document in much the way the contemporary plea roll of a king's justice was neither, though the fact that they were never called into the treasury, the final test of an official document, led them rapidly to a completely private status.[33]   Since the rolls were not those of a court of record, they could have no more incontestability than that possessed by the court whose proceedings they comprised, and thus the question why were these rolls not of record is an unreal one, based on a confusion between record and roll similar to that which led Professor Woodbine to attempt to reconcile the county's lack of record with the undoubted existence of county rolls by emphasizing their connexion with

---

[31]*Leis Willelme,* c. 24 (Liebermann, *Gesetze der Angelsachsen,* vol. I, at p. 510) : "De hume ki plaided en curt, en ki curt que ceo seit, fors la u le cors le rei seit, e hume lui met sure, k'il ad dit chose, qu'il ne voille conuistre, s'il pot derehdner par un entendable hume del plait oant e veant, qu'il ne l'averad dit, recovré ad sa parole." Glanvill, *De Legibus,* lib. viii, c. 9.   At a time when a complaint against a judgment is not distinguished from an accusation against the judge who made it, the statement that the king's court is of record may only be the equivalent of the assertion that false judgment does not lie against it.

[32]Plucknett, "New Light on the Old County Court" in 42 *Harvard Law Review* (1929), at pp. 639 *ff.;* Woodbine, "County Court Rolls and County Court Records" in 43 *ibid.* (1930), at pp. 1083 *ff.;* Plucknett, "A Note on the County Rolls" in 43 *ibid.* (1930), at p. 1111; Lapsley, "The Court, Record and Roll of the County" in 51 *Law Quarterly Review* (1935), at pp. 299 *ff.*

[33]In the London eyre of 15 Edw. II, Staunton J. asked what became of the rolls of a sheriff who was removed from office.   Did he retain them, or were they taken to the treasury?   He was told that the sheriff kept them.   "Of a truth, then," said Mutford J., "they who bring actions before sheriffs get but their labour for their pains ('Donqes cels qe pledent devant les viscontes perdent malement lor travayle')." This extract from Lincoln's Inn Hale MS 141, f. 48 is printed by Dr. Bolland in *Y.B. 5 Edw. II* (Selden Society, 1916), at p. xviii, n. 3.   In the Kent eyre of 6 & 7 Edw. II, when various county rolls were being called for by the justices, the sheriff came to deliver up all the common pleas of the county, but the justices refused them. *Y.B. 6 & 7 Edw. II* (Eyre of Kent) i, at p. 23.   Cf. Lapsley, *op. cit.,* at p. 315.

the sheriff's office and labelling them sheriff's rolls. In other words, the rolls were not incontrovertible records in the technical sense because the court's oral record (upon which the ancient distinction between courts of record and courts not of record was based) was not incontrovertible. Nevertheless the rolls did embody at least part of the proceedings of the county court; and might serve to refresh the suitors' memory of events that had occurred there: indeed we know that the roll was consulted by suitors charged with the task of making a record of the court's action.[34] The further question remains, why was not the simple entry sent, why did not the (controvertible) entry substitute for the (controvertible) record brought by the four knights? The answer, we venture to think, lies here: the old county court's record, just as that of the king's court in the late twelfth century, was its memory. As we have endeavoured to indicate, due to many causes, the chief of which is the pressure of increased litigation, entries upon royal rolls expanded, and the roll itself grew from a writing intended to serve as a memorandum of the assignment of days and other exact data that might easily be forgotten and to supply a narrative and brief statement of facts as an aid to memory, into a full and detailed account of court proceedings, and finally into the *recordum* itself. The county roll did not pass through these stages. There is no need to visualize a strong antagonism between sheriff and suitors: both were essential to the proper functioning of the court, and the fact that the roll was compiled by the sheriff's office was not the reason for its failure to substitute for the record based on the memory of suitors. The explanation lies rather in the fact that the county roll, originating as an aid to memory,[35] never passed beyond that point. Had it become necessary to rely upon the rolls rather than upon the memory of the suitors, another result might have been reached, but memories were long and suits not too frequent in the communal courts, and since the written record would still be controvertible, there was no effort made by the treasury to take the rolls into custody, nor were they ever asked for by the royal judges.[36]

---

[34]Several cases are discussed by Mr. Lapsley, *op. cit.*, at pp. 307 *ff.*, especially 312-4.

[35]The entries remain brief and stereotyped. The names of the parties, the cause of action, the essoins, the attachments and the names of those who make them, the stage at which the case rests in this particular county court, the fines and amercements, are all that appear. Woodbine, *op. cit.*, at p. 1092, n. 31. Their resemblance to the early plea rolls of the royal court is close. Mr. Lapsley (51 *Law Quarterly Review*, at p. 311, n.) presents a comparison between the entry on the roll and *recordum* in the Chester county court which illustrates the difference admirably.

[36]The Willicot case (*C.R.R.*, vi, pp. 202, 208, 228-30; *Placit. Abbrev.*, at p. 85a), has been discussed at length by Mr. Lapsley both in the paper cited above and in

The record of the county court continued to be made by four knights who came before the judges and recorded in much the way we observed Pateshulle, Fauconberg, Gesting, and Crepping, former judges of the bench, recording before the judges then sitting at Westminster, though there is here an interesting series of stages to which we now turn.

At the time of our earliest plea rolls the record of the county was made by four knights "missi pro comitatu ad faciendum recordum comitatus",[37] who came and recorded orally what had occurred at a session of the county court at which they had been present. How far the story told by the knights was a repetition of the record agreed upon by the county in response to the *recordari facias* we cannot say; Glanvill seems to recognize the knights as simply bearing the county's record,[38] but we must avoid visualizing in the early thirteenth century any mere repetition of a precise story formulated by the county and only transmitted by the knights. Later, as an aid to memory, the record agreed upon in the county is written down, probably by the sheriff and the knights, and then read by them before the superior court. Contemporaneously, the writ to the sheriff begins to include the instruction to have the *recordum comitatus* sent "sub sigillo suo" which clearly indicates that, just as the roll had become the record of the king's courts, the written account of county proceedings had become its record.[39] In the late thirteenth century the knights will merely present and avow it, and will no longer, even in form, make it.[40] Thus the oral record of the county, made *ad hoc,* and "redactum in scripto" becomes the county record: it remains, however, still as completely controvertible as it had been earlier, and, in addition to inertia, the reason for the continued presence of the four knights lies here. An action of false judgment against the county court was in origin not so much a form of appellate procedure for the correction of errors as an action in which the suitors were defendants, liable to amercement, and in appropriate cases,

---

the *English Historical Review,* vol. XLVII, pp. 179-93. In it the sheriff is ordered to cause Walter the clerk to come with the roll of the county "ubi loquela inbreviata est", but this is not to aid the court in determining the *recordum* of the county, that is brought by the four knights, but to aid the prior in developing his case, to show that the words "nec venit nec" had been written between the lines in another hand. For the writ ordering the sheriff to cause Walter to come "cum rotulo suo" the prior paid one mark.

[37]*C.R.R.,* i, pp. 44, 227, 393, 445; ii, pp. 260, 269; iv, p. 293; v, pp. 45, 160; vi, pp. 228, 376. Woodbine, *Glanvill, De Legibus* (New Haven, 1932), at pp. 239-45.

[38]Glanvill, *De Legibus,* lib. viii, c. 10.

[39]Bracton, *De Legibus,* fo. 149b. *B.N.B.,* ii, at pp. 172, 195, 195, n. 5, 197, n. 4; iii, at pp. 9, 149, 165, 365. In criminal matters the practice is much earlier: *C.R.R.,* vii, pp. 110, 115, 169.

[40]Sayles, *op. cit.,* at pp. 63, 131; *Y.B. 19 Edw. 111* (Rolls Series), at pp. 479-80.

to the payment of damages.[41]   The action gradually lost a portion of its character as an accusation of the court, for by Glanvill's time, the knights who represent the county, who are in fact the county,[42] no longer need defend their record by battle.   When the truth of the record is denied, and in the thirteenth century, with the growth of pleading, it becomes possible for the plaintiff to plead more than a flat denial and both to admit and deny parts of the record,[43] the knights defend it, and even in Edward's time, when they need no longer do more than present the written record, they remain as quasi-defendants.

II

The earliest distinguishing characteristic of a court of record is the indisputability of its oral record.   As we have indicated, a second point of differentiation appears in the parchment roll, identified with the record, which stamps the court that keeps it as one of record.   Soon other differences appear as lawyers begin to construct theoretical bases for procedures and powers they found courts in practice exercising, and these new definitions remain side by side with the old.   The writ of false judgment was the means by which judgments of the county or other local courts were brought to the royal courts for review, and since these courts were not of record, it becomes possible to express their status by the statement that where a writ of false judgment rather than error lies the court is not one of record.   In the same way, these courts were popular courts in the sense that judgment was given by the suitors, and this is rationalized into the statement that where suitors are judges there a writ of false judgment and not error lies, and since that writ lies only from a court not of record, then where suitors are judges they do not hold a court of record.[44]   The history of the county court illustrates these rules aptly, for though it was clearly not a court of record as early as Glanvill,[45] under certain circumstances it bore record as completely as did the central courts at Westminster, and the decline of this dual jurisdiction affords an example both of the new definitions of courts of record which were becoming current and of the curious loss of record in the county court.

---

[41]Pollock and Maitland, *History of English Law* (1923), vol. II, at p. 666.

[42]*C.R.R.*, iii, pp. 136-7, 140; v, pp. 16-7; vi, pp. 173, 383. *B.N.B.*, iii, at p. 366.

[43]*B.N.B.*, ii, at pp. 37, 197, *passim.   Cf.* Pollock and Maitland, *History of English Law*, vol. II, at pp. 608-15.

[44]Holdsworth, *History of English Law* (1924), vol. V, at p. 159.

[45]Glanvill, *De Legibus*, lib. viii, c. 9; Bracton, *De Legibus*, fo. 156b; Hengham, *Summa Magna*, c. 4; W. A. Morris, *The Early English County Court* (Berkeley, 1926), at p. 128.

Both Bracton and Fleta describe a twofold jurisdiction in the county, in the second of which the sheriff heard pleas as *iustitiarius regis* by virtue of an *ad hoc* delegation of authority by means of the writ *justicies*.[46] In this capacity as royal judge the sheriff possessed record. But what is clear in the thirteenth century is far from clear in the fifteenth. In 1486, after a writ of admeasurement of pasture had been removed to the bench by *certiorari*, the defendant claimed that it should have been removed by *pone, recordari,* or false judgment, since the admeasurement was made not before justices but before the sheriff:

> *Jenney* (for the defendant) : The admeasurement was made by the sheriff who is not a justice, for the suitors are judges in the county court, just as in a writ of *justicies*. *Danby*: In *justicies* the sheriff is judge, not the suitors, for the writ reads *quod justices T. etc.* and thus is a commission and command to the sheriff who holds the plea as a justice, and well he may, for the plea is not *in pleno comitatu* . . . *Littleton*: On the contrary, neither in *justicies* nor in any viscontiel action is the sheriff judge, but only the suitors, for he has no court except the county court and can hold no pleas except there—if he does it is *coram non judice*. And thus in replevin the command is *replegiari facias*, yet it is held in the county and the suitors are judges; and so here, for the *justicies* has no other effect than to allow him to hold pleas involving more than forty shillings. And if they (the suitors) were not judges then one could not have false judgment, for this writ lies only against suitors, but on a judgment given under *justicies* false judgment lies, proving that the suitors are judges. *Quod Choke and Needham affirmavit.*[47]

The justices are here directing their attention more to the question of the proper writ than to a distinction between courts of record and courts not of record, but that problem receives discussion elsewhere:

> *Moyle*: In debt it cannot be pleaded that the plaintiff had recovered before on the same bill or contract in the county under a *justicies*, or in any other court not of record, unless he had sued execution. But the matter is otherwise in a court of record.[48]

---

[46]Bracton, *De Legibus,* fo. 108, 155b-156; Fleta, ii, c. 43; Plucknett, "New Light on the Old County Court" in *42 Harvard Law Review* (1929), at pp. 644 *ff.;* Woodbine, "County Court Rolls and County Court Records" in 43 *ibid.* (1930), at pp. 1107 *ff.;* Morris, *The Mediaeval English Sheriff* (Manchester, 1927), at pp. 73, 198.

[47]*Y.B. 7 Edw. IV. Hil. 27* (1468). See also: *Y.B. 39 Hen. VI. Mich. 5* noted in *Brooke's Abridgement,* Justicies 6: "Nota que in court baron, hundred, et county, les suitors sont judges, et hoc cibien in brief de droit patent direct al court baron, in *justicies,* come sur auters suites que sont la per plaint sans brief." Also: *Y.B. 3 Hen. VI. Pasch. 2* (1402) ; *Y.B. 7 Hen. VI. Mich. 17* (1429) ; *Y.B. 34 Hen. VI. Pasch. 2* (1456) ; *Y.B. 21 Edw. IV. Mich. 46* (1482) ; *Y.B. 16 Hen. VII. Mich. 6* (1501).

[48]*Y.B. 9 Edw. IV. Hil. 10* (1470) ; *Y.B. 34 Hen. VI. Trin. 13* (1456) : "*Little-*

Coke expounded the medieval rules ably in *Jentleman's Case.*[49] The question as there raised was whether in a writ of right patent directed to the lord of the manor, or in a writ of right close directed to the lord of ancient demesne, or in a writ of *justicies* directed to the sheriff, the court held by virtue of the writ was or was not a court of record. It was argued that the lord, the bailiff, or the sheriff was constituted judge by the writ since it was directed to him and not to the suitors, and that "as the writ is of record and constitutes a new judge, then the authority of the judge being by the king's writ, the court must be one of record". This Coke vigorously denied: the writ is sent to the lord or sheriff because the court baron is the lord's court, the county court the sheriff's, and the writ is sent to him to whom the court belongs. Further, the suitors are judges, and since they hold no king's writ, they hold no king's court. Also, a writ of false judgment and not error lies whether the plea be by writ or not, and as false judgment lies only from a court not of record, these courts are not of record. The view reached by Coke differs completely from that expressed in Bracton, Fleta, and Britton: to them the sheriff hearing pleas by delegated authority, and thus as *iustitiarius regis,* clearly had record, though his court did not necessarily keep a roll. At first sight, therefore, we are tempted to conclude, as did Mr. Pike in a similar instance,[50] that Coke has perverted his sources, but as we have shown, there is adequate Year Book evidence to indicate that he is correctly interpreting the law of the fifteenth and sixteenth centuries. The distinction between proceedings by the county court and proceedings in the county court had been lost, or in other words, the king's county court and the sheriff's county court had become the same institution. With this merger the sheriff's privilege of record vanished.

Coke is here defining courts of record along ordinary and accepted lines, repeating, in fact, the precise words of Littleton a century and more earlier, but he is responsible in large measure for the curious modern

---

ton: If a *justicies* is sent to the sheriff, even though it is an original writ, the party will never be allowed a writ of error on it, but only false judgment. But if judgment is given in a franchise, there error will lie. *Moyle*: On a judgment given in the county under *justicies,* as you say, false judgment and not error lies. But if the writ of *justicies* is removed here by *pone,* as can well be done pending the plea, Sir, in that case after plea and judgment given in this court, the party doubtless will have a writ of error and not false judgment. . . ."

[49] 6 Rep. 11b. *Coke Litt.* 117b; *Coke Inst.,* ii, p. 312; iv, c. 55; Crompton, *L'Authoritie et Jurisdiction des Courts* (1594), at pp. 230-2.

[50] Holdsworth, "The Influence of Coke on the Development of English Law" in *Essays in Legal History* (Oxford, 1913), at p. 304.

definition of a court of record as one that can fine and imprison,[51] and in reaching this definition there is every reason to believe that he used cases to give, if not a wholly new meaning to the distinction, at least a new emphasis to it.[52]   The extent to which his precedents justify him is the investigation to which we now turn, though it must be preceded by some remarks upon the meaning of the word "fine".   In the thirteenth and fourteenth centuries, the king's justices had no power to impose a fine —no tribunal of the period is ever said to impose a fine. What the judge can do is impose a sentence of imprisonment and then allow the culprit to "make fine", that is to make an end (*finem facere*) of the matter by paying or finding security for a sum of money.   In theory the fine is a bilateral transaction, a bargain; it is not "imposed", it is "made".[53] Down to the middle of the sixteenth century this is recognized usage, but at about that time, and perhaps during the half century preceding it,[54] there are indications that the mechanics of the practice are only half understood and that the fine which terminates indefinite imprisonment has been confused with the fine in its modern sense of a pecuniary mulct.   This is perhaps natural, for as early as the statute of 45 Edw. III, c. 1 there is mention of a fixed statutory penalty corresponding to the modern fine, and from the time of Edward IV on, a fixed payment is the common statutory method of punishing minor offences.[55]   Similarly, imprisonment for a fixed term had become the punishment for many acts,[56] and thus

---

[51]*Halsbury's Laws of England* (Hailsham's ed.), vol. VIII, at p. 527.

[52]Holdsworth, *History of English Law* (1924), vol. V, at pp. 158-9, nn. 3, 5.

[53]Pollock and Maitland, *History of English Law* (1923), vol. II, at p. 517; *Y.B. 16 Edw. III* (Rolls Series), at p. 170 (1342): "*Thorpe*: You will find by the record that it was adjudged that John should be taken, and you will not find by the record that he has made fine ('qil ad fait fyne') ; wherefore, for the King, we pray that the body may remain [in prison].   *Pole*: By this suit [attaint on a writ of trespass that passed against John] we are to annul the first suit just as much as by a writ of error, wherefore we shall not make a fine which may afterwards be defeated.   *Hillary*, C. J.: Truly you shall do so in either case, and you shall be in custody until you have made fine ('et vous serrez en garde si la qe vous eiez fait fyn')."

[54]Thomas Marowe's reading on the peace, printed in Putnam, *Early Treatises on the Practice of the Justices of the Peace in the Fifteenth and Sixteenth Centuries* (Oxford, 1924), at pp. 286-414, affords some instances of the new usage: p. 369 ("al primer foitz que il soit troue coulpable, il serra amercie et paiera fyne") ; p. 373 ("ils serront toutz punys pur ceo si soit present deuaunt Justicez de peas pay fyne") ; ("fut al comen loie fynable").   Sir John Fox (*The History of Contempt of Court* (Oxford, 1927), at pp. 164 *ff*.) dates the change between 1558 and 1625.

[55]Fox, *op. cit.*, at p. 152.

[56]As early as the Statute of Westminster I terms of imprisonment became common: Pollock and Maitland, *History of English Law* (1923), vol. II, at p. 517.

what had been essentially one transaction—imprisonment followed by release upon payment of a fine—might easily be regarded, now that the word fine was associated with a pecuniary penalty independently imposed, as two. The transition to its new meaning was further facilitated by the fact that though in theory the culprit was committed to prison and made fine to be released, in practice the imprisonment frequently did not occur. He would be instructed to pay or find security for the payment of the fine, and only in the event that this was not possible would the sentence of imprisonment be enforced. Payment of the fine had become the main object, and its dependence on the condition precedent of a real term of imprisonment lost from view. But the old books were filled with references to imprisonment and fine, and since fine in its new sense had no apparent connexion with imprisonment, the words in the old cases are taken to mean this: that wherever one may be fined, imprisonment may follow to enforce the collection of the fine. It is this which leads Brooke to use indiscriminately the two phrases "il serra imprison et ferra fine" and "il ferra fine et serra imprison".[57]

In Coke's writings the word is used only in this new sense: in *Beecher's Case*—

> In touts actions *quare vi et armis*, come *rescous, transgressiones vi & armis &c.* si judgement soit done vers le defendant, il serra fine et imprison, car a chescun fine imprisonment est incident; et toutz foitz quant le judgement est, *quod defendens capiatur,* ceo est tant a dire *quod capiatur quousque finem fecerit*.[58]

A passage in his commentary upon Littleton illustrates equally well that Coke regards imprisonment as appendant to the fine, and the fine itself as the end of the offence rather than of the imprisonment.

> Fine, *finis*. Here "fine" signifieth a pecuniarie punishment for an offence or a contempt committed against the King, and regularly to it imprisonment appertaineth. And it is called *finis* because it is an end for that offence. And in this case a man is said *facere finem de transgressione etc. cum rege,* to make an end or fine with the king for such a transgression . . . . And to an amerciament imprisonment belongeth not, as it doth to a fine or ransome . . . . And aptly a redemption and a fine is taken to be all one; for by the payment of the fine he redeemeth himself from imprisonment that attendeth the fine, and then there is an end of the businesse.[59]

---

[57] *Brooke's Abridgement,* Imprisonment 2: "Vide titulo 'fine pur contemptes' per totum, que in chescun case ou home ferra fine il serra imprison, et cesty que dedit son fayt demesne, et est troue verz luy, sera imprison et ferra fine." See also Imprisonment 19, 100; Fine pur contempts 3, 5; Amerciaments 56.

[58] 8 Rep. 59b; *Griesley's Case,* 8 Rep. 38a, 41a; *Godfrey's Case,* 11 Rep. 42a, 43b.

[59] *Coke Litt.,* 126b-127

Throughout his work Coke discards the expression "to make fine", which made it clear that the offender thereby made an end to his punishment, and substitutes for it the phrases "to fine", "to be fined", "to impose a fine",[60] thus permitting a double penalty for common-law offences which formerly had had but one. In this it is probable that he is not consciously misconstruing sources but adopting contemporary usage, and his statement in Rolle's report of *Godfrey's Case*: "What is the difference between a fine and amercement? For denying deeds, for force and contempts, fines are but amercement",[61] is no departure from Lambarde's observation that the original distinction between fines and amercements is no longer retained with strictness.[62] That Coke is using "fine" in the sense of a pecuniary penalty independent of a prior sentence of imprisonment but enforceable by it, there can be little doubt, and in so far as this is a departure from older usage we must expect precedents brought forward in support of his definition of a court of record as one that can fine and imprison to fall aside the point.

In *Griesley's Case*[63] we find the first appearance of the quotation from Fitzherbert's *New Natura Brevium* which forms the corner-stone of that portion of Coke's theory concerned with the power to fine. "If a man be convicted before the sheriff in the county of a recaption, he shall be only amerced, but if he be convicted thereof in the Common Pleas he shall be fined; and the reason of this difference is, because the county court is not a court of record, and therefore cannot impose a fine, for no court can fine but such court which is a court of record. Vide F.N.B. 73d. And by these differences you will the better understand your books, which are plentiful in these matters." It appears again in *Beecher's Case*,[64] with the added ornament of a Latin translation: "quia nulla curia quae recordum non habet potest imponere finem, neque aliquem mandare carceri, quia ista spectant tantummodo ad curias de recordo", and with the citation to Fitzherbert supplemented by two cases—8 Edw. IV. 5 and 34 Hen. VI. 24. It is once again brought forward in *Bonham's Case*,[65] and finally in *Richard Godfrey's Case*,[66] where another case is added, and the definitive theory of courts of record stated. Fitzherbert is dealing only with the writ of recaption, and in an action upon the writ, he says,

---

[60]Fox, *The History of Contempt of Court,* at pp. 181-2. *Cf.* p. 153.
[61]*Bullen* v. *Godfrey,* I Rolle 74.
[62]Lambarde, *Eirenarcha* (London, 1581), lib. iv, c. 16.
[63] 8 Rep. 38, at p. 41.
[64] 8 Rep. 58, at p. 60b.
[65] 8 Rep. 110, at p. 120.
[66] 11 Rep. 42, at p. 43b.

if one is convicted before the sheriff he will be amerced and render damages for the contempt; but if he be convicted before the justices he will make fine and likewise render damages for the contempt.[67] There is no mention of record and, in fact, no reason or authority for the diversity is supplied. The rule, at least in part, seems to have its origin in a passage in Bracton's treatise,[68] reproduced in Fleta.[69] Bracton's words are: "Et si per ballivos tuos per quos averia praedicti A. secundo replegiata fuerunt et per alios legales homines convinci poterit de secunda captione, et pro una eademque occasione, tunc praedictum B. ita castiges per gravem misericordiam, ut castigatio illa in casu consimili aliis timorem tribuat delinquendi." Bracton is here reproducing the words of the royal writ to the sheriff, and it will be noted that he is to punish B by heavy amercement. The passage appears in Britton[70] in slightly changed form: "Whosoever shall be convicted of this offence 'en primes soint les damages agardez al pleyntif, et puis soit le distreignour puni par prisoun et par fin; ou nous maunderoms en tiel cas a nous viscountes, qe si troevent tiel trespas estre fet encountre nostre pes, qe hastivement facent tiel punisementz par enprisounement des cors de tiels trespassours et par grevous amerciementz, qe autres par ensample de eux soint chastiez en cas semblables'." In Britton's version there apparently are two forms of punishment—imprisonment and fine, and, when the sheriff is judge, imprisonment and heavy amercements—and this passage we take to be the authority for Fitzherbert's rule. The words "fine" and "amercement" seem to be used in the same sense, as they are in 20 Edw. I, stat. 3, but in the light of their various and conflicting uses, we do not pretend to the formulation of a clear distinction between the two terms.[71] It is sufficient for our present purpose to point out that Fitzherbert is referring to procedure only under the particular writ of recaption, and that any connexion between his statement and the problem of courts of record is the fabrication of Coke and not Sir Anthony. In defence of Coke we should make it clear that the passage was printed in an authoritative book, which was included among those "most necessary and of greatest authority and excellency", and that it must certainly have stated the law to the satisfaction of that learned judge, Sir Anthony Fitzherbert, who set it

---

[67]It will be noted that, in accordance with his custom, Coke has altered Fitzherbert's "he shall make fine" to "he shall be fined".

[68]Bracton, *De Legibus*, fo. 159.

[69]*Fleta*, at p. 103.

[70]*Britton* (ed. F. M. Nichols, Oxford, 1865), vol. I, at p. 154.

[71]An earnest but unsuccessful attempt to distinguish amercements and fines has been made by Sir John Fox, *The History of Contempt of Court*, at pp. 118 *ff*.

there. To Coke and his contemporaries its authority was undeniably high.[72]

With the supplementary cases cited in conjunction with the passage from Fitzherbert in support of the statement that no court but a court of record can fine, we may deal very briefly. The case in 8 Edw. IV. 5, which we take to be 8 Edw. IV, Trinity 17, has no apparent connexion with the argument. That of 34 Hen. VI. 24 deals in part with one who denies the deed of his ancestor which is found against him. Fortescue, in the exchequer chamber, is of the opinion that he would not be fined, as he would be had the deed denied been his own, but only amerced. There is no indication that the penalty varied with the court in which the matter was being heard; indeed, to make Fortescue's argument intelligible, the penalty must be taken to vary with the deed denied. But two of the cases cited in *Griesley's Case* offer stronger support for Coke's contention, and since *Griesley's Case* is the first appearance of Coke's new definition,[73] we venture to suggest that it owes its origin in large part to arguments put forward in them. In the first of these,[74] the steward in a court leet had twice commanded the bailiff to draw a panel, which the bailiff had twice refused. The steward thereupon placed a fine of 40 shillings upon him, for which the lord now brings an action of debt. The question presented was this: can the steward in a court leet fine, or technically phrased, is the sum demanded in the present action liquidated and certain enough to support an action of debt, or need the assessment be "affeered"?

> *Cotesmore*: There are in this court fines and amercements, and amercements are affeered by the country and fines are assessed by the discretion of the justices. And if a juror at the bar will not swear, you assess a fine upon him or put him in prison at your election; and if the people at a sessions make a great noise and disturbance, the justices have power to command them to keep silence under a penalty. So also the steward, who is justice in the leet, if they [the suitors] will not do their office, has power to command them under a certain penalty. And the leet is the oldest court in the land and has power to enquire of all manner of felonies and treasons, except the death of a man and the rape of a woman . . . . *Rolfe*: The steward, the bailiffs, the suitors,

---

[72]For a perhaps too sympathetic view of seventeenth-century standards of legal scholarship and of Coke's standards in particular, see: Plucknett, "Bonham's Case and Judicial Review" in 40 *Harvard Law Review* (1926), at pp. 30-41; *cf.* Hazeltine, "The Historical Background of Selden's Dissertatio ad Fletam" in Ogg, *Ioannis Seldeni Ad Fletam Dissertatio* (Cambridge, 1925), at pp. xix *ff.* Hazeltine, "Selden as Legal Historian" in *Festschrift Heinrich Brunner* (Weimar, 1910), at p. 579; F. M. Powicke, *Sir Henry Spelman and the "Concilia"* (British Academy, vol. XVI).

[73]In the sixth volume of his reports Coke had used the ordinary definition: see note 49, *supra;* beginning with the eighth volume (1611) the new definition appears.

[74]*Y.B. 7 Hen. VI. Mich. 17.*

and the men impanelled are the court, and if none are present but the steward, there is no court. Thus he has no power to do anything. . . . *Elderker*: If one breaks into my close and destroys my crops, I cannot assess the damages as certain and bring a writ of debt, for one cannot be his own judge. So in this case, he could be amerced and it would be affeered by the oaths of his peers, for otherwise the lord would be his own judge. For the steward is not in fact judge in the record, the suitors are judges, for if a writ of false judgment is brought, it is brought against the suitors . . . . *Paston*: As far as his [the steward's] power extends it is equal to that of the justices. . . .

In the second case,[75] the defendant, a tithingman, refused to make a presentment in a court leet, and he was consequently "amerced in the discretion of the steward" as, the plaintiff said, was permitted by the custom of the court. In an action of debt for the amount, the defendant sought to wage his law, to which the plaintiff demurred:

> *Newton* . . . he who is judge in the leet is judge of record, for the leet is the king's court for the time being, especially since the steward can inquire into treason and felony . . . affrays and assaults etc. which proves that it is a court of record, and therefore the steward had power to amerce him [the defendant] for not filling his office. It is similar to a case in which the sheriff and the coroners, who are officers of this court, do not attend to their duties, for then you have power to amerce them a sum certain in your discretion, an amercement which need not be assessed in any other way; so here. . . . *Chantry*: On the contrary, the plaintiff is barred by the statute of Magna Carta, that no one be amerced but *secundum quantitatem delicti,* and that was not done in this case. The amercement should have been affeered by the suitors, which was not done; therefore the action is not maintainable, for otherwise the statute is without effect. . . . *Fulthorpe*: . . . that which you say, that he is a judge of record, I freely grant, but that does not prove that he can amerce a man in his discretion. . . . *Candish*: On the contrary; to that which is said about the amercement being contrary to law I cannot agree, for he [the steward] is a judge of record and has the power, if there is an affray before him in the court, to commit those who do it to prison, and he can assess a fine upon them in his discretion, without need for it to be affeered. . . .

We postpone discussion of these cases until we have presented the cases Coke brings forward in support of the second half of his contention, namely, that only those courts are courts of record which can commit the defendant to prison.

In *Alfrid Denbawd's Case*[76] Coke puts the matter positively. "The reason why the defendant shall not wage his law when the account is made before auditors, is upon the Statute of Westminster II, c. 11, for now this statute has made the auditors judges of record, because they

---

[75] *Y.B. 10 Hen. VI. Mich. 22.*
[76] 10 Rep. 102b, at p. 103.

have power thereby to commit the defendant to prison, which none can do unless they be judges of record; and with this reason, *sc.* that they are judges of record, agree 20 Hen. VI. 41 and 10 Hen. VI. 24*b*. 25*a*." In *Bonham's Case*[77] he resorts again to a case of auditors: "A plea of trespass *vi et armis* doth not lie in the county court, hundred court, *etc.* for they cannot make a record of fine and imprisonment; and regularly they who cannot make a record cannot fine and imprison. And therewith agrees 27 Hen. VI. 8." Now it was settled law in the fifteenth century and earlier that if one is accountable to another, and duly accounts before auditors who find a certain sum due, then he can be sued for that sum by an action of debt, for the account had the effect of liquidating the claim. Further, in defence to the action, the defendant could not wage his law on the general issue of *nihil debet*.[78] In a sense, therefore, the auditors had record, since one could not resort to wager of law against their findings and since these were regarded as sufficient to support an action of debt, but there is a line of argument in the cases connecting the action of account with the Statute of Westminster II, c. 11, and it is this that Coke emphasizes and transforms into a new theory. Procedure in the action of account had been made particularly stringent by the statute which enacted that a bailiff, who had been found by auditors, appointed by the lord or assigned by the court, to owe his lord a stated account, should be arrested, "and by the testimony of the auditors of the same accompt, shall be sent or delivered into the next gaol of the king's in those parts". Once in prison he could then have recourse to the court of exchequer to determine disputed details "if he can find friends who are willing to bring him there by mainprise". On the basis of this statute, limited to manorial bailiffs,[79] but in the later middle ages regarded as the basis of the auditors' powers, Coke erects his theory of courts of record. To indicate how this was accomplished we must examine the precedents he cites.

In 20 Hen. VI. 41 the defendant had accounted before one auditor, and had been found to be in arrears. In an action of debt he attempted to wage his law:

---

[77] 8 Rep. 114, at p. 120.

[78] *Y.B. 13 Rich. II* (Ames Foundation), at pp. xlviii, 95-7. For the action of account see: Ames, *Lectures on Legal History* (Cambridge, Mass., 1913), at p. 116; Belsheim, "The Old Action of Account" in 45 *Harvard Law Review* (1932), at p. 466; Jackson, *The History of Quasi-Contract in English Law* (Cambridge, 1936), at pp. 27-8.

[79] Belsheim, *op. cit.*, at pp. 471, n. 32, 482 *ff*.

> *Yelverton*: . . . in a writ of debt on arrears of account the defendant cannot wage his law. And the justices were of various opinions whether he should have his law or not, and then *Newton*, "per avis de touts ses compagnons, dit": he shall have his law, because the account was not before auditors assigned, who are judges of record, but before one auditor who is not a judge of record, no more than if the defendant had accounted before the plaintiff himself and had been found in arrears,[80] in which case he would have his law. And the statute speaks of account before auditors.[81]

In 10 Hen. VI. 24 the auditors had found the bailiff or bailee not indebted to the testator, but on the contrary, the testator indebted to the bailiff, who apparently had turned over to his lord money in excess of that found due by the auditors. The bailiff promptly brought an action of debt against the executrix of the lord, and the question presented was whether the claim was liquidated and certain:

---

[80]In 1389 (*Y.B. 13 Rich. II* (Ames Foundation), at pp. 20-2) in an action of debt to recover the balance found due after the defendant had accounted to the plaintiff, it was objected that the plaintiff cannot sue on an account rendered to himself, for in such a proceeding he would be his own judge. This point was abandoned, and issue taken on the fact of an alleged arbitration. By the early fifteenth century the argument that plaintiffs in similar circumstances were judges in their own case met with little success, and an informal accounting was regarded as grounding an action of debt for the agreed sum: *Y.B. 7 Hen. IV. Pasch. 17; Y.B. 34 Hen. VI. Trin. 4.*

[81]*Y.B. 20 Hen. VI. Hil. 4*: The defendant had similarly been found in arrears before one auditor. "*Newton* demanded of the serjeants whether in this case the defendant could wage his law. *Markham*: In a court of record a plaintiff counted on a writ of debt for arrears of account, and it was found that the account had been before one auditor; the judges allowed him [the defendant] to wage his law, and then the record was removed to the King's Bench by writ of error, debated there, and finally reversed. *Fortescue*: There was a similar case in the Exchequer, and it was adjourned into the Exchequer Chamber, and there, with the assent of all the justices, he was ousted of his law. *Ascough*: No sir, the case in the Exchequer concerned [an account before] two auditors, and it was this: the bailee had paid more than he had received, and he brought debt for this surplusage, and the lord wished to wage his law, but was ousted. *Fortescue*: No sir, it is rather as I said it, for if it had been the lord I believe he would have waged his law. *Newton*: At common law the bailee could wage his law upon the finding of auditors against the lord, and similarly, the lord could wage his law against the bailee on a surplusage. After the statute, the auditors can commit the bailee to prison, but they cannot commit the lord, for at common law the auditors could commit neither the bailee nor any other person, but after the statute they can commit the bailee. Therefore, etc. But I believe that at common law, if the account was heard by one auditor, the bailee could wage his law . . . . *Ascough*: Go to the Exchequer and see the record: and it was just as he had said, a surplusage found before two auditors, and the lord had been ousted of his law. And then *Newton* 'par avis de touts ses compagnons disoit Qu'il ait la ley'."

Newton: . . . before the Statute of Westminster II an account was no more of record than an arbitration, but by the statute the auditors are judges of record to hear the account, and if the bailee is found in arrears before them, they have power to commit him to prison. But if it is found that the lord received a sum in excess, they [the auditors] cannot commit him to prison, for the excess of the account is at common law, just as it was before the statute, and therefore this action cannot be maintained against the executrix, for the law does not charge her with a duty due by the testator unless due by matter of record or by a specialty. . . . *Strange*: The statute made the auditors [misprinted "executors"] judges of record to hear the account, and if the lord is found indebted to the bailiff, that is part of the account. Thus it is a debt of record by the statute, and as to what was said earlier, that this case is not within the statute since the auditors may not commit the lord to prison, that does not prove that this case is without the statute, for the auditors are judges of record to hear the account. . . . And it is another provision of the statute that gives power to the auditors to commit to prison, which proves nothing but that the whole account is of record.[82]

In the case cited by Coke in *Bonham's Case*—27 Hen. VI. 8—there is no mention of record or courts of record. It illustrates simply the power of the auditors to commit to prison.

No one of the cases he brings forward clearly supports Coke's contention. That the auditors were judges of record in the sense that wager of law was not permitted against their finding, and in so far as their finding was regarded as sufficient to charge an executor, we may grant. But that they constituted a court of record "because they have power to commit the defendant to prison", or that their power to imprison is due to their status as a court of record, is far from the minds of the serjeants and judges who engage in the discussions set out above. In the second excerpt Newton uses the statutory provision for imprisonment simply to prove the lord not within the statute, and Strange is clearly of the opinion that the auditors are judges of record quite apart from any power to imprison they may possess. Nevertheless the juxtaposition of imprisonment and record in the cases might suggest to an uncritical mind that a true connexion exists between them, and it is this, perhaps, coupled with Coke's own authority and reputation as a common lawyer, that led to the wide acceptance of his definition.

With respect to the first of the two cases set out to prove that no court but a court of record can fine, the participants in the argument are concerned with the steward's power to fine, and Cotesmore and Paston very clearly consider his action proper since the leet is comparable to the courts at Westminster where such action is permitted. There is no word

---

[82]*Y.B. 38 Hen. VI. Mich 14*: a very similar case in which the defendant was permitted to wage his law.

of record despite the fact that an action of debt had been brought. In the second case Newton's remarks afford some basis for Coke's contention, but he too is concerned to picture the exalted nature of the court in order to draw an analogy, which he does, to the central courts in which the judges might fine. Fulthorpe admits that the steward is a judge of record, but sees no connexion between that and his power to fine. Candish's argument likewise affords Coke support, but he is using imprisonment and fine in its old sense, quite differently from Coke, and justifying the amercement as a fine which terminates a term of imprisonment. His words might serve more easily to buttress the imprisonment half of Coke's definition, though we believe that this would go far beyond Candish's understanding of them.

Just as the auditors' power to imprison is made the reason for their record, so the steward's power to assess a fine upon which debt may be brought is made to indicate, and at the same time, is drawn out of the statement, that the leet is a court of record.   That Coke was able to assemble some authority for his definition is clear, for these cases and their arguments might well appear to support his view, especially if read rapidly and uncritically, but it is equally clear that his definition was new and completely his own. Much more clearly his own is his further distinction in *Godfrey's Case* between courts like the central courts of common law which could both fine and imprison, and courts, like courts leet, which could fine but not imprison.[83] His final definition that the true court of record must be able both to fine and imprison is completely without authority. We think it quite evidently aimed at the court of chancery which had the power to imprison but, though it exercised it, not, in Coke's opinion, the power to fine.[84]

<h3 style="text-align:center">III</h3>

It now remains to turn briefly to an attempt to ascertain the reasons behind Coke's insistence upon his definition.   That it was designed to

[83]This is expressly contradicted by Coke's words in *Griesley's Case* and by the cases cited in it; also by *Coke Litt.*, at p. 117b, and the *Complete Copyholder* (London, 1764), at p. 35; Hearnshaw, *Leet Jurisdiction in England* (Southampton Record Society, 1908), at p. 134.

[84]*Commons Debates 1621* (New Haven, 1935), vol. II, p. 259 ("It was questioned in Francis Englefield's case whether the Lord Chancellor may put a fine upon anyone in Chancery for not performing a decree there, and it was resolved he could not. So 22 Ed. 4. For he can set no fine; if he do it is only *in terrorem*, and so it is 10 Hen. 7, and so it was adjudged in the Exchequer when Sir Edward Coke was Attorney. Yet the Lord Chancellor doth so now and doth sue for it in the Petty Bag Office") ; p. 265, p. 327 ("The Chancery cannot set a fine because no court of record") ; vol. III, p. 98; IV, p. 195; V, pp. 68, 104; VI, pp. 85, 433.

cripple the newer courts which the common lawyers regarded as their rivals—the council, the star chamber, the chancery acting as a court of equity, the admiralty, the ecclesiastical courts—is the commonly received impression.[85] If Coke's view that only courts of record could fine and imprison was correct, these courts had no legal right to exercise these powers, but this would be true only if the test of a court of record were made that detailed in the *Termes de la Ley*: the presence of a formal Latin record enrolled upon parchment. Of this characteristic as a test there is little mention in Coke's later writings. During the period the power to fine and imprison was habitually exercised by the council, star chamber, chancery, admiralty, and high commission, and it is difficult to believe that even Coke cherished the thought that they might be deprived of these powers because their proceedings were not properly kept in accordance with common-law custom. Whether or not this thought lay behind his formulation, and we believe that it played at most a minor part, it is clear that in this field his remarks had little or no effect.[86] Elsewhere, however, they bore magnificent fruit, for it was with more than a casual eye toward parliament that they were framed. Coke had determined that parliament should again become the judicial body that it had been in the fourteenth century, the highest court in the land, which would mean a court above the council-made courts as well as at the apex of the common law. It was the last step in the war he had been waging for the supremacy of the common-law courts over the courts of equity.[87] Not long after the appearance of Coke's definition in the eighth volume of his *Reports,* the house of lords, urged by a small group in the commons, in which Coke was powerful, assumed the power to act both as a court of appeal and of original jurisdiction, a power for which, in Hargrave's words, "perhaps antient precedents may be wanting". That the lords, and the commons as well, should be courts of record was imperative, but neither kept a formal Latin record enrolled on parchment, and both were open to the assertion that the suitors were judges. If, however, the power to fine and imprison, legally and rightfully exercised, characterized the court using these powers as one of record, the problem would be satisfactorily solved. Thus in the Belasyse diary Coke is reported to have said, "The

---

[85]Holdsworth, *History of English Law* (1924), vol. V, at pp. 159-61.

[86]*Ibid.,* at p. 160.

[87]F. H. Relf, *Notes of the Debates in the House of Lords* (Royal Historical Society, 1929), p. xiv. The entire introduction which supplements, in turn, Sir Francis Hargrave's introduction to the 1796 edition of Sir Matthew Hale's *The Jurisdiction of the Lords House of Parliament*, is of much importance in this connexion.

howse of commons is a Court of Record, for 1, it grants priviledges in accions of anie value, whether reall or personall, and stayes suites in Courtes of record; 2, it holds plea of accions above 40 *s.*; 3, it imprisons in the towre; 4, it fines. *Ergo* a Court of Record, for these are the proper effects of a Courte of Record."[88] When with more dispatch than discretion the commons pronounced judgment against Floyd, and immediately received word from the king denying that they had any part in judicature, Coke reiterated what he had previously maintained. "He that sayes this house is not a court of record, I would his toung might cleave to the roofe of his mouth. He that thinkes we have no Judicature speaks ignorantly; he that saith we have in all cases is deceived much too."[89] Coke was able to establish both the lords and the commons as courts of record, and thus from his black-letter books with their technical questions of wager of law and account he was able to raise a harvest of great importance in English constitutional history. His definition of courts of record was instrumental in the lords' assumption of judicial power, and strengthened very considerably the commons in the second decade of the seventeenth century. His doctrine was new, though on the surface fortified with precedents from the middle ages, for he knew well that without such support it would have availed nothing. The whole is but another phase of the long struggle between parliament and council, and it adds still another proof to what is already marvellously clear: that in the history of that conflict Coke's influence cannot well be over-estimated.

---

[88]*Commons Debates, 1621,* vol. V, p. 146; vol. II, p. 349 ("The lords of Parliament are a court of themselves and so is the house of Commons, proved thus: 1, what court can grant privileges is a court of record. But the House of Commons can do this. *Ergo* the House of Commons is a court of record. 2, what court can hold pleas of actions above 40*s.* is a court of record. But so can this. *Ergo.* 3, what court can fine a man, that is a court of record. But this can do so. *Ergo.*"); vol. III, pp. 181-2; vol. IV, pp. 312-3.

[89]*Commons Debates, 1621,* vol. III, pp. 138-9.

20

DR. BONHAM'S CASE*

TO students of the origins of American constitutional law and theory no judicial utterance of Sir Edward Coke can surpass in interest and importance his so-called *dictum* in Dr. Bonham's case, decided in the Court of Common Pleas in 1610.[1] It is widely regarded as foreshadowing not merely the power which American courts to-day exercise in the disallowance of statutes on the ground of their conflict with the constitution, but also that very test of 'reasonableness' which is the ultimate flowering of that power. We turn here to a determination of these questions: to what extent does Coke's own intention sanction the modern application of his doctrine, and also, on what grounds does the doctrine rest.

In April, 1606, Thomas Bonham was summoned to appear before the president and censors of the Royal College of Physicians for practising medicine in the city of London without their certificate. A fine of one hundred shillings was imposed upon him, and he was forbidden under pain of imprisonment to practise physic until he had been admitted to do so by the college. Bonham continued to practise, however, and in October he was resummoned. This time he defaulted, and was sentenced in his absence to a fine of ten pounds. Early in November he again appeared, in response to a third summons, and refused either to pay his fine or to refrain from further practice, both on the ground that he was a doctor of medicine of the University of Cambridge, and that therefore the Royal College of Physicians had no jurisdiction over him. In the words of the reporter, he said 'he had practised and would practise within the city, as he conceived he might lawfully do'. Thereupon the censors committed him to prison in the Counter of Fleet Street, whither he was conveyed by the servants of the president and censors. Bonham now brought an action of false

---

* A paper read before the American Historical Association, December 30, 1937.
[1] 8 Rep. 114 a; 2 Brownl. 255. The literature upon Bonham's case is voluminous and repetitious: McIlwain, The High Court of Parliament (1910) 286 ff.; Plucknett, 'Bonham's Case and Judicial Review' (1926) 40 Harv. L. Rev. 30; Corwin, 'The "Higher Law" Background of American Constitutional Law' (1929) 42 Harv. L. Rev. 367 ff.; Allen, Law in the Making (2nd ed. 1930) 265; Haines, The Revival of Natural Law Concepts (1930) 32-36. Other literature will be found collected in these discussions.

imprisonment against the leading members of the Royal College of Physicians.

The pleadings of the defendants set forth that letters patent dated 10 Henry VIII had incorporated them as the Royal College of Physicians, with powers to fine practitioners in London who were not admitted by them, and further general powers to govern all the physicians in London and district with fine and imprisonment. In all cases one-half of the fine was to go to the King, and one-half to the college. This patent was confirmed twice by statute, with the addition of a general command to all gaolers to keep such persons as the president and college shall commit to them without bail or mainprise, until delivered by the president and censors, or their successors. It was pursuant to these statutory powers that the college claimed to have committed Dr. Bonham.

Protracted argument followed, to which we will return shortly. For the present we may turn directly to the judgment of the Chief Justice, Sir Edward Coke. He regarded as decisive two legal points. In the first place, a proper construction of the statute indicated that the censors did not possess the power to fine and imprison unlicensed, as distinct from incompetent, physicians; and secondly, even if they did, they had not pursued it aright. It is the fourth of the five reasons adduced in support of the former of these propositions that has since become so famous. Coke pointed out that the censors were to receive one-half of the fines, and therefore are not only judges but parties in any case that comes before them. It is an established maxim of the common law that no man can be judge in his own case. 'And it appears in our books that in many cases the common law will controul acts of parliament and sometimes adjudge them to be utterly void: for when an act of parliament is against common right or reason, or repugnant, or impossible to be performed, the common law will controul it and adjudge such act to be void.'

The generally received opinion is that Coke was here appealing to natural law, or higher law, or fundamental law. 'Although Coke was no canonist', says Sir Frederick Pollock, 'we can be pretty sure that his theory was ultimately derived from the canonist doctrines prevailing on the continent',[2] and in this he has been generally followed by contemporary scholars. They have had some difficulty in explaining the appearance of the principle in Bonham's case. They likewise have been troubled

---

[2] The Expansion of the Common Law (1904) 122.

by *Rowles* v. *Mason*,[3] decided two years afterward, which they
are forced to regard as a retreat by Coke from the position he
had taken earlier. The fact that the statement as interpreted
makes no appearance in Coke's Institutes, though the last three
Institutes appeared when Coke was quite safe from imprisonment
in the Tower, also has been a constant source of embarrassment.
Nevertheless, the belief that Coke in Dr. Bonham's case. was
invoking the doctrine that there were superior principles of
right and justice which Acts of Parliament might not contravene,
is widely held. Without disputing the general truth of this
proposition, we believe that some light may be thrown upon the
problem by approaching it from the private law rather than
from the constitutional law side, and we suggest that to some
extent at least, later doctrines of natural law have been reflected
backward upon Coke's statement, giving it a content it did not
in fact have. His words have been read so long in the light of
theories Coke did not contemplate that it is difficult now to
dissociate them. It is nevertheless to this that we now turn.

The statute under consideration was a negative statute. The
words of the patent were clear: no one should practise medicine
in the city of London and district if he be not admitted by the
letters of the president and college, sealed with their common
seal. Now it was a general principle of statutory interpretation
that statutes phrased in the negative superseded and defeated
common law. A negative statute could neither be extended to
include cases in like mischief, or narrowed to exclude cases
within its express words. It must be taken literally as it stands;
as Coke remarks elsewhere, a statute in the negative is necessary
to be observed. This is the burden of Justice Walmesley's
remarks, as we see them in Brownlow's report of Bonham's case:
Walmesley ' doth not know of any case where the words of the
statute are negative, that they admit any interpretation against
that but only one, and that is the statute of Marlbridge,
chapter 4, which provides that no lord shall distrain in one
county, and the beasts distrained drive into another county, in
which case, though that the words are negative, yet if the lord
distrain in one county, he may drive the beasts to his manor in
another county, of which the lands, of which the distress was
taken, were held, but it is equity and reason in this case, that
the statute should admit such exception, for it is not of malice,
but for that, that the beasts may remain within his fee, but in
the principal case there is not the like reason or equity '.

Similarly in Coke's summary of the arguments made for the defendant college, the question of statutes negatively phrased appears again : ' They (the defendants) relied upon the letter of the grant, ratified by the said act of 14 Henry VIII, which is in the negative, *scilicet, Nemo in dicta civitate, etc.* And this proposition is a general negative, and *nemo* excludes all; and therefore a doctor of the one University or the other is prohibited within this negative word *nemo.* And many cases were put where negative statutes shall be taken *stricte & exclusive,* which I do not think necessary to be recited here.'

Thus an obvious way out of the difficulty—by excepting from the general words of the statute graduates of the Universities— was closed. It was even more completely closed by another section of the Act of 14 Henry VIII which regulated persons practising medicine outside London. They were likewise to be examined and certified by the college, but with one exception : graduates of Oxford and Cambridge were to be permitted to practise outside London without examination. The absence of this proviso in the portion of the statute relating to practice in London made it clear that in that case the exception was not to be made. Nevertheless the plaintiff relied completely upon this point, and at least one of the justices, Justice Daniel, agreed with him, for he said that a doctor of physic of the one University or the other was not within the body of the Act, and if he were, that he was excepted by the said later section of the Act. But the Chief Justice did not speak to this point, which, we may add, was quite proper.

Coke turned instead to a construction of the letters patent of the college. The provisions were that none should practise in the city of London if he be not admitted by the college. For every month an unlicensed physician practised there, he was open to a fine of one hundred shillings. A second clause provided that the college should have the overseeing, and searching, correcting and governing of all the physicians of the city, including foreign physicians practising there, and the power to punish them for improper practice by fines, amercements, imprisonments of their bodies, and other reasonable and fitting ways. Coke's contention was ' that the censors have not power by the letters patent and the act to fine or imprison any for simply practising physic in London, but only for ill, and not good use and practice of physic '. This he proved by five arguments : (1) The clauses are distinct and parallel, and therefore the one does not extend to the other, for a definite penalty of one hundred shillings is attached to the first clause, but no definite penalty is attached to the second. The intention of the makers of the statute, says Coke, must have been to have the penalties for inexpert practice vary with the injuries done in that practice, and thus they left it to the college to fix punishments in each case. But the college was not given that discretion in the first clause. Therefore the two clauses are distinct, and imprisonment cannot attach to one who falls only into the class of unlicensed practitioner. (2) The harm that accrues by improper practice concerns the body of man, and therefore it is reasonable that the offender should be punished in his body, that is, by imprisonment. But he who practises physic in London in a good manner, though he doth it without a licence, yet it is not any prejudice to the body of man. (3) The time of a month is fixed by the first clause, and a man doth not offend the statute unless he practise in the city of London a month. But no time is fixed in the second clause, and if a man practise improperly within a month, he doubtless would be punishable. Thus the two are distinct. (4) ' The censors can't be judges, ministers, and parties. Judges to give sentence, ministers to make summons, parties to have the moiety of the forfeiture. One cannot be judge in his own case, and it appears in our books that in many cases the common law will control Acts of Parliament and adjudge them to be utterly void. For when an Act of Parliament is against common right or reason, or repugnant, or impossible to be performed, the common law will control it and adjudge such Act to be void.' (5) If the two clauses were not distinct, an unlicensed physician would be liable to a fine of one hundred shillings, fixed by the statute, after practising a month, and also to fine and imprisonment, under the second clause, for the same thing. But this is absurd, for no one should be twice punished for the same offence. Thus the second clause must be understood to apply only to improper, rather than to both unlicensed and improper, practice.

These are the arguments that Coke brought forward to indicate that the two clauses of the patent were distinct; that therefore the college's´ power to imprison was confined to imprisoning physicians guilty of improper practice; and that therefore Dr. Bonham's imprisonment had been illegal. As we examine them, all but the fourth seem to be directed toward that end. It may be, as has been urged, that the fourth argument embodied a favourite argument of Coke's, which he was anxious to publish, so anxious, indeed, that he did so by placing it in a group of arguments with which it has no apparent connexion. This, of course, is unfounded. The fourth argument was directed, just as the others were, toward an interpretation of the statute which on its face seemed to make Dr. Bonham's imprisonment lawful. We must keep well in mind the fact that the question of the legality of Bonham's commitment was the only question before the Court in this action of false imprisonment against the defendant college. In view of the first three and the fifth of Coke's arguments, it seems reasonable to suppose that the Act was not meant to provide for the imprisonment of merely unlicensed, as against incompetent, physicians. But if Bonham did not fall within the provisions of the second clause, he seemed very clearly to fall into those of the first. He therefore might be fined; indeed this fine Bonham had refused to pay. Now it was clear law that to every fine imprisonment was incident. Coke himself had said those very words in *Beecher's Case*, decided a few months before.[4] Thus the college, if not directly permitted to imprison Bonham under the second clause of the Act, was entitled, if entitled to fine at all, to commit him until his fine was paid. Coke's fourth argument is directed toward the fine and its consequent imprisonment. It may be reproduced as follows: just as it would be absurd to interpret the statute to permit an unlicensed physician to be fined one hundred shillings at the end of a month, and also to be punished by imprisonment during the month, for the one offence of engaging in practice without a licence, so it would be absurd to interpret it to permit the college to be party and judge, that is, to assess fines in which it shares. Even though the statute apparently gives the college power to fine unlicensed physicians, when upon investigation we find that the college has a direct, pecuniary interest in those fines, it would be impossible, without absurdity, to adhere even to words so unambiguous. It therefore cannot fine. Thus the fine placed upon Dr. Bonham was not legally placed upon him, and therefore the imprisonment incident to it was unjustified. All five arguments, then, converge to prove Bonham's false imprisonment; all five take their proper place as interpretations of the statute. Coke's fourth point proves to be not a *dictum*, but a very material portion of his argument. And finally, though Coke's fourth argument is phrased in very wide terms, it visualizes no statute void because of a conflict between it and common law, natural law, or higher law, but simply a refusal to follow a statute absurd on its face.

Far from ' evincing a receptive and candid attitude toward

---

[4] 8 Rep. 59 b.

natural law ideas, a fresh influx of which from the continent was
already setting in ', the argument is derived from the ordinary
common law rules of statutory interpretation, with which, we
may add, Coke doubtless was more familiar. Let us state the
words again: ' When an act of parliament is against common
right or reason, or repugnant, or impossible to be performed,
the common law will controul it and adjudge such act to be
void.' Repugnancy in statutes was quite familiar to seventeenth-
century lawyers. In a contemporary treatise on statutory interpretation, preserved among the Ellesmere papers at the Huntington Library, we find it treated in these words: ' If the words of a
statute be contraryant or repugnant, what is there then to be
said? And surelie therin we ought to make our construction as
nigh as we can so that nothing be repugnant. Yet if it cannot
be avoided, so that a repugnancy must needs be, then is the thing
repugnant void.' [5] A repugnancy, then, is a contradiction; it
occurs when a statute provides one thing, and then through
oversight perhaps, its opposite. When we are faced with a
repugnant statute we are first to construe it so as to save its
words, but if that is impossible, then our author tells us, ' are
the former wordes good, and the latter, because they make a
jarre by reason of the repugnancy, shalbe omitted '. There is
no conscious constitutional problem raised here, but only one
of statutory construction. We are looking at a statute from the
point of view of a judge called upon to apply it in a particular
case. Since a provision and its opposite cannot both be applied,
the later contradictory words are regarded as of no effect. How
simple to carry this idea over to the case in which a man is both
party and judge. To be sure, that is not a direct repugnancy:
if it were, none could object, for even Lord Ellesmere, who
did not approve of those who declared statutes void for being
contrary to reason and common right, made two exceptions: ' I
speak not of impossibilities or direct repugnances.' Though not
technically a repugnancy, certainly a statute making a man
judge in his own case and a self-contradictory statute might well
be regarded as cognate, and as Coke, with the facts of Bonham's
case before him, turned over his precedents on statutes repugnant
and statutes impossible to be performed, his theory of a statute
against common right and reason took form. There can be no
doubt, we think, that it was from these precedents, rather than
from any natural law theories, that Coke's argument stems. It
will be remembered that his fourth argument was one of five

---

[5] El. 2565, fo. 7-7 b.

interpreting the statute in Bonham's case. We see that it is phrased in the technical language of statutory interpretation. But two years after Bonham's case, in *Rowles* v. *Mason*, Coke felt that common right or reason and repugnancy were roughly equivalent: 'if there is repugnancy in statute or unreasonableness in custom, the common law disallows and rejects it, as appears in Dr. Bonham's case'.⁶ This is, likewise, the tone of all the relevant passages of the Institutes.⁷

Further light on the meaning of Coke's fourth argument is supplied by the precedents he cited in its support. These have been examined many times, most recently by Mr. Plucknett, who clearly felt that they did not support the idea of a fundamental law which limited Crown and Parliament indifferently. With this we may wholeheartedly agree, for as we have indicated, the probabilities that such a theory existed in Coke's mind are small. But we need not therefore offer apologies for Coke's *bona fides* or for his Year Book scholarship, for Coke doubtless felt it unnecessary to support a theory of unconstitutional legislation when propounding one of strict statutory interpretation. In Cessavit 42, cited by Coke from Fitzherbert's Abridgement, and in *Copper* v. *Gederings*,⁸ an earlier case with which it is in complete accord, the Court quietly ignored an unambiguous statute, just as Coke did in the instant case. Mr. Plucknett tells us that in neither of the earlier cases was the nature of statutes questioned or the constitutional issue raised. Nor was it in Dr. Bonham's case. *Tregor's Case* ⁹ is a trenchant comment upon the situation in Bonham's case, and the interpolations by Coke introduce an idea of some superior ' right ' only when read in the light of St. Germain's and Fortescue's natural law. Certainly the legislator who conferred upon the Royal College of Physicians the power to fine and imprison, and thus established it as a Court of record,¹⁰ would have repented of his hasty piece of work when he found that the president and censors were judges of record, no more open to attack for false imprisonment than were the judges of the King's Bench who committed a defendant to prison. Bound by no common law rules, required to hold no public trial, and in addition, permitted to have half the fines collected, they would indeed have had ' power to correct or punish any of the subjects of the kingdom at their pleasure '.

---

⁶ 2 Brownl. 198.
⁷ Corwin, *op. cit. supra*, n. 1, p. 374, n. 32.
⁸ Y. B. 3 Edw. II, 105.
⁹ Y. B. 8 Edw. III, Pasch. 26.
¹⁰ Thorne, ' Courts of Record and Sir Edward Coke ' (1937) 2 Univ. of Toronto L. Jour. 24. See above, pp. 243-68.

Fitzherbert's Annuitie 41, though an opinion only, is clearly in point with the meaning we are giving to Coke's fourth argument, and so too are the Elizabethan cases on the conflict between prerogative and statute. These cases, then, support no theory of higher law, binding upon Parliament and making Acts that contravene it void. Nor does Coke entertain that theory. We can agree with Mr. Allen's statement that they are ' cases merely of strict interpretation which seem to have produced a result other than that which was intended by the legislator ',[11] though not with his general discussion of Bonham's case. When the fundamental law theories have been put aside, we can understand Coke's refusal to acknowledge any substantial error in his writings, and his repetition of the offending passage in Bonham's case word for word in reply to the questions put to him in 1617 by the King, apparently at the suggestion of Bacon and Yelverton.[12] We can understand his words in *Rowles* v. *Mason* and his later expressions in the Institutes, and similarly the appearance of his doctrine in the language of statutory interpretation and as the fourth of five arguments on the interpretation of the statute in Dr. Bonham's case.

It remains only to account for such criticism as Ellesmere's, the accumulation of which was a material factor in forcing Coke's removal from the bench. We know that judges had wide powers of statutory interpretation, but Coke's disregard of the express words of the Act probably went beyond them. Though even this is not clear, for our manuscript treatise on statutory interpretation permits a statute ' to be taken contrary to its words to escape injustice, for statutes come to establish laws, and if any iniquity should be gathered of them, or if any absurdity or contraryty should follow, they do not so much deserve the name of laws '. The cases Coke cited technically support his view, but they were early cases, and the feeling was prevalent that Acts of Parliament should not be disregarded if clear and unambiguous. This we take to be the meaning of Ellesmere's remark implying that the King and Parliament should be left to judge what was common right and reason.[13] Then, too, members of the council, such as Bacon and Ellesmere, might very well have a conception of statutes different from that entertained by common lawyers and judges, though we do not believe that Ellesmere regarded Coke's argument as meaning more than this: that unambiguous statutes would not be enforced

---

[11] Allen, Law in the Making (1930) 266.
[12] 6 Bacon, Works (1803 ed.) 405.
[13] McIlwain, *op. cit. supra*, n. 1, p. 293-4.

if unreasonable results might follow.   Ellesmere's qualifying adjective : ' I speak not of impossibilities or *direct* repugnances ', seems to indicate that to him, Coke's theory was directed toward interpretation broadened to include indirect repugnances, that is, contradictions not on the statute's face.   Finally, anything coming from Coke was open to suspicion.   Coke's argument was soon to be read in a new light, and to bear fruits across the sea, but it is difficult to believe that it contained an appeal to fundamental, higher, or natural law.   It furnished a form of words which soon became separated from the case in which they had been uttered, but when they are returned to their proper place, Coke's ambitious political theory is found to be not his, but the work of a later generation of judges, commentators, and lawyers.

INDEX